The Moral Imagination

CONFRONTING THE ETHICAL ISSUES OF OUR DAY

EDWARD TIVNAN

Simon & Schuster
NEW YORK   LONDON   TORONTO   SYDNEY   TOKYO   SINGAPORE

SIMON & SCHUSTER
Rockefeller Center
1230 Avenue of the Americas
New York, New York 10020

SIMON & SCHUSTER and colophon are registered trademarks of
Simon & Schuster Inc.

Designed by Eve Metz
Manufactured in the United States of America

10 9 8 7 6 5 4 3 2 1

Library of Congress Cataloging-in-Publication Data
Tivnan, Edward.
    The moral imagination : confronting the ethical issues of our
day/Edward Tivnan.
        p.   cm.
    Includes bibliographical references (p. 269) and index.
    1. Ethical problems. 2. United States—Moral conditions.
    I. Title.
    BJ1031.T57   1995
    170—dc20   94-43331
                                                          CIP

ISBN: 0-671-74708-8

To Marilyn, Maisie, and Nell

Contents

Introduction

This is *not* the book to end all arguments about morality, a kind of *World Almanac* or *Baseball Digest* for settling moral disputes. This is a book about arguments, good arguments but *different* arguments for and against five issues that have been nagging the American conscience for decades or longer: abortion, suicide, euthanasia, capital punishment, and racial justice.

We Americans are inclined to think that if we debate an issue long enough, we will come to some sort of agreement. In *The Moral Imagination,* I try to show that complex moral issues are unlikely to have simple solutions, that no one—"conservative" or "liberal"—has special access to The Truth, and that in a society as diverse as our own, disagreements about fundamental moral problems are likely to be fundamental, and thus irreconcilable. In the land of truth, as one great historian of philosophy has often advised, there are many mansions.

But isn't this a recipe for moral chaos? Surely, some things are simply right or wrong. They are indeed. But we are likely to disagree on what they are. How often have you yourself been conflicted over what to do? (That, after all, is the definition of a moral dilemma: to want two incompatible things at the same time.) I will argue in this book that in a democracy a certain amount of intellectual chaos is inevitable and even good. But I will also argue that the only way we can create a decent society out of so many versions of what Americans think is "decent" is to understand why we disagree so strongly and learn to live with our disagreements, all the while fighting for our convictions (but never forgetting that we might actually be wrong). This requires what I call "moral imagination."

Life-and-death matters used to seem simpler to decide. Most Americans were members of communities or religious groups that passed on their moral principles to their members, who were not inclined to dissent. But religion's role is not what it used to be; ethnic groups have fragmented or been assimilated. America no longer seems to be "one nation indivisible under God." But our moral dilemmas remain; we cannot walk away from them: Is abortion murder? What about your father suffering the interminable pain of cancer—should you help him die? Is capital punishment more than mere vengeance? Should an African-American be given special consideration for employment or educational opportunities, even if a white candidate is better qualified?

The issues that make up this book were once discussed mainly by moral philosophers, theologians, constitutional scholars and members of the boards of Catholic hospitals. The same problems are now the flashpoints of dinner-party disputes, newsmagazine cover stories, and demonstrations in the streets. Americans take the issues of this book so seriously that men have been killed for disagreeing. These days we all seem to have an opinion about abortion, suicide, euthanasia, the death penalty, and affirmative action. Trouble is, most of us don't know what we are talking about.

"I don't know what to believe anymore" has become an American refrain. And if you don't know what to believe, how are you supposed to teach your children what they should believe? Few of us, however, have the time to read what philosophers, theologians, constitutional scholars, and medical ethicists have to say (and even fewer penetrate their prose). In the chapters that follow, I have tried to collect the best arguments on all sides of the debates over abortion, suicide, euthanasia, capital punishment, and racial justice. In some cases, those arguments are as old as Plato and Aristotle; in others, they are as new as today's news.

I have tried to lay out those arguments simply and clearly, free of academic jargon, with no ax to grind. My goal has been to paraphrase and summarize each position as accurately and as efficiently as I could. I have used some direct quotations, but I have also taken the liberty of avoiding the typical third-person attribution (e.g. "according to the Harvard philosopher John Rawls . . ." or "as Kant argued . . ."). For while I was eager to use an author's shiniest phrases and most memorable comments, I found that the arguments came out clearer and more forceful when packaged as a kind of speech or conversation—as if the reader had cornered one of my sources in a room and said,

"Okay, Professor, let me hear your opinion on . . ." The arguments featured here are from the writings of authorities on each issue, men and women who have devoted a good part of their careers to thinking, teaching, and writing about the moral, medical, and constitutional issues in this book. I have tried to make the sources of the arguments I have used clear; specific references can be found in the notes. I apologize here to my sources for any mistakes or misrepresentations I have made in their arguments (and quickly point to the consolation that my readers may become theirs).

I begin my survey of a moral issue with a brief account of its history. Anyone frustrated by the moral chaos of contemporary life might find some solace in the fact that the greatest thinkers in history have expressed their opinions about all these issues—and have been no more successful at resolving them than we have. That, I assure you, made it easier for me to offer my own opinion at the end of the chapter. But I hasten to add that it is only that, one man's effort to confront the ethical issues of our day.

In Chapter Six, "One Nation, Many Disagreements," I try to explain why moral disagreement is inevitable in America, a pluralistic democracy that was designed to deal with philosophical, religious, and ideological clashes. No one person or group in such a society has *the* answer, the final solution, The Truth about how we all ought to live (or die). There are good arguments on all sides of all of these issues; it just depends on who you are, where you are from, and what your view of life is. Inevitably, my values will clash with yours.

How to minimize this clash of values and shape a decent society from our moral differences (or in spite of them) is the subject of my final chapter, "The Moral Imagination." Readers over forty-five will identify this notion with the literary critic Lionel Trilling, who remarked in a 1947 essay that "for our time the most effective agent of the moral imagination has been the novel of the last two hundred years."[1] For Trilling, the novel forced the reader to question "his conventional education" by opening him up to the complexities of life. "It taught us," writes Trilling, "the extent of human variety and the value of this variety."

The novel no longer has the kind of moral status Trilling gave to it even among the best-educated Americans. In my final chapter, expanding on some ideas I have found in the works of the philosophers Isaiah Berlin and Richard Rorty, I suggest that the new agents of the moral imagination are the kinds of arguments I have featured in this book, the differences of opinion over moral issues that have evolved in the United States over the past twenty years. Such arguments, in the press, in politics, in the classroom, in the dining room, and in the streets are today's proof of the "human variety" that a genuine, open democratic society is bound to be. Devotees both of the religious Right and "politically correct" Left are inclined to grumble about that variety. I argue that we should appreciate it. Moral progress is impossible without disagreement. But the most productive kind of disagreement demands moral reflection—trying to understand why others believe what they do. And that requires, I believe, moral imagination.

But first let's see how good these moral arguments are. I begin with the most perplexing moral dilemma confronting us today and the most incendiary—abortion.

1. *Abortion*

THE ISSUE

Over the past twenty years in the United States, abortion has become the most viciously divisive religious, moral, political, and legal issue since slavery. Simply to mention the word "abortion" is to raise the temperature in the room.

Why this is so is the least discussed aspect of this overdiscussed issue—and illuminates why Americans have so much trouble even talking about, never mind resolving, topics that touch their most fundamental beliefs about life and death. Abortion has been legal for more than twenty years, and each year 1.6 million legal abortions are performed. But the controversy over these two facts has become mired in rhetoric on both sides. The arguments are familiar to everyone: rights of the fetus versus rights of the mother, "unborn child" versus "lump of cells," "murder" versus the constitutional right of privacy to choose to end a pregnancy. None of these arguments, as I will try to show in this chapter, is easily dismissed. Each is strong and persuasive—*on its own terms*.

And this is the problem: Opponents in the abortion debate refuse to accept the other side's terms. Hard-line Christian opponents of abortion are unlikely to become advocates of choice. Their differences are fundamental, and thus irreconcilable. Each side looks across the barricades and sees a criminal.

Abortion—and virtually every other "moral" issue worth discussing—raises a fundamental question about the system of governance we inhabit: How does a modern, constitutional democracy resolve the inevitable clash of values that is the very definition of a pluralistic society?

With great difficulty, it turns out. Americans are inclined to believe that if we argue about an issue long enough, we will eventually arrive at a consensus. This is not always so, especially in the culturally, religiously, and ideologically charged area of morality. Yet, historically, in America, there has been a way out of moral, religious, and philosophical battles, a typically *American* way—political and legal compromise. The men who invented America knew that the only way a nation of so many different kinds of people with so many different—and contradictory—views and values could survive was if each group *tolerated* the differences of the others. The history of abortion bears this out.

Abortion and the American Legal Tradition

In late-eighteenth-century America, early abortions—that is, before the mother felt the fetus moving (known as quickening)—were legal. English common law tradition viewed the human embryo as something less than a person. Even postquickening abortions were not considered indictable offenses. The Christian churches accepted abortions before quickening. Thus, at the time that the Constitution was written, the framers, like most Americans, would have been comfortable with abortions in the first weeks of pregnancy.

By 1857, influential members of the ten-year-old American Medical Association were lobbying hard against legal abortion. Eager to professionalize American medicine and to protect women from the risks of abortion, the AMA sought to eliminate the charlatans. Advances in reproductive biology after 1950 proved that actual conception occurred long before quickening, suggesting that the human embryo was more of a baby than had been thought. Doctors began arguing for the fetus's right to life. Less admirable was the belief among some white Anglo-Saxon physicians, concerned about the social consequences of increased immigration, that legal abortion would only further diminish the falling WASP birthrate and thus endanger, as one doctor put it, "our most intelligent communities."[1]

It was this opposition to prequickening abortions among doctors rather than theologians that stirred up religious opposition to abortion in the late nineteenth century.[2] Between 1860 and 1880, U.S. states and territories signed into law forty new or revised statutes that banned abortion, though generally with one exception: "the preservation of a woman's life," a decision that was only the doctor's to make. By the turn of the century almost every state had passed a law against abortion. *Illegal* abortions, of course, continued, performed by sympathetic doctors, charlatans, and outright butchers. In 1930, 18 percent of all abortions in the United States ended in the death of the mother. During the Depression doctors sympathetic to the need for abortion stretched their definition of a "life-threatening" pregnancy to include poverty. In the 1940s doctors added *the psychiatric* problems of pregnancy to the list of what might threaten a mother's life. A 1940 survey showed that 22 percent of American women had one or more abortions between marriage and age forty-five.

To decrease their legal liability, doctors urged hospitals to set up review boards to determine which abortions were therapeutic and thus necessary. Soon, and inevitably, the threat of lawsuits over differing interpretations of "necessary" abortions scared off many doctors from performing even abortions they considered legitimate. The medical profession began to insist that the abortion laws be clarified.

In 1959 the American Law Institute revised its Model Penal Code to advocate expanding the doctor's discretion in most abortion laws to cover not only life-threatening pregnancies but also those that, in the doctor's opinion, critically impaired the mother's physical or mental condition. The code also permitted abortion if the child would be born with "grave physical or mental defects," or if the pregnancy was the result of rape or incest. The ALI also proposed that two doctors be required to certify that the abortion was justified. But, finally, it took two highly publicized cases to push the medical profession—and American public opinion—in the direction of favoring increasing the class of exceptions to the ban on abortion.

The Shift Back to Legalization of Abortion

In 1962 an Arizona mother pregnant with her fifth child realized that she had taken thalidomide, a tranquilizer that had caused horrible birth defects in Europe. A doctor scheduled her for a legal abortion, but when a newspaper interview she had given to alert other women to the dangers of thalidomide appeared, the hospital, afraid of being criminally liable for the death of the fetus, canceled the abortion. After her challenge failed in court, the woman flew to Sweden for a legal abortion.[3] According to a Gallup poll, 52 percent of Americans supported her decision.

Between 1962 and 1965 a German measles epidemic broke out in the United States, causing 15,000 babies to be born with birth defects. Nine California doctors were charged with performing illegal abortions on women exposed to measles. According to a strict reading of the abortion law, the possibility of bearing a deformed baby did not qualify as endangering the life of the mother. Doctors who adhered to the long-standing liberal attitude that the emotional or psychological risk of bearing a deformed child might constitute just as much a threat to a woman's life as a physical complication were stunned.

Also in the 1960s the availability of the birth control pill and the IUD made contraception more than a matter of good luck. Reliable birth control also allowed more women to join the workforce, either for personal fulfillment or out of economic necessity. From 1950 to 1970 the percentage of white working women nearly doubled.[4]

But artificial birth control was far from foolproof, and even the most conscientious users of the pill might end up pregnant. For a woman whose job was crucial to the economic survival of her family, an unwanted pregnancy could be a financial disaster. Feminists argued that it was impossible for women to achieve equality with men as long as they were unable to choose whether to be pregnant or not. Among most feminists, the right to choose abortion became fundamental.

In 1970 the American Medical Association publicly supported legalization, leaving the decision to abort up to the "sound clinical judgment" of the physician.[5] That year Hawaii became the first state to repeal its ban on abortion. New York soon followed. In 1972 the American Bar Association proposed its Uniform Abortion Act, based on the New York law, as a model for every state. A congressional commission also pointed to the New York law as the nationwide model. By 1973, thirteen states had liberalized their anti-abortion statutes along these lines.[6]

But most states were awaiting word from the Supreme Court.

The Battle of the Rhetoric Begins

In 1973 the Court ruled, 7 to 2, in *Roe* v. *Wade,* that a woman's decision to have an abortion is a private choice and therefore protected by the U.S. Constitution, at least until the end of the first trimester. Later in the pregnancy, the High Court ruled, a state may intervene, but only to make sure that the abortion procedures do not endanger the life of the mother. After "viability," the moment when the fetus is capable of living outside the womb (approximately the beginning of the final third of the pregnancy), the Court gave its allegiance to the "potential life" of the fetus and ruled that the state may "regulate, and even proscribe" an abortion—except when the mother's life is in danger.

Writing for the majority, Justice Harry Blackmun, a conservative jurist who was appointed to the Supreme Court by President Richard Nixon, pointed out that in the American legal tradition, "the unborn have never been recognized in the law as persons in the whole sense," and thus did not have the same legal rights as the rest of us. Blackmun noted that doctors, philosophers, and theologians do not agree when life begins. And although some Americans might truly believe that the fetus is a full-blown person, the seven-justice majority wisely fell back on the American principle of philosophical and religious tolerance, arguing that the state could not overcome a woman's right to end a pregnancy "by adopting one theory of life," in this case, a minority view, namely, that life begins at conception.

Roe v. *Wade* defined the battle lines between the opponents and advocates of abortion for the next twenty years. Calling themselves prolife, the forces against abortion, mainly groups of conservative and fundamentalist Christians who found themselves politically aligned with their traditional theological nemesis, the Roman Catholic Church, argued vigorously for their "theory of life": that, contrary to the Court's opinion, human life begins at the moment of conception, that the fetus is indeed a "person," and aborting it is an act of homicide, *pure and simple.*

Supporters of *Roe* v. *Wade* insisted they were in no way "prodeath," nor even in favor of indiscriminate abortion. They were simply "pro-choice," advocates of a woman's private right to *choose* to end a pregnancy. The pro-abortion forces also pointed out that public opinion polls showed that most Americans, including people personally opposed to abortion, supported a woman's right to make her own decision about pregnancy without the interference of the state.

Opponents of abortion chipped away at the privacy right of *Roe,* and the Court ruled in 1979 that a state could require pregnant minors to get the consent of either a parent or a judge.[7] But by then the anti-abortion forces recognized that they had only two real options: lobby to amend the Constitution, or get the Court to overturn *Roe* v. *Wade.* After several unsuccessful attempts to gain the two-thirds majority needed to amend the Constitution, the anti-abortion forces decided that if they could not change the law they would change the judges who interpret the law. Since the President nominates members of the federal judiciary, to create an anti-abortion Supreme Court the opponents of abortion would have to help elect an anti-abortion President.

In 1980, Ronald Reagan was their man, and the right-to-lifers worked hard on his behalf. President Reagan did not forget. In a speech to participants in a March for Life Rally in 1985, he reasserted his belief that "abortion is taking the life of a living human being" and that there is no constitutional right to an abortion. Such support in the White House emboldened the extreme elements of the pro-life camp to take to the streets outside abortion clinics, harass the workers at what they called "killing centers," and try to "rescue unborn children" by persuading women to reconsider their decision to have an abortion. Militant abortion opponents bombed abortion clinics.[8]

During his two terms in office Reagan appointed more than half the members of the federal bench and replaced three of *Roe*'s seven-justice majority in the Supreme Court.

President George Bush continued his predecessor's public opposition to abortion. In 1989 the Court, now led by a dissenter in *Roe*, Chief Justice William Rehnquist, made a significant retreat from abortion rights. The Court ruled, 5 to 4, in *Webster* v. *Reproductive Health Services,* to reverse a court of appeals decision and uphold a Missouri law that declares life begins at conception and prohibited state-funded clinics and state employees from performing abortions when the mother's life was not in danger and ordered clinic physicians to test for the viability of the fetus if they suspected that it was at least twenty weeks along. In the majority decision, Chief Justice Rehnquist made it clear that the government has an interest in protecting human life not just after viability but throughout pregnancy. For the Court majority, a woman's right to decide to terminate her pregnancy was a mere "liberty interest," which Rehnquist in his dissent in *Roe* had compared to a woman's "right" to drive a car or choose a certain job. In a separate opinion, Justice Antonin Scalia, a Reagan appointee, a Catholic, and the most conservative member of the Court, went so far as to declare that he was in favor of overruling *Roe. Webster* indicated that another Reagan appointee, Justice Anthony Kennedy, opposed abortion, while Justice Sandra Day O'Connor, Reagan's first appointee and the only woman on the Court, seemed willing to restrict access to legal abortion.[9]

The message of *Webster* was clear to anti-abortion legislators: though abortion was still technically legal so were regulations limiting abortion. Bush continued Reagan's effort to appoint Supreme Court justices hostile to *Roe*. In 1990, when Justice William Brennan, the most liberal member of the Court and another member of the *Roe* majority, retired, President Bush nominated David Souter, a New Hampshire jurist who was politically conservative but no ideologue. During Souter's Senate confirmation hearings the only issue that the senators and interest groups seemed to care about was the judge's position on abortion, which he deftly kept to himself, as he had every right to do. *Justice* Souter, however, soon tipped his hand.

In May 1991 the Court ruled, 5 to 4, in *Rust* v. *Sullivan,* to uphold federal regulations that bar employees of federally funded family planning clinics from *all* discussions of abortions with their patients. This meant that the 4 million women who annually use some 4,500 clinics around the country could be refused basic medical information about abortion. If a pregnant woman asks about abortion, the doctor must legally tell her that the clinic "does not consider abortion to be an appropriate method of family planning."[10] Souter cast the deciding vote.

An editorial in the *New York Times* noted that "even people who aren't poor, ignorant and utterly dependent on such a clinic would construe such a statement from a doctor as meaning, 'You can't have an abortion.' "[11] Justice Harry Blackmun, the author of *Roe,* in his separate dissent wrote angrily: "A woman seeking the services of a Title X clinic has every reason to expect, as do we all, that her physician will not withhold relevant information regarding the very purpose of her visit."

With Bush's appointment in 1991 of Clarence Thomas to replace the retiring Thurgood Marshall, another of those who had voted for *Roe,* legal abortion looked doomed.[12]

The 1992 Surprises

In June 1992 the Supreme Court surprised both sides of the abortion issue: In a 5-to-4 decision, *Planned Parenthood* v. *Casey,* a challenge to a Pennsylvania law regulating access to abortions, the High Court reaffirmed what it called "the essence" of the constitutional right to abortion. The majority said that *Roe* v. *Wade* established "a rule of law and a component of liberty we cannot renounce." It also pointed out that the 1973 decision had acquired a "rare precedential force" and could be overturned only "at the cost of profound and unnecessary damage to the Court's legitimacy." The Court upheld parts of Pennsylvania's Abortion Control Act, including requiring a woman applying for an abortion to wait twenty-four hours before having it and a teenager to have the permission of at least one parent or a judge. There was another surprise in the sixty-page decision: it was written by Souter, Kennedy, and O'Connor—the three Reagan-Bush justices.

The assault on *Roe* had been pushed back. In November 1992 the anti-abortion forces took another severe blow with the election of the Democrat Bill Clinton. In the first days of his presidency, Clinton struck down the Bush administration's federal gag order on mentioning abortion in clinics receiving federal funds. Abortion opponents redoubled their efforts. So did the extremists among them, assassinating two doctors in Pensacola, Florida, who had regularly performed abortions.

The Next Round

The battle over abortion in the United States is hardly over, but as it moves into the next round both sides might profit from keeping in mind abortion's history here. Since the U.S. Constitution was written, most Americans, including the legal and medical establishments, have not viewed *early* abortion as "murder." The majority of the current U.S. Supreme Court, most of them appointed by two presidents who vigorously opposed abortion, do not believe abortion is "murder." In fact, most Americans, including women who personally oppose abortion, believe women have a constitutional right to choose to end a pregnancy.[13]

Of course, poll numbers, or even a Supreme Court majority, do not make something *morally* correct. And no one, including the Supreme Court, can settle moral issues like abortion once and for all. In a strong sense (which I will be arguing throughout this book), moral debate over such issues as abortion is never settleable to the final satisfaction of all sides. That is why when what ought to be a private moral issue—whether a woman may terminate a pregnancy—turns into a public debate or lawsuit, the state or the courts must come up with a political, legal, or constitutional compromise. The Court did not say Americans should not debate which theory of life is best, but just that such a debate is a moral and personal one.

With this in mind, let us examine the arguments for and against abortion.

AGAINST

The Traditional Argument: "We Are All Fellow Fetuses"

Dead babies are what the abortion issue comes down to—murder, *legalized* murder, to be sure, but murder plain and simple, nevertheless; in fact, abortion in the United States is the very definition of mass murder.

Each year doctors perform an estimated 1.6 million legal abortions in our country—an unborn child is killed every twenty seconds.[14] At the current rate, by the end of 1995, twenty-two years after the Supreme Court ruled that abortion is a woman's constitutional right, the body count will have risen to 35 million dead babies. This is nothing less than a "silent Holocaust."[15]

Richard Selzer, a surgeon who is the author of *Confessions of a Knife* and other books, has described walking down the street in Manhattan in 1973 and stepping on something "soft." Upon examination, he saw "a tiny naked body, its arms and legs flung apart, its head thrown back, its mouth agape, its face serious. . . ." It resembled a bird, but it was too big. Perhaps, he thought, it was a rubber doll, an item from the jokestore.

"Look," said one passerby, "it's a baby." Others pointed out more of "these little carcasses upon the street." Dr. Selzer realized with horror that he had stepped on a "dead baby." The scene turned even more bizarre. Police arrived, roped off the area, and stood guard. "Ambulance attendants scoop up the bodies . . . little more than a dozen pounds of human flesh," recalled Selzer. The official explanation from a nearby hospital is as straightforward as it is horrifying: Aborted fetuses weighing one pound or less are incinerated. Those weighing over one pound are buried at a city cemetery. Evidently, a plastic bag marked HAZARDOUS MATERIAL that was to be taken to the cemetery got mixed up with the garbage. The bag had fallen off a garbage truck. It was, said the hospital director, "a freak accident."

This disgusting and careless scene on Seventy-third Street neatly sums up the casual attitude toward human life embodied in the abortion movement. Spread a year's worth of abortions—1.6 million tiny baby corpses—on the sidewalk in front of the Supreme Court building, and you would have a second American Revolution.

The Religious Argument: The Sanctity of Life[16]

"Pro-life" says it all: every human life is valuable in itself, including fetuses. The Bible, New Testament as well as Old, is unequivocal: Human life is given and taken back by the Creator, always under his
protection (Genesis 2:7, Proverbs 15:11). Man is made "in the image of
God" (Genesis 9:5–6), and life is a gift and responsibility (Matthew
25:14–30). "Before I formed you in the womb of your mother, I knew
you. Before you were born, I consecrated you . . ." (Jeremiah 1:4–5).
Or Psalm 139:13–16:

> It was you who created my inmost self, and put me together in my
> mother's womb. . . . You know me through and through, from having
> watched my bones take shape when I was being formed in secret, knit-
> ted together in the limbo of the womb. Your eyes beheld my informed
> substance, and in your book they were all written: the days that were
> ordained for me, even before those days were begun.

What distinguished the early Christians in the Greco-Roman world
was their commitment to protecting human life from its beginnings.
"They procreate, but they do not reject the fetus," is how one early pagan writer described Christians.[17] The heart of the Christian message
has been that each individual, created in the image of God, endowed
with a spiritual soul, has the right to life. According to early Church
teaching, "You shall not kill by abortion the fruit of the womb and
you shall not murder the infant already born. The one who will be a
man is already one."[18] The theologian Tertullian (c. 160–c. 220) condemned abortion as "murder."[19] In the thirteenth century, St. Thomas
Aquinas, Christianity's most influential theologian whose philosophy
still dominates the Roman Catholic Church, taught that abortion was
a grave sin against "natural law."

In modern times the Catholic Church, through its councils, decrees, and papal encyclicals, has confirmed its unwavering opposition
to abortion and infanticide as "abominable crimes."[20] In 1991, Pope
John Paul II vigorously scolded his fellow Poles for their high abortion
rate: "Each and every child is a gift from God. That gift is always price-
less, even if it is sometimes difficult to accept."[21] And while the Church
sanctions the emancipation of women from unjust discrimination, it
asserts that no one can free women from what nature demands of
them. Their freedom is limited by the rights of others, namely, in the
case of pregnancy, the unborn child's right to life.

This "Catholic view" is shared by numerous other Christian groups and Orthodox Jews. Opposition to abortion is widespread on the Indian subcontinent. Terminating pregnancy is called "murder" in the Vedas, the classical texts of Hinduism. Muslim leaders in Pakistan and India also condemn abortion as "murder."[22]

The Fetus Is Definitely a Person: The Scientific Argument

In *Roe* v. *Wade* the Supreme Court pled that it was not in a position to resolve "the difficult question when human life begins." This is preposterous. Science long ago decided that from the moment of conception that genetic speck is already who we will be. Present in that fertilized egg are the forty-six chromosomes that determine each person's unique genetic identity. As one geneticist told the Senate Judiciary Committee in 1981,

> Life has a very, very long history, but each individual has a very neat beginning, the moment of its conception. . . . To accept the fact that after fertilization has taken place, a new human has come into being, is no longer a matter of taste or of opinion. The human nature of the human being from conception to old age is not a metaphysical contention, it is plain experimental evidence.[23]

The evolution of the fetus into what we identify as a human being is swift and definitive: By twenty-five days the heart starts beating, by thirty days—just two weeks past the mother's first missed period—the fetus, a mere quarter inch long, has eyes, ears, a mouth, a kidney, a liver, and a brain that by forty-five days is making waves that can be recorded on an EEG. The milk teeth are already forming, and the fetus is already moving slightly. By sixty-three days the fetus can make a fist.[24]

Such scientific facts belie the notion that the fertilized egg is something different from the person it eventually will become. The fetus is a "potential person" in the same way that teenagers are potentially middle-aged. From conception every one of us is in a constant state of becoming. Is there a significant difference between the baby that is born and the "fetus" it was five minutes before? And what about that fetus coming to term and one a few weeks younger? As you follow this argument backwards toward conception, the notion that there is some qualitative difference in "personhood" between an infant and a fetus self-destructs. When *Life* magazine published photographs of the fetus in 1965 the doubts of millions that the fetus was a baby vanished.[25] As the Protestant theologian and pioneer in medical ethics Paul Ramsey once declared in opposition to abortion, "We are all fellow fetuses."[26]

The Constitutional Argument: "Slaves Were Not 'Persons' Either"

According to *Roe*, "legal personhood does not exist pre-natally." In 1857 the Supreme Court ruled in the infamous Dred Scott decision that a black slave was the "property" of its master and therefore not qualified to be a "legal personage."[27] But after the Civil War, Congress ratified the Fourteenth Amendment to the Constitution which guaranteed legal rights to black Americans.

The Supreme Court once discriminated against slaves on the basis of skin color, concluding that they were not "legal personages"; now the Court's criterion for "legal personhood" is the unborn child's environment. Living in the womb, the unborn child can be killed, legally. Outside the womb—if only for a minute—killing that same child is murder.[28]

The Horrifying Facts of an Actual Abortion

Most arguments for abortion pretend that terminating the pregnancy is the equivalent of a session in the dentist's chair, beneficial to the mother, humane to the fetus. "Safer than childbirth" is the common refrain. In fact, abortion is physiologically intrusive for the mother, interrupting an array of natural bodily functions aimed at nourishing and protecting the baby. For the unborn child, abortion is a gruesome death.

Most women who "choose" abortion have no idea what is about to happen to them. There are six common methods of abortion:[29]

  (1) Suction Aspiration: The method of choice in 90 percent of abortions performed during the first twelve weeks of pregnancy. After general or local anesthesia, the mother's cervix is dilated. A hollow tube with a knifelike tip (suction curette) attached to a suction machine is inserted into the womb. Strong suction literally tears the baby into pieces, which are vacuumed into a container.

(2) Dilation and Curettage: D&C is similar to the suction method, except for the weapon of choice: a loop-shaped knife (curette) that cuts the baby to bits and scrapes the pieces out through the cervix.

(3) Dilation and Evacuation: D&E is similar to the D&C procedure and is used up to eighteen weeks into the pregnancy. The doctor inserts a "grasping forceps" (a kind of pliers with teeth) into the uterus to snare part of the fetus. Since the baby's bones are already calcifying, the abortionist will have to twist and tear the fetus apart. The process is repeated until the unborn child's body is entirely dismembered and removed. If the head is too large to be pulled out, it is crushed.

(4) Saline Injection: Used for late second and third trimester abortions. A saline solution is injected into the amniotic sac for the baby to breathe and swallow. After one or two horrific hours, the baby dies of a dreadful combination of salt poisoning, dehydration, hemorrhages of the brain and other organs, and convulsions. Used for late second and third trimester abortions, the procedure eventually induces labor, and within twenty-four to forty-eight hours the baby is delivered, dead or dying. The salt solution often literally strips off the baby's skin.

(5) Prostaglandin Abortion: Used for abortions performed in the second half of pregnancy. The doctor injects the amniotic sac with prostaglandins—hormones required in the natural birth process—which induces the birth of an infant usually too premature to survive outside the womb. A saline injection is often used to assure that the baby is born dead, which is believed to be less upsetting for the mother and hospital staff.

(6) Hysterotomy: Similar to a Caesarean section, the hysterotomy is used if the saline injection or prostaglandin abortion has not worked. The doctor cuts open the abdomen and lifts out the baby, usually alive. The umbilical cord is clamped, and the child dies, though often not without a struggle.[30]

The Fight Goes On

It is not surprising that thousands in the right-to-life movement have taken their battle to the streets in an all-out effort to prevent this slaughter of innocents. Some have gone to jail and suffered solitary confinement; others have burned and bombed the "killing centers" that abortionists would prefer to call "clinics." A few have gone so far as to kill the killers.

Violence is not everyone's style. And it would be a tragedy that in a dedicated effort to stop innocent deaths more innocent people were killed. Catholic and other pro-life groups have advised abortion opponents to create political and public relations strategies to defeat legalized abortion as a substitution for violence. But when else is violence justified if not to stop mass murder?

IN FAVOR

The Argument for "Choice"[31]

Pro-choice advocates do not *favor* abortion over birth; they simply support reproductive freedom—that is, women should have the choice to end an unwanted pregnancy.

That abortion is murder requires a logical leap that stretches the limits of the language. "The fetus is an innocent person," argue the right-to-lifers, and, as everyone—including liberals and feminists—can agree, killing an innocent person is cold-blooded murder and thus morally reprehensible. But pro-choice advocates do not concede the fundamental principle of the right-to-life movement: that a fetus is a "person." The fetus, especially in its earliest stages, is certainly not a person—at least not in any way that most people understand that word. To call the fetus a person is like calling an acorn an oak, a seed a rose, a blueprint a house, cake ingredients a cake.

Personhood is a philosophical or theological issue, not a biological one. Although the Roman Catholic Church, Orthodox Jews, and some fundamentalist Christian sects may sincerely believe that personhood begins at conception, certainly not all Christians and many Jews, as well as millions of others not tied to any organized religion, believe that fetuses are persons. As Justice Blackmun noted for the Court majority in *Roe,* no consensus exists among theologians and philosophers for when personhood begins.

The Appeal to Science Produces Only
Another Scientific Theory

The National Right to Life Committee has played the declarations of certain geneticists and "fetologists" to the hilt: at conception, all forty-six chromosomes that determine a person's unique genetic identity are present. But, as clever lawyers have always known, "expert witnesses" can be found on both sides of almost every issue, and abortion is no exception.

Cell biologist Charles Gardner has taken aim at the fetuses-are-us argument and, at the very least, blasts away its air of certitude.[32] According to him, after conception, a complex series of cell and molecular divisions occurs, each stage responding to the preceding *random* division. "There is no program to specify the fate of each cell," notes Gardner. "Each stage brings new information, information that will change as the body pattern changes." One single cell may contribute randomly to the formation of several different body parts. "With this layering of chance event upon chance event the embryo gradually evolves its form." Not only is the person that the embryo is to become not programmed in the fertilized egg, not even so much as a fingerprint is already there. The ovum is in no way, argues Gardner, "a prepackaged human being."

That at conception something has begun is not controversial. But to call a minute-old embryo or a three-month-old fetus a person is to beg the question.

The fetus is only a "potential person" which looks increasingly human as it develops from the speck of a fertilized egg to a full-term infant ready to exit its mother's womb. Whatever one thinks of *Roe*— and many supporters of choice find the Court's decision flawed—the Court evaded the issue of "personhood" because it saw that giving a fetus legal rights would be a judicial catastrophe.[33] States have already prosecuted crack and cocaine abusers for "delivering" drugs to their fetuses, and a Florida woman was actually convicted of such a crime after she admitted to taking cocaine the night before she gave birth to an addicted baby.[34] What's next—drinking or smoking cigarettes or pigging out on jelly donuts, which we all know to be filled with heart-stopping cholesterol? Could the state prosecute a woman for manslaughter if she threw herself down the steps, causing a miscarriage? Can a fetus be a person in Florida but not in New York?

Over the years we have listened to theologians, philosophers, constitutional scholars, and the medical profession about abortion. We must now begin listening to women.

The Feminist Argument: Autonomy with a "Different Voice"[35]

Many women suffer for no other reason than that they are women. Unwanted pregnancy is a dilemma that a man can share, perhaps; sympathize with, maybe, but fully understand, never.[36]

Feminists now recognize that abortion crystallizes the most fundamental issue of feminism—the autonomy of women. "No woman can call herself free who does not own and control her own body," declared Margaret Sanger, the pioneer of birth control in the United States. The French philosopher and patron saint of feminism Simone de Beauvoir viewed pregnancy, which she called the "slavery of reproduction," the greatest obstacle to female liberation.

Who controls a woman's body? Their husbands or lovers? The courts? The right-to-life movement? Is there a man (or woman) alive in our country today who would seriously claim that women do not have the right to control their bodies? If someone did make such a claim, would anyone take him seriously? Feminists do not want to be men, or even to be "like men"; they want only to be *equal* to men, to have the same rights as men, to be paid the same as men in the same jobs, to be able to choose as freely as men. In the 1960s the increasing availability of reliable birth control made it possible for women to choose when they wanted to have a family. A giant step toward the liberation of women, birth control did not, however, free them entirely from the dilemma of unwanted pregnancy. No method of contraception is perfect.[37]

Listen carefully to the hard-line opponents of abortion, examine their propaganda, catch their focus: the fetus is a person, that's a baby in there, with a right to life. Look at the photographs of fetuses, look at aborted fetuses. They look like us, say the anti-abortion camp.

But there is one important factor missing in all those photographs of fetuses: the mother. The fetus is not hanging on a hook in the nursery or suspended in space, awaiting the stork. The fetus happens to be surrounded by its mother; it is in a very real sense *part* of its mother. A woman is not merely a vehicle of birth. Nor is she a warehouse for the "unborn child," as a federal judge with a knack for metaphor recently put it, "holding it captive."[38]

The right-to-life movement claims to be a defender of "motherhood." Yet, the anti-abortion camp's insistence that the fetus is an "independent person" devalues the first nine months of motherhood. Without the mother a fetus cannot grow. She nurtures and sustains the fetus. She *creates* a child. Each week of pregnancy brings a different relationship to that fetus. There is nothing trivial about that pregnancy. The fetus not only inhabits the mother's body, it is also *part* of her body. The health of the mother affects the health of the fetus.

Unfortunately, in the heat of the feminist renaissance in the 1960s, too many advocates of choice adopted an unnecessarily extreme position by arguing that the fetus was some kind of "primitive form of life," a mere "lump of cells," a jelly that had no more significance in a woman's body than her appendix. "Abortion is a health issue, not a moral issue," was a favorite slogan of the early feminist movement.[39]

Few would go so far today.[40] The fetus is more than a vestigial organ, if only because it is human, alive, and developing, and will at one point be able to live on its own. It is also the way we all come to be. For that reason alone the fetus should have some special status. Nevertheless, as a fetus, it cannot be discussed independently of its mother; by definition, that is what a fetus is—a human embryo growing in the mother's womb. *Separate* from its mother, the fetus is a "baby."

For many women, facing the issue of abortion is the first time they have had to make a decision for themselves that no one else, finally, can make. It is their body at risk, their fetus at risk, their personal, family, and financial future at risk. In fact, women may make moral decisions differently from men; they may speak in a "different voice," as the Harvard psychologist Carol Gilligan suggests in *In a Different Voice,* a provocative and controversial (even among feminists) book about how women grow morally. According to her, while men look to logic and reason to help them decide what is best to do, women's moral choices are based on "a feeling for the complexity and multifaceted character of real people and real situations."[41] Faced with a moral dilemma, women, Gilligan points out, are inclined to ask not what is right or best or reasonable or the rule, but "who am I hurting?"[42]

In a study of twenty-nine women aged fifteen to thirty and of diverse ethnic and social backgrounds grappling with the dilemma of unwanted pregnancy, Gilligan found that again it was not "rights" or "rules" that shaped their decisions but the "ethic of care."[43] For these women, the dilemma of abortion was an agonizing and guilt-provoking crisis, but one, finally, that gave them the opportunity for, in their words, "a new beginning" and a chance "to take control of my life."

For the first time in their lives, these women claimed they experienced the "power of autonomy" to make a decision without their father, boyfriend, or husband.

In 1970, Kate Michelman was a thirty-year-old mother pregnant with her fourth child when her husband announced that he was leaving her for another woman. "I had no car, I couldn't get credit because I had no husband, and I had three children to feed," Michelman later told a newspaper reporter. "I understood at that moment the kinds of choices women have to make and how they affect the very fabric of a woman's life."[44]

Michelman opted for an abortion, and the hospital scheduled her for a legal abortion. But while lying in a hospital bed awaiting the procedure she was informed that the hospital would not allow the abortion unless she had the written permission of her husband—the man who had already left her (and their fetus) for another woman! Michelman got her abortion (the hospital tracked down her husband, who gave his permission), but she also recognized that "I had absolutely no control over my own life."[45]

For most women, abortion is an agonizing decision. Something went wrong. They had not planned to have a baby. And what the anti-abortion forces never concede, particularly those who support contraception (and polls show that even among American Catholics 95 percent use artificial contraception), is that something goes wrong a lot of the time. In fact, of the 6 million pregnancies every year in the United States, more than half are unintended. Even using the pill, the most effective method of birth control, the pregnancy rate runs from 4 to 9 percent.[46] The highest percentage of abortions are among poor, unmarried black women, for whom pregnancy or another child can be a tragedy.[47]

"Life is like that," say the hard-liners. "We all have to suffer the consequences of our actions [i.e., ordinary sexuality]; life is full of contingencies which we have to cope with." But if one out of two pregnancies is accidental, then unwanted pregnancy is the norm and not the exception.

Abortion as Self-Defense

Twenty years ago the MIT philosopher Judith Jarvis Thompson articulated in a sharp, original way what many women faced with an unwanted pregnancy have felt about abortion: it is an act of self-preservation.[48] Professor Thompson concludes that the concern over the personhood of the fetus distracts us from the real question of whether the state has a right to force us to support any life against our will. In a now-famous "thought experiment," she asks you to imagine waking up attached to a famous violinist with a deadly kidney ailment. You alone have the right blood type to help, and he is now tied to your circulatory system. Disconnect him, and he will die. Fortunately, he will not be attached to you forever; nine months is all he requires, or maybe just twenty-four weeks.

"Well, maybe, for nine months," you say. How about for eighteen years (i.e., the time until most children finish high school and might be able to support themselves)? And remember: violinists are persons, and all persons have a right to life. Thompson suggests that most of us would find this "outrageous," and no law would justly force you to be the violinist's life-support system. The violinist may have a right to life, but he definitely does not have a right to use your kidneys, unless you have given him that right. Thompson notes that too often the participants in the abortion debate "refuse to grant to the mother that very status of person which is so firmly insisted on for the fetus."[49]

As Thompson points out, in Anglo-American law there is no general obligation for anyone to be a hero. By any other measure, to require a woman to put her life at the service of someone else's life is an act of discrimination.

An Equal Right to Choose

Banning abortion imposes a huge burden on women only. If women are to be equal to men, they must be as unhindered in reproductive matters as men. A free society allows many different kinds of personal choices; control over sexual reproduction ought to be one of them.

Despite the overheated rhetoric of the right-to-life camp, most women do not have abortions for trivial reasons. Nor do most women take their decisions to have an abortion lightly. Usually, it is a matter of last resort: they cannot raise the child alone as a single parent, they cannot face giving up the child for adoption, they are not psychologically or financially equipped to assume caring for a severely deformed, retarded, or handicapped child. Abortion is never an easy decision. And although that might not be apparent to those who oppose a woman's right to end a pregnancy, if there is a right to choose to end a pregnancy it exists no matter what others might think of the reasons for that choice. A decision must be made. A free decision, an autonomous decision. A choice. How could such a process be considered immoral? In the face of violent opposition, pro-choice advocates will continue to point out that in the United States individual moral decisions are the prerogative of individuals. Most Americans, including those who personally oppose abortion, believe that the option of legal abortion—the choice—ought to be available. And so far, the Supreme Court is inclined to agree.

"PRO-LIFE FEMINISM"

The conventional perception is that if you are a feminist you must be an advocate of abortion. Historically, however, such founding mothers of feminism as Susan B. Anthony, Elizabeth Cady Stanton, and Victoria Woodhull all opposed abortion on the grounds that it was just one more way that men oppressed women, particularly poor women. "Pro-life feminism" is undergoing a renaissance, and thousands of women, well educated, professionals and intellectuals, have joined such national pro-life organizations as Feminists for Life, founded in 1972 by two women who were expelled from the National Organization for Women (NOW) for opposing abortion, and JustLife, a coalition of Catholics and Protestants who support a "consistent life ethic." Members share the view that anyone who believes, as Christians must, that every person has been created in the image of God must fight against nuclear arms, support government programs to create jobs, health care, housing, and food for America's poor, and oppose abortion.[50]

The following argument is based largely on the writings of Sidney Callahan, a professor of psychology at Mercy College in New York and a well-known Catholic writer and feminist who opposes abortion. She is the wife of Daniel Callahan, a pioneer in medical ethics and the founding director of the Hastings Institute, who is pro-choice and has written a book on abortion and lectured widely on his position. The Callahans have been interviewed often and have appeared in public together debating their own long-standing dispute about the morality of abortion. They are a striking example of how even the best informed

and most thoughtful people can disagree deeply on a moral issue—
even when they are happily married.

True Feminism Is Opposed to Abortion: Sidney Callahan

Abortion is not a prerequisite for total fulfillment as a woman. Nor is
abortion the sine qua non of female equality. You can be a feminist and
also be pro-life.[51] Pro-life feminists view abortion as one more "human rights movement" in the tradition of the fight against slavery, capital punishment, and nuclear arms, and the fight for women's suffrage
and aid to the poor.[52]

"The fetus is not a person." Does this major premise of the traditional feminist argument for abortion sound familiar? How about: "A
slave is property, not a person"; or "Women are inferior to men." Indeed, women were once seen as somehow not fully developed until
they were incorporated into the "one flesh" of marriage. Women, too,
were not so long ago considered the "property" of their husbands.
Philosophers stray too far afield for analogies to justify abortion: it is
not like rescuing a drowning child; it is not like being hooked up to a
famous violinist. Pregnancy is not like anything.

Yet a few things about the fetus are not controversial: it is alive, it is
human, it is innocent, it is powerless. If there is one value that distin-
guishes "liberalism," it is its concern to protect the innocent and the
powerless. What is more innocent and more powerless than the fetus?

Typically, feminists contend that the fetus—read "early" fetus—is
obviously different from you and me, hardly a person. The criteria for
personhood that pro-choice feminists usually offer are self-conscious,
rational, desiring, and social. Throw a brick over your shoulder on
any big city street and you will hit a "person" who is unlikely to meet
such high standards. (And none of us when we are asleep.) What child
under two would measure up? Yes, many women who suddenly find
themselves unintentionally pregnant are terrified or miserable or anx-
ious or crazed with stress. Yes, women are alone in the face of the
dilemma of abortion. Like all refugees from nonpersonhood, they are
left to fight for themselves. Feminism has become a rallying point for
women fed up with male aggression and dominance who are convinced that there is a better way to live. Feminism is a struggle for justice and equality. But "women will never climb to equality and social
empowerment over mounds of dead fetuses."[53]

Moral Responsibility Is a Communal Responsibility

No pro-life feminist would dispute the difficulties that bearing an unwanted child entails. But feminists have focused too hard on "choice."
Autonomy is not the ultimate model of moral responsibility. Morality
also requires us to accept the accidents of life as well as be part of a
family, a community, and a society.

Parents have moral obligations to their children. Women, even accidentally pregnant, have a moral obligation to the new innocent life
that depends only on them. The rights of fetuses come from their dependency, their innocence, their weakness. Our obligation to these innocents stems from our sense of community, of solidarity. How can we
condemn cruelty to the Kurds or Jews or Palestinians or the poorest
Americans and not wince at the prospect of killing a human life inside
our own body? How could any woman claim that a life she helped create, something she is now nurturing inside her own body, is not "like
us"? What is more "like us" than our own children?

The "Feminist Fallacy"

Many women have fallen victim to the "phallic fallacy"—namely, that
to be equal to men requires becoming more like them. But feminism's
true goal is that women as women can make a significant, and equal,
contribution to every aspect of human life and be rewarded equally.

Women *are* different from men, and nowhere is this more indisputable than in matters of sex and reproduction. Sex for women is different—more complex, more intense, more extended in time, and more
risky physically, psychologically, and socially. It is significant (and not
surprising) that nineteenth-century feminists advocated sex with deep
emotional bonds and security—sex, but not without love; sex, but not
without chastity and monogamy; sex, but not without fidelity.

Historically, feminists have fought for women to be protected
against rape, for mothers to be ensured child support, for older
women not to be abandoned when their sexual attraction fades. The
male reverence for orgasm has encouraged "recreational sex"—sex
for pleasure only, sex for conquest, sex for "fun." What feminist is not
fundamentally opposed to this version of sexual fulfillment? It is this
male ethic—"free sex" (i.e., no-cost sex) as opposed to liberated sex—
that encourages men to abandon their pregnant girlfriends, their
wives, and their children. Legal abortion legitimizes male irresponsi-

bility. Indeed, "abortion helps a woman's body be more like a man's."[54] *Roe* v. *Wade* has removed the last defense women had against male sexual demands: "I don't want to risk getting pregnant."

Toward the "Feminization of Sexuality"

The only aspect of sexuality that men and women share is the orgasm, and as is often the case in our male-dominated world, it is only what men find important that counts. When male psychologists discuss "peak experiences" they laughably discuss athletic events—the perfect basketball game, the grand slam.

Is there a peak experience that beats birth? Female sexuality is a unique potential trust. Pro-life feminists believe that "women will only flourish when there is a feminization of sexuality." Orgasm, pregnancy, birth, and nurturing are all involuntary experiences of the female body. Historically, feminists were right to rebel against patriarchal demands. But the "feminist mistake" was to reject the nineteenth-century feminist ethic of love, chastity, and fidelity in favor of a male ideal of "having it all"—namely, sex without responsibility.

Helping Women in a Man's World

Instead of committing so much thought and energy to justifying abortion, feminists should devote themselves to rethinking sexuality, femininity, and reproduction. Has the availability of abortion slowed the progress of birth control research? Shouldn't our anger be turned against the drug companies rather than against women who enter an abortion clinic?[55] Science and the laws are already rewriting the boundaries of motherhood and reproduction. Test-tube babies, surrogate mothers, fetal surgery, and the abortion pill are already challenging the old arguments for and against abortion. We must face up to the moral and social implications of these advances.

We must also work for women's rights in the workplace, for day care, for flexible schedules and maternity leaves, and for an environment free of sexual discrimination and harassment.

Pro-life feminists have an important role in guiding that vision for our daughters and granddaughters.

A MIDDLE ROAD

The official Catholic position is known, indeed is notorious in certain circles, for its extreme position on the pure immorality of abortion. But individual Catholics do not always toe the hard line, particularly in the area of sex (contraception, extramarital sex, divorce, and homosexuality quickly come to mind). The Catholic philosophical and theological tradition is apparently vast and complex enough to accommodate liberals, conservatives, and everyone in between. Here is a summary of a much anthologized argument for why a Catholic can support an early abortion:

"A Liberal Catholic's View": Joseph F. Donceel, S.J.[56]

Traditionally, Catholic philosophy has held that it is the "spiritual soul" that makes an organism a human being. Today most Catholics believe that the soul is infused in the human body at *the moment of conception.* For most of the Church's history, however, Catholic philosophy and theology have held that "the human soul was infused in the body only when the latter began to show a human shape or outline and possessed human organs." To abort a fetus when it looks like a person is a grave sin. Before this stage, however, the embryo is alive— but only as a plant or an animal is alive. The fetus may be *evolving* toward personhood, but in the early stages of pregnancy it is not a person. This view was most famously articulated by St. Thomas Aquinas (1225–74), whose views were adopted as the official philosophy of the Christian Church before the Reformation and dominate Roman Catholic thought to this day.[57]

St. Thomas, like other great medieval theologians influenced heavily by the writings of Aristotle, believed in hylomorphism—namely, that the human body is the result of the union of the soul and the "cosmic stuff" that gives it its shape. The soul is to the body as the shape of the statue is to the actual statue. The embryo is no more a person than a block of marble is Michelangelo's *Pièta*. The Catholic Church officially adopted the hylomorphic view of man at the Council of Vienne, in 1312, and "for centuries her law forbade the faithful to baptize any premature birth which did not show at least some human shape or outline."[58]

Why the shift away from Aquinas on the issue of abortion? "In the early seventeenth century, as a result of poor microscopes and lively imaginations," physicians saw little people with arms and legs in embryos a few days old, and argued from this that humans are "preformed." Further impetus came with the popularity of the view of the French philosopher René Descartes (1596–1650) that the human body and the human soul are each complete and separate substances, connected only by divine intervention. It was the soul's presence that caused the body's evolution. One more possible explanation of the shift in Catholic opinion away from Aquinas is the Church's early opposition to the theory of evolution. With hylomorphism, Aquinas admitted to a kind of evolution taking place in the womb, from embryo, to fetus, to child.

Now that the Church has finally accepted the evolution of the human species, why not the evolution of the embryo? Contemporary philosophy opposes Descartes's strict dualism between the soul and the body, and no one is any more certain about the moment the fetus is infused with a soul to become a person than precisely when the innocent child becomes a responsible moral agent. If so, why abandon hylomorphism?

Therefore, according to at least one centuries-old view in Catholic theology and philosophy which holds that neither the embryo nor early fetus is an actual person with a soul, it is not immoral to terminate an early pregnancy, "provided there are serious reasons for such an intervention."

"Sanctity of Life" as a Pro-Choice Argument: Ronald Dworkin[59]

Neither side in the abortion wars has an argument to offer that the other can accept. Disagreement is fundamental and would seem therefore to be irreconcilable: the fetus is an unborn child and abortion is an act of murder, or the fetus is a collection of cells, not yet a child any more than a just fertilized egg is a chicken. Compromise is impossible. The best we can hope for between these two camps is a "pale civility, the kind of civility one might show an incomprehensible but dangerous Martian."[60]

But this is so only if we persist in seeing the argument in these terms. In fact, the way the abortion argument is usually posed is wrong and based on a "widespread intellectual confusion" which, once identified, opens up at least a "responsible legal settlement" that will satisfy both sides of the abortion battle.

Both sides of the abortion battle do not always stick to the logical consequences of their rhetoric. According to the polls, most Americans support a woman's right to an abortion. According to a 1992 Gallup poll, 52 percent of American Catholics think that abortion should be legal in "many or all" circumstances and 33 percent in "rare" circumstances. The best evidence suggests that American Catholic women are no less likely to have an abortion than women in general. Other fundamentalist opponents of abortion, including many state legislators, are willing to sanction terminating a pregnancy when the mother's life is at stake or in cases of rape or incest.[61]

These opinions are "baffling" if we accept the seriousness of the argument that abortion is murder. If opponents of abortion really believed aborting the fetus is murder, it would remain murder in all cases, no matter the mitigating circumstances. No less baffling is the ambivalence toward abortion among those who believe that women have an absolute right to choose to end a pregnancy. "Liberals" are inclined to argue that the fetus, hardly a person, has no rights; yet few liberals are willing to concede that an abortion is no less grave than a tonsillectomy. Like conservatives, liberals appear to presume that "human life has moral significance, so that it is in principle wrong to terminate a life when no one's interests are at stake."[62]

What most people, on both sides of the abortion divide, really seem to believe is that "the fetus is a living, growing human creature and that it is intrinsically a bad thing, a kind of cosmic shame, when human life at any stage is deliberately extinguished."[63] Christians and feminists, liberals and conservatives seem to be generally opposed to destroying human life because they believe that in some deep sense life is "sacred."

WHAT DOES IT MEAN TO SAY THAT "LIFE IS SACRED OR INVIOLABLE"?

"The sacred is intrinsically valuable because—and therefore only once—it exists."[64] To be "intrinsically" valuable is to be valued *independent* of what people enjoy or want or need. A great painting is valuable not for the pleasure it gives or for the amount of money it might be worth, but because it is simply wonderful.

We are inclined to view both art and people as *creations*. And just as an artist creates a picture, we believe that God (or nature) has created humans and their environment. We believe that humanity should flourish and survive not because it is a matter of justice for those who follow us, but because of "our instinctive sense that human flourishing as well as human survival is of sacred importance."[65] But it is also crucial to note that we are selective about survival. Just as we believe the work of a major artist is more sacred than the work of a minor one, that the survival of the Siberian tiger is more important than that of a species of snake or shark, we also believe that certain lives deserve saving over others.

WHAT IS MORE SACRED—THE LIFE OF THE MOTHER OR THE FETUS?

It depends on how you view the effects of death. Traditionally, both conservatives and liberals seem to agree that a premature death is "a waste." How great the waste is likely to depend on the stage of life at which it occurs. This helps explain why liberals are no less comfortable than conservatives with a late-term abortion: It is not merely because late fetuses look more like infants or that they are more sentient; it is also because "Fetal development is a continuing creative process . . . after implantation, as fetal growth continues, the natural investment that would be wasted in an abortion grows steadily larger and more significant."[66] The mother's emotional attachment to the growing child in her becomes stronger. What started as a genetic speck is now looking, and feeling, more like a baby.

It is here in this area of "waste" and "frustration" of created life that liberals and conservatives have their strong philosophical and religious differences. Those who believe that God (or nature) creates life are more likely to believe that the deliberate destruction of the fetus is morally wrong. However, if you believe that it is *man* himself who has control over life and that life's creative value derives from how much a person—and not God—contributes to that life in terms of training, personal choice, and commitment, you will be more inclined to believe that the frustration that an unwanted pregnancy might create for a woman's life could be a greater evil than the premature death of a fetus.[67]

Seen in these terms, the conflict over abortion is hardly about the rights of the fetus versus those of the mother. The argument can now be seen as a "difference of emphasis" on how an investment in life can be frustrated.

"WASTING LIFE": TWO VIEWS

The fundamental issue of the debate over abortion can be summarized in this question: Is the frustration of a biological life, which wastes human life, nevertheless sometimes justified in order to avoid frustrating a human contribution to that life or to other people's lives, which would be a different kind of waste? If so, when and why?

Conservatives answer a flat no to the first question. Abortion is murder and as such it is not justified. But even for conservatives, there seem to be exceptions, which suggests that not even they see abortion as murder pure and simple. Only a minority view abortion as not justified even to save the life of the mother. Other opponents of abortion believe that terminating a pregnancy is morally permissible in cases of rape and incest.

Liberals justify abortion by expanding the realm of exceptions beyond those dire circumstances to how much the birth of the fetus will affect the quality of the lives of the mother and her family. If the fetus will inevitably have a "seriously frustrated life," liberals believe abortion is justified, particularly so in the case of a severe physical deformity that would create a miserable and painful life for the child and parents. Liberals also believe ending the life of a fetus is justified if the birth would severely affect the lives of the mother and the rest of the family. Given the respect liberals have for the intrinsic value of human life, "liberals are especially concerned about the waste of the human contribution to that value."[68] Measuring this waste in frustration rather than just loss, liberals believe such waste is much greater when a teenaged mother's life is ruined than when an early-stage fetus's life is ended.[69]

This has nothing to do with comparing the quality of the mother's life with that of the child had it been allowed to live.

> Recognizing the sanctity of life does not mean attempting to engineer fate so that the best possible lives are lived overall; it means, rather, not frustrating investments in life that have already been made. For that reason, liberal opinion cares more about lives that people are now leading, lives in earnest, than about the possibility of other lives to come.[70]

Thus there can be a common ground in the abortion issue for liberals and conservatives. While both sides are bound to continue to disagree, they might recognize that their disagreements are "at bottom *spiritual*." That alone is cause for optimism because in America we have learned that "real community is possible across deep religious grounds." This "common commitment to the sanctity of life . . . is a unifying ideal we can rescue from the decades of hate."[71]

"The Seamless Garment": Cardinal Joseph Bernardin[72]

As Dworkin rightly notes, "spiritual" disagreements have never been a major obstacle to political unity in our nation. American Catholics have worked hard to acclimate their beliefs, supervised by an essentially medieval, absolutist empire based in Rome, within a modern pluralistic democracy. In the heat of the abortion debate, the most central American value is often overlooked—religious tolerance. An influential segment of the Catholic intellectual community has made an impressive effort to pose its arguments against abortion in the context of religious tolerance and what they see as the Church's moral—and political—obligation to help shape society. An important voice in this movement is Joseph Bernardin, the cardinal archbishop of Chicago, who argued on several occasions in the 1980s that if Catholics were serious about "respecting life," then they must extend that respect from fetuses to the poor, the criminal, and the victims of war and other forms of violence.[73] Cardinal Bernardin's argument:

"Human life is both sacred and social." On those two truths about the human person, Catholic teaching rests. "Because we esteem human life as sacred, we have a duty to protect and foster it at all stages of development from conception to natural death and in all circumstances. Because we acknowledge that human life is also social, society must protect and foster it."[74]

Catholic teaching has always recognized certain exceptions to this sanctity of human life—for example, self-defense and capital punishment. But modern technology forces us to pay even more careful attention to the restrictions on these exceptions, for while war has always threatened life, "the weapons produced by modern technology now threaten life on a scale previously unimaginable." This new technology creates a "new range of moral problems"—in genetics, abortion, capital punishment, modern warfare, and the care of the terminally ill.

How should we decide what to do and what not to do? No single answer is available to all these problems; each requires its own analysis. "But they are all linked!" Solving these moral problems requires a "consistent ethic."

Society's policies and practices about life are determined, ultimately, by its attitude toward life. "When human life is considered 'cheap' or easily expendable in one area, eventually nothing is held as sacred and all lives are in jeopardy."

So the theological foundation of the "consistent ethic" is one that grows out of Catholic thought—a theological system that refuses to treat moral issues in an ad hoc fashion and holds that central to morality is the defense of the person. According to Catholic theology, a person is made in the image of God, a person's dignity must be affirmed, and the society and the state exist to serve the person.

These positions are behind the U.S. bishops' stand on such diverse issues as nuclear policy and abortion. This is much more than a mere political position; it is a "moral vision" for how the Catholic Church can influence the shape of morality in the United States.[75]

RELIGION AND PLURALISM IN AMERICA

In America, different groups hold different—and incompatible—views about religious and moral matters. This is the definition of "pluralism."[76] Fundamental also to the American system is religious tolerance. But tolerance is not, as some mistakenly seem to believe, about expelling religious views and values from the society; it is about giving them space to play a role in the public discourse. The Church in America, as the eminent Jesuit historian John Courtney Murray pointed out, has a right to speak out on political matters. The Church will, however, have to recognize that issues of medical ethics and social policy are complex; "the moral dimensions of our public life are interwoven with empirical judgments where honest disagreement exists." But such "empirical complexity" should not necessarily silence religious or moral views.

How do you achieve a moral consensus in a religiously pluralistic society? "By a process of debate, decision making, then review of our decisions."[77] Reaching a consensus about legislating morality is never easy, but in the past we have managed as a society to struggle with morality and come up with some answers as to whether or not to try to legislate how our fellow citizens ought to behave in public. Mistakes are made. Society, for example, recognized that making the consumption of alcohol illegal was a mistaken intrusion into private morality and beyond the province of the law. But in the case of civil rights, especially in housing, education, employment, voting, and access to public facilities, legislating against racial discrimination was crucial to public order.

The opponents of civil rights for African-Americans were no less convinced that you could not legislate morality than those who opposed Prohibition. When he was told that the law could not be used to legislate morality, Dr. Martin Luther King Jr. used to say that "the law could not make people love their neighbors, but it could stop their lynching them." The law can shape the moral consensus as well as result from it. Catholics have an obligation to make sure their views about morality are part of the general moral and legal debate over such life and death issues as caring for the terminally ill, capital punishment, modern warfare, genetic engineering, and abortion.

CONSTITUTIONAL BATTLE OVER ABORTION, PROS AND CONS

This section is a summary of the constitutional arguments for abortion and the criticism of these arguments. Rather than grouping all the arguments against the courts' right to enter the abortion argument and then follow with the counterarguments, I think it is more helpful (and striking) to see them together, first the argument against the role of the courts in settling abortion (CON) and then the counterargument in support of the Supreme Court's position (PRO). This summary leans heavily, though not only, on Laurence Tribe's more lengthy attempt to settle abortion's place in our constitutional rights in his book *Abortion: The Clash of Absolutes* and Ronald Dworkin's more recent effort in his book *Life's Dominion.*[78]

Con: Legislators, not judges, should decide the legality of abortion. For courts to decide that a woman has a right to an abortion is undemocratic. Such important social issues should be left to congresspeople and state legislators, the elected officials representative of and responsible to their constituents.

Pro: An independent judiciary, by definition, is undemocratic, but the job of striking down laws that the Court decides violate the Constitution is the linchpin of the American constitutional system. "Should a legislature, through the democratic process, enact a law that transgresses the guarantees contained in the Constitution, the federal courts have not merely the power but the obligation to strike that law down."[79]

Con: Roe protects a woman's "right to privacy," which is never mentioned in the Constitution. Some states have legally banned abortion. Supreme Court justices have overturned those laws on the basis of disagreement with the majority decisions of duly elected representatives of the people of those states. *Roe* is a clear example of judicial power out of control.

Pro: To be sure, the word "privacy" is not in the Constitution. "But the guarantees of the Constitution are not like itemized deductions. The Constitution contains broad provisions whose meaning requires judicial interpretation."[80] And that is what judges do. The current consensus among legal scholars (and the majority of the Supreme Court) is that a woman's fundamental right to privacy is provided for by the "liberty clause" of the Fourteenth Amendment: "No State shall . . . deprive any person of life, liberty, or property, without due process of law." Historically, the Court has interpreted this to protect individual rights from government intrusion. In fact, the Court has decided that the protections of the Bill of Rights, which Congress (but not necessarily state legislatures) is *prohibited* from curtailing, are extended to states by the liberty clause of the Fourteenth Amendment.

The framers of the Constitution clearly did not intend the Bill of Rights to apply to the states, but the Supreme Court has applied those protections via the Fourteenth Amendment, and no sitting justice has disagreed.

Con: Opponents of *Roe* argue that only those rights mentioned in the Bill of Rights should be applied to the states—freedom of religion, speech, the press, assembly, and the right to petition; the right to bear arms; the right to quarter troops; the right to be secure from unreasonable searches and seizures; the right to a fair and speedy trial; the right not to be tried for the same offense twice, and just compensation for property. "Privacy" is not on the list.

Pro: What these opponents of *Roe* fail to mention is that Article IX of the Bill of Rights explicitly states, "The enumeration in the Constitution of certain rights, shall not be construed to deny or disparage others retained by the people." Thus the Constitution itself warns us that the Bill of Rights is not necessarily an exhaustive and ultimate list of our protections.

The Right to Privacy in Sexual Matters

Earlier in this century the Supreme Court made it clear that Americans have, in Justice Louis Brandeis's famous phrase, "the right to be left alone." In two landmark cases in the 1920s the Court ruled that a state does not have the right to "foster a homogeneous people"; parents have the right to "direct the upbringing and education of children under their control."[81]

The Court first recognized that Americans have a fundamental right in sexual matters in 1942 (*Skinner* v. *Oklahoma*) by invalidating a state law that allowed anyone convicted two or more times of "felonies involving moral turpitude" to be sterilized. The Court declared that the right to reproduce was "one of the basic civil rights of man," and warned of turning this power over to the state, thus risking it to end up in "evil or reckless hands." In 1965, in *Loving* v. *Virginia,* the Court recognized another fundamental protection that is certainly not listed in the Bill of Rights—"the right to choose one's spouse"—by declaring Virginia's law against interracial marriage unconstitutional.

The same year the Supreme Court ruled that married couples have the right to decide to use contraceptives (*Griswold* v. *Connecticut*). Seven years later, in *Eisenstadt* v. *Baird,* the Court struck down a Massachusetts law that made it more difficult for unmarried people to get contraceptives. According to Justice Brennan, if "the right of privacy means anything, it is the right of an individual, married or single, to be free from unwarranted governmental intrusion into matters so fundamentally affecting a person as the decision whether to bear or beget a child."[82]

It is important to note that the same issue is at stake in *Roe*—the right to have sex without having a baby. It is also important to note how recent these rights are. The difference is that a fetus is already in place, and the right not to have it necessarily requires that the fetus be killed.

And therein lies the problem, for those who oppose abortion and for the Supreme Court: two conflicting, fundamental rights—a woman's right to make reproductive decisions and a fetus's right to life.

Does the fetus have a right—a *constitutional* right—to life? The Supreme Court has refrained from acknowledging that the fetus has the same legal rights as the rest of us.

The Court's Way Out—So Far

In *Roe* the Court carefully avoided calling the fetus a "person" and decided there was no precedent for granting a fetus constitutional rights. Abortion, according to *Roe,* is not "murder"; thus the fetus is not deprived of its constitutional right to equal protection.

But the same majority sidestepped a definition of what a person might be, thus avoiding committing the Court or the country to one "theory of life"—and thence to legal chaos and oppressive implications (e.g., pregnant drug abusers charged with child abuse or illegally delivering drugs to children, parents charged with raising their children in unsafe, polluted environments, pregnant women prone to miscarriage forced to give up their fetuses to surrogate mothers). If a state can decide whether or not the fetus is a person, we would have a bizarre situation in which a fetus could be a person in one state and not in another. (And what would prevent a state from declaring other things—trees, perhaps—persons, too?)[83]

Abortion and Sex Discrimination

In *Skinner* (1942) the Court declared that the right to control reproduction is "one of the basic civil rights of man."

But not of women, according to the opponents of abortion. And that raises the charge of sexual discrimination. Men do not need abortions, and thus limiting them or banning them will not affect their personal control over their own sexuality. An abortion ban or even restrictions on ending pregnancy will shape, if not harm or destroy, the lives of many women.[84]

A law against abortion will, in effect, discriminate against an entire sex, denying them equal protection under the law.

The Problem with Privacy: Catharine MacKinnon[85]

Not all feminists support *Roe*. For some radical feminists, who still believe that abortion is fundamental to a woman's right to equality, *Roe* misses the point altogether. The most forceful proponent of anti-*Roe* feminism is the radical feminist and constitutional scholar Catharine MacKinnon. A summary of her argument:

"*Roe v. Wade* presumes that government nonintervention in the private sphere promotes a woman's freedom of choice." Feminist research and analysis, however, has discovered that it is precisely in that "private sphere" (i.e., in the privacy of their homes) that women are more susceptible to male dominance and force, particularly in sexual matters. ". . . for women there is no private. . . . Feminism confronts the fact that women have no privacy to lose or to guarantee."[86] Privacy law assumes women are equal at home, although according to a massive (and horrifying) amount of statistical evidence it is mainly in private that women are beaten up, forced into sex, and exploited as domestic laborers. Privacy allows men to dominate women, with legal impunity.

This right to privacy is a right of men "to be let alone, to oppress women one at a time."[87] *Roe* is a way for men to control the consequences of sex and thus enhance its availability. Abortion allows women to have sex on the same terms as men, without consequences.

Feminists, however, are less concerned with getting more sex than in establishing who actually defines sexuality and therefore defines women. The Supreme Court's view of abortion only preserves the status quo: that men define sexuality and thus perpetuate the inequality of women. True equality and genuine freedom for women would include not the right to have as much sex as men without consequences, but the *right to refuse sex*. "Abortion policy has never been explicitly approached in the context of how women get pregnant; that is, as a consequence of intercourse under conditions of gender inequality; that is, as an issue of forced sex."[88]

The Court has cited that the right to privacy guarantees a woman's access to contraceptives and abortion. But in 1981, in *Harris v. McRae*, the Court ruled that this right to privacy did not mean that medically necessary abortions were covered by Medicaid. According to the

Court, a woman's decision to abort or not to abort was protected by her right to privacy, but the government could only finance her decision to have a baby.

Is that a free choice? What does a poor woman do—risk having the child, regardless of the medical dangers because it is at least covered by Medicaid, or try to come up with the money to do the medically necessary thing and have an abortion?

The Court has not convinced women that it is prepared to grant them real freedom, which demands real equality. Abortion should not be merely a privacy issue; it is about a woman's right to control not only reproduction but her very sexuality. And in the arena of sex, most women are well aware that they are nowhere near equal to men.

IN MY OPINION

Ten years ago my wife and I attended a small dinner party, four couples around a long table, all friends, nothing special. Somehow, the conversation turned to abortion. Two of the men denounced abortion as a moral outrage, nothing short of murder. Educated in Catholic schools and colleges, these two men had married Catholics, had children, and divorced. Both had remarried. In their mid-forties, they had fallen away from the Church and admitted only to being "cultural Catholics." Though they disdained the Church's bans on premarital sex and contraception, they supported the Vatican's categorical opposition to ending pregnancy.

Suddenly, the four women at the table turned on these two men with a passion and ferocity that surprised the women themselves. How dare they dismiss the agonized choices of millions of women as "murder"! Were they so anti-women that they could show no compassion for a woman facing an unintended pregnancy that will disrupt, maybe even ruin, her life and family? Within minutes the wives of these two men were so angry with their husbands that they were in tears.

On the way home, my wife explained to me the reason for the tears: Those women had had abortions—at the urging of the two men who had just expressed their opposition to abortion so vehemently. One of the women, already in her late forties, was childless and was likely to remain so. The other was eager to have a child, but her husband, older and already the father of two, was reluctant. (They eventually had a child.)

I learned a few things that evening: (1) The right-to-life camp has hypocrites among its number, and some are my friends; (2) women, even upper-middle-class, well-educated women with loving, sympathetic husbands, are not always free in sexual and procreative matters; and (3) abortion will never be only a theoretical debate. It is a blood and guts issue, particularly for women.

And so I enter this arena cautiously. To claim to have resolved the issue once and for all is foolish; even to write another word when so many people have written so much seems presumptuous. Who hasn't heard all the arguments? And, as I have tried to show in this chapter, there are sophisticated and persuasive arguments on both sides of the abortion divide. The traditional position against abortion has a logical perfection: all human beings have a right to life, and to kill intentionally is murder; abortion is killing a human intentionally and therefore murder. There is a simplicity to that argument—except if you cannot accept the crucial premise—namely, that a fetus is a human being like you and me, a person with rights. For the pro-choice camp this premise is pure nonsense.

And we are back to the fundamental problem again. Each side states its argument and the other side looks at it in horror and incomprehension. The conservative points to the similarities between us and the fetus; the liberal focuses on the essential differences. One concentrates on late pregnancy, while the other zeroes in on the earliest days of human life. Both sides see each other as criminals. And so the anti- and pro-abortion positions stretch out like two parallel lines, heading off into infinity, never to meet. As Einstein once said, "It's harder to smash prejudices than atoms." Can we get beyond the screaming and say something new about the morality of abortion?

I think we can, but only if we understand why people feel they have a right to scream for or against abortion. We can move beyond the abortion stalemate only if we understand why one person's moral conviction can seem to another person a mere prejudice. Abortion has become a lesson in the complexity of moral issues in a pluralistic democracy. Moral conflict is inevitable in the United States, where people's fundamental religious, ideological, and ethical positions are bound to clash with the opinions of others from different traditions. Just as Catholics and atheists are bound to disagree, or Republicans and Democrats, or feminists and proponents of traditional "family values," so will those who view the fetus as a full person and those who see the fetus as something quite less than that.

But historically in our country, opposing groups have not disagreed about *everything*. In an important sense that is the idea of America—one nation in which people of all sorts of backgrounds and political ideals can exist. *E pluribus unum*—out of many, one—is the official American motto.

And in America, therefore, there is, I believe, only one place to be in the abortion debate, and that is in the middle—willing to accept the majority opinion, judicial compromise, and the possibility that no matter how strong your moral convictions about ending the life of fetuses, pro or con, you might end up in the minority, but always with the option of fighting for your own moral beliefs and trying to convince others to adopt your own view of the world.

My own position, up front: I support legal abortion. But I am also exceedingly uncomfortable with the number of abortions performed each year in this country. No matter how minimal one's respect for the fetus is, killing 1.6 million fetuses is a lot of killing, too much in a society that claims to value human life, which a fetus indisputably is (though it is not necessarily a "person"). Pro-abortion activists do not generally tolerate any wavering, but we must be honest: it would be better if abortions were not necessary. But abortions are necessary, a fact that most reasonable Americans have always recognized.

The Main Flaw in the Argument Against Abortion

Abortion is either murder or it is not, and if it is murder there ought not to be any exceptions, including rape, incest, and even the mother's life.[89] The fetus is not responsible for the pregnancy; no matter how violent or repulsive was the sexual act that led to conception, the fetus remains an innocent party whose life may not be sacrificed. The mother and the fetus's right to life are identical, or they are not.

Why is it that most of us find the implications of this fact draconian, unfair, even cruel? Even the toughest laws against abortion allow for exceptions. Examining exceptions to the rules often tells you more about the rules (not to mention the rulemakers).

Woman versus fetus. This matchup remains the heart of the abortion debate. *Roe* drew the lines clearly: A pregnant woman has the right to end her pregnancy only as long as the fetus cannot survive without its mother. At "viability" the state must protect the interests of the fetus. But, as abortion opponents have rightly argued, why, at twenty or so weeks does the fetus gain a constitutional right not to be killed? What is essentially the difference between that fetus one minute (or millisecond) after viability and one minute (or millisecond) before? One can even conceive of technological advances that will make it possible for the fetus to survive outside the mother virtually from the moment of conception. The fetus will not gain moral standing from an arbitrary time frame.

Thus, abortion opponents return to the fundamental conflict: woman versus fetus, one intentionally conspiring to destroy the other. Right-to-lifers are appalled by the killing; the pro-choice faction, not always appalled enough, tends to evade the fact that killing is really at issue.

But finally and inescapably, abortion is about loss of life. "Terminating the pregnancy," before or after viability, is simply an indirect way of saying "*killing* the fetus." To meet the moral dilemma of abortion (literally, two goods in conflict: a revulsion against killing the innocent versus a woman's right to freedom and equality), we have to meet the reason for that dilemma—the killing—head-on. To legalize abortion is to legalize killing and violate the principle that most agree is, and ought to be, central to any morality: the sanctity of life.

The Sanctity of (Some) Life

I suspect that the moral ambivalence about abortion among some members of the pro-choice camp is due to wondering whether they might indeed be murdering a child. No feminist has ever disputed that the fetus is alive or human. Supporters of abortion also believe in the sanctity of life.[90]

But few people are absolute pacifists who believe that life is always sacred and that killing is always wrong. Killing, for most people, is therefore not *intrinsically* wrong. It is permissible in self-defense, for example, or in a just war. Some believe killing may take the form of punishment for heinous crimes or that it acts as a deterrent. We also make life and death decisions for ourselves all the time—whether to smoke or drink or do drugs or ride a motorcycle or eat as much cholesterol as we please. That is what freedom is about. The real question in the abortion issue is how much freedom ought women to have over their own lives and bodies. Are they free to end something so intensely personal and physical as a pregnancy? And if they are not, then what other liberties might they be forced to give up?

The anti-abortion camp contends that no woman is free to choose to kill an "unborn child," an innocent, defenseless victim—that is, *except to save the life of the mother or in cases of rape and incest*. Such exceptions undercut the argument that abortion is murder, as I have argued. But these exceptions also seem to suggest a way of looking at the relationship between the mother and the fetus which explains our intuition that when a mother's life is at stake, the fetus ought to be sacrificed.

Relating to Fetuses

Imagine your pregnant wife is dying. The doctor confronts you: "It's either the fetus or her. Your choice."

What is your choice? For me, the answer is not merely easy, but categorical: "Save my wife." How could it be otherwise? I have no relationship with that fetus. In fact, suddenly, that fetus has lost its innocence. Quite the contrary: That fetus has become the enemy, part of a conspiracy to kill my wife. I love my wife. I would miss her; her death would throw my life, and my children's lives, into misery and chaos.

I will not miss the fetus, in any recognizable sense of "miss." The fetus is replaceable. (I won't be able to tell the difference between it and the next fetus my wife bears.) One reason the right-to-life camp focuses on late pregnancy is that not only does the fetus look more like us, but after several months of pregnancy the mother, the father, and the rest of the family have begun to think of the fetus as a member of the family. Plans are being made. The pro-choice camp prefers to focus on the faceless, indeed shapeless, embryo, sidestepping the fact that it is nevertheless alive and very human. But the issue facing both sides of the abortion argument is the same: How does one relate to the fetus?

With difficulty, I'm afraid. Although fetuses are certainly alive, and definitely human, they are not necessarily little people with all the moral and legal rights that go with that status. In American law, the fetus has never had legal standing. And while Operation Rescue militants may march around abortion clinics carrying tiny coffins, no church body requires that families bury miscarriages. Any woman who called the funeral parlor about "losing her baby" in the third month of pregnancy would be considered overwrought. If she referred to the lifeless embryo as a "stillbirth," her audience would be shocked.[91] Any woman who has ever experienced a spontaneous abortion knows that no matter how painful or sad or tragic the event was, that bloody fetal stuff that wouldn't even fill a Dixie cup was not a child. (To call a miscarriage an "accidental death" seems stretching the language.) I would suggest that the death of a fetus by abortion is equally sad or tragic.

Fetuses Are Different from You and Me

The kind of life that abortion ends is the same as that ended by miscarriage—something more than an unnecessary human organ, an appendix, say, but something quite less than a person with full moral standing and constitutional rights. And though fetuses are certainly "potential persons," so are spermatozoa, and few would argue that contraception (or masturbation) is a crime.

That more mature fetuses look a lot like persons has often been used as the clinching argument for their being persons. Much has been made of magazine photographs and film of the fetus in utero appearing to be very much an "unborn child." It is often argued that if you could see the fetus, indeed hold one, then no one would want to kill it. But this seems more a psychological phenomenon than a moral one. In war it is easier to kill the enemy from a B-52 than with a bayonet. "Moral distance" also seems to account for the fact that we will mourn a close friend who has died of AIDS and not shed a tear for the millions in Africa who will die of the same disease (until we see the pictures of the children, and then the compassion flows).

But fetuses, in spite of their superficial likeness to us, are not like us in one significant way: They are not conscious in the way we are. They have no desires, no thoughts, no dreams. Fetuses, I suggest, resemble *dead* persons more than fully alive persons. According to the medical ethicist Robert Veatch, "Any systematic medical ethic needs to show consistency between the point at which moral standing begins and when it ends."[92] And thus we might be able to understand better when moral personhood begins by fixing on when it ends. For Veatch and other philosophers, you cannot kill someone who is already dead.

As the Oxford philosopher Jonathan Glover has argued, "consciousness" is the minimum requirement for the name "living person." Without the brain integrating bodily functions, a person becomes less than human (i.e., in what doctors and lawyers call a "persistent vegetative state"); not conscious, the "person" is more like a breathing corpse. Such unconsciousness resembles death more than life.

The unconsciousness of the early fetus is not unlike that of the patient in a "persistent vegetative state." Neither is able to communicate with the world; neither is a genuine person. (Another similarity, weirder than substantive: comatose patients often shrivel into a fetal position.) Brain-dead patients are no longer "one of us." (I will discuss this in Chapter 3, "Euthanasia.") Fetuses are *not yet* one of us. They may be the basis of our community, and potential members, but full membership is not yet theirs.

This standard of consciousness can also explain why even supporters of abortion are uncomfortable with late abortions. As the fetus grows, so does its physiological equipment for consciousness. Not sentient, the early fetus resembles a comatose adult; the late fetus, especially one capable of surviving outside the womb, resembles a conscious adult. *Resembles.* I am drawing analogies here, trying to redescribe the fetus in a way that might point to the difference between it, at various stages, and a child, and then an adult. It is, I think, the only way to allow us to discuss abortion again in a way that takes us beyond the screaming. This standard of consciousness, I think, is a good one for life and death decisions.

And so if it comes down to a decision between the life of the fetus and the life of the mother, then the fetus will be sacrificed—not without careful thought, to be sure. If a pregnancy or new baby is only a minor disruption for a woman's family or for her career or for her state of mind, then abortion seems wrong. But if there is a good reason, if there seems no alternative or the only way to prevent some kind of economic or family disaster, if abortion is the last resort, then killing the fetus, I believe, can be a genuinely ethical decision, a kind of reluctant act of survival, of self-preservation, a kind of "killing in self-defense."

The Right to Autonomy and Self-Defense

All of us know women, young and older, who have experienced the emotional chaos of an unwanted pregnancy. Add the complication that the woman's husband pressured her into sex or her boyfriend refused to use a condom, and the resistance to bearing that child seems to take on some moral force. Does a woman have a moral obligation to turn her body and soul over to that fetus for the next nine months, not to mention the next eighteen years until the child is really prepared to live without the support of its family?

Part of the force of Judith Jarvis Thompson's famous analogy comparing an unwanted pregnancy to discovering suddenly that you have become the life-support system of a famous violinist is that it is hard to argue that the violinist's life is more important than the woman's—a position that most right-to-lifers seem to adopt with respect to the fetus without a thought.

Yet the flaw in Thompson's thought experiment is that being pregnant is not quite enough like being hooked up to a violinist. For starters, that violinist is not a part of you in the way a fetus is. And as much as a woman might resent the fetus that is threatening her future, as the pregnancy progresses she is likely to develop a bond with the growing being inside her. If she bears the child, she is likely to love it as mothers do. After nine months, Thompson's woman is unlikely to take the fiddler to her breast.

But Thompson offers another analogy that has been overshadowed by the famous violinist and that resonates, I think, even more for women. Thompson asks us to

> suppose you find yourself trapped in a tiny house with a growing child. I mean a very tiny house, and a rapidly growing child—you are already up against the wall of the house and in a few minutes you'll be crushed to death. The child on the other hand won't be crushed to death; if nothing is done to stop him from growing he'll be hurt, but in the end he'll simply burst open the house and walk out a free man.[93]

I suspect that one reason Thompson's argument for abortion, published in an academic journal two years before *Roe,* has achieved a firm position in philosophical and feminist circles is that for the first time a respected professional philosopher articulated in the language of philosophy the fear—and lack of freedom—that ordinary women feel when faced with an unwanted pregnancy.

For Thompson, abortion is not an abstract issue but one that strikes at the very heart of what it is to be a woman in control of her body and future. While the opponents of abortion tried to focus the argument on the rights of the fetus to live, she turned the argument back to the mother's right to choose to live the kind of life she wants. Undeniably, abortion is a decision to kill the fetus, but it is not necessarily a decision *against* life, as Ronald Dworkin has rightly pointed out. Advocates of choice also believe in the sanctity of life; but for them, the woman's life, the life of an indisputable *person* who has invested decades in becoming who she is, takes precedence over the life of a potential person.

For Women, Birth Is Something Not Yet Totally Under Control

The arguments against abortion seem to assume that the woman was somehow in control, that because she had sex she is responsible for the pregnancy that resulted from it. This, too, I think, accounts for why even opponents of abortion are willing to make exceptions for rape and incest where a woman was *forced* into sex; since she was not in control of her pregnancy she cannot be held responsible for it and should therefore have the legal option of ending it. Yet a woman who is pregnant accidentally is no more in control of her pregnancy than a victim of rape or incest. Her pregnancy is a lot less dramatic, but it is no less involuntary. Why should she be more morally responsible for that pregnancy than a woman who is raped or the victim of incest?

No wonder that feminists believe the pro-life forces to be not only anti-women but anti-sex. Only someone committed to the deeply conservative view that the sole purpose of sexual intercourse is procreation would argue that a woman who does not want to be pregnant must remain so. Certainly, many women who get pregnant do so irresponsibly or, in the case of many teenagers, ignorantly; others simply should be more careful about contraception. But many who are careful still get pregnant and should have the right to make their own private moral decision about how to proceed with their lives. We are in no position to judge.

The Real Culprit in Abortion—Sex

Abortion is about sex, so it is curious that in the thousands of words written about abortion, pro and con, very little gets said about sexual relationships.[94] The pro-life side typically derides contemporary sexuality as overeroticized, pointing to the common usages of "casual sex" and "recreational sex." For them, sexuality has an obvious purpose—procreation—and thus has a special, almost sacramental role in their view of life and the family.[95] Pro-life women insist that advocates of abortion are too eager to destroy the link between sex and procreation.[96] Pro-life *feminists* contend that they see "procreation as equal to the values of love, desire, and unity."[97]

Such concessions bear all the signs of a public relations decision. The "equality" that opponents of abortion give to sexuality is not unlike the equality some concede to women—and then pay them less or hire a less qualified man. Recognizing that in the final years of the twentieth century only a minority, and not even most theologians, believe that sex is only for procreation, the right-to-life propagandists have anointed sex as an "equal" to love and affection between married couples.

But their discomfort with sexuality, and its risks, shows. It is a cross that our Western Christian tradition has forced us all to bear. Since the early Church of the Roman era, Christians have viewed celibacy as a higher calling and tried to "live like angels." In the Roman world, the clearest manifestation of Christian asceticism—and the most incomprehensible to contemporary Romans—was the Christian community's insistence on sexual abstinence.[98] By the late fourth and early fifth centuries, the great theologian Augustine was teaching, contrary to earlier Christian theory, that free will was an illusion, man was a "captive" of his desires, a victim of Adam's "original sin"—"all of us were that one man who fell into sin through the woman who was made from him."[99] The best evidence of the effects of original sin, for Augustine, was sexual desire.[100]

Human sexuality had become a bare necessity, more a danger to the soul than an extension.[101] For the next fifteen centuries the official position of Christianity and then the Roman Catholic Church was that sexual intercourse was only for procreation—until 1965, when Pope John XXIII's Vatican Council to reform the Catholic Church finally recognized that sexual intimacy between married couples is as important to the sacrament of marriage as procreation.

The sanctity of family life and the role of the woman in it is an appealing notion. Who does not want to think his or her life is sacred, his career a vocation? But to glorify procreation and claim that it is the only point of sex is to fly in the face of biology. Both men and women are ready for sex in a flash. The accidental consequences of sex, however, can be more time consuming. Women get pregnant and, traditionally, have borne the burden of child care. To take on those considerable responsibilities ought to be their decision.

The Unreal World of Pro-Life Feminism

The pro-life feminists agree that women have not gotten a fair shake. One of their best reasons for opposing abortion is that it allows men to get away even more easily with exploiting and abandoning women. The pro-life feminists are absolutely right about this. Public opinion polls show that men are more inclined to support abortion than women, and many of those men are in the pro-choice camp not because they are feminists, but because they know that the easy availability of abortion assures that even "accidents" can be erased. A woman's last-ditch argument against sexual intercourse—"I am afraid of getting pregnant"—is trumped.

But pro-life feminists also presume an "order, purpose, meaning, and goodness" in the world. For them, "life is good . . . a precious gift and is better, far better, than the absence of life."[102] Finding this "meaning" and "purpose" is, they say, "the challenge of life." And part of that challenge is dealing with the unexpected—such as an unwanted pregnancy. Sidney Callahan, one of the most articulate proponents of this view, explains that feminists like her, whose politics and theology tend to be to the left of most of those in the anti-abortion movement, share with them a "basic trust toward life" and thus "hope in a future that will work."[103]

But these pro-life feminists do in the end stress "pro-life" over "feminism." For Callahan, your position on abortion finally entails committing to a certain "configuration of emotions." The pro-choice camp is committed to autonomy and self-realization and independence. The favored emotional response is that of the "rational, pragmatic human being." For feminists active in the right-to-life movement, sacrifice and love are the dominant emotional responses. It is impossible to oppose love and sacrifice. Who does not want to believe that purpose and order dominate the universe? But it is impossible, particularly at the end of this murderous century, to believe that love and sacrifice, or order and purpose, can prevail.

For Callahan, it is not the individual's rights that have priority, but the community's, and the fetus is crucial to the life and future of the community. The fetus should not be seen so much as an "isolated individual," but as a new entry into "the collective life of the species" with automatic equality with its fellow members.[104]

But what kind of equality is that? The pro-life feminists seem not to have taken into account that, even by their own feminist position, women are *not* equal. Pro-life feminists like Callahan have taken what she herself concedes is a "romantic" view of the world. She would also be the first to admit that the "configuration of emotions" that encapsulates pro-life feminism is a Christian one, which stresses love of others and sacrifice, even if it entails suffering.[105] Life is full of accidents and "contingencies" that we have to deal with, the argument goes, and accidental pregnancy is among them.

But surely such a view is more than romantic or religious; it is, in the eyes of opposing feminists, contradictory. Such an accepting view of the world requires pro-life feminists to abandon the central point of their feminism—namely, to do away with the unnecessary suffering that women undergo by virtue of being something they have no control over, being a woman.

The pro-life feminists, mainly comfortable, educated, middle-class Christian women by the looks of their groups and the tenor of their literature, are not willing to concede the battle of feminism or the life of the unborn to the point of view and the experiences of the poor, young, unmarried, mainly black women who have the highest percentage of the abortions in this country (and constitute the highest percentage of single mothers)—women who often have no choice in contraception or sex, women who are more likely to be abused and raise children who will be abused, women whose standing in their male-dominated "communities" is not very high. If an unwanted pregnancy is a "challenge," it is a challenge for these women that they are unprepared to meet. They do not have a chance. For these women, the world does not seem very harmonious or ordered or reasonable or even fair. Moreover, if half the pregnancies each year are involuntary, the accidental pregnancy is hardly a mere "contingency" of sexual relations; it is the norm.

Abortion and Women's Liberation

For any woman who thinks (even secretly) that she is the equal of any man, let her get accidentally pregnant by a husband who opposes abortion. One of the most maddening aspects of the abortion controversy is that men and women who would fight the government to the death if Congress deprived them of any one of their "rights," no matter how debatable (e.g., the right to carry an automatic weapon), are willing to take to the streets to ensure that half the citizens of their own country (not to mention their wives and daughters and *themselves*) should be deprived of the freedom to decide not to be a mother.

After twenty years of feminism, two decades of concessions by even the most wooden-headed of men, and women, that a woman's lot in life traditionally began at less than zero, women remain unequal. That women have decided that they want to be "in control" is not surprising. That they have not managed to take control of anything, in the political world or in business or science or academia, is not surprising either.

Women are still largely responsible for raising children. Yet the same women are in no position to assure that the economy will allow them decent jobs, housing, food, and day care. Indeed, it is amazing that women will even listen to what a man might have to say about pregnancy and abortion.

In only one area of sexuality (dare I say life?) have women gained control—choosing to end a pregnancy. It is not surprising that they are willing to fight against giving it up.

Just as feminists had, and perhaps still have, a certain ideological reluctance to concede any moral status to the fetus, the right-to-lifers seem unable to admit their own hostility to women's fight for equality. Both men and women resent the challenge to the status quo; both sexes have a lot riding on the old conventions.

Feminism is not supposed to be at issue; the lives of fetuses are. Nevertheless, the pro-life community does not generally display much sympathy even when confronted with the lives of such "born children" as black male teenagers who now die at an alarming rate; nor do they much care about the futures of poor, black, unmarried teenaged girls, the prime candidates for the abortion clinics. If the right-to-life camp is so concerned about the future of the unborn, they ought to be lobbying for better housing and health care for the poor, better child care, and more jobs. (The pro-life feminists have recognized the importance of this implication of "pro-life"; and the Catholic bishops finally have added social and health-care concerns to their own efforts to fight abortion.)

And anyone who is really concerned about cutting down those 1.6 million abortions a year would extend their demonstrations from abortion clinics to the doorsteps of the drug companies in the contraception business. Surely a genuine commitment to the sanctity of life demands diverting some of that impassioned energy from attacking family clinics to lobbying Congress to pay more attention to those American families mired in poverty and social chaos.

Different Theories of Life: Welcome to America!

For those who say I can't impose my morality on others, I say just watch me.

Joseph Scheidler
Executive Director
Pro-Life Action League

I do not expect opponents of abortion to read my argument on behalf of legal abortion and immediately cross over to the pro-choice camp. I have simply laid out my "theory of life" (to borrow from Justice Blackmun) and moral convictions about abortion. They have theirs. Moral convictions are, by definition, the ideas and beliefs we should be willing to go to the wall for; they ought not to be changed or abandoned too easily. But they ought not to be rammed down anyone's throat either, as the anti-abortion activist Scheidler has suggested. His urge to impose his views on me, to make me into him, is positively and fundamentally un-American.

Pluralism assures moral dilemmas. We are bound to disagree with our neighbors. Indeed, we are bound to disagree with ourselves. Most of us hold contradictory beliefs and values: justice versus mercy, sanctity of life versus love for our wife, law and order versus compassion for the poor. My own Catholic tradition has clashed with the urban, intellectual, liberal, postmodern world I live in. Look at yourself. If you have changed, if you no longer accept all the tenets of your childhood, if you have rejected the definition of values cherished by your family, if you have questioned the dogmas of your church or synagogue, then welcome to America.

The social scientist Kristin Luker has shown that among abortion activists each side divides on economic, educational, religious, and political grounds.[106] The pro-life movement is dedicated to a religious view of life: that our lives are in God's control, that we must suffer life's burdens; they are eager to preserve the traditional nuclear family and the priority of childbearing and parenting for women. Across the divide Luker finds a pro-choice movement that reflects opposite viewpoints. Those who support abortion tend to be more secular and dedicated to the liberation of women from traditional roles as breeder and mother; for them, women must have the right to pursue whatever goals they might want and choose how having a family might fit into that kind of life.

Luker's conclusions seem a little too neat. I know people in both camps who are hardly as committed to their position as the people she interviewed. The pro-life feminist position—held by well-educated, upper-middle-class feminists who are uncomfortable with easy access to abortion—is a clear counterexample to Luker's divided world. In fact, one of the consequences of the abortion battle is that the extremes of both sides have presented such stark, inflexible options that most of us have gravitated to the inevitable good gray middle. Polls show that as many as 70 percent of Americans believe that the government should not interfere with the decision to have an abortion.[107]

And that is how it should be. No discussion about abortion can take place on the extremes. Warfare is inevitable there. Scheidler and I have a fundamental disagreement; our values, theories of life, and "configuration of emotions," as Sidney Callahan might put it, clash. In Dworkin's terms, our differences are basically "spiritual"—Scheidler and his fellow opponents of abortion value all life at its earliest stages absolutely (I don't know Scheidler's position on whether abortions ought to be allowed for women pregnant from rape or incest), whereas I am inclined to think that the mother's life is more sacred than the fetus's.

That our disagreement is merely spiritual gives Dworkin hope. Throughout its history our nation has proved that people with spiritual, religious, and political differences can live together, not only peaceably, but productively.

I am less hopeful. For me, the cultural and religious warfare over abortion has undermined the genius of the U.S. political system and pointed to its most fundamental dilemma. A democratic society built on the premise that everyone has a right to have his say is threatened if someone says, "I know the truth and the rest of you had better follow me, or else." One of the most troubling results of the abortion wars is that this vicious clash of opposing values, this inability to allow others to choose what they think is right, may be final proof that the American experiment in pluralism is foundering.

And that is truly an American tragedy.

A Suggestion

There is, however, an exit out of the abortion mess—an American way out. All parties in the wrangle ought to remind themselves that the idea of America is an expanding, pluralistic democracy that willy-nilly seeks to accommodate, by laws and constitutional system, all sorts of different political, moral, and religious beliefs. Whether abortion is an evil or a necessary good is included among those beliefs. The Supreme Court cannot finally arbitrate that dispute. All the Court can do is seek a legal compromise that does not violate the Constitution. This is what *Roe* tried to do, for better or for worse.

Justice Blackmun explained in *Roe* that the belief that the fetus is a person is simply one "theory of life." Ironically, Cardinal Bernardin is more helpful here. And for those who might think that I have been too harsh on the Catholics in this discussion, let me confound them further by giving a Prince of the Church the last word.

Bernardin concedes that in a country like ours, where people have been raised in different cultures and traditions and adhere to different religions, we are bound to disagree over moral issues. The cardinal values religious tolerance. But, as he points out, tolerance does not mean that religious views must be banished from political discussion. Quite the contrary: Religious (and moral) views have their place— namely, to help shape the moral vision of America. Catholics, or anyone else, have a constitutional right to try to *persuade* others through "a process of debate, decision-making . . ." that their view of abortion, or any other moral issue, is the right one. That is how a "moral consensus" is achieved in a pluralistic democracy, not by imposing values on those who would rather act otherwise.

All sides have to be ready to accept that the courts and politicians have a different task, a different moral obligation. Their job is to achieve a consensus, too, and in doing so someone's "theory of life" will lose, usually the minority's. In the juridical and legislative debate over abortion, the pro-choice movement is likely to prevail. But that does not mean that the anti-abortion minority must remain silent. Their moral conviction is that abortion is wrong; thus they have a moral and political obligation to try to persuade the rest of us to see abortion from their point of view.

But those who oppose abortion and those who favor it must recognize that their debate is more than an argument about the rights of fetuses versus the rights of mothers, or "murder" versus privacy or freedom. Underneath the rhetoric of both sides, abortion is, finally, a debate about the idea of America—how moral differences get settled in a society where those differences are bound to run sharp and deep. Americans are inclined to believe that if they debate an issue long enough, they will arrive at the ultimate resolution of the issue. In morality, however, our differences might be so fundamental that we will never agree.

That is not necessarily a bad thing. Moral progress is impossible without moral disagreement. The kind of blood and guts clash of values that the abortion controversy has provoked reminds us of the seriousness of the issue. If any discussion should raise the temperature in the room, it should be one about life and death. But moral progress also requires that we *listen* to what others have to say about abortion—and suicide, euthanasia, capital punishment, social justice and every other issue we care about deeply as individuals and a community—and then consider the possibility that we might actually be wrong. Moral progress is also impossible without moral reflection.

2. Suicide

THE ISSUE

"Suicide," the French writer and Nobel Prize winner Albert Camus once wrote, "is the only truly serious philosophical problem."[1] For what is more serious than the choice between living and dying? As Camus realized, if life is not worth living, if it is meaningless or absurd, then why bother going on? But if life is truly sacred, whose life is more sacred than your own?

Suicide might also be the only truly personal moral problem. You lie, you cheat, you break your promise, you steal money or your neighbor's wife—in every instance of immorality that you can think of, what you do hurts someone else. But suppose you decide to commit suicide because you have become a burden to yourself, to others, even to society, and no children are involved, and your suicide will not plunge your family into economic ruin. Why is such a suicide not the rational, even moral thing to do?

Some societies have believed that suicide can be a good thing. That doesn't mean these people viewed life as less worthwhile than we do; they simply believed that a life of endless pain or disgrace was not a life worth living. Their standards, or values—what they view as "good"—are different from our own. If, as in the world of the medieval Japanese samurai warrior or the Homeric hero, the avoidance of shame is at the center of what constitutes a good man, then a life of shame is not worth living. In the Western religious tradition, however, life itself is a central moral value. It is God's property, not man's, and thus sacred. Secularists, too, believe life is sacred. For in a human world without

God what is more sacred than man? And if we belong not to God but only to ourselves, surely we have a right to dispose of our own selves as we see fit.

Yet who does not flinch at the thought of suicide? Self-destruction has an air of, if not madness, then certainly mystery. Can people actually *choose* to kill themselves, rationally? Can self-destruction actually be the moral, the good, thing to do?

Against God and the Community

Greek literature and history are filled with suicides. When Jocasta discovers she has married her own son Oedipus, "carried away by pain," says Homer, she hangs herself. Rather than remarry, Dido hurls herself on her husband's funeral pyre. To avoid capture, soldiers in antiquity often committed mass suicide. The oligarchs of Corcyra, trapped in a building by the Athenians in 425 B.C. during the Peloponnesian War, killed themselves, according to Thucydides' graphic description, by "thrusting into their throats the arrows shot by the enemy, and hanging themselves with the cords taken from some beds that happened to be there, and with strips made from their own clothing."[2] In A.D. 66 a thousand Jewish zealots trapped by the Romans on Masada committed mass suicide.

In Athens and other Greek states, at certain times suicide was sanctioned by the state. Citizens suffering from old age, illness, sorrow, or disgrace could petition local authorities for the right to commit suicide; magistrates maintained official supplies of poison for this purpose.

The most eminent philosophers of ancient Greece, however, condemned suicide, mainly for religious reasons. The followers of Pythagoras (sixth century B.C.) taught that man's immortal soul merely resides in the body, as in a tomb, where it undergoes a process of atonement and purification. At death, successful souls will return to their divinity, while the rest, half baked as it were, will move into another body and try again. The Pythagoreans compared suicides to military sentinels who have abandoned their posts without the order of their commander, namely, god.

Plato (427?–347 B.C.) echoes the Pythagorean opposition to suicide in his dialogue *Phaedo,* an account of the last days of his legendary teacher Socrates (470?–399 B.C.); and in the *Laws,* Plato declares that suicides ought to be buried in solitary, nameless graves.[3] Aristotle (384–322 B.C.), Plato's most famous student, also opposed suicide.

"The Road to Freedom"

The best-known advocates of suicide in the ancient world were the Stoics. Seneca, the most celebrated Stoic philosopher in Rome during the reign of Nero and a philosophical mentor of the emperor himself, proselytized for the right to kill yourself as the ultimate choice and the best evidence that man was rational and free. In A.D. 65, Nero believed that Seneca was part of a plot to replace him with a popular member of the Roman aristocracy and he ordered Seneca to kill himself. According to the historian Tacitus, Seneca obeyed. Three years after he ordered Seneca's famous suicide and in the face of another conspiracy to destroy his cruel regime, Nero panicked, tried to escape Rome, and, according to Suetonius, to avoid capture, stabbed himself in the throat and died.

The Sin of Suicide

While some cultures share the Roman Stoics' appreciation of the noble suicide (e.g., Japan's notorious hari-kari, suicide by disembowelment, and the Eskimo practice of allowing old people to freeze to death for the good of the community), the Judeo-Christian tradition has condemned self-destruction. The Talmud does not explicitly forbid suicide, but later rabbinic authorities condemned suicide as a sin even worse than murder. No duty is more important in Judaism than the one of preserving life, including your own.

In the Christian tradition, suicide is no less than "self-murder." Yet neither the Old nor New Testament explicitly condemns suicide. Samson pulled down the Temple on himself and the Philistines. After Jesus was condemned, as recorded in the Gospel According to Matthew 27:5, Judas Iscariot, the disciple who had betrayed Jesus, tried to repent by returning the thirty pieces of silver he had been paid. When the chief priests turned him down, Judas "cast down the pieces of silver in the temple, and departed, and went and hanged himself." The implication of this brief passage is Judas, given the enormity of his disgrace, made the right decision.

Ironically, the most virtuous Christians of the early Church, indeed the Christians' Christians, were the martyrs, the men and women who rather than deny their religious beliefs preferred to be thrown to the lions, pitted unarmed against gladiators, stabbed, roasted, and torn to bits. And although the Romans persecuted Christians and hunted them down, many so-called martyrs were notorious for provoking Roman magistrates to sentence them to death, some actually volunteering.

For Christians, dying for their beliefs was an imitation of Christ's death on the cross, and the quickest route from this world to the next one. "Your blood," wrote Tertullian, one of the most eminent of the early church fathers, "is the key to Paradise."[4] Christian prisoners, wrote the martyr Bishop Cyprian, were eager to "quit men in order to stand among angels, to become the colleague of Christ in suffering."[5] Ignatius, whose celebrity as a martyr was assured by his prison diary which survived, describes his "lust" for death.[6] Preferring the next life to this one, many martyrs were outright suicides.

It would be cynical to say that all martyrs chose death out of self-interest rather than religious conviction. But the rewards of a violent death for the glory of God, in heaven and on earth, were tempting. Martyrdom was considered a "second baptism" and wiped out all previous sins. The virgin's rewards in heaven were calculated to be sixty times greater than those of an ordinary Christian's; a martyr's were a hundred times greater.[7] On earth, dying for Christianity was a sure way, albeit a desperate one, to feed and shelter one's family; the early Christian community supported a martyr's survivors.

The Christian Backlash Against Martyrdom

In the fourth century, the Donatists, the dominant Christian sect in North Africa, reportedly went so far as to insult non-Christians and their rituals in hopes of being prosecuted and executed. Puritanical Christians who saw themselves as a kind of Noah's Ark of perfection in a corrupt society, the Donatists awaited the opportunity for martyrdom. When it didn't come, devotees were known to take matters into their own hands and hurl themselves off a cliff.[8]

By the fifth century, however, Christianity was no longer a rebel sect but the official religion of the Roman Empire, and its hierarchy looked askance on a radical Christian sect's lust for martyrdom. Nor were the Donatists some tiny group on the radical fringe, as some writers on suicide have suggested.[9] In fact, when St. Augustine (354–430) returned to his home province of North Africa from Rome in 388, the Donatists were the dominant Christian sect in Africa, with three hundred bishops, and were a formidable obstacle to the success of *Roman* Catholicism in that part of the world. To bring the self-righteous fanatics into line, Augustine actually persecuted the group with, according to his biographer Peter Brown, "police measures"—a startling example of a great Christian persecuting other Christians. In sermons against Donatism, Augustine denounced suicide as "monstrous," nothing but self-homicide.

Over the next century, the Roman Church officially condemned suicide in a series of edicts, eventually denying Christian burial to anyone who killed himself (just as Plato advises solitary burial in the *Laws*) and ruling that even those who tried but did not succeed would be excommunicated. And thus suicide, once the quickest route to heaven, had become a mortal sin that prohibited its victim from entering the Kingdom of God. In his *Summa Theologica,* the most influential Christian theological text ever written and still the basis of much Roman Catholic thinking, St. Thomas Aquinas (1225–74) repeats Augustine's position, also echoing Plato's and Aristotle's arguments against suicide.

From Mortal Sin to Capital Crime

The predominance of the Christian Church in medieval life assured that its laws would become the laws of the state. In England, the suicide was denied a Christian burial and his property was confiscated. Dante placed suicides deeper in hell than heretics and murderers.

Yet a fascination for the courage and romance of suicide remained among later thinkers. Renaissance writers resuscitated the famous suicides of ancient Greece and Rome. Shakespeare gave us the passionate and tragic suicides of Romeo and Juliet, Ophelia, Cassius, and Othello. The issue was not about to disappear, for as John Donne expressed it in 1608, "in all ages, in all places, upon all occasions, men of all conditions, have affected it, and inclin'd to doe it."[10]

"A Sickely Inclination"[11]

Donne (1573–1631) wrote *Biathanatos*, the first defense of suicide in the English language, concluding that taking your life does not necessarily contradict the laws of nature, reason, or God and is therefore not always morally abominable.[12] He argues that each case must be judged individually.

Donne's interest in suicide was evidently no academic exercise. In the preface to *Biathanatos*, he admits in a personal and confessional tone that is more in tune with our own century than the early seventeenth, "I have often such a sickely inclination." At least one Donne scholar has argued that the poet's learned and exhaustive examination of what he called "self-homicide" adds up to a primitive essay in psychology.[13]

A. Alvarez in his study of suicide, *The Savage God*, argues that Donne's life and work reveals that the great poet suffered from an "annihilating depression."[14] The Elizabethan courts, however, rejected such fine distinctions. Suicide remained morally and legally wrong. The property of suicides was confiscated, their bodies were hanged in shame and buried at a crossroads, a stake through the heart. Only if the family could prove insanity was the suicide allowed a Christian burial.[15]

The Right to Kill Yourself

The great thinkers of the Enlightenment, with their passion for the individual "rights of man," their contempt for the Roman Church's absolutism, and their impeccable classical educations, resurrected the Stoic justifications of suicide. Killing yourself, in the opinions of such eighteenth-century rationalists as Montesquieu, Rousseau, Voltaire, and the Scotsman David Hume (1711–76), was not only a private act but a fundamental human liberty. Hume's essay "Of Suicide," published at least twenty years after his death, was quickly suppressed and attacked from the pulpits of Great Britain.

The anti-suicide forces had no trouble lining up their own philosophers. To the ancient claim that suicide was a mark of freedom, John Locke (1632–1704) argued that life was an "inalienable right" and its preservation a fundamental law of nature. For the great German philosopher Immanuel Kant (1724–1804), a minister's son, our lives belonged to God, and suicide was "an abomination."[16] England, however, did not budge. The newspapers fueled the public's fascination with suicide with such enthusiasm that the English were inclined to agree with the perception abroad that suicide was "the English malady."[17]

The "Science" of Suicide

The new religion of the post-Enlightenment world was science, and doctors, in Britain as well as France, sought the physiological causes of self-destruction. Their theories were diverse and not always "scientific." Suicide, they argued, was due to bad weather, rich food, the shape of the skull, brain injuries, insanity, even masturbation. The remedies were even nuttier: drinking cold water, being doused with cold water, taking laxatives, listening to soothing music. One German physician suggested that the suicidal patient be hung from ropes while someone stood next to him shooting off a gun or threatening to light his body aflame.[18]

While the philosophers of the Enlightenment had argued that suicide was the ultimate act of rationality, the physicians of the nineteenth century examined cases of suicide and concluded that since no rational person would want to kill himself, all suicides must be lunatics, and thus not morally responsible for killing themselves.

It was a dubious kind of intellectual "progress." In the course of a few hundred years, the act of self-destruction had proceeded from being a mortal sin against God to a heinous crime against the community to a sure sign of lunacy. The only constant was that people continued to commit suicide.

The "Modern Era"

In 1897, Emil Durkheim, a French intellectual who devoted his life to proving that the new discipline of sociology was not only a science but would also provide a science of ethics that could guide social policy, published *Le Suicide,* an ingenious effort to examine the social forces that propelled people toward self-destruction. Durkheim concludes that the statistical fact of self-destruction was symptomatic of something wrong in the relationship between the individual and his society. According to him, "the term suicide is applied to all cases of death resulting directly or indirectly from a positive or negative action of the victim himself which he knows will produce this result." Every suicide could be classified ("scientifically," of course) into three categories: The "egoistic" suicide was not properly integrated into society (e.g., he was without any religious or family attachments) and thus on his own was more likely to self-destruct. The typical "altruistic" suicide lived in a primitive group and was so absorbed in the community that its conventions and goals became his. As examples, Durkheim cites Indian suttee, the ancient Hindu practice of the wife immolating herself on the pyre of her dead husband; and the army, a more modern, and Western, example of a community where the individual is expected to sacrifice his life for the good of others. (The two classic examples of the altruistic suicide in contemporary philosophical literature are Captain Lawrence Oates, the member of the British explorer Captain Robert Scott's second Antarctic expedition in 1912 who walked off to his frigid death to increase the odds of survival for his companions, and Father Maximilian Kolbe, a Catholic priest imprisoned in Auschwitz during World War II who volunteered to die in the place of a Jewish man with children.) The third type—the "anomic" suicide— was a man whose social position changed so suddenly (e.g., by a death in the family or a devastating divorce) that, overwhelmed by "anomie," he could not cope and killed himself. Durkheim points out that extreme economic fluctuations, both depressions and booms, increase the number of suicides.

Such explanations of why certain groups of people kill themselves, however, do not account for why certain individuals suffering an economic collapse, say, or a death in the family shoot themselves, while most soldier on. What was needed was not a theory of what makes society tick, as Durkheim had suggested, but a theory that aims to understand the *motivation of each individual,* at least according to the newest and most fashionable theorists in Europe, the psychoanalysts. Freud and his followers viewed suicide as the neurotic result of the murderous instincts in every one of us. The impulse to kill someone else you might have loved is turned against the image of the beloved that lives on in your ego. To kill the other, you kill yourself.[19] Freud later suggested that the suicide's "death instinct" overwhelms his more healthy natural urge to preserve his own life and that of the community.[20]

Contemporary Arguments

As recently as 1980 the Roman Catholic Church reaffirmed its opposition to suicide, noting that Catholicism teaches that "life is a gift of God" and that suicide "is to be considered as a rejection of God's sovereignty and loving plan."[21] The Vatican also pointed out the spiritual benefits of suffering.

Yet even the rigid dogmatists of the Roman curia have recognized that in the case of suicide "at times there are psychological factors present that can diminish responsibility or even completely remove it."[22] What precisely those "psychological factors" are, and what their relationship to all suicides is, of course is another matter. Clearly, depression is a common culprit. In a study of the seventy-three cases of suicide of people sixty-five and older in Chicago during 1990, all but two had a "psychiatric disorder."[23] If the depression can be treated successfully, suicide specialists have found that the urge to commit suicide disappears.[24]

But if today's suicidologist can tell us only that suicide is connected to depression, then we haven't got much further than John Donne's notion in the seventeenth century that suicides are victims of "a sickely inclination."

Depression may be a common cause of suicide, but not all suicides are depressives and not all depressives kill themselves. Some people just want out.

Can such behavior be called moral? Is suicide really the ultimate sign of human freedom or merely an affront to God and the community? Or do all suicides have to be a little bit crazy because it is impossible to make a "rational" decision about something no one really knows anything about—what it is like to be dead?

The answers to these questions, it seems, have not changed much since antiquity.

AGAINST

We know that suicide was legal in certain Greek states, including Athens. But the Athenian democrats questioned everything, including democracy itself. Suicide was no exception, and Plato, clearly one of the most fervid critics of the standards of Greek democracy, weighed in on the subject. In the *Phaedo*, Plato uses his account of Socrates' last hours with his friends as an opportunity to explain why suicide is wrong. Ironically, some contemporary philosophers point to Socrates' death as a classic case of the rational suicide: against the advice of his friends to flee Athens, Socrates willingly accepted the lethal dose of hemlock—and thus, the argument goes, committed suicide.

Plato gives Socrates a *religious* argument against suicide, which he is quick to footnote as a "secret doctrine." The reference is to the disapproval of suicide among the Pythagoreans, the followers of the "pre-Socratic" philosopher and mathematician Pythagoras, who founded a mystical sect in the sixth century B.C. Believers in the transmigration of souls, the Pythagoreans followed moral and dietary practices aimed at purifying the soul for its next embodiment.

"We Are God's Possessions": Plato[25]

"Tell me then, Socrates, why is suicide believed to be wrong? I have certainly heard Philolaus, when he was staying with us, say that it's not right, and others as well, though I've not yet figured out what any of them was talking about."

"Don't give up," said Socrates. "For the day may come when you understand. Perhaps this seems strange to you that other things which are evil may be good at certain times for certain people, death is the only exception, and why when a man is better dead, he is not permitted to be his own benefactor, and must wait for someone else's help."

Cebes laughed gently. "Aye, it's so," he said, lapsing into his own dialect.

"Put in that way, I admit that it seems inconsistent, though perhaps it has some justification. But there is a doctrine, whispered in secret, that we men are stationed in a kind of guardpost from which we cannot release ourselves or run away. This is a great mystery which I cannot understand very easily. Yet, Cebes, this much I believe is true: that the gods are our keepers and we men are their possessions. Don't you agree?"

"I do," said Cebes.

"And if one of your possessions were to destroy itself without any signal from you that you wanted it to die, wouldn't you be furious with it and punish it if you could?"

"Absolutely."

"So if you look at the matter in this way, it's not unreasonable to say that a man should not kill himself until god summons him, as is now the case with me."

But Plato was apparently no absolutist on the matter of suicide, as the following passage from the *Laws,* generally considered to be his last work, suggests. It is significant to note the mitigating factors that Plato lists here. Later Christian opponents of suicide tend to echo Plato's religious arguments against killing yourself without noting his compassion for certain cases of suicide. This passage suggests that Plato thought that suicide was justified in some instances.

"THEIR TOMBS SHALL BE ISOLATED . . ."[26]

What about the man who kills the most beloved and closest person to him—what penalty should he suffer? I mean, of course, the man who kills himself, either violently robbing himself of his destiny, not ordered to kill himself by the state, nor forced into it by great suffering or some inescapable misfortune, nor by falling into some kind of disgrace that is unmanageable and intolerable. But he inflicts upon himself this unjust penalty out of lazy and unmanly cowardice . . . For those thus destroyed, first, their tombs shall be isolated—not even one tomb next to theirs; and second, they should be buried in those sections of the 12 districts that are barren and nameless, without note, neither with gravemarkers nor names to indicate their tombs.

"Cowardice and an Injustice to the Community": Aristotle

In Aristotle's theory of morality, virtues are central, and the central virtue is "courage." For Aristotle, the main test of courage is not to be bothered by death "in any situation." Suicide, he implies, would be the coward's way out of life.

About what sort of dreadful things, then, is the brave man afraid of? About the greatest? For surely no one is more likely to stand up to what's terrifying. Death is the most terrifying thing. For it is the end, and for the dead man nothing seems either good or bad. But the brave man would not be bothered by death in any situation, at sea, for example, or diseases. . . . He will be properly called courageous who is fearless in the face of a noble death and all those sudden events that involve death, the worst of which relate to war. Yet also at sea and the face of diseases the man of courage fears nothing. . . .[27]

A man cannot treat himself unjustly, so when a man kills himself, it is not a crime against himself but against the state (the polis, or Greek city-state).

> When someone, contrary to the law, voluntarily hurts someone else— when he hasn't been hurt—he acts unjustly. And by voluntary I mean the person who knows whom he is affecting and by what. But the person who voluntarily stabs himself out of anger does so contrary to right reason which the law does not allow. Therefore, he is acting unjustly. But against whom? *Surely, against the community, and not himself.* For he suffers voluntarily, and no one can be treated unjustly voluntarily. This is also the reason that the state punishes; a certain loss of civil rights is attached to the person who kills himself because he has treated the community unjustly. [my italics][28]

Traditional Christian Opposition

Christianity's official opposition to suicide began with St. Augustine's arguments against self-destruction in the fifth century. St. Thomas Aquinas added his gloss some eight hundred years later. Their debt to Plato and Aristotle is clear:

"THOU SHALT NOT KILL"—EVEN YOURSELF: ST. AUGUSTINE[29]

Life is a gift from God, and to reject life is to reject God himself. Above all, to kill yourself is to kill a man; therefore, suicide is murder and against the Sixth Commandment: "Thou shalt not kill." This extends to all forms of self-destruction, for all sorts of reasons: asceticism, protection of your chastity, *even martyrdom,* which is no less a sin than common suicide. Suffering is a test of a soul's greatness.

If taking your life were ever morally permissible,

> Why should a liberated spirit enmesh itself again in the manifold hazards of this life, when it is the easiest thing in the world for him to stave off everything by snuffing out his life? . . . Why waste time in those exhortations we address to virginal purity, or widowed continence, or

conjugal fidelity? We have simpler short-cuts for avoiding all danger of sin: we can urge everyone, the moment he is cleansed of his sins at the baptismal font, to rush himself of the death.[30]

A person who did this would be "silly . . . mad." Since no occasion to kill yourself is more justifiable than this, and this would be mad, then there is no justifiable suicide.

What about such famous biblical suicides as Samson and the virgin martyrs of the early Church who chose death rather than rape? Their deaths are justified only because these men and women killed themselves under "divine command." Anyone not sure that God wants them to kill themselves should know that suicides "are not received after death into that better life."

"A SIN AGAINST GOD, COMMUNITY AND SELF": ST. THOMAS AQUINAS[31]

Suicide is "altogether unlawful" for three reasons:
  (1) Everything naturally loves itself and tries to keep itself in existence. Self-destruction is contrary to this natural law of self-preservation.
  (2) Every part belongs to the whole. Every man is part of a community, and thus belongs to it. And so, following Aristotle, "by killing himself he injures the community."
  (3) God says, according to Deuteronomy 32:39, "I will kill and I will make live." Life is "God's gift to man," and it is God who is in control of that life. And thus whoever kills himself sins against God, "even as he who kills another's slave, sins against that slave's master. . . ."
Suicide is thus a sin against God, the community, and the self, a sin against love and justice. And even though man is "master of himself" by virtue of his free will, "the passage from this life to another and happier one is subject not to man's free will but to the power of God." Nor is suicide blameless in an effort to escape unhappiness or evil, even rape. It is an example of choosing a "greater evil" to escape lesser ones.

The ancient Greek and Christian arguments—that suicide is against your interests, the community's interests, and above all God's interests—are echoed in the anti-suicide position of one of history's greatest moral thinkers.

"Contrary to the Highest Duty": Immanuel Kant[32]

Suicide is "the intention to destroy oneself" and thus flies in the face of what every living thing in nature seeks above all—self-preservation. Man is endowed with free will, but that does not mean that it is in his power to kill himself. Indeed, "to use the power of free will for its own destruction is self-contradictory. If freedom is the condition of life it cannot be employed to abolish life and so to destroy and abolish itself."

Some believe that it can be not only permissible to commit suicide, but even heroic. This is false. The highest duty we have as men is self-preservation. Without life, we cannot perform any of our other duties. The suicide "robs himself of his person." Free will is useless, indeed it will not exist, without life. For that reason, suicide "goes beyond the limits of the use of free will."

Suicide is not an abomination because life is so important. Even more important than life is morality, and to kill yourself is certainly to violate morality. Suicide is inadmissible in any moral system because it "degrades human nature below the level of animal nature and so destroys it." To destroy yourself is to discard your humanity and thus treat yourself as a thing.

Suicide may even seem heroic and moral: "For if a man is capable of removing himself from the world at his own will, he . . . can retain his independence and tell the rudest truths to the cruelest of tyrants." But this "semblance of morality" vanishes once we realize that man's freedom cannot exist unless it rests on a solid, unchangeable condition: "that man may not use his freedom against himself to his own destruction."

Advocates of suicide also harm the community, for in any state that allowed or even honored suicide what would restrain men from "the most dreadful vices"?

Death is not our choice to make. "God is our owner; we are his property; His providence works for our good." It is up to God and God only when we leave this life. We are but "sentinels" on earth waiting for God to recall us from our post. The suicide is a "rebel against God."

Twentieth-Century Philosophical Opposition

Ludwig Wittgenstein, the Cambridge philosopher who is considered by most professional philosophers to be the greatest philosophical genius of the twentieth century, grappled with the issue of suicide throughout his life. In childhood, three of his older brothers killed themselves. According to his most recent biographer, Ray Monk, Wittgenstein himself contemplated suicide at various times in his life. "The best for me, perhaps," he wrote in 1920 to the British philosopher Bertrand Russell, who had been his mentor, "would be if I could lie down one evening and not wake up again."[33]

In spite of his thoughts about ending his own life, Wittgenstein, who was raised a Catholic through both his mother's and father's families, had Jewish roots, remained intellectually ambivalent about suicide right up to his death from cancer in 1951 at age sixty-two. Wittgenstein's last words were, "Tell them I've had a wonderful life."[34]

"THE ELEMENTARY SIN": LUDWIG WITTGENSTEIN

If suicide is allowed, then everything is allowed. If anything is not allowed, then suicide is not allowed. This throws a light on the nature of ethics, for suicide is, so to speak, the elementary sin. And when one investigates it it is like investigating mercury vapour in order to comprehend the nature of vapours. Or is even suicide in itself neither good nor evil?[35]

In a letter to a close friend Wittgenstein wrote:

I know that to kill oneself is always a dirty thing to do. Surely one *cannot* will one's own destruction, and anybody who had visualized what is in practice involved in the act of suicide knows that suicide is always a *rushing of one's own defences*. But nothing is worse than to be forced to take oneself by surprise.

Of course it all boils down to the fact that I have no faith![36]

Were Socrates and Jesus Suicides?

"Suicide" is commonly defined as "taking your own life" or "rejecting God's gift of life." According to Durkheim, you can commit suicide "indirectly" by doing (or avoiding) something that results in your own death. Critics have pointed out that such a wider view of suicide would throw moral doubt on some of the most inspiring deaths in history.

SUICIDE VERSUS SELF-SACRIFICE: TERENCE M. O'KEEFE[37]

We are inclined to view the deaths of Socrates, the Christian martyrs, Captain Oates, and Father Kolbe as admirable. Morally, we applaud such acts as heroic. Father Kolbe is a candidate for sainthood, and Christianity itself is based on Jesus' acceptance of death. But if suicide is merely killing yourself, or allowing yourself to be killed and thus rejecting God's gift of life, does that mean Socrates, Oates, the martyrs, Father Kolbe—and Jesus!—were morally wrong? What is the difference between those deaths and suicide?

Intention is the main difference. "To intend to terminate one's own life—this is the distinguishing mark of the act of suicide. To bring about the termination of one's life by so arranging the circumstances that one dies but with the intention of bringing about some other state of affairs, is not suicide."[38]

Oates was not eager to die, but decided his death would increase the odds that his companions might live. (In fact, they, too, died.) Father Kolbe, all things being equal, did not want to end his life; he simply wanted to save the life of a fellow concentration camp inmate whose family needed him. In neither case was death their primary intention. On the contrary, their real goal was to *save* lives, and if they had had another way of accomplishing that they would have chosen it rather than death. Such deaths are "instrumental" in achieving other ends, and thus are not to be counted as suicides.

"Suicide" might be redefined as "the act of a person who noninstrumentally intends his death."[39] A possible method of distinguishing between such self-sacrifice and straight suicide is: If the dead person could be miraculously revived, what would his reaction be? The "true" suicide would wish he were dead, while the heroic self-sacrificer would be delighted to be alive (though, of course, such a person might be willing to face death again if there is still no alternative to saving the other's life).

IRRATIONALITY OF SUICIDE: PHILIP E. DEVINE AND JOYCE CAROL OATES

The traditional argument in favor of suicide, dating from the ancients, is that suicide is a free and rational act. A "precondition" of rational choice is that you know what you are choosing, either from your own experience or that of others. But the suicide chooses death, and no one can "know" death in this way. We may know what a corpse is or how people die; we may know the consequences of death for those left behind (e.g., grief, financial ruin), and we may try to explain the experience of death or imagine it by certain "myths" or metaphors such as "death is an everlasting sleep" or "the absence of life." But death is finally, and certainly, something quite different from all of the above. "Human beings characteristically find themselves in profound imaginative and intellectual difficulty when they attempt to envisage the end of their existence."[40] Therefore, suicide is *not* a rational choice. Our very inability to describe death with any accuracy is proof of the "opaqueness of death."[41]

Suicides are inclined to romanticize death. But death is not some kind of "sleep" or beneficent "nonexistence" or the road to freedom. Death is "Deadness—mere, brute, blunt, flat, distinctly unseductive Deadness."[42] And while there might be suicides which are inevitable, the only way to preserve your dignity or escape immeasurable pain, "the act of suicide itself is a consequence of the employment of false metaphors. It is the consequence of the atrophying of the creative imagination: the failure of imagination."[43]

Anyone who believes that suicide is a romantic answer to life's pain or even an expression of "art" is a fool, and a deranged one at that.

IN FAVOR

The contemporary debate over the "sanctity of life" has split between those who hold that life is good no matter what and those who argue that it is the "quality of life" that counts. The pro-life contingent often acts as if the "quality of life" standard is some kind of fly-by-night, modern, "humanistic" view of life. People-centered it is, and definitely of the secular persuasion. But the position that each man controls his life, and death, that living well takes precedence over simply living, is as old as Stoicism, a school of philosophy founded in about 300 B.C. in Greece which also thrived in Rome at about the time Christianity was born. (Stoic asceticism—the disapproval of passion, overindulgence, and unjust thoughts—influenced the early Christians.)

A passionate Stoic defense of the individual's control over life, and death, has come down to us from Seneca, a Roman philosopher for whom wisdom is the key to goodness:

"The Quality of Life, Not the Quantity": Seneca[44]

"Mere living is not good, but living well." The truly wise man is concerned with the "quality of his life." Once that quality disintegrates, "he sets himself free." He does this carefully, thoughtfully, and bravely.

Those who argue that suicide is evil, that we should simply wait for the end "decreed by nature," are merely depriving us of our freedom. "The best thing which eternal law ever ordained was that it allowed to us one entrance into life, but many exits. . . . Tranquility can be purchased at the cost of a pin-prick." If it is reasonable to die rather than to live, die. "The foulest death is preferable to the cleanest slavery."

Suicide, according to five of the greatest minds in the Western Tradition—Plato, Aristotle, Augustine, Aquinas, and Kant—is a sin against God, the community, and the self.

Another of the superstars of Western Philosophy targeted each one of these traditional arguments:

"To Restore Men to Their Native Liberty": David Hume[45]

God, the Almighty Creator, has put the world and all its contents into operation, things animate and inanimate, all matter and animals. To govern "every particle," he has established laws "general and immutable." The inanimate parts of the world proceed "without regard to the particular interest and situation of men," while men "may employ every faculty with which they are endowed" to secure their happiness and self-preservation.

Yet nature affects man, and man affects nature. Great rivers block the passage of man, who also can channel the same rivers so that their power energizes machines. The world is full of differences, yet there seems to be a "harmony and proportion" to it all—"the surest argument of Supreme Wisdom."

If this is true, if such general laws govern the universe, if the lives of men and animals are dependent upon these laws, is it criminal to disturb their operation? In particular, is it criminal for a man to encroach upon God's province by killing himself?

"This seems absurd." For if life and death were the province only of God, and suicide were to interfere with God's rights, "it would be equally criminal" to save my life as to destroy it. "If I turn aside a stone which is falling upon my head, I disturb the course of nature; and I invade the peculiar province of the Almighty, by lengthening out my life beyond the period, which, by the general laws of matter and motion, he had assigned it."

God has given us many powers for which we ought to be thankful; among them is prudence over our own lives. Why would we not be allowed to use this freedom? Is it because human life is more important than other kinds of life? "But the life of a man is of no greater importance to the universe than that of an oyster." Don't the Christians teach that when something bad happens to me, that it is God's will, that "I ought to be resigned to Providence," and that what men and nature do are actually the "operations of the Almighty"? "When I fall upon my sword, therefore, I receive my death equally from the hands of the Deity as if it had proceeded from a lion, a precipice, or a fever." If I can try to avoid calamity by whatever skills I have on hand, or if I am allowed to endanger my life for glory or friendship and am called a "hero," why is it that if a man "puts a period to his life from the same or like motives" he is called a wretch or miscreant?

What about the argument against suicide (made by the Pythagoreans, Plato, and Kant, though Hume does not credit them) that God places us in a particular station, like a sentinel, and when we desert it on our own we are guilty of rebelling against God? If I owe my birth ultimately to God, who guides the "chain of causes, of which many depended upon voluntary actions of men," that resulted in my life, then my death, no matter how voluntary, cannot happen without God's consent. If pain or sorrow "make me tired of life," then it is actually God that has recalled me from my station.

"A BREACH OF OUR DUTY TO OUR NEIGHBOR OR SOCIETY"?

If it is not against the law to resign my position because of illness or old age and devote my life to "fencing against these calamities," why can't I "cut short these miseries at once" by suicide? My death will do no harm to society; in fact, if my misery or pain keeps someone else from being more useful to society, then "my resignation of life must not only be innocent but laudable."

SUICIDE MAY OFTEN BE IN OUR OWN INTEREST

If old age or illness or bad luck makes my life seem worse than death, then it is in my interest to end it as soon as possible. "I believe that no man ever threw away life while it was worth keeping."

Contemporary defenders of suicide share Hume's opinion that suicide can sometimes make very good sense, while also echoing the Stoic view that death may be preferable to a miserable life. The best known "quality of life" proponent is Joseph Fletcher, notorious for his advocacy of what has been called situation ethics. The Oxford philosopher Jonathan Glover also argues that a good suicide depends on whether life is worth living.

"Quality of Life, Not the Sanctity of Life": Joseph Fletcher[46]

The basic error of most traditional morality, particularly of a religious nature, is its commitment to eternal absolutes. For the typical Christian moral theologian, certain acts (e.g., abortion, birth control, suicide) are wrong because they are *intrinsically* wrong or evil. In humanistic ethics, "no action is intrinsically right or wrong . . . nothing is inherently good or evil."[47]

What makes an action right or wrong? It depends: "When suicide helps human beings, it is right. That is, we have a right to do it. What makes it right is human need."[48] A set of moral principles, external absolutes that supersede all human needs (e.g., Plato's "Forms," the Bible's Ten Commandments, the Vatican's position that abortion is always wrong or suicide is always murder) can easily put us into a situation that the "moral" thing to do is the most callous or cruel act available.

Some cultures have honored various kinds of suicides (Japanese hari-kari, Hindu suttee, Buddhist self-immolation); others abhor it (in the Koran, suicide is condemned more than murder because it interferes with kismet, Allah's control of life and destiny). Even primitive cultures in Africa and America considered suicide a taboo. Greek philosophers opposed it; Roman philosophers celebrated it. The Catholic Church has viewed suicide as a heinous sin for fifteen hundred years.

Common to most of these views is that life is a kind of "property" that either belongs to God or to the person living it. Those who believe that life belongs to the person living it have traditionally been more willing to sanction suicide. For these moralists, as long as the suicide does not hurt others (family or friends, for example), "when it is truly and only a personal choice, it is right."

"SUICIDES ARE SICK PEOPLE" IS BASICALLY SILLY

Doctors and psychiatrists are inclined to think that suicides are "out of their gourd," mainly because doctors and psychiatrists are more likely to deal with "false suicides" whose threats or attempts are evidence of emotional or mental stress. We don't often hear from the successes.

While some suicides might be mentally disturbed, not all are. We now have plenty of evidence that people can end their lives carefully, rationally, indeed ethically. Thousands of terminally ill people have chosen to kill themselves; hundreds of thousands of others have signed living wills instructing relatives and friends to end artificial life-support systems for them when they are no longer able to make that choice themselves. Whether we choose to kill ourselves or authorize others to pull the plug and allow us to die, the goal is the same—death. Is it right to let cancer kill us, slowly and painfully, and wrong to decide to cheat that pain and time and kill ourselves? "Every person's fight with death is lost before it begins. What makes the struggle worthwhile, therefore, cannot lie in the outcome. It lies in the dignity with which the fight is waged and the way it finds an end."[49]

No life is absolutely sacred. Life must be measured in relation to other values. For many people, simply living or surviving, either in psychological misery or physical pain, is not enough. Life is not necessarily an end in itself. Suicide, as Camus pointed out, is "the only truly serious philosophical problem"—and thus cannot be taken, as a given, to be evil or good. Nothing is intrinsically good or evil, including life or death. "Quality is always . . . contingent. The full circle is being drawn. In classical times suicide was a tragic option, for human dignity's sake. Then for centuries it was a sin. Then it became a crime. Then a sickness. Soon it will become a choice again. Suicide is the signature of freedom."[50]

Criteria for the Good Suicide: "Is Life Worth Living and How Will It Affect Others?": Jonathan Glover

"To kill oneself can sometimes be the right thing to do, but much less often than may at first sight appear."[51] Many argue that suicide is not even a moral question, that the urge to kill yourself is merely an irrational sign of some kind of mental disturbance and thus must be viewed (and treated) as a "medical" problem. Others contend that suicide is merely a matter of "free choice," none of anyone else's business—but simply a matter of deciding whether your life is worth living. On the contrary: "The consideration of a possible act of suicide raises moral questions, for the person himself and for other people, of the same complexity as other acts of killing (e.g., murder, abortion, infanticide, assisted euthanasia, capital punishment, political assassination)."

Of the suicide who knows what he is doing and has time to deliberate about his actions, two questions are relevant: (1) If he doesn't commit suicide, what would his life be like, "would it be worth living"? and (2) How will his decision to die or live affect others, not only relatives and friends but the entire community?

It will not be easy, of course, to predict the future. But it is not unusual for people to contemplate suicide without considering some other alternatives such as changing jobs, leaving a family, leaving a country, going to a psychiatrist—extraordinary and often traumatic changes in life, but far less radical than killing yourself.

And what sort of life is worth living anyway? Who is to tell? "One test has to do with the amount of life for which you would rather be unconscious. . . ." Just as we may prefer anesthesia for a painful operation, we might choose as an antidote to a painful life "permanent anaesthesia"—death. Yet others might prefer pain to no life at all, while still others might believe that brief periods of intense happiness are enough to make up for longer periods of misery. "Our estimates of the quality of our lives are especially vulnerable to temporary changes of mood, so that the only reasonable way to reach a serious evaluation is to consider the question over a fairly long stretch of time."

Nor is it easy to gauge the effect that suicide might have on others—family, parents, friends. One source of evidence might be the accounts of families which have experienced a suicide. A successful suicide may also deprive the community of a valuable and productive member. Suicide may be the right thing to do but not "without the most careful thought about the effects on all those emotionally involved."

"WE ARE MORALLY OBLIGED TO INTERVENE . . ."

The moral dilemma for someone thinking of preventing another from killing himself is actually more complicated than deciding to commit suicide: like the suicide, he must evaluate the effects of the act, but he also must decide whether it is right for him to get in the way. For those of us who do not advocate "paternalism" (i.e., that it is always right to interfere in other people's lives), these are two different questions.

And if we are entitled to interfere, how far can we go? Is persuasion the limit, or coercion; how much? ("This problem is clearly illustrated by the use of forcible feeding on people killing themselves by hunger strike.") Are doctors and hospital workers morally obliged to revive the attempted suicide who is rushed to the emergency room?

One guiding principle is: "It is desirable where possible to save a worth-while life." If we believe that a person considering suicide has a "life worth living," then reasoning with him and trying to persuade him to reconsider his decision is "always legitimate." Reasoning with someone will in no way step on his autonomy, and if it succeeds it will save a worthwhile life. (Of course, the suicide can always reconsider and try again.) The downside is that the person kills himself anyway, a result no worse than the original one.

If persuasion fails, "it is legitimate to restrain him by force from his first attempt, or even several attempts." But if after we intervene several times, and he persists in wanting to kill himself, to continue to prevent him forcibly "is a total denial of his autonomy in the matter." The hunger striker has had plenty of time to consider the consequences of his protest. Always in the case of a rational person contemplating his own self-destruction we should, all things being equal, "respect his decision."

Of course, we cannot always know what is going on in the mind of the suicide, particularly one who experiences periodic, but nevertheless persistent moods of suicidal depression. All in all, it is better to err on the side of interference. The fact is that "someone calmly determined to kill himself will have other opportunities."

IN MY OPINION

> It's a durn mystery, you know, in spite of all we've written about it.
>
> Dr. Karl Menninger, after a lifetime
> of research into suicide (1984)[52]

In two thousand years of arguments for and against suicide, this remark may be the most honest thing an "expert" has ever said about the issue. "A durn mystery" it is, and this may be the best reason not to rush to judgment about either the rationality or morality of suicide.

Writers have been arguing about suicide since the time of Plato, and among suicide's opponents at least, most of what they have written is simply patronizing. The suicide has been either portrayed as a sinner and criminal or as a lunatic. Other cultures, of course, have honored suicides as heroic responses to public shame or humiliation. In this discussion, however, I intend to stick to the Western tradition, which has been ambivalent about self-destruction; great thinkers can be lined up on either side. I also want to rule out obviously *irrational* suicides, acts of self-destruction where people are either out of their minds or in such a state of deep clinical depression that they have no idea what they are doing. The American novelist William Styron has described his own harrowing bout of suicidal urgings as a "despair beyond despair"—a "veritable howling tempest in the brain" that he eventually realized had been brought on by what amounted to an overdose of prescription drugs.[53] (Some will argue that no suicide, no matter how apparently rational, can know what he is doing. I will try to answer that objection.) Nor will I discuss "heroic" suicides, cases where people, such as Captain Oates or Father Kolbe, or even Socrates or Jesus, offer their lives to save others or as an example of self-sacrifice.

I want to focus on personal acts of self-destruction and make an argument for suicide being rational and moral, sometimes. History and literature abound with evidence of suicides who are quite rational, *deadly* rational. Self-destruction is hardly an impulsive act among those who put their things in order, write notes to friends and family, and make elaborate plans, sometimes for months, to make sure they are prepared to die. They end their lives not because they have lost their minds. On the contrary, their minds are very much on the case. So eager are they to erase their pain, psychological or physical, that they are willing to end the condition for all other action—life itself. They want to escape, they must escape. The writer Virginia Woolf experienced bouts of "madness" from adolescence, probably severe depressions that sent her to bed for weeks at a time. At age sixty, after one of the most productive and successful literary careers in the twentieth century, Woolf, sensing she was about to descend into her own personal hell once again and might not ever come out of it, wrote a note to her husband to that effect, went down to the river, puts rocks in her pockets, and drowned herself.

Few of us have trouble at least understanding why a man or woman racked by the pain of terminal cancer wants out. It seems a reasonable thing to consider, though not always necessarily the right thing to consider. (I will discuss why in the next chapter, "Euthanasia.") Why, then, is the psychic pain of the suicide any less agonizing? Virginia Woolf clearly saw another bout of depression as a kind of terminal state from which she would not return; she recognized that, in one sense, she was dying. As the Russian writer Boris Pasternak wrote about the 1930 suicide of the poet Mayakovsky and others who decided that death was preferable to life under Stalin: "And, as we bow in homage to their gifts and to their bright memory, we should bow compassionately before their suffering."[54] On August 24, 1991, three days after an attempted coup by a group of high Soviet officials collapsed (the beginning of the end of the kind of totalitarian madness that drove Mayakovsky to despair), Mikhail Gorbachev's special advisor on military affairs, Marshal Sergei Akhromeyev, killed himself in his Kremlin office. He left behind a note: "Everything I have worked for is being destroyed." Akhromeyev, a former chief of staff of the Red Army, had devoted his life to the Communist Party, the Soviet Union, and its army. All three were dying, and Akhromeyev decided to beat them to it.[55]

It is not surprising for someone who has never felt a suicidal urge to think that anyone who kills himself must be crazy. But what about a Mayakovsky or a Virginia Woolf? Can you ever kill yourself in a morally responsible way?

I think you can, though not in as many cases as most pro-suicide people might like to think. But there is such a thing as a "good suicide," a fact, I believe, that explains why even the best efforts of the greatest minds in Western thought to develop a good argument against suicide have failed. Plato, Aristotle, Augustine, Thomas Aquinas, and Kant all attack suicide lamely, in my opinion, and invitingly. (It is not often that you have the chance to carve up the arguments of such a star-studded lineup.)

A Sin Against God, the Community, and the Self?

Behind the traditional opposition to suicide sits an omnipotent God. The argument is as old as Pythagoras and was echoed by Plato through his mouthpiece Socrates in the *Phaedo:* "The gods are our keepers, and we men are one of their possessions. Don't you think so?"[56]

Augustine agreed, as did Aquinas and Kant. As recently as 1980 the Roman Catholic Church issued a "Declaration on Euthanasia," reaffirming the traditional Christian view that life is "a gift of God's love," and that any attempt on a human life is "a crime of utmost gravity," "a refusal of love for self," and a "flight from the duties of justice and charity" owed to your neighbors and community.[57] But if you do not believe that there is a Superior Being who controls all life, then man alone is in charge and can decide when to make his final exit. But even a religious man is likely to wonder, as Hume so cleverly, and persuasively in my opinion, points out: "Were the disposal of human life so much reserved as the peculiar province of the Almighty, that it were an encroachment on his right for men to dispose of their own lives, it would be equally criminal to act for the preservation of life as for its destruction."[58] If doctors are not criminals, neither are suicides. Hume argues that everything we do must be "equally innocent or equally criminal." And if God has placed us as "sentinels" (as Pythagoras, Socrates, and Kant contend), if he guides all causes, then that includes death, "however voluntary."

Hume, too, disposes of Aristotle's argument that suicide injures the community: if I can resign from office because of old age or illness and spend the rest of my life "fencing against these calamities," why does ending them once and for all—by suicide—hurt society any more? Hume also rightly points out that some people might be burdens to society or prevent other people from being more useful. In such cases, "my resignation of life must not only be innocent, but laudable."

Hume might also have pointed out that some people are not only burdens to society, they actually threaten the community and everything it stands for. What community would not benefit from the disappearance of its thieves and murderers, not to mention its torturers or tyrants? Did Hitler's suicide (surely, one of his most rational career decisions) harm the community?

Hume also takes on the argument that suicide is a sin against the self: "That suicide may often be consistent with interest and with our duty to ourselves, no one can question, who allows that age, sickness, or misfortune may render life a burden, and make it worse even than annihilation. I believe that no man ever threw away life while it was worth keeping." At least no *rational* man. To this day, the opponents of suicide seem unable to imagine how any sane man could take his life.

I believe this betrays their failure of imagination.

The Rational Suicide

Seneca shows that suicide can be so rational that a man will find a means, no matter how limited his opportunities may be. The Roman Stoic reports on the case of a "wild beast gladiator" who, before he was sent into the arena against the hungry lions, asked for permission to visit the latrine. Out of the sight of the guards, the gladiator grabbed a stick with a sponge ("devoted to the vilest of uses") and stuffed it down his throat, choking himself to death. "What a brave fellow!" says Seneca, adding that "the foulest death is preferable to the cleanest slavery." The opponent of suicide Kant echoes Seneca when he praises the innocent man sentenced to the galleys who "would rather die than live as an object of contempt."

Who could disagree? Such suicides among condemned men in the first century resonate even more strongly in our own, an age that has seen terrors far worse than anything Nero achieved. No one knows how many of the millions who perished in Stalin's gulag or Hitler's camps or Pol Pot's killing fields (to mention only three cases of mass murder in our murderous century) died by their own hand. We mourn those murdered masses and honor the survivors. Following Seneca and Kant, we should praise the men and women who by their own self-destruction deprived the torturers of the pleasure, indeed the self-righteousness, of murdering them. Under the most inhumane circumstances, these people salvaged their humanity and died. Even someone who believes that life is a "gift of God" can reach a stage where it seems his duty to return the gift. Not all lives are sacred.

Imagine yourself a political prisoner, say Winston Smith in George Orwell's *1984* at the mercy of the torturer O'Brien, who explains that you must be tortured rather than simply shot because "the object of torture is torture." You await having your head stuck into a cage of hungry rats. The example is fictional but by no means unreal, for if this weren't already the Century of Mass Murder, the twentieth century might be called "the Century of Torture."

Or imagine yourself one of the 253 men who have been executed in the United States since 1976, when the Supreme Court allowed the states to resume capital punishment. Do you bravely walk out to face your killers, or do you, just as bravely, deprive them of their spectacle? The spy carries with him his cyanide pill to deprive his torturers of the pleasure they get from making him scream, so why not the criminal?

And what about the victim of psychic pain, the kind of personal shame, for example, so piercing that every waking moment is torture? Joyce Carol Oates has called the urge to suicide a "failure of the imagination."

On the contrary: not to see it from the suicide's point of view is a failure of imagination.

Imagining Suicide

Oates wonders whether you can "freely choose" suicide—"a state of being that has never been experienced except in the imagination and, even there, *only in metaphor.*"[59] Agreed: no one knows what death is like. Agreed: it is likely to be worse than most lives.

But is death worse than *all* lives? Therein lies the real failure of imagination. Joyce Carol Oates is concerned that the suicide is a victim of a false metaphor, that he or she thinks death is some kind of "serene, transcendental, Platonic 'all-knowing non-existence,' and not biological 'deadness.' " That may be true of many suicides, but not all of those bent on self-destruction are such wide-eyed romantics. Many are quite aware that they are choosing "deadness," and that is exactly the metaphor they want. They prefer that blank nothing to the misery of life.

Imagining what it is like to be dead is not the issue. *Imagining what it is like to prefer death to life is.*[60] And what is "life" anyway? Any life?

A life of cancer pain? A life of Alzheimer's disease? A life awaiting the electric chair? A life of slavery? Or shame? A life of AIDS?

We have heard enough reports, in brilliant as well as melodramatic detail, from people and families who have experienced all of these conditions; they are the stuff that great novels (and awful TV movies) are made of. Mayakovsky did not think a life under Stalin's boot was worth living and shot himself. "I don't recommend it for others," he wrote, but for him suicide was a rational solution.

Even those of us who could never do such a thing can try to put ourselves into the head of such a man and imagine the enormity of the suffering that made him put a gun to his head. Mayakovsky penetrated the mystery of suicide and embraced death. What would it take for us to make such a decision? If every man has his price, what is the price of suicide? As Pasternak, who survived the same horrors that his friend Mayakovsky and others could not, so kindly put it, "we should bow compassionately before their suffering."

One problem is that Christianity, the most adamant opponent of suicide, has tried to make a *virtue* of suffering.

The Virtue of Suffering or the Vice of Cruelty?

Suffering in the Christian tradition has, as a 1980 Catholic document put it, a "special place in God's saving plan; it is in fact a sharing in Christ's passion and a union with the redeeming sacrifice which He offered in obedience to the Father's will."[61] Thus, suffering is the closest Christians can come to experiencing the redemptive pain Christ suffered on the cross—not an argument bound to win over most people in grave physical or psychological pain. Even the brutal, non-Christian "deadness" that Joyce Carol Oates refers to might seem preferable. Indeed, to demand that a person in such suffering persist in life, though well intentioned at first, could evolve into an act of cruelty.

If any moral system is to meet the challenges of the twenty-first century, it will have to be opposed to cruelty in all forms.[62] But even if a certain suicide is good or right, don't we have a moral obligation to stop someone from killing himself?

Getting in the Way

Suicides ought to be prevented, *but not always*. Conceding that some suicides are rational and justified, I must ascertain that *this* potential suicide, the one I can stop, is rational and moral. If a friend tells me that he can take an overdose of sleeping pills and find himself in the arms of his girlfriend who has just been killed in an auto accident, I have a duty to warn him that this is not necessarily so. Many suicides may have, as Oates has pointed out, an overly romantic notion of dying, or what the philosopher Gerald Dworkin has called "evaluative delusions" about death.[63]

And if my friend seems depressed or disoriented, I should try to help him, calm him down, keep him out of harm's way, until he can get to a doctor. If he calls the "suicide hotline," I will assume he is reaching out for help. Or if I catch him composing a suicide note or accidentally read his diary and discover that he is contemplating suicide, I should try to persuade him to reconsider his decision, to think about it a bit more. And if I know that his suicide, no matter how rational, will hurt his wife and family, and leave them destitute, then I must inform him that his decision is wrong.

Letting people alone, as John Stuart Mill argued, "should be the general practice."[64] Coercing people "for their own good" assumes that your good is the only plausible one, that you alone have a line on what is good not only for you but for everyone.

But we cannot assume that *everyone*—even every middle-aged adult—is as reasonable as John Stuart Mill. Some people ought not to be left alone, and many suicides fall into that category. I agree with the Oxford philosopher Jonathan Glover: My interference does not violate the liberty of my friend the suicide in any substantive way. After I stop him, if he still believes suicide is the best decision for him, he will get another chance.

Even Mill concedes that there are exceptions to his own absolute opposition to the universal urge to play the "moral police." Preventing suicide is one of those exceptions. Suicide is a special moral case because of its irrevocability: the successful suicide is in no position to change his mind. Nor can he base his decision, as Mill advises, on "personal experience." No one has any such experience of death.

But how often may we interfere with the suicide? I suspect that each of us will know when we arrive at the limit. I myself would be willing to intervene several times—once, twice, three times. After that, I should examine my own intentions. Am I the fanatic? Interfering with another's decision to kill himself more than several times will begin to seem like a career. Suicide is not necessarily an appalling act. It is usually construed so because, historically, the Christian world has been appalled by suicide. Suicide has had a bad reputation, and that has a lot to do with St. Augustine.

The Problem with Augustine

Hard-pressed to come up with a proper *theological* condemnation of suicide—neither the Old nor New Testament approves or disapproves of suicide, as Augustine concedes—Augustine resurrects Plato's arguments: life is a "gift" of God, man is but a sentinel awaiting God's call, to choose to die before then is to rebel against God. From the historical record, however, it appears that Augustine's attitude toward suicide was much influenced by Church politics—namely, his effort to undercut the popularity of Donatism in Africa. Augustine's not-so-Christian contempt for the Donatists rang through his famous sermons attacking this bizarre branch of Christianity: "The clouds roll and thunder, that the House of the Lord shall be built throughout the earth: and these frogs sit in their marsh and croak—We are the only Christians!"[65] To discredit the Donatists, Augustine had to discredit their central principle: the glorification of martyrdom.

He succeeded. The Donatists were declared heretics and suppressed. In the twelfth and thirteenth centuries in southern France, the Albigensians recreated the fashion for martyrdom, and were declared heretics by the Vatican and destroyed by the Inquisition.

Both groups, however, had a kind of pure Christian logic on their side. Augustine admitted as much when he raises the question why a newly baptized Christian, to escape the risk of accidentally dying in a state of sin, doesn't rush out and kill himself before he can submit to temptation.[66] Augustine simply dismisses such behavior as "mad." But it presents a logical difficulty that suicide's most famous Christian opponents have solved only with waffling. Augustine's condemnation of suicide, and the Donatists' taste for martyrdom, without condemning the celebrated martyrs of the early Church, required some fancy footwork: suicide is wrong—except if God commands it.

Though Augustine, Aquinas, and today's Roman Catholic Church, as well as other conservative Christian churches, are all appalled by suicide, God apparently does not have a problem with people killing themselves for His greater glory.

For the past sixteen hundred years, such ironies have inspired commentators to try to redefine suicide in order to count out such "altruistic" versions as martyrdom. This is the same weakness in the argument against suicide that forces contemporary philosophers personally appalled by self-destruction to look for ways to define suicide so that the deaths of Socrates, Jesus, Captain Oates, Father Kolbe, IRA hunger strikers, and any other individual who intentionally chooses death for "a higher cause" do not count as "self-murder."

Of course, these arguments beg the question, Whose "higher cause"? And why doesn't a rational and good man's decision to end his life for good reasons measure up to such a "higher cause"? Indeed, from the point of view of the secular man his own "cause" is as high as causes can get.

And so for him, suicide can be both the rational and the moral thing to do.

3. Euthanasia

THE ISSUE

One nagging irony of modern life is that while medicine is now better able to save lives, it also can prolong suffering. Modern medicine, in fact, has learned how to cheat death, manipulate it, even metamorphose it into a high-tech version of Snow White's sleep. An indisputably terminal cancer patient who would have met a quick death a century ago can now be kept alive for years by radiation and chemical therapies, by intravenous nutrients, or just by hospitalization. A comatose patient can be kept alive for decades on nutrition and hydration machines.

Once the least ambiguous event in life, death has become increasingly difficult to pinpoint. Americans now die quite differently than they did a century ago, when tuberculosis and influenza were the scourge, and the last place a sick person wanted to end up was the hospital, where he was more likely to die by contracting another patient's infection than by the illness that hospitalized him. Today most of us will die in a hospital, where many doctors, buoyed by technological advances in saving the critically ill, believe it is their duty to do everything possible to keep patients alive.

Others, however, do not. They believe that responsible medicine has to recognize that, at some point, death is inevitable, and everything must be done to help that patient die with a minimum of suffering. In fact, 80 percent of hospital and nursing home patients will succumb only after someone (the patient himself, a doctor, parents, relatives, or friends) makes the decision that it is time to let the patient die.[1]

Helping someone die is called euthanasia—Greek for "easy death" or "dying well." Traditionally, in discussions of euthanasia, a basic distinction has been made between "passive" euthanasia (i.e., letting someone die, either by not intervening to prolong life or by turning off life-sustaining equipment) and "active" euthanasia (i.e., taking direct action to end a life by, say, giving a lethal injection to a terminal cancer patient). Active euthanasia is what most people have in mind when they talk about "mercy killing."

For the past twenty-five years most Americans have seemed to favor the legalization of euthanasia, at least when the question is put to them in the most positive way. In 1977 the National Opinion Research Center, which surveys religious views, found that 59 percent of their respondents thought doctors should be allowed to end the lives of patients "who could not be cured," if the patient and family request it.[2] In a 1986 poll conducted by Roper, 62 percent felt that euthanasia "should be allowed by law," 27 percent said it "should not be allowed," and 11 percent either did not know or had no answer. In a 1987 Field poll, 64 percent believed that one "should have the right to ask for and get life-ending medication," 27 percent believed they "should not have the right," and 9 percent were undecided.

In a 1992 *Family Circle* survey of "national values," people were asked whether they thought it was "fair" to prosecute a man for killing his terminally ill wife. Sixty-six percent thought not.[3] Indeed, in both the National Opinion Research Center and *Family Circle* polls, at least half of those who claimed to be deeply religious and frequent churchgoers were still willing to permit euthanasia.

To many, the notion that no dying person should be obliged to live out his days in misery seems merciful. And the medical and legal professions and mainstream churches largely agree: patients who are being kept alive only by life-support machines and have no reasonable hope for recovery ought to be allowed to die. There are even some moderate medical ethicists who concede that in exceptional situations voluntary active euthanasia might be morally right—but not in enough cases to warrant legalizing assisted suicide.

Like the abortion issue, the noise in the debate over euthanasia comes from the extremes—the "quality of life" advocates of legalization versus the "sanctity of life" advocates, who oppose allowing dying patients a quicker death under any circumstances. Stripped of their rhetoric, however, both sides share something in common: a passion for life. How they *perceive* life is where they differ. And, inevitably, how you view life will affect how you view death.

Like the abortion debate, the argument over euthanasia exposes how important our personal views of life are to our moral and political convictions. Traditionally, personal religious or spiritual or moral preferences have been outside the domain of the government, which has tried to avoid imposing a particular view (i.e., what constitutes life, or a "good death") on those who might not share that view. Over the past twenty years the courts have been called on to arbitrate the different attitudes that patients, families, and doctors have toward life and death. And by and large the courts, like most Americans, seem to prefer compassion to dogmatism—a position that has ancient roots.

Euthanasia's Ancient History

The ancients seem to have had few qualms about committing suicide, and the same held for euthanasia.[4] In the fourth century B.C., Socrates, according to his protégé Plato, derided a doctor whose cures promoted the notion of "lingering death" and praised Asclepius, the god of healing, noting that "bodies which disease had penetrated through and through, he would not have attempted to cure . . . he did not want to lengthen out good-for-nothing lives."[5] Plato, who generally opposed suicide, allows it in cases of someone in "great suffering."[6] Aristotle, as we saw in the last chapter, opposed suicide as an affront to the community and proof that the individual lacked the central virtue of any good man, courage.[7]

State-approved suicide existed in ancient Greece where Athenian magistrates kept on hand a supply of hemlock, the poison of choice, for any citizen who had obtained the Senate's permission to "abandon life." Among the Romans, too, suicide and euthanasia flourished. Zeno, the founder of Stoicism, hanged himself at ninety-eight.

The Ambivalence Toward Suffering

The traditional Jewish and Christian position on suicide and helping someone die is absolute; it is a moral duty to prolong life.[8] Yet by the Renaissance, with its advances in science and medicine and cultural reaffirmation of Greek and Roman values, Christian theologians began to argue for allowing the terminally ill to die. In 1595 a Spanish scholar first pointed out the difference between prolonging life by "ordinary" and "extraordinary means" (medical treatment or surgery that caused horrible pain). Great thinkers of the sixteenth and seventeenth centuries—Sir Thomas More, Francis Bacon, John Donne—began to endorse euthanasia, arguing that scientific advances that kept patients alive also increased their suffering. In the eighteenth century, the Enlightenment's commitment to rationality and the individual rights of man encouraged philosophers to explore arguments on behalf of a merciful release from suffering; throughout the next century they began to speak of the right to "die well" and have an "easy death."[9]

In the 1930s voluntary euthanasia societies organized in England and the United States lobbied for legislation that would allow individuals to "apply" for the right to die, provided they could prove they were suffering from a fatal disease. Doctors were more willing than ever to discuss their responsibilities to a dying patient, and a growing number of mercy killings made the headlines on both sides of the Atlantic. Juries seemed unwilling to convict people who had helped spouses or children die. Indeed, opinion polls indicated that more than 40 percent of Americans favored euthanasia for physically and mentally deformed infants as well as "hopeless invalids." In a similar British poll 69 percent supported euthanasia.[10] Yet British and American legislatures, along with the medical establishment, opposed the practice.

One government, however, was notoriously receptive to euthanasia: Nazi Germany. On September 1, 1939, Hitler ordered all state institutions to report on patients who had been ill for five years or more or who were unable to work. In the interests of creating an Aryan utopia, 250,000 Germans were killed. None of them asked that their lives be ended, nor were their families consulted—a classic example of "involuntary euthanasia," or murder.

The Focus of Intellectual Debate

Since World War II two points of view have dominated discussions of the ethics of euthanasia: the Catholic "ordinary-extraordinary" distinction, as refined by several prominent Catholic theologians and adopted by Catholic hospitals; and the belief of Protestant ethicist Joseph Fletcher, who argued that in an age of swift medical advances doctors dedicated to "the sanctity of life" had lost sight of "the quality of life." For Fletcher, a former head of the Euthanasia Society of America, a life spent in an irreversible coma or in agonizing pain is not a life worth living.[11]

Interestingly, it was a comment made by Pope Pius XII in 1957 that opened up the debate about the limits to prolonging life. At an international medical conference in Rome, a Catholic anesthesiologist had pointed out to the pope the dilemma faced by modern hospitals whose technology to sustain life was available to patients who did not want it, or for whom it was futile or prohibitively expensive. In reaffirming the Church's ban on euthanasia, the pope said that patients have a duty "to take the necessary treatment for the preservation of life and health." But he added a caveat: "Normally one is held to use only ordinary means—according to circumstances of persons, places, times and cultures—that is to say, means that do not involve any grave burden for oneself or another." Withdrawing medical technology, the pope explained, was not a case of "direct disposal of the life of the patient, nor of euthanasia in any way."[12]

The pope's commonsensical position on prolonging suffering artificially is too often ignored by religious and medical opponents of "easy death."

Learning How to Cheat Death

Despite significant advances during the 1960s in surgery, resuscitation methods, and intensive care, health professionals were deciding to let patients die every day. And there were not just the terminal, but also the very elderly and babies so horribly deformed and physically limited that no one could offer a prognosis of "a meaningful life" for them. Privately, doctors were saying, "Enough, let the poor thing die." But it wasn't until the 1970s that they began talking publicly about the reality of euthanasia. One reason for this was the "Johns Hopkins Case," reported in 1973.[13] After seeking some spiritual advice, the parents of an infant born with Down's syndrome and duodenal atresia, an intestinal blockage that can be repaired, decided that a mongoloid child was better dead and refused permission for corrective surgery. Fifteen days later the child died of starvation. Most commentators were appalled by the simplistic standards of "deformity" and "suffering" applied in the case, and many disagreed with the parents' decision. But such cases were not as rare as most people thought. In the prestigious *New England Journal of Medicine* two doctors reported that among

299 deaths in the special-care nursery of the Yale–New Haven Hospital between 1970 and 1972, forty-three—14 percent—were infants with multiple birth defects to their bodies, hearts, and central nervous systems. In each case, doctor and parents agreed that the chance the infant had for a "meaningful life" was either extremely poor or hopeless; treatment was ended.[14]

In 1973 the American Medical Association issued their guidelines, declaring that the use or termination of "extraordinary means to prolong the life of the body when there is irrefutable evidence that biological death is imminent is the decision of the patient and/or his immediate family."[15] The trouble was, where biological death would have been "imminent" a decade before, machines were now available to extend life. While infants with all sorts of ailments could not be cured, they could be saved easily. And comatose adults in "persistent vegetative states," shrunken and curled in fetal positions, could be kept alive literally for decades by machines. For every patient and family member eager to "pull the plug," there was a doctor and hospital administrator who was not, either out of moral qualms or fear of litigation. It was inevitable that such a case would end up in court—and as a weekly melodrama in the pages of *Time* magazine.[16]

The Karen Ann Quinlan Case

On April 15, 1975, after an evening on the town that began with tranquilizers and ended with gin and tonic, a twenty-one-year-old New Jersey woman passed out, went into a coma, and was rushed to a hospital where she was hooked up to a respirator. Karen Ann Quinlan never regained consciousness.

In September her parents, practicing Catholics, finally convinced that a miracle was not forthcoming, requested that the doctors pull the plug and allow their daughter to die.

The doctors refused. They had put the young woman on a respirator to save her life, and Karen Ann Quinlan met none of the medically accepted criteria for determining death: she responded to pain, and her brain showed electrical activity. The Quinlans went to superior court, which ruled that "there is no constitutional right to die that can be asserted by a parent for his incompetent adult child."[17] In spite of his own "sympathy" for the Quinlan family, the judge said that "judicial conscience and morality" told him Karen's doctors had acted properly.

In March 1976 the New Jersey Supreme Court reversed the lower court, ruling that the patient's right to privacy flowed to the right of the doctor to act according to his "best judgment" and the right of a guardian to act on a comatose patient's behalf. Critics of the Quinlan decision charged that the New Jersey Supreme Court had "gone a long way to obliterating the distinction between voluntary and involuntary euthanasia and weakening the legal protection of life from involuntary euthanasia."[18]

The Legal Right to Die

The year 1976 became a watershed one in the debate over treating the critically ill. Two Boston hospitals published guidelines for when treatment could be discontinued, and California became the first state to pass a "Natural Death Act," which gave citizens the right to refuse life-sustaining machines.

In 1983 a President's Commission for the Study of Ethical Problems in Medicine and Biomedical and Behavioral Research published *Deciding to Forgo Life-Sustaining Treatment,* aimed at helping doctors, legislators, "competent and informed patients," and their families to make decisions about when to stop life support. "Health care professionals," according to the report, "serve patients best by maintaining a presumption in favor of sustaining life, while recognizing that competent patients are entitled to choose and forgo any treatments, including those that sustain life."[19] In the more difficult case of "incompetent patients" (i.e., infants and those in irreversible comas), the commission recommended that state courts, legislatures, and hospitals make provisions allowing patients to designate others to make decisions for them. The commission made it clear that dying patients and their families must be allowed to make decisions about when treatment should end and how they should be cared for in their final days.

By 1994 forty-five states and the District of Columbia had legislation authorizing both living wills and "health-care agents" that allow people to go on record against prolonging their lives in the event of an irreversible coma.[20]

A Right to Artificial Nutrition and Hydration?

By the mid-1980s the euthanasia debate had shifted to machines that deliver nutrition and water to patients who would otherwise die. In 1984 the Washington State Supreme Court allowed the parents of a twenty-two-year-old woman blinded and brain-damaged from a rare fatal disease to remove her from a nutrition machine, even though she was sensate and could swallow liquids. In 1986 the AMA's Ethical and Judicial Affairs Council weighed in, declaring that, with the consent of the family, physicians could withhold "life-prolonging medical treatment"—including food and water—from the dying and those in irreversible comas. A furor resulted. Upwards of 1.25 million people in U.S. hospitals at any given time cannot feed themselves and are attached to various kinds of nutrition and hydration machines, some by tubes directly to the intestines. Ten thousand or so of them are in a coma or a persistent vegetative state. Horrified, many ethicists and doctors underlined the distinction between pulling the plug of a respirator and starving someone to death. In the meantime, doctors and lawyers across the country were eagerly awaiting word from the U.S. Supreme Court, which had already accepted the first case to question whether among all the rights in the Constitution there exists "the right to die."[21]

CRUZAN V. MISSOURI

On January 11, 1983, a twenty-five-year-old Missouri woman flipped her car off the road. A rescue team was able to restore her breathing and heartbeat at the scene and rushed her to the hospital. However, as a result of probable brain damage, Nancy Cruzan never regained consciousness or responded to rehabilitation. To ease feeding, doctors implanted artificial food and water tubes, only to be told by the young woman's parents to stop the nutrition and hydration machines—and allow Nancy to die. The hospital refused without court approval. The best medical guess was that Nancy Cruzan might live another thirty years in this condition.

A Missouri lower court decided that a patient in Cruzan's condition had a fundamental right under the state constitution and U.S. Constitution to refuse or ask for the withdrawal of "death-prolonging procedures." The court also found that conversations Cruzan had five years earlier with a roommate indicated that she would not wish to live hooked up to machines.

The Missouri Supreme Court disagreed. Because Nancy Cruzan was alive, argued the court, her parents did not have the common-law right to terminate her care. Cruzan's statements to her roommate were "unreliable," argued the justices, and not sufficient to give her parents the right to end treatment. In fact, no one had the right to decide to end her life without the kind of formal living will sanctioned by Missouri law or "clear and convincing" evidence about her intentions. The court also suggested that "broad policy questions bearing on life and death" should be settled not by the courts but by legislatures.[22]

In 1990 the U.S. Supreme Court finally ruled, 5 to 4, that no one had the right to terminate Nancy Cruzan's life except Nancy Cruzan. In the opinion of the majority, choosing to end a life was such a "deeply personal decision of obvious and overwhelming finality" that a state may legitimately try to protect this element of choice by imposing strict guidelines for evidence about a person's beliefs on how he or she wants to live and die. Not even Nancy Cruzan's parents could interfere. In a separate decision, Justice Antonin Scalia, agreeing with the majority, lamented that he would have preferred that the Court announce that "the federal courts have no business in this field." Scalia noted that the courts have left the prevention of suicide up to the states. He also pointed out that the moment when a life becomes "worthless" and efforts to preserve life become "extraordinary" or "inappropriate" are "neither set forth in the Constitution nor known to the nine Justices of this Court any better than they're known to nine people picked at random from the Kansas City telephone directory."

Scalia failed to divulge his reasons for believing that state legislators had any better understanding of the limits of life than thousands of people picked at random from the telephone directory. Nor did he explain how they could draft laws on the right to die in the face of hundreds of different cases. For this reason, the AMA opposes the adoption of legally binding policies. Many doctors insist that the decision to end a life or to let a life end belongs within the traditional limits of the doctor-patient relationship or between a doctor and the patient's family. They also argue that if the law takes over this area, then the opportunity for "base, evil, calculating, conniving motives," according to one doctor, "is wide open." But other physicians argue that they need legal guidelines to avoid malpractice suits.

The Cruzan family's agony finally ended after the state of Missouri withdrew from the case in the fall of 1990, allowing a county probate judge in Carthage, Missouri, to rule that the Cruzan family had the right to stop the artificial feeding of their comatose daughter. Nancy Cruzan died twelve days afterwards.

Voluntary Euthanasia: "Mercy Killing" or Just Plain Killing?

Opponents of all forms of euthanasia expressed their concern that the inevitable next step was actively helping patients die. As if to prove them right, the state of Michigan decided not to prosecute euthanasia advocate Dr. Jack Kevorkian for helping an Oregon woman suffering from Alzheimer's disease die. In May 1991 a Michigan court acquitted a man who had helped his cancer-stricken wife to end her life.[23]

Suddenly, euthanasia, once a topic for college and medical school seminars, was back on the front pages. In 1991, Derek Humphry, co-founder of the Hemlock Society, published *Final Exit,* a slim book filled with detailed instructions for how a terminally ill patient might hasten his death. Within days the book was at the top of the *New York Times* best-seller list. Later in the year the national media ran stories about Washington State's Initiative 119, which asked voters, "Shall adult patients who are in a medically terminal condition be permitted to request and receive from a physician aid-in-dying?" Although voters defeated the referendum, nationwide polls indicate that support for euthanasia still remains strong. Arthur Caplan, director of the Center for Biomedical Ethics at the University of Minnesota, called the battle over active euthanasia "the most important bioethics decision of the post-war era."[24]

Dr. Kevorkian single-handedly kept the issue in the news by assisting twenty other people to die. When he was arrested in 1994 for breaking a new Michigan law against physician-assisted suicide, Kevorkian staged a hunger strike to protest the law, which he and his attorney argued had been drafted and passed expressly to stop his work. Kevorkian was acquitted later in the year. In November, Oregon voters approved a new law allowing doctors to prescribe lethal drugs to patients in the last six months of life.

The Dutch Experiment[25]

Advocates of legalized euthanasia point to the Netherlands, where doctors and hospitals have accepted mercy killing and physician-assisted suicide as a patient's right, helping some three thousand terminally ill die each year. Yet what is not often made clear is that euthanasia is still *illegal* in the Netherlands, and the current law calls for twelve years' imprisonment for anyone who "takes the life of another at his or her explicit and serious request." Nevertheless, it is true that no doctor has been penalized for euthanasia in twenty years, and the Dutch have come to tolerate mercy killing.

The main reason for this is that Dutch doctors have established specific conditions for euthanasia that require the patient to request euthanasia freely and frequently, and as a result of careful consideration. Doctors will act only if the patient is terminally ill, with no hope of improvement and in severe pain. They will also have to consult another physician and file a report with the coroner. After a police investigation a prosecutor reviews the findings, consults with the attorney general, and then decides whether to prosecute.

In the Netherlands it is usually the family doctor who helps the patient die, always with a large dose of barbiturates (which causes a coma) and then an injection of curare (which stops the breathing and the heart). If the patient can kill himself, the doctor simply provides the right dose of barbiturates. A recent study reveals that most people die at home.

Who chooses this method of death is surprising. A recent Dutch study revealed that men and women seem to seek euthanasia in equal numbers. The average age for men was sixty-three; for women, sixty-six. Voluntary euthanasia was rare among people over seventy-five and rarer for men and women over eighty-five. Typically, they are cancer patients who fear "dependence, loss of dignity, humiliation and pain."[26]

There is, however, an alternative to all this.

The Hospice Movement

Dating from the care and shelter of the poor afflicted with cancer, tuberculosis, and other diseases in nineteenth- and early-twentieth-century Dublin and London, the modern hospice movement is largely the brainchild of Cicely Saunders, a researcher in pain control for advanced cancer patients who founded St. Christopher's Hospice in a London suburb in 1967. Conceived as an alternative for patients for whom a hospital was no longer appropriate, St. Christopher's is both a place that cares for the dying and does research on how to deal with terminal diseases.

Over the past two decades the hospice movement has found enthusiastic support in Canada and the United States. Hospice Inc., the first American program, was incorporated in New Haven in 1971 and began to thrive with state and federal support. According to the National Hospice Organization, there are more than two thousand hospices across the nation caring for 275,000 patients.

Hospices aim for comprehensive care of the terminally ill, taking advantage of the skills of health-care professionals from many different disciplines. Some hospices offer only home care, while others have their own building and rooms that are considerably "homier" than hospital wards. Whatever the case, all hospices share the same goal: viewing death as a natural part of life which, like birth, can be made easier with professional help.

In the past decade, federal agencies as well as state legislatures have made various tax and insurance provisions to make sure terminally ill Americans and their families can turn to a hospice program. More than 40 percent of employers now offer a hospice-care benefit. Many now argue that advances in geriatric medicine and hospice-care will end the euthanasia debate.

Perhaps, but for now the debate rages on, and the questions remain the same as they were in the time of Socrates: Do we have a right to expect an "easy death"? If so, do we have the right to expect our doctor to help us, to stop our suffering by hastening our end? Is it part of a doctor's job to not simply let us die, but kill us? Is there a *moral* difference between "mercy killing" and withdrawing an artificial respirator or nutrition machine? Is "life" on a respirator really life? Is a "life" of relentless suffering really life? Should euthanasia be legalized? What are the moral and social consequences for a society that allows this kind of "legal killing"?

AGAINST

Traditional Religious Opposition

The Bible, both Old and New Testaments, is absolutely unequivocal about life and death being in God's hands alone.[27] That means, say religious absolutists, hastening death in any way, even for a suffering, terminal patient, is an interference in God's domain—and thus homicide. This pro-life position, now identified with Christian hard-liners, first flourished among the ancient Jews, whose beliefs are practiced today by their religious descendants known as Orthodox.

ORTHODOX JEWS

For Orthodox Jews, even if a dying man who has previously refused life-sustaining equipment is in unbearable pain, wants to live no longer, and slips into an irreversible coma, no one has the right to end his life except God. Even adjusting a terminal patient's pillow, say the Orthodox, is to risk death. Only when death is certain and just hours away can any interference be tolerated. On the other hand, saving a life is so important even the Sabbath or the laws of the Torah can be violated.[28]

The other branches of modern Judaism—Conservative, Reform, and Reconstructionist—join the Orthodox in their opposition to active euthanasia; intentionally killing a patient, no matter how much their suffering, is morally unjustified under any circumstance. The traditionally liberal Central Conference of American Rabbis argues against such "mercy killing" in words that could have been written by conservative Christians: "Human life is more than a biological phenomenon; it is the gracious gift of God; it is the inbreathing of his spirit. . . . Man is the child of God, created in his image. . . . Thus, human life, coming from God, is sacred, and must be nurtured with great care."[29] The majority of Jews and their rabbis, however, recognize a difference between "active euthanasia" (i.e., taking positive steps to end a life) and "passive euthanasia" (i.e., standing back and allowing someone to die).

THE CATHOLIC POSITION

In the Catholic tradition there is no justification for euthanasia, defined as "an action or omission which of itself or by intention causes death, in order that all suffering may in this way be eliminated."[30] As in its opposition to abortion, the Church's ban on euthanasia is rooted in the biblical commitment to the "sanctity of life." According to the famous Vatican Council convened by Pope John XXIII in 1962, "euthanasia is opposed to life itself." Causing a death, even to end suffering, is an "infamy" and thus a crime against humanity.[31]

In 1980 the Vatican issued a specific "Declaration on Euthanasia," which reminded the faithful of St. Paul's words: "If we live, we live to the Lord, and if we die, we die to the Lord."[32] In underlining its position, the Vatican felt compelled to link euthanasia with abortion: "It is necessary to state firmly once more that nothing and no one can in any way permit the killing of an innocent human being, whether a fetus or an embryo, an infant or an adult, an old person, or one suffering from an incurable disease, or a person who is dying."[33] Nor is anyone permitted to ask to be killed, and certainly no "authority" has the right to recommend or permit an act of euthanasia. According to Christian teaching, suffering, particularly at the end of one's life, is a natural human condition; more important, suffering allows us to share in the painful sacrifice that Christ himself made to save mankind.

Recognizing that it cannot require people to be saints, the Church permits painkillers, though those that cause unconsciousness need special attention, for at the end of our lives, we must, in full consciousness, not only be prepared to handle family obligations, but also to meet Christ.[34]

Since the sixteenth century Christian moralists have noted that no one is ever obliged to fight off death with "extraordinary means." But with today's "miracle drugs" and fast-moving medical advances, once extraordinary treatments have become the ordinary machines of the modern intensive-care unit. To help doctors, patients, and their families make life and death decisions, the 1980 Vatican declaration offered specific "clarifications":

- To relieve suffering and perhaps even benefit humanity, a patient may accept even experimental and risky medical techniques, though the patient can consent to interrupt them if they fall short of expectation, though only with the advice of doctors and consultation with family members.

- Doctors might also help determine whether the patient's investment in the medical techniques and personnel is "disproportionate" with the results; they may also help decide whether the "strain of suffering" on the patient is not in proportion to the results.
- Any patient who decides to use the "normal means," even when new techniques are in use, and dies is not committing suicide. "On the contrary, it should be considered an acceptance of the human condition."
- When death is imminent, and new techniques will only prolong life in a "precarious" and "burdensome" way, it is permissible to refuse such treatment. The doctor who accepts this decision has no reason to reproach himself for failing to help a dying person.

Thus, the position of the Catholic Church is quite clear: active euthanasia is murder, but voluntary passive euthanasia—refusing "extraordinary" care—is morally permissible. On November 10, 1984, American bishops sought to influence the growing "right to die" debate by publishing "Guidelines for Legislation on Life-Sustaining Treatment." The three-page report stresses "the distinctive approach" of Catholic theology to the question of life and death and recommends that any legislative debate should not sacrifice "a firm commitment to the sacredness of human life."[35]

THE PROTESTANT DENOMINATIONS

Only a few of the major Protestant denominations have an official position on euthanasia. But most have studied the issue and, like the Catholic Church, are opposed to active euthanasia and sympathetic to refusing or terminating "extraordinary" treatment.

Typical are the American Baptists, with more than thirty denominations, independent, diverse, and democratic. The largest—the Southern Baptist Convention organized in Georgia in 1845—has no stated policy on euthanasia, but its Christian Life Commission actively opposes euthanasia on the grounds that "human life, from fertilization until natural death, is sacred and should be protected, not destroyed." The Southern Baptists oppose infanticide and active euthanasia, "including efforts to discourage any designation of food and/or water as 'extraordinary' medical care for some patients."[36]

In 1989 the American Baptist Churches of the U.S.A., formerly the

Northern Baptist Convention and later the American Baptist Convention, published guidelines on "death and dying" that dealt primarily with decisions to forgo life-sustaining treatment. The document supports living wills and advises families to respect the patient's wishes. The Episcopal Church and the Lutheran Church—Missouri Synod have both opposed active euthanasia, though the more liberal Lutheran Church of America has shown sympathy for withdrawing extraordinary care in certain cases. In 1986 the United Methodist Church agreed with a committee of the National Conference of Catholic Bishops that "excessive procedures" to prolong the lives of the terminally ill could be abandoned in good conscience. The Reformed Presbyterian Church, which also includes some Congregational churches, seems to have gone the furthest in considering the possibility that euthanasia is not inconsistent with Christian respect for the sanctity of life. The preface of their 1983 report on euthanasia includes appendices showing examples of a living will and a request for "active euthanasia."[37]

But when it comes to the bottom line—actively ending a patient's life—Protestants, Jews, and Catholics all equate it with murder. And the American medical establishment agrees.

Doctors Must Not Kill: Leon R. Kass, M.D., and Albert Jonsen[38]

> *I will neither give a deadly drug to anybody if asked*
> *for it, nor will I make a suggestion to this effect . . .*
> Hippocratic Oath

Doctors heal, not kill—even at a patient's request. While much has changed in medicine since the days of Hippocrates, the general horror of the medical profession toward administering a "deadly drug" remains.

The American Medical Association's position on euthanasia is unequivocal: "A physician should not intentionally cause a death." Making doctors killers changes the aims of medicine and the perception of doctors, says the AMA, placing them on the "slippery slope" of morality. Besides, no matter how much they might sympathize with a patient's desire to end his life, most doctors are repelled by the prospect of killing someone. Legalized "aid-in-dying" would give a much too easy way out for a physician frustrated by his inability to help a patient. Moreover, how easily will doctors be able to care wholeheartedly for patients when it is always possible to think of killing as a "therapeutic option"?[39]

And what of those patients who do not want to die but know they have become such a burden that others would prefer that they do? More troublesome still is that most candidates for mercy killing—comatose, deformed infants, mentally ill patients, or those suffering from Alzheimer's—are in no position to request it. In Holland, for example, where the repeated request of the patient is the prime standard for euthanasia, the government is finding that an alarming percentage of doctors have performed euthanasia *without* the patient's request. Physicians, too, can be tempted by their compassion, and the Hippocratic oath has presumed as much, setting at least three outer limits on a doctor's behavior: no break of confidentiality, no sexual relations with patients, and no dispensing of deadly drugs.

Doctors must be compassionate, but not so compassionate that they redefine what doctors do. "The physician-euthanizer is a deadly self-contradiction."[40]

In fact, there is much that can be done to "enhance the *lives* of those who are dying."[41] Physicians can learn how to withhold or withdraw machines that are burdensome and degrading. They can follow the lead of the hospice movement and encourage their patients to be courageous about death and provide adequate relief from pain and discomfort. By eliminating the patient, legalized euthanasia may actually undercut advances in pain control and care for the dying.[42] "The present crisis that leads some to press for active euthanasia is really an opportunity to learn the limits of the medicalization of life and death and to recover an appreciation of living with and against mortality."[43]

Against Socializing Death: Daniel Callahan[44]

In life and death matters the law has been clear on one thing at least: each of us has control over our own person, and that includes the power to make the decision to end medical treatment and die. I can say, "Enough, pull the plug."

But *you* ought not to have the right to end my life—even if you are a doctor, or even if I have signed over that right to you. Unlike suicide, active euthanasia is a *social* act; by definition, it cannot happen without the involvement of someone else.

For that reason, euthanasia and assisted suicide ought not to be legalized. Legalization would change the traditional role of the doctor, require government regulations, and add another category of permissible killing in our society at a time when the existing ones—killing in a just war and capital punishment—are under attack. "Civilized societies have slowly come to understand how virtually impossible it is to control even legally sanctioned killing. It seems of its nature to invite abuse and corruption."[45]

We are free, but not to do anything we want. The great British philosopher John Stuart Mill noted in his classic essay "On Liberty" that no civilized society has ever extended the right of self-determination to permit its citizens to sell themselves into slavery. "The principle of freedom," Mill wrote, "cannot require that he should be free not to be free." Slavery corrupts the slaveholder as well as the slave. So will euthanasia. It is *our* life, and only ours to end. "To allow another person to kill us is the most radically imaginable relinquishment of sovereignty, not just one more way of exercising it."

Nor does it make any difference that you hand over your own body to someone else to relieve your unbearable suffering. How much suffering is too much? By whose standard—the patient's, the family's, the attending physician's? After all, one man's threshold of pain may hardly faze another. When you hand over the right to kill yourself to another, you have also exchanged your values about life and death with his.

This step takes most people, especially doctors, in a direction they do not want to go, for if it is the doctor's moral standards, and not the patient's, which are in control, then the doctor is in a position to decide to kill a person who is in pain but not physically able to request euthanasia. Can a person who is not suffering or dying ask a doctor to kill him? If the doctor has the right to decide when his patient should die, has he now undertaken a duty to *kill* people? Are there certain grounds on which the doctor can deny the request for euthanasia from a competent person?

There are no objective standards to help answer any of these questions.

Legalized euthanasia would be a major change in the way society operates, a change not justified by the relatively small number of people whose pain could not be relieved any other way. Assisted suicide is substituting one evil (pain and suffering) for another (legalized murder). If the twentieth century has taught us anything, it is that "killing is a contagious disease."

Opposition to Withdrawing Nutrition and Hydration Support

After the Cruzan case, the euthanasia debate expanded into a new area: Was it morally permissible to withdraw artificial nutrition and hydration from a dying or comatose patient?

FAILING TO PROVIDE FOOD AND DRINK IS NEVER MORAL: ROBERT BARRY[46]

Stopping life-sustaining food and fluid is simply involuntary euthanasia. While patients continue to live once a respirator is shut off—Karen Ann Quinlan survived a decade, much to the amazement of her physicians—when food and drink are cut off, patients die. Food and drink are not "medical treatments," like an appendectomy or coronary bypass; nor can they be considered "extraordinary" care.

But the best reason for believing that assisted feeding is morally required is that it is a decisive, *objective standard* for not withdrawing treatment. Quality of life measures will differ from patient to patient, family to family (e.g., the cost of treatment might be "burdensome" to a poor family without medical insurance but a drop in the bucket to a wealthy family). But if food or fluid will keep the person alive, then that should be decisive for not withdrawing such support.

Starvation and dehydration amount to intentional killing—by, not incidentally, a cruel, repulsive method. With more than a million critically ill Americans on some form of artificial nutrition each year, the prospect of cutting them off would result in mercy killing of Nazi-like proportions.[47] Only when it is medically impossible to provide food or fluid, or when the mode would require extreme pain, should a patient be deprived of it.

DANGERS OF WITHDRAWING NUTRITION AND HYDRATION: DANIEL CALLAHAN[48]

One revolts against this option for emotional reasons—feeding the hungry has always been the most basic act of charity. There is also a genuine suspicion that the "denial of nutrition may in the long run become the only effective way to make certain that a large number of biologically tenacious patients actually die." Given the increasing number of aging and chronically ill patients, is there not a danger that dehydration and starvation will become "the nontreatment of choice"?[49]

Withholding fluid and food looks horribly like trying to kill an innocent person.

IN FAVOR

"Death with Dignity"

"A persistent vegetative state" is how the Missouri Supreme Court summarized the condition of Nancy Cruzan. "She is not dead," noted the court. "She is not terminally ill."[50] Because of this, the U.S. Supreme Court agreed with the state court: not even her parents had the right to let Nancy Cruzan die.

"A persistent vegetative state." The words hardly do justice to the horror to which the Court's majority condemned Cruzan—and her family: three decades, perhaps, of lying in a hospital bed, fed by tubes delivering food and water to her stomach. She had permanent brain damage, no consciousness, and no chance of recovery. Would any person want to continue such a life, given the choice? How does the "life" to which Nancy Cruzan was doomed differ from death?

The U.S. Supreme Court's four dissenters zeroed in on the real problem with the case, and the crucial issue in the euthanasia debate: the American legal system can ensure that a human vegetable—"a passive prisoner of medical technology"—will remain so for the rest of her life.[51] The dissent raised the toughest issue in the euthanasia debate: What is the morality of helping a person who is not technically dying to die? Such an act goes against every convention in Western religious—and medical—tradition.

The Court majority cited the provision of the Fourteenth Amendment that no state shall "deprive any person of life, liberty, or property, without due process of law." In his separate dissent Justice Stevens stressed that "the best interests of the individual" must prevail over those of the state. He charged that central to Missouri's policy was "an effort to define life, rather than protect it." Stevens went so far as to question whether the kind of life Nancy Cruzan had was even using the word "life" in a way commonly understood or "as it is used in both the Constitution and the Declaration of Independence." He stressed his discomfort with the notion that life is merely a "physiological condition or function." Echoing a refrain usually heard from right-to-life groups, Stevens noted life's "sanctity is often thought to derive from the impossibility of any such reduction."[52] To be only biologically alive is to lose the very *humanness* that makes life sacred. That Nancy Cruzan was alive at all was due solely to the success of modern medicine.

Who wouldn't prefer to be spared such "success"? In what way is a life like Nancy Cruzan's "sacred"?

The Problems with the "Sanctity of Life": Jonathan Glover[53]

Most would agree that a necessary principle in any system of morality worth the name would be some version of "the sanctity of life"—that is, killing people, by its very nature, is always wrong. Yet what about capital punishment and killing the enemy during war? Obviously, those who allow for exceptions do not believe that killing is always inherently wrong. To them, killing is *generally* wrong. A utilitarian, for instance, bases his moral decisions on maximizing happiness, so killing someone is wrong because it will deprive him and his family of happiness. Another person might believe it is always wrong to kill someone who does not want to be killed. In both examples, a belief in the sanctity of life does not enter the thought process.

But for someone who believes in the absolute sanctity of life (as do the right-to-lifers) even a life spent in an irreversible coma is valuable. Yet most would agree that a life like Nancy Cruzan's looks very much like death. Of course, to label her condition "death" requires a redefinition of that term, or at least a transformation of the criteria by which we conclude someone is dying or had died. Redefining death, however, should not be an obstacle. Modern medicine and its artificial heart-pumping and breathing machines have already forced doctors and lawyers to rethink their notions of death as the loss of electrical activity in the brain. (To be on the safe side, some have argued that the best standard would be a "double test"—the shutdown of respiratory and circulatory functions *plus* brain death.) But for someone horrified at the prospect of living the life of Nancy Cruzan, whose brain showed electrical activity, brain death will not be an adequate standard.

The best new definition of "death" is "loss of consciousness." "Those of us who think that the direct objections to killing have to do with death considered from the standpoint of the person killed will find it natural to regard life as being of value only as a necessary condition of consciousness."[54] Nor is consciousness a value in itself, for anyone who believes that will have trouble arguing that human lives are more valuable than animal lives, particularly animals with a high level of consciousness.

Some would argue that the best criterion for life is that it is "a life worth living," and that seems to require a life that is more than mere biological life or even mere consciousness. Certainly it is risky to try to list what in fact makes any life "worth living," and the criteria are bound to change from person to person. Yet you do not have to make such a list to agree that "if life is worth preserving only because it is the vehicle for consciousness, and consciousness is of value only because it is necessary for something else, then that 'something else' is the heart of this particular objection to killing. It is what is meant by a 'life worth living' or a 'worthwhile life.' "[55]

For those who accept euthanasia, "sanctity of life" will have to yield to another standard: "quality of life."

"The Quality of Life": Joseph Fletcher and Glover

To live as a vegetable is not really living; to be doomed to a life of irreversible coma is no life at all. The person is dead—his or her "humanness" has disappeared. "The highest good" is not mere biological life, but the "well-being" of a person, his or her integrity.[56]

Discussions of euthanasia skate by the real issue: Is it morally justifiable to take the initiative in death, for ourselves and others we love?[57]

If you value the well-being of a person above everything else, then the answer is yes. If you value fairness to a person, a family, a community, yes. It is a difficult decision, to be sure. Few can end even the most hopeless life with ease. But that is a psychological problem, not an ethical one.[58]

This is not to say that once a person's life is determined to be not worth living he should be killed. Even if everyone else could agree that a patient's life is so miserable, so full of pain, so burdensome to his family and society that it is not a worthwhile life, it is still *his* life, and the assessments of others are so often mistaken only a "monster of self-confidence" would feel justified in overriding the patient's judgment. (Respecting an individual's own decision thus rules out involuntary euthanasia or any kind of Nazi-style "mercy killing.")

Of course, not everyone is in the physical or mental condition to make such a choice. What is to be done about them? The alternative is clear, though unsatisfactory: Someone else must attempt to put himself in the position of that person and try to imagine what he gets out of life and make a choice. Admittedly, we risk the chance of making a terrible mistake. But the risk of being wrong is less than the risk of prolonging an unspeakable existence. In such cases, the "undiluted act of killing may not be a wrong act, but an act of a decent generous person."[59]

Isn't this "playing God"? Yes, but science plays God every day. Medicine interferes with nature as a matter of course and presents us with moral dilemmas that never bothered our grandparents. Such advances increase our moral responsibilities. In our modern world, even those of us who believe strongly in God know we must make many "life and death" decisions without God's help.

Anyone who still recoils at the prospect of euthanasia must face up to the following question: How does "mercy killing"—what the AMA and most religions abhor—differ from what most doctors and religions accept—pulling the plug and letting a terminally ill patient die?

"Passive" and "Active" Euthanasia Are Morally the Same: James Rachels[60]

There is, in fact, no *moral* difference between withholding treatment and actively inducing a patient's death. The AMA's position—that withdrawing treatment is ethical, while lethal injection is not—is illogical. Active and passive euthanasia are morally equivalent. Either both are acceptable or both are not. Those who accept passive euthanasia ought to be able, morally, to accept killing the same patient directly, and for the same reasons: to end unnecessary suffering for a person who is dying.

In practical terms, by simply withholding treatment and allowing the patient to die, doctors are letting the patient suffer *more*. So-called active euthanasia is quicker and thus more humane.

Once the decision is made that it is better that the person be allowed to die, then the mode of death is morally the same. Surely one would prefer to use the most humane and less cruel method. Doctors and hospital staff often complain about the "ordeal" of watching a child wither to death after food and water machines have been unplugged. A lethal injection would avoid such ordeals.

It is often argued that the real difference between killing and letting die is in the *intention*. Any doctor who stops treatment so that his patient will die has acted wrongly. The doctor who stops treatment because it is useless has acted admirably, even though he knows his action will hasten death. But death is not his intention.

Surely, this is wrong. The act itself is what is important and the reasons for it. Good reasons make the act good, not the intentions. Both doctors are doing the same thing (letting a patient die) for the same reasons (prolonging life is not only useless but will also increase the patient's suffering). That one doctor plans that death might tell us something about his flawed character, but not about the morality of the act itself.[61]

The AMA's opposition to active euthanasia forces doctors into the indefensible moral position of choosing cruelty over compassion. The absolute prohibition of killing an innocent human being leads to consequences few moral thinkers would accept.

Legalize It: Rachels, Fletcher, Marvin Kohl,[62] and Hemlock Society

State prosecutors, courts, and juries are not inclined to condemn "mercy killers." The unfortunate result: a large gap between the law and practice. If no one wants to prosecute mercy killing, then why have a law against it?

Abuses of legalized euthanasia are bound to occur, but it is doubtful that the number of those abuses will swell to the point where they outweigh the benefits. Legal killing does not turn everyone into legal killers or even increase the amount of illegal killing. Soldiers who are allowed to kill others in war seldom return home to careers as professional murderers.

For the past decade national polls have shown that the public supports euthanasia. Evidence of that support has come in jury verdicts that fail to convict mercy killers. The fairest solution is for legislatures to write the laws so that a plea of mercy killing can be an acceptable defense against a charge of homicide.[63] As consenting adults, terminal patients and their doctors ought to be free to choose euthanasia.

"The Hemlock Manifesto"

The best-known and most outspoken publicist for active voluntary euthanasia for the terminally ill is the Hemlock Society, a nonprofit corporation that was founded in 1980 in Los Angeles and is now headquartered in Eugene, Oregon. The society's notoriety is largely due to the writing and public relations skills of its co-founder, Derek Humphry, author of *Final Exit,* which has 100,000 paperback copies in print.

From the outset the Hemlock Society has stressed that its aim is to lobby for the legalization of assisted suicide for the *terminally ill*—a person who is "likely, in the judgment of two examining physicians, to die of that condition within six months."[64] According to the Hemlock Manifesto, "incurable distress" does not legally justify euthanasia "unless it is a product of terminal illness."

Doctors must respect a patient's wish not to have his life extended, and they also have a "duty" to inform others that a patient has requested assistance in dying. The Hemlock Society also believes doctors ought to be legally required to hasten a patient's death or arrange to find someone who will. They recommend that patients contact an attorney for advice and put their wishes in writing.

Religious Support of Euthanasia

Among the traditional Protestant denominations only the two most liberal appear to sanction euthanasia: the Unitarians and the Universalists, who joined forces in 1961 to become the Unitarian Universalist Association.[65] Stressing individual freedom of belief, democratic principles, and the search for truth through science, the groups feel that every human personality is valuable.

In 1978 the Unitarian Universalists declared their support for the living will. In 1988 the church's General Assembly backed the Durable Power of Attorney for Health Care, legislation allowing patients to appoint a proxy to make life and death decisions if they are incapacitated. The Unitarian Universalists also declared their support for active euthanasia, advocating "the right to self-determination in dying, and the release from civil or criminal penalties of those who, under proper safeguards, act to honor the right of terminally ill patients to select the time of their own deaths."[66]

In 1990 the Rocky Mountain Conference of the United Church of Christ adopted a resolution to affirm "the right of persons under hopeless and irreversible conditions to terminate their lives and emphasize that Christian understanding and compassion are appropriate with regard to suicide and euthanasia."[67]

THE RELIGIOUS ARGUMENT FOR PASSIVE EUTHANASIA: RICHARD A. McCORMICK, DANIEL MAGUIRE, AND CHARLES CURRAN

The inviolability and primacy of life is central to the Christian vision of the world. Yet not even traditional Catholics see life as an absolute good, an end in itself. It is life that is a precondition of so many other "goods" or values.[68] "Life, death, all temporal activities are in fact subordinated to spiritual ends," said Pope Pius XII to a group of Catholic physicians in 1957.[69]

A life is not to be lived only for the sake of living. An infant so grossly deformed or mentally limited or doomed to a life of constant surgery and pain will not even have the potential for sharing in any higher good.[70]

Modern medicine has stripped death of its naturalness; almost every death becomes a decision between prolonging life and accepting the inevitable. Death has become a moral decision. How to decide? One method is to ask, Is there a potential to aim for any good beyond mere biological living, an opportunity to have relationships with others? But in hopeless cases, the Catholic Church has pointed to the way of compassion. In fact, on the issue of letting such hopeless cases die, the Church is, ironically, way out ahead of the courts. Neither the Missouri Supreme Court nor the U.S. Supreme Court was willing to give Nancy Cruzan's family the right to end her life.

But the Church shows no such queasiness nor does it expect anyone to go beyond "ordinary means" to prolong a life. Hopelessly unconscious patients on respirators, Pius XII told the doctors in 1957, are "virtually dead."[71] In such cases, said the pope, "the soul may have actually left the body."

Catholic moral theologians have viewed intravenous feeding in the same way. Others have gone even further and suggested that you have to give special justification for prolonging the lives of patients where "the personality is permanently extinguished."[72] Otherwise, keeping "a breathing corpse" alive is "irrational, immoral and a violation of the dignity of human life."[73]

Existing behind "the wall of their own solitude," the patients do not even know whether they are living or dying.[74] Such patients do not even respond to human care. What is left of their life has only one good remaining: their living organs may be harvested to bestow life on another person. Once death has begun, helping it along is not usurping God's role. Neither the patient nor anyone else, no matter what he or she does, will have any *ultimate* control of what is happening. The patient will die. Passive euthanasia only hastens the inescapable.[75]

A MIDDLE ROAD

"Dying Well": Arthur J. Dyck and Paul Ramsey

Life is sacred, but only to a point. And deciding when someone ought to die based on the "quality of life" is much too subjective a standard. Whose standard of "quality"? There is a better standard for when to stop treatment: the patient must be dying.

In life we make many choices, not the least of which are about our health—what we will eat, how much we rest, how much exercise, to smoke or not, to take certain kinds of medication and not others. Call them life choices. Our final choice is how to die. But a person "does not choose death but how to live while dying."[76] For the dying person, life is no longer a genuine alternative. The only choice is how to manage those last moments. For the Christians, "We are stewards and not owners of our lives." But part of the stewardship, by definition, requires living life to its end. In the process, the dying person is in no way "usurping" God's role or invading his dominion. The final life choice of how to live while dying is just another decision in one's stewardship of life.[77]

The goal is the thing. If we choose death as an end, then the means to that end is only . . . death. Choosing to "die well" is quite another matter. Relieving suffering so that someone can move toward the inevitable—namely, death—is different from intentionally ending someone's life. Ask any physician: he knows when he is trying to kill someone, or ease suffering so someone can die well. We have a moral obligation to save a person's life, to reduce pain and suffering, but when death is the inevitable next step, our obligation becomes one of *caring* for the dying person—not helping him die more quickly, as Kohl and others have suggested, but simply helping him die.[78] This preserves the physician's professional obligation to "do no harm," while maximizing kindness and minimizing suffering.

Outdated Distinctions: Paul Ramsey[79]

Stopping treatment for dying patients should not be called "negative" or "passive euthanasia." Doctors have always decided that, at some point, further treatment is useless, and the dying process should be allowed to follow its course.

Nor is it correct to say that *treatment* has stopped altogether. What has been abandoned is *curative* treatment. After that decision is made the next one is how to care for the dying person—how to allow that person to "die well."

Nor does the traditional distinction between "ordinary" and "extraordinary" means of treatment help clarify matters. The sixteenth-century Catholic moral theologians who conceived the distinction between prolonging life by "ordinary" and "extraordinary" means were not thinking about keeping dying or incurable patients alive. The original goal of the ordinary/extraordinary distinction was to find an *objective* standard to distinguish between choices that were suicidal and ones that were reasonable given what was necessary to save a person's life (a long journey, horrible disfigurement, surgery before the discovery of anesthesia). It is unlikely that those medieval thinkers had ever imagined that it would be anyone's medical *duty* to prolong a patient's dying.[80]

Today the ordinary/extraordinary distinction has shifted to patients who are dying and not dying, to patients who can refuse "extraordinary" treatment that might indeed be burdensome to them and patients in no position to make that choice because they are in a coma or are infants. It is a dangerous shift, for while a patient may have the right to refuse special treatment that neither he nor his family can afford or that will only delay his imminent death, it is quite another matter for someone else to make this decision. The danger is that "extraordinary" will become a signal that will allow doctors or families to stop treatment for people who are not yet dying.

The real danger in the continued use of the ordinary/extraordinary distinction in sustaining the lives of patients who are unconscious but not dying is that it already looks very much like the first step onto the slippery slope toward active, involuntary euthanasia.[81]

The urge is an understandable one: we all want to find some *objective* standard that makes us comfortable in our decision to let a patient or loved one die. "Extraordinary" means, however, is not the standard we are looking for.

WHO DECIDES?

Patients, their families, and doctors need some standard on which to base their choice to continue or end treatment. The best possibilities are: (1) a reasonable decision on the part of the patient to refuse treatment, and (2) the doctor's best medical decision that "no further treatment is indicated."[82]

The problem with the first is that one man's reasonable decision might seem foolish to another. The patient is not free to do wrong. No matter how competent and intelligent the patient might be, his decision to refuse treatment will never be as informed as his physician's. A wholly subjective decision is in danger of abandoning standards altogether. A conscious, competent patient with an incurable disease might make a decision to refuse treatment, but only after the patient has discussed this decision with his doctor and shared it with his family.

What about unconscious patients? Simply because an individual can choose to die, does not necessarily mean his parents or family can make the same choice for him. Family or guardians must pay particular attention to the medical care that physicians indicate. Disagreements are possible, but they have to be real disagreements based on the medical facts and possible treatments available. Parents might argue that a particular treatment is "too burdensome" for them, too expensive or too emotionally draining. Yet what is burdensome for them might be the only route to life for the patient.

The only authority who knows whether a particular treatment might give a patient another chance to live is the doctor. It is the doctor, too, who knows that a patient, although alive, has no chance to live—that he or she is beyond medical care. The doctor should not make this judgment based on "quality of life" criteria. The medical criteria for care are *physiological*.[83]

The issue is a simple one: Is the person dying or not? Physicians have an obligation to sustain all life. "Terminally ill" and "incurable" are medical judgments. The distinction between dying and nondying patients is crucial and can be made only according to what the physical condition of the patient indicates. This is the only reliable objective standard.

To leave the decision up to the subjective deliberations of others is to open the door to involuntary euthanasia. Such criteria as "privacy," "best interests," and "quality of life" are too subjective to base the decision of ending a person's life on. When a person is incompetent to say "Please pull the plug," the only way anyone else can determine that it is indeed time to cease treatment and end a life is when that treatment is known only to prolong the dying process.

Dying is the criterion for abating treatment. Then the question becomes, "what will ease?"[84] Otherwise, we end up treating incompetent, unconscious patients or defective newborns as if they were competent patients refusing treatment—and thus erase the line between voluntary and involuntary euthanasia.

Support for Withdrawing Nutrition and Hydration

Catholic moral theologians and medical ethicists can also be found taking a middle-of-the-road position over the morality of removing nutrition and hydration assistance to patients on life-support machines.

"CAPTIVES OF OUR TECHNOLOGY": JOHN PARIS[85]

"The artificial provision of nutrition and fluids is not the same as providing ordinary food and water to a patient."[86] The medical machines now available are able to sustain life for decades, but they are not able to cure the patient. So a patient who would have died under normal circumstances can be hooked up to a machine that can keep his vital organs functioning for two or three decades. To keep a person alive in such cases only by machines once all medical technology has failed to cure the patient or restore him to a relatively normal condition is to make us "captives of our technology."[87]

Although some Catholic right-to-life advocates have resisted the removal of life support for religious reasons, the Catholic tradition has always allowed dispensing with medically useless or burdensome treatment. The "save at all cost" mentality, which is in evidence even among prominent physicians, is an extreme view. When the patient's condition is *futile* or extremely burdensome, withdrawing nutrition and hydration support is "designed not to hasten the death by starvation or dehydration, but to spare the patient the prolongation of life when the patient can derive no benefit from such prolongation."[88]

The question that doctors and families must ask is not merely, Can we keep this patient alive? Medical technology can keep virtually anybody alive artificially. The more important question is, What kind of life are we saving? So-called quality of life decisions cannot be avoided. If the patient has no hope of being cured, if the patient would not live except by artificial means, then, according to Catholic teaching and the consensus view of the American medical and legal professions, artificial support can morally be withdrawn.

Life is more than merely existing biologically.

Exceptions to the Rule of "No Active Euthanasia"

As Paul Ramsey has argued, we must always care for the dying. Opposed to active euthanasia even when patients want it, Ramsey has also maintained that to decide to allow terminal patients to die when they are unconscious is a dangerous step down the slippery slope to active euthanasia. But Ramsey is willing to entertain some exceptions to his rule "always care for the dying." Robert Veatch, another well-known medical ethicist and one much admired by Ramsey, and James Childress, a professor of religious studies and medical education, share Ramsey's concern about legalizing euthanasia and also point to some possible exceptions to their own opposition to active euthanasia. Each, however, has a slightly different position on what constitutes the "standard" for when one can, if not legally at least morally, hasten a dying patient's death. Their arguments:

EXCEPTIONS: RAMSEY[89]

When a patient is irreversibly ill, when our care achieves nothing, makes no difference to the patient's living or dying, when there is no significant moral difference between letting the patient die or helping him die—when the patient is already out of our hands and in God's—

involuntary euthanasia is morally permissible. "There is no obligation to continue to do the useless."[90]

The obvious case is an anencephalic baby, a child born without a brain, and thus a "baby born dying."[91] In fact, because such a child is without a brain, the primary organ of the body, it is even difficult to describe this human thing (for it is definitely human, and perhaps only that) as born "alive." It is certainly born "brain dead," an acceptable definition of dead among the medical profession. And without artificial support for the vital organs, heart and lung death is quick to follow.

Another possible exception is a baby—or unconscious adult—with an incurable disease that causes such insurmountable pain that the patient is "beyond the reach of the human caring community."[92] The patient is clearly dying, nothing more can be done, nor can the patient detect anything that is being done. There is no "quality of life" decision here, simply a medical one. More important, the person who decides to end the life, such as it is, does so in full knowledge and belief that euthanasia is wrong, and thus, in helping the patient die, becomes a "conscientious objector" to the rule against directly killing the sick and dying.

The Church of England's study pamphlet on euthanasia is quite sensible on this issue:

> It is perfectly consistent to argue that morally speaking euthanasia is permissible in some extreme cases, but that it would be wrong to alter the law to allow it in such cases, because this might inescapably, in practice, let in cases in which euthanasia should not be allowed by law. The law is a blunt instrument for dealing with moral complexities. . . .[93]

That there is no obligation to continue to do the useless is not a subjective evaluation of the patient's state of suffering or any other "quality of life" judgments. It is simply a fact of medical care.[94] Christian love and medical care may have their limits, and when those limits are reached, the dying patient should be helped along to his death.

EXCEPTIONS: ROBERT VEATCH[95]

Decisions about continuing or stopping medical treatment are all subjective. Finally, in spite of the equipment and the laboratory tests, the doctor must make a judgment call. The real issue is whether the treatment is *useless* or a serious burden to an individual patient.

The best way to decide whether to continue treatment is from the patient's perspective. An Orthodox Jew or devout Catholic is likely to value prolonging all life, even vegetative life, and that probability should be factored into a doctor's decision. If the patient were competent, what would he do? Some people cling to life more avidly than others, and that has nothing to do with "objective" medical standards.

The obvious danger for patients in no condition to make their own decisions is that the final choice is left to a surrogate who now has the chance to decide to end a patient's life for reasons that are either dumb or malicious. The preference ought to be for guardians who are not strangers and who will follow his "standard of reasonableness"— namely, that treatment is no longer useful and not a social or economic burden for the patient himself or his family.

Killing another human being is "prima facie wrong" and any legal policy in its favor would involve "great danger." That does not mean there could not be cases, exceptions, where actually killing the patient might be the most moral thing to do. Helping a patient to die who was in relentless and intractable pain or for whom an artificially prolonged life would be an economic burden could be morally permissible. Such rare instances of euthanasia should not be legalized; instead, doctors or family members who believe there is no alternative to euthanasia should be prepared to help the patient die as an act of "civil disobedience."

EXCEPTIONS: JAMES CHILDRESS[96]

When a patient is in no condition to decide to reject or withdraw life support, the decision must be made by the family and friends. They are more likely to know the patient's position on having his life prolonged unnecessarily; in cases where the patient's opinions are not known, a series of surrogates are available who would act with the patient's best interests in mind, beginning with family and friends and progressing to doctors, other health-care professionals, and then to obvious strangers such as hospital committees and the courts.

Active euthanasia is generally wrong, but there are rare exceptions when it is morally permissible to kill a person who is dying and in agonizing pain. Indeed, in such rare cases, killing "may be an expression of love, mercy, kindness, and care."[97] Prudence rules against legalizing active euthanasia, which is bound to be abused. The only solution is *conscientious objection.* (Unlike civil disobedience, a political act aimed at a social change or even changing the law, conscientious objection usually stems from personal moral and religious views.)[98]

The Best Alternative: The Hospice Movement[99]

The decision to stop medical treatment is part of what medicine is all about. Once that decision is made, medical care becomes comforting the dying (who might also be called the "still living").

Traditionally, the best argument for direct euthanasia was that for certain kinds of terrible, relentless pain death was the only exit. But advances in modern medicine and caring for the dying are making pain a thing of the past. Even the dreaded "cancer pain" can be controlled in virtually all cases. The most impressive advance in making death easier is the hospice movement, which focuses on assuaging the emotional and physical pain of terminal illness. Instead of prolonging life, the modern hospice aims to make sure that what life is left is as comfortable and meaningful as possible.

Central to the hospice idea is effective pain-control management. Hospice care is directed at controlling symptoms and not the disease with the minimum of diagnostic studies and invasive therapies. Hospice physicians believe that they have mastered pain so well to make euthanasia a moot issue. As Cicely Saunders, the founder of the modern hospice movement, has said, "If you relieve a patient's pain and if you can make him feel like a wanted person, which he is, then you are not going to be asked about euthanasia. . . . I think that euthanasia is an admission of defeat and a totally negative approach. One should be working to see that it is not needed."[100]

Hospice care involves an all-out effort to confront the criticisms that hospital care of the terminally ill too often prolongs life unnecessarily via various machines, does not deal with pain effectively, ignores the other residual miseries of illness, gives no emotional support to patients, and divides the care between so many doctors and nurses and health-care "professionals" that the patient sees himself as someone warehoused until his bed is once again free, ready for the next victim. The major goal of the hospice is to help the patient and his or her family come to terms with the fact that death is near and inevitable, and try to maximize the quality of the time that is left. The staff of a hospice focuses on the final care of the dying and tries to use and adapt medical technology to this kind of care.

Hospice patients are likely to spend time at home or in more congenial homelike settings with easy access to friends and family or among a staff whose goal is to be the least like a hospital as possible to the dying. Hospitals can be terrifying and demeaning. But the most striking difference is the costs. The hospice philosophy is to provide the best care regardless of ability to pay.

Dying is usually not only about coping with pain. The terminally ill also face psychological, social, financial, and legal problems. Hospice care seeks to attend to anything that might be an obstacle to a comfortable death. The hospice idea involves a "multidisciplinary" team approach to helping the dying, which includes just about everyone who might be able to add his or her expertise to the case: doctors, nurses, social workers, physical therapists, chaplains, even volunteers.

Reformulating the Euthanasia Debate

Traditionally, the debate over euthanasia has been divided between those committed to the "sanctity of life" principle, who believe that we have no moral right to intrude into God's (or nature's) domain, and those who believe we have the moral right to avoid ending our otherwise happy lives in pain or coma or dementia by choosing to "die with dignity." The philosopher Ronald Dworkin has recently argued in a book-length essay about abortion and euthanasia that underlying the rhetoric of the liberal and conservative adversaries in the debates over both issues is a common commitment to the "sanctity of life." The fundamental difference between both camps, Dworkin explains with great insight, is their own spiritual, personal, or philosophical views about the "cosmic importance of life itself."[101]

Dworkin's redescription of the abortion debate is summarized in the "Abortion" chapter, pages 35–41. His position on euthanasia follows. The similarities will be obvious, for it is the central argument of Dworkin's book that "the mortal questions we ask about the two edges of life have much in common."[102]

A RESPONSIBILITY FOR DYING YOUR WAY: RONALD DWORKIN

Supporters of helping terminally ill people die are inclined to argue that competent, conscious patients who plead to be allowed to die should have their wish granted as a matter of "autonomy."

But why should we care if an unconscious, incompetent patient hooked up to a machine (like Nancy Cruzan) is allowed to die or live? If Nancy Cruzan is not consciously suffering, or if her family is not overburdened with the cost of her care (which reportedly was the case), why should we care whether she lives or dies? Most of us do. Some think it is appalling that a person should be allowed to continue living for decades in such a vegetative condition; it is, they argue, "in the person's best interests" to die. Others are horrified when the plug is pulled. (When a Missouri court decided not to press the state's case to keep her alive and accede to her parents' wishes, several of her nurses protested and wept.)[103]

Some of us are not indifferent to what happens to us or those we love in similar circumstances because we believe that human life is intrinsically valuable, and euthanasia, like abortion, can be seen as "an insult to God's gift of life."[104] Atheists, too, may share this sense of the "sanctity of life."

Though traditionally seen as an argument against euthanasia, the principle of the sanctity of life may turn out to be a "crucial argument for . . . euthanasia."[105]

LIFE'S "CRITICAL INTERESTS"

To understand how people view death, we must first take a look at how they view life. No matter our religious beliefs, most of us seem to care about living a "good life." And while our definition of "living well" includes good experiences (e.g., travel, fine restaurants, walking in the woods, seeing *Casablanca* for the twelfth time), we also seem to have strong convictions over what makes life genuinely worthwhile—such "critical interests" as close relationships with children and friends, success in work. These are not just important or in our interests; without these, our lives would be worse.

In fact, these "critical interests" are likely to be so important to our lives (and our sense of what life ought to be) that if we never achieve them, then we might conclude, like Leo Tolstoy's Ivan Ilyich, that our lives have been "wasted." And regardless of our religious beliefs, these fundamental convictions about life have a "pervasive influence" on our moral and political beliefs, including those about euthanasia.[106] Stephen Hawking, the almost totally paralyzed cosmologist, has managed to live an extraordinarily productive life; but a professional ath-

lete similarly stricken might find Hawking's existence intolerable.
"None of us wants to live our lives out of character."[107]

It is thus understandable why many people resist the idea of the
state being able to legislate some general view of how to live and die.
Each of us should be able to make provision for our future care; and if
that is impossible, the decisions should be left to relatives or friends
who have intimate knowledge of what our best interests are.

"SANCTITY AND SELF-INTEREST"

Conservative opposition to all forms of euthanasia rests on a belief
that deliberate death is a "savage insult to the intrinsic value of life"—
even when that death might be in the interest of the patient. Such revulsion to taking any life is central to many religious traditions, and
both Justices Rehnquist and Scalia reflected it in their decisions in the
Cruzan case.

But suppose we insist that the *human* contribution to life is as important as the divine (or natural), and that, too, should not be wasted?
Believing that life is sacred, we want *our* life to go well, *we* want to be
responsible for its direction, *we* don't want that life wasted. Anyone
who takes this view of life is likely to believe that lingering near death
on machines, comatose, does not respect the sanctity of his life, but
dying does.[108] As in abortion,

> the critical question is whether a decent society will choose coercion or
> responsibility, whether it will seek to impose a collective judgment on
> matters of the most profound spiritual character on everyone, or
> whether it will allow and ask its citizens to make the most central, per-
> sonality-defining judgments about their own lives for themselves.[109]

To say that someone must end his life in a way that you believe is right,
but "he believes a horrifying contradiction of his life, is a devastating,
odious form of tyranny."[110]

IN MY OPINION

If euthanasia is so wrong, as religious minorities and the medical profession argue, why do so many people think it is right? Why is Dr. Kevorkian a hero to many? Why did *Final Exit* walk out of the bookstores? The answer has nothing to do with morality and a lot to do with fear. People are now considering euthanasia because they fear that they will "live" out their final days hooked up to a machine, unconscious, in a state that looks very much like death.

Few contemporary ethicists dispute that a terminally ill patient in great suffering has the right to kill himself. Even the Catholic Church does not flinch at a dying patient rejecting "extraordinary" treatment and thus choosing to die. But killing an irreversibly dying patient is something that makes most doctors queasy. Their business, they point out, is *healing* not killing.

But let's not talk of what "doctors" should do or "people" should not do. Let's talk about what *we* should do as doctors and as people now that medical science can prolong dying for decades and call it life. Euthanasia is no longer some abstract professional, legal, or philosophical debate. At a time when most of us will die in hospitals and then only when someone makes a decision to let us die, euthanasia has become an intensely *personal* story about Granddad or Mom or me.

The issue of euthanasia is, finally, a simple one: Is it morally right *for me* to help someone die, to kill that person, out of compassion and mercy?

Dying Is No "Abstract Issue"

"Do everything you can." Those were my father's last words to his doctor before he died of cancer at the age of seventy-three. For twelve years he had fought prostate cancer, skin cancer, and lung cancer (metastasized from the prostate). He was as successful as anyone fighting the losing battle against cancer can be. "Whenever I feel lousy," he confided to me, "I get myself over to the track and walk three miles." He had become a professional cancer patient. His fight against cancer was an obsession that grabbed his mind more than any job he had ever held. But then he had always preferred living to working. He wouldn't give up. Neither would his cancer.

Finally, he began to lose his appetite, and weight. His face thinned so much that his head became more ears than visage. For the first time in his life, and mine, he began to look his age, maybe a bit older. It didn't help that sometimes the pain cracked through the medication. The running track became a memory. Then the worst: "It's spread to my liver," he announced matter-of-factly. He was medical expert enough to know what that meant. A "hospice nurse" had been sent to consult with him about special care. He shrugged it off to me, but I overheard him talking to a relative on the phone: "A hospice nurse came by, and you know what that means."

The end came more quickly than either of us thought, mercifully. He was staying with my sister, and early one morning she heard him having difficulty breathing. She called the ambulance, which rushed him to the hospital. "Do everything you can" were his last words to the doctor before he slipped into unconsciousness. The doctor knew that fluid from his lungs was simply drowning his heart. "Everything" that the doctor could do was not much. But honoring a dying man's request (and avoiding any legal complications), the doctor tried to jump-start my father's heart. It did not respond, and my father died. Had his heart kicked back on, he would surely have been, as the doctor put it, "incapacitated." Right then I realized that if my father had lived on in a "persistent vegetative state," I could never think of him as my father. My father was many things, both admirable and flawed, good and bad, but he was no vegetable (though there were times when he seemed to mistake himself for a hot tamale).

When my father asked the doctor to "do everything you can," he did not, I am sure, have coma in mind. In fact, months before, in sounder mind and body, he had chosen to inform his doctor and the hospital, in writing, that he did not want to be kept alive by machines. My sister, who was caring for him, agreed. So did I.

The more I think about his fight with cancer, the more I realize that what he meant was "Do everything you can—*to bring me back to the way I am now, or better.*" I recall him telling me proudly that his doctors considered him a "medical miracle." Just when the disease seemed to be about to finish him off, his body would fight back, and he would get better. On that final day he was hoping for another "miracle." Earlier in his treatment he had confided to me, "It will get me eventually." It seemed an honest prognostication. But I now realize my father had anticipated being able to fight off that "eventually" forever. He had gone over to the other side. He had become more the high-tech doctor than his own high-tech doctor.

Death Is Part of Life

In this era of high-tech medicine it takes some effort to remember that people simply used to die. After disease struck or a body wore out with age, there was not much anyone could do. You hoped death would come without too much pain, but one thing was certain: it would come.[111]

Now it can be put off for decades. (Doctors estimated Nancy Cruzan might have survived for *thirty years* on artificial nutrition and hydration.) Traditionally, Christians have looked upon death as an "evil," only to be transcended by "everlasting life." But death is neither evil nor good, it is simply death, the end of life, as natural as birth—and the one milestone that we have a lifetime to prepare for. It seems at once futile and absurd to resist it, either psychologically or by "life-sustaining machines." Without such machines, no doctor or patient or family member would ever question the notion of "letting the patient die." The issue should be no different even in the face of the machines. The idea of a "lingering death" is an invention of medical science. Since Socrates, thoughtful people have been skeptical, even appalled, preferring an "easy death" to an unnecessary life.

The most important criterion for an easy death is: Is the patient dying? The second should be: Is there anything medicine can do to prevent him from dying, apart from prolonging the patient's life artificially? If the patient is, in Ramsey's elegant phrase, "beyond care," then the patient should be allowed to die. *Indeed, if the patient is beyond care, a doctor should have to provide a special justification for keeping him alive.*

But Can It Ever Be Morally Right to Kill Someone?

What if my father had been less a fighter, more resigned to death, more—this seems right to me—like me? What if during my final conversation with him when I knew it had spread to the liver, he had confided to me that the end was approaching, that he feared vegetablehood, that he did not want any machines, that he did not want my sister and me or any doctor to have to feel guilty about ending it for him? What if he had asked me to provide him with a lethal overdose of barbiturates?

I am no killer; the thought of killing someone (anything) is repellent to me. And to hasten the death of your own father, to be what the ancients called a parricide . . . the mind recoils.

Yet, if my father had suddenly killed himself, I would have been stunned but, given the circumstances of his health, understanding. He had made all sorts of choices about how to live his life (to go to war, to quit smoking, to overwork, to eat too much, to drink too much, to stop drinking, to become an ideal cancer patient), and now he had judged how to end it. His family no longer depended on him, and his magnanimous federal employees' health insurance protected him—and us—from financial disaster. If his suicide was not the result of a momentary depression, not an example of a desperate man reaching out, if he had thought it through and decided that, at age seventy-three, he wanted to end it now, that would have been his right.

I would have had no problem advising his doctors to shut off life-support machines. But consider this possible exchange:

"I'm pleading with you, father to son," he says.

"Anything, but please don't ask me to commit murder," I reply.

"I'm not asking for murder. It's mercy I want. You're begging the question."

He's right. He touches my arm and comforts me, the one who should be comforting him. My mind races: murder has never occurred to me as something someone might want to happen to him.

"I'll write a letter swearing that it was my idea, that I hounded you, that I swore that I would haunt you for life unless you helped me die," he says. He looks at me hard. "*Help* me die. I want it. I've lived long enough. I'm dying, and I don't want to spend the rest of my life doing it." Then he manages a smile; that naughty twinkle in his eye that the pain, the chemo, the anxiety of oblivion seemed to have erased, reappears. "It would be un-American of you." He waits for my raised eyebrow to lower. He shrugs: "Fast food, why not fast death?" Then he adds: "Besides, juries never convict in these mercy killing cases."

I tell him I will have to think about it, discuss it with my wife, maybe even a lawyer. He is asking me to take risks that could destroy my own future. Juries are inclined to be lenient, but what a disaster should I appear before a majority of hard-liners!

"I have been a good father," he says. "I was always there for you. Now you have to be there for me."

I leave. Euthanasia is no longer an abstract issue. Whatever my views, I must make a decision. And this is what runs through my mind: He is my father, and I owe him not only my life but the seeds of any success I have had. "A just man pays his debts," Socrates said. In my scenario, was my father asking for justice?

It is an intriguing aspect of this moral dilemma that the just thing, the rational thing, the compassionate thing, indeed the moral thing, might be to kill someone. It is this irony—that it seems so right to do what otherwise seems so wrong—that instills my decision to commit euthanasia with moral conviction. My decision is bound to involve many factors: notions of justice and fairness and duty and responsibility. And emotions. Too often the philosophers and lawyers leave out the emotions, the guilt, fear, sympathy, the confusions, the love that must be factored into such a momentous moral decision.

What could be admirable about ignoring a parent's last wish, and then watching his death drag out in pain, misery, loneliness, and bitterness over his son's cowardice? On the basis of every system of ethics I can think of—maximizing his and my and society's happiness (utilitarianism), looking to the results (consequentialism), avoiding cruelty (liberalism), treating a person as an end not a means (Kantian liberalism), putting myself in his position (universalizability), responding emotionally to it (emotivism), reacting to the specifics of the situation (situation ethics), being fiercely rational (humanism)—helping my father to die is the moral thing to do. And surely accomplishing a parent's last wish, after careful consideration of his condition, is the very definition of Christian charity.

To be sure, only a murderer would help someone die without a pang. But only a man with the morals of a murderer could be so cruel as not to consider seriously helping his father die. If the act is as justifiable, morally, as anything you have ever done, then do it. Then do it.

The Sanctity of Death

Christians often talk of "a good death," and the end I have imagined here seems better than its painful, dragged-out, lonely, unconscious alternative. Moral theologians have been skeptical about extending life by "extraordinary means" because, among other things, they believe that a dying person has the right to be able to prepare himself for death. Many people now enter death from a state of unconsciousness too much like death itself. Already "dead," they die. When Pope Pius XII in 1957 questioned the virtue of prolonging lives already judged terminal, he suspected that unconscious patients on respirators are "virtually dead." In these cases, the pope told a group of doctors, "the soul may have actually left the body."[112]

The pope's intuition seems right to me. Life is more than a breathing corpse. And putting off death is not necessarily life. As Plato pointed out, what separates Asclepius, the god of medicine, from his successors was that he resisted saving "good-for-nothing lives."

Death, however, remains the greatest of mysteries. In the Christian tradition the hope of death is a new kind of life, "everlasting life," *sanctity*. If we can believe in the sanctity of life, why not the sanctity of death? If death can be sacred, why not helping someone to die?

"Life is a divine loan," say the Christian ethicists. If so, then a life lived in unending misery or pain or unconsciousness is a bad loan that ought to be called in. Such prolonged misery is not worthy of a merciful God. Christians are too enamored of suffering; for them it is the closest approximation to re-enacting "The Way of the Cross," Christ's ultimate agony and sacrifice. Yet not everyone can be expected to be a hero or a saint. Traditionally, the Catholic Church, in spite of its opposition to euthanasia, has allowed fighting pain with "extraordinary means." I would propose that one such extraordinary way to fight off pain might be assisted euthanasia. If, according to the Catholic Church, it is preferable to be conscious to prepare to die, if dying is only a matter of time, if the dying patient wishes to forgo the machines that only extend that time (extending the pain and the cost in the process), if he just wants to "get it over with," before he is too out of it to know what is happening and to be able to prepare properly to meet his maker, then what is the evil in that?

Karen Ann Quinlan was alive and dead—biologically living, but, as the phrase goes, dead to the world. Her life was neither savable nor worth living. In Pope Pius XII's terms, her soul had already left her body. In my terms, what made her not only human, but Karen Ann Quinlan, had gone. Only a body remained. Shutting off life support meant nothing to Karen Ann Quinlan.

But what about terminal patients who are conscious? They are different from Quinlan in two ways: they are much more than breathing corpses, and they are dying. But like Quinlan, their lives are not savable; they are beyond care. And thus there seems no difference between pulling the plug on a comatose patient whose life cannot be saved (passive euthanasia) and helping another patient, competent but equally incurable, die (active euthanasia).

The Real Similarity Between Active and Passive Euthanasia

Active and passive euthanasia have two things in common: in both cases the patient is dying, and they prevent a miserable death.

If in my own hypothetical case I were asked *why* I had decided to help my father die, I would explain that my aim was not simply to kill someone. Rather, I wanted to do the most fair and reasonable and caring—and therefore moral—thing I could do to abate his misery and help him toward death. It is not really my *intention* that is at issue, as some philosophers have argued, it is the *reason* I intend to do what I do.

Why did I decide to help kill someone? Because he was dying and was ready to die. Because living any longer would not cure him, but only allow the disease to make his remaining days even harder to bear. Because he had no alternative except a prolonged dying attached to a machine. And most important, because he asked me to help, and for good reasons. Surely, I would have to help him have the best death possible. To do otherwise would have been cruel, unjust, and thus immoral.

Every day thousands of doctors make a similar call: that because no available care can save the life of a patient, he or she must be allowed to die. It is a medical and human decision. The AMA recognizes that allowing patients to die is an ethical decision. (So did Pope Pius XII.) But if the doctor decides to speed up that death with a lethal injection, why is that not, according to the AMA, equally ethical? Does the distinction between active and passive euthanasia really make sense? James Rachels says no: the end result is that the patient dies; there is no moral difference, though he adds that letting a patient die is likely to increase the suffering and therefore make the death worse, which looks like a moral difference to me.

The difference between active and passive euthanasia is in the intention, according to Rachels. "Is the intention deadly?" asks one of Rachels's critics. "If so, the act or omission is wrong."[113] The doctor who pulls the plug does not intend to kill the patient. This looks like fancy footwork to me. The doctor surely knows that as soon as he unplugs the machine the patient will die. To say that killing him is not the doctor's *intention* is technically true. But this logical tactic seems disingenuous, a safety valve for queasy doctors who hate, understandably, to find themselves losing lives instead of saving them. In fact, the doctor's intention in pulling the plug is to let the person die. Death is the goal in both acts, as Rachels points out. What is significant is that mischief is involved in neither.

If I help my father die, my intention is not "deadly." Quite the contrary. To be sure, it is possible to murder a dying person. If my father is terminally ill, but the prognosis is that he will last six months—too late for me to pay off my gambling debts and avoid having my legs broken—I could decide to hasten his end in some clever way and gain the benefits of his insurance policy. That would be murder. It would also be murder if I walked into my father's room, saw a tube accidentally fall from the machine, and stood by as he suffocated to death. These are the malicious acts of commission and omission that the AMA seeks to avoid, not acts of true compassion on the part of doctors and the families of dying people.

Murder is the ultimate cruelty. Making sure a loved one dies well—I am not sure what the name of it is—is certainly the opposite of cruelty.[114]

That is not to say that there is no line between killing and letting die. There is a difference, though it is not one of consequences or intentions or acts or omissions. The crucial difference is found in why the same doctor can be comfortable with letting a patient die a slow, painful though "natural" death, and abhor the thought of helping him die more quickly and with less pain by lethal injection. The notion that separates mercy killing and letting a patient die is *responsibility*.

The reason I hesitate to immediately grant my father his wish to die is that though death is his decision, by asking me to help him die, his death now also becomes *my* decision. And if I decide to hand over to my father a handful of barbiturates that will send him into a deadly coma, I am now an accomplice in his death. His death will now be *my* responsibility. If he kills himself without my help, it is not my responsibility.

The difference—and moral convenience—of pulling the plug and letting someone die is that it is not a direct act of killing. Without the machine, the person dies; he is not killed. The doctor has, as it were, left the room. He is not responsible for the patient's death. The disease killed the patient, not the doctors.

What is the best thing to do?

My moral dilemma is a classic example of one person's values clashing: I do not have the soul of a murderer, but I do not have the soul of a torturer either. The idea of killing someone makes me recoil, but the idea of pulling the plug and watching the same person die of starvation appalls me, too. But a crucial fact remains: my father is dying. Nothing can save him, which is why, if he were connected to a life-support machine, few doctors would hesitate to pull the plug. And it is also why I would decide to help my own father die, someone I love, someone who loves me, someone I owe much to, someone who is depending on me, someone who has given me the opportunity to grant his last request so that he can die a happy, autonomous man, rather than a man so unconscious, so "dead" that he will not even know how pathetic and miserable and unhumanlike he has become in his last day.

The question that I have to ask myself is, What responsibility can I live with? Will I feel more guilty about standing back and watching him shrivel up and die than if I hand him a packet of barbiturates? When my children ask me, "How did you help make Granddad's final moments comfortable and happy?" is it easier for me to answer, "I stood back and let nature take its course—it was a hideous, inhumane sight." Or can I say, "He wanted to die, and I helped him go through with it. He was brave, and I tried to match that bravery."

This is the answer I could best live with. Helping him die is my version of pulling the plug. And what would I say when the police come? And then to the jury, if it came to that? "My father was a dying man," I would say. "Nothing could stop his dying, no doctor, no machine. I agonized over it and then acted. But I did not really kill him. It was a matter of stages. His disease was already killing him. All I did was help him from the penultimate step to the final one. I gave his killer—the disease—a hand. The disease and I were 'accomplices.' He had begged that the disease speed up his death, but the disease could not respond. *I* could respond, and so I did the *human* thing. I helped him die. And I can live with that."

Allow Euthanasia, but Don't Legalize It

In the best of all possible worlds, a place where doctors and families were reasonable, careful, selfless, kind, and genuinely compassionate, I myself would press for the legalization of euthanasia. But not in this world.

Curiously, the philosophers and medical ethicists seem most respectful of the medical profession. Paul Ramsey hinges his own view on "medical indications," a kind of "Doctor knows best" policy. Even Jonathan Glover, a hardheaded rationalist who approves of euthanasia, is inclined to say things like, "It seems to me worth trusting doctors not to take life unjustifiably."[115]

Now, maybe. But always? We baby boomers are aging fast, 75 million of us. It is conceivable to me that young doctors will be looking over their wards of dying baby boomers wondering whether they can afford the time and spend the money to consider every case of "letting die" on its merits. With the possibility of so much illness and old age and dying in our future, I am inclined to assume the worst. The slippery slope is bound to be a very crowded location.

Daniel Callahan's arguments against institutionalizing killing are persuasive. He is right to worry about turning over a life and death decision to someone who might not share the patient's views about life and death or have more pressing concerns (i.e., a hospital wingful of younger and richer patients who have a better chance of being treated successfully). Callahan is right to worry about abuses. Temptations are bound to increase as medicine continues to become less a vocation and more a business, and a ferociously competitive one where costs increase as the economy shrinks. But I am less worried than Callahan about hurting the feelings of the medical profession.

CARE FOR THE DYING

In a 1991 cover story about euthanasia, *Newsweek* cited a case of a sixty-nine-year-old woman dying of emphysema and inoperable lung cancer. The doctor advised hooking her up to a life-support machine. The woman's daughter disagreed, and so, finally, did the patient. According to *Newsweek*, "the doctor bristled. 'If that were *my* mother, I'd do it,' he said." The family ignored him, and the next day the woman died quietly.[116]

This is a doctor who is unable to face death, and, therefore, in my opinion, not a good doctor. The family should not have had to justify their decision to let a woman beyond care die. The doctor should have had to justify prolonging such a life. It is an uncomfortable irony of the euthanasia debate that those most opposed to helping patients die an easy death—the medical profession—are the same group whose machines have made it *harder* for their patients to die naturally.

Doctors may think of themselves as only "healers," but when a patient is incurable the physician should also know how to help care for dying people, which might also mean helping them to die. And while it is understandable that many doctors are uncomfortable with ending lives rather than saving them, it is not improbable that some men and women would view helping people die as just another step in medical "care." (Or caring.) Dr. Kevorkian has argued that the only reason patients seek him out is that their own doctors are unwilling to deal with their dying. He has suggested that a new specialty in the final stages of life might be created where physicians would explore methods to help people die, including better painkillers, dealing with the psychological effects of dying (the loneliness of illness can be tougher to handle than pain), and psychological counseling for patients and their families.

That said, this new specialty begins to look a lot like an existing alternative—the hospice program, barely mentioned in the philosophical and medical literature on euthanasia. An eminent medical school professor explained to *Time* why the medical profession acts as if hospice care had not been invented. "Hospice doctors are considered to be on the margin of medical malpractice," he said. "They are not thought of as real doctors because they don't try to cure people. They just help them die."[117] Professional prejudices aside, surely the hospice approach (or some refinement of it) is precisely what will cancel out the debate over the morality of euthanasia.

Finally, the euthanasia debate comes down to the issue of medical care in dying. We all want to be helped to die well. Tragically, doctors, in their efforts to save lives, are now saving lives that should not be saved. It is not enough to pull the plug and then stand back and let a patient die. The doctor must be able to pull the plug and help that patient die easily and well and in as much comfort, physical as well as psychological, as can be devised. And if a competent patient, not yet on life support, but certainly dying requests help in speeding up the process, doctors must face up to the fact that this, too, is part of their responsibility—the care to which patients are entitled.

The impulse toward euthanasia is, in the end, a defensive move. It is a cry for a more compassionate and more complete system of care for the dying. There comes a time when the dying person is "beyond treatment." But that same patient is never beyond care.[118]

True Death with Dignity

Euthanasia advocates often appeal to the notion of "death with dignity." What do they mean? Where is the dignity in the face of the indignity of death? The answer, from euthanasia supporters at least, seems to be in the notion of autonomy, of control: a dignified death is one where the individual makes the decision when to die; the patient is in total control.

It is one opinion, couched, too, in relative terms. An autonomous death is more dignified than a death where the person is not in control, in fact, so out of control that the patient has no idea that he is dying or being allowed to die.[119] Yet, as Daniel Callahan has pointed out, we may have become too concerned about being *in control* of every aspect of our life, including our dying. Autonomy need not be the measure of a dignified death. *Care* should determine the quality of dying, for even a patient who is not in control can receive devoted care, can be given such comfort that we all could agree that this is a dignified death.

A dignified death is one that we ourselves would be happy to undergo. Dying ought to be the most personal of all decisions. The state has no place here. Yet even according to this standard, neither active nor passive euthanasia will measure up. Personally, I would prefer not to have my life prolonged unnecessarily. Personally, I would prefer not to have to kill myself to avoid a drawn-out and painful death. Personally, I would prefer not to have to beg my doctor or relatives to inject me with a lethal dose of barbiturates.

There is no dignity in that. I would prefer to die at home surrounded by my family, the pain dulled, and holding the hands of my children. That to me is death with dignity and, given the genius of modern medicine, not too much to ask for.

4. Capital Punishment

THE ISSUE

> *Life for life, eye for eye, tooth for tooth, hand for hand, foot for foot, burning for burning, wound for wound, stripe for stripe . . .*
>
> Exodus 21:23–25

> *One penalty was assigned to almost all transgressions, namely death, so that even those convicted of idleness were put to death and those who stole salt or fruit received the same punishment as those who committed sacrilege or murder. Therefore Demades, in later times, made a hit when he said that Draco's laws were written not with ink but with blood.*
>
> Plutarch, "Life of Solon"

The history of the death penalty is itself a story written in blood and mercy. From the time men first wrote down their laws and punishments, the penalty of death has been at the top of their lists, the ultimate penalty. The ancient Babylonian code of Hammurabi (about 1750 B.C.), like biblical law, was based on the "eye for an eye" code of vengeance. Eleven centuries later the Athenian ruler Draco's code (c. 621 B.C.) eliminated the problem of judicial discretion by executing all criminals. But such bloody laws were not easily enforceable, and Draco's successor, Solon, soon offered a new set of laws that set execution for only the severest crimes, like murder and treason.

One thousand years later the Roman Republic's Twelve Tables could only be called draconian. Convicted traitors were beheaded; perjurers were thrown off the Tarpeian Rock, and murderers were scourged and drowned to death. According to the Roman version of retribution—the *lex talionis* (i.e., the law of reciprocal punishment), murderers deserved to be killed. In the early years of the Roman Empire, as its legal system became more refined, the death penalty—now including crucifixion—was used for fewer crimes, and even for them the alternative of fleeing into exile was available.[1]

In the Middle Ages, the pendulum swung back to barbarity. Ordinary robbers and brawlers were beheaded. A less bloody treatment was reserved for women—they were drowned. According to the standard work on the subject, *A History of English Criminal Law and Its Administration from 1750,* by the end of the fifteenth century, English law recognized eight major capital crimes: treason (including unsuccessful attempts and conspiracies), "petty treason" (wife killing a husband, but not the reverse, of course), murder (killing with "malice"), larceny, robbery, burglary, arson, and rape.[2] By 1688, another forty or so crimes had been added, and over the next century death became mandatory for literally *hundreds* of offenses, mainly related to property. Gallows dotted the landscape and were used as geographical landmarks in the way that gas stations are today ("You leave Frampton, Wilberton and Sherbeck, all on the right, and by a gibbet on the left, over a stone bridge . . .").[3] In 1757 a convicted killer was driven in a cart through the streets of Paris to the scaffold, where the hand that had wielded the murder weapon was set on fire. The executioner proceeded to tear flesh from the condemned's body with pincers, pour oil over each wound, and then attach his limbs to four horses, which tore them off. The wriggling torso was then incinerated.[4]

The first execution in the American colonies took place in Virginia in 1622. The crime: theft. Following the English common law traditions of the sixteenth and seventeenth centuries, colonial America established the death penalty, though for fewer crimes. The first statute in the Massachusetts Bay Colony lists a dozen capital crimes: murder, manslaughter, witchcraft, idolatry, blasphemy, poisoning, man-stealing, bestiality, sodomy, lying in a capital trial, rebellion, and adultery. Before the end of the century, rape, arson, treason, and theft of anything over forty shillings merited death. The Quakers of Pennsylvania, however, limited the death penalty to treason and murder; the Royal Charter of South Jersey, with strong Quaker influence, abolished capital punishment.

But the other American colonies followed English law, and by the time of the American Revolution, many of the colonies had set death for such major crimes as murder, treason, rape, robbery, burglary, and arson. Horse theft sometimes made the list, as did inciting a slave rebellion. The execution of choice was usually the rope.

In the eighteenth century, the Europe of the Enlightenment, with its emphasis on "the rights of man," demanded a more humane system of punishment. Voltaire and Montesquieu argued for the abolition of the death penalty in France, but they were only following the lead of Cesare Beccaria (1738–94), an Italian criminologist and economist. In his *Essay on Crimes and Punishments,* considered the most influential book on the reform of criminal justice ever published, Beccaria, only twenty-six years old, systematically attacked secret judicial proceedings and the use of torture; he also advocated the abolition of the death penalty.[5]

America's Beccaria was Benjamin Rush (1745–1813), a signer of the Declaration of Independence and a brilliant doctor who was known as the "Hippocrates of Pennsylvania." Rush's writings questioned the Bible's commitment to capital punishment and argued that hanging not only did not deter crime, it probably increased it, a radical view for its time which has been taken up by some death penalty abolitionists today.[6] For Rush, the state has no right to kill its citizens. An early psychiatrist, he viewed crime as a disease that could be cured. His notion of "Houses of Reform" that would try to reshape the lives of individual criminals inspired first Philadelphia's Walnut Street Jail, built in 1790, and eventually the American penitentiary system.

In the nineteenth century, while the rest of the world was backing away from what many perceived as the barbarities of capital punishment, various American states were embracing execution and displaying true Yankee ingenuity in coming up with crimes that deserved the ultimate punishment: a second forgery offense, distributing seditious literature among slaves, stealing banknotes, dueling. Highway robbery and bigamy qualified in North Carolina, perhaps the harshest state of the Union before the Civil War. In 1835, New York was the first state to ban public executions, and several other states followed. Michigan abolished the death penalty in 1846 except for treason, and Rhode Island did the same in 1852 (except for murder by a prisoner serving a life sentence).

During the first decades of the twentieth century the abolitionists seemed to have the upper hand. Nine states banned capital punishment. But within four years, five of those states had restored the death penalty. No state banned capital punishment until Alaska and Hawaii, still territories, in 1957. The last public executions had taken place in Kentucky and Missouri in 1936 and 1937. Since then, executioners have done their work behind the walls of America's prisons.

Into the early 1960s the list of capital crimes still contained some surprises: committing a crime while armed with a machine gun (though not necessarily firing it) in Virginia, "forcing a woman to marry" in Arkansas, and "desecrating a grave and foeticide" (i.e., abortion) in Georgia.[7] Yet though the list of capital crimes was long, the number of convicts actually executed for those crimes was not. Neither juries nor judges were eager to give the death penalty. The 3,862 lawful executions between 1930 and 1980 were for only eight crimes—murder, rape, armed robbery, kidnapping, sabotage, espionage, burglary, and aggravated assault by a prisoner serving a life term. By the late 1960s, only six states used the gallows, eleven had gas chambers, Utah continued to allow a convict to choose between hanging and a firing squad, and the rest used the electric chair, invented in New York in 1888 and considered a step forward in finding a "painless" way to put someone to death.

In 1964, Oregon outlawed the death penalty, and during the next year Iowa and West Virginia followed with outright bans. Vermont did away with executions, except for a second unrelated murder and killing a police officer, and New York set the death penalty only for cop killers and inmates serving a life term for murder who killed prison guards. Meantime, most European nations had abolished the death penalty or simply ignored the laws on the books. Then in 1967, in the midst of the far-reaching social changes of the notorious 1960s, abolitionists sued California and Florida, the states at the time with the most inmates on death row, on the constitutional ground that the death penalty violated the Eighth Amendment's provision against "cruel and unusual punishment." The cases persuaded the Supreme Court to stay all executions until it could decide on the constitutionality of capital punishment. The Court took its time, and for the next decade there was a virtual moratorium on the death penalty, based on the implicit understanding among the states that the Supreme Court would soon rule on the issue. No American was executed until 1977, when the Utah murderer Gary Gilmore resisted all attempts to prevent his execution and elected to end his life in front of a firing squad. By then, however, the Supreme Court had spoken.

"Cruel and Unusual Punishment"?

> *Excessive bail shall not be required, nor excessive*
> *fines imposed, nor cruel and unusual punishment*
> *inflicted.*

> Eighth Amendment to the Constitution

While individual states banned the death penalty, capital punishment seemed immune to constitutional attack. In 1890 the Court ruled that electrocution was not unconstitutional. In 1968 and 1971 the Court ruled that capital punishment was not in violation of the "due process" and "equal protection" clauses of the Fourteenth Amendment. Until 1970, mostly, the High Court avoided the constitutional issue by settling in favor of the defendant on specific grounds or by simply deciding not to intervene in death penalty cases.

Then in 1970, in *Ralph* v. *Warden,* the Court ruled that the death penalty for rape where "the victim's life was neither taken nor endangered" constituted "cruel and unusual punishment" because it was "disproportionate" to the severity of the crime.[8] Two years later the California Supreme Court held that the death penalty itself violated the state constitution's provision against "cruel and unusual punishment." In 1972, while the California case was being fought, the Supreme Court was considering the merits of three other capital punishment cases, one involving a convicted murderer in Georgia, the other two Georgia and Texas rapists. All three men were black. In *Furman* v. *Georgia,* the decision that dealt with the three cases, the Court ruled, 5 to 4, that because trial juries were free to sentence convicts to death or to life without any sentencing guidelines, the death penalty, as administered in 1972, was "cruel and unusual punishment in violation of the Eighth and Fourteenth Amendments."[9]

The five-justice majority was so fractured in why it had reached this decision that each justice delivered a separate opinion—243 pages worth, earning *Furman* the record as the longest decision in the history of the Supreme Court. But the justices seemed to agree on some things: that the death penalty as administered by U.S. courts was capricious, discriminated against the poor and black, and did not deter crime. "Under these laws no standards govern the selection of the penalty," wrote Justice William O. Douglas. "People live or die, dependent on the whim of one man or of twelve." Douglas pointed out that the statutes were "pregnant with discrimination," which was not compatible with the idea of equal protection implicit in the ban on "cruel and unusual" punishments. Justice William Brennan denounced the death penalty as a "lottery," and Justice Potter Stewart compared it to being "struck by lightning." Justice Byron White concluded that death was imposed so rarely that it could not have any real effect on the criminal justice system. For Justice Thurgood Marshall, the Eighth Amendment prohibited the death penalty for all crimes and under all circumstances.

Even in dissent, Chief Justice Warren Burger was quick to concede that if he were a legislator, he would join Marshall and Brennan in opposition to the death penalty "or, at the very least, restrict the use of capital punishment to a small category of the most heinous crimes." Nevertheless, Burger and the three other dissenters argued that there is no evidence that the founders saw the death penalty as "cruel and unusual punishment"; in fact, the language of the Constitution itself explicitly acknowledges the power to impose capital punishment. (The Fifth Amendment, for instance, guarantees that the death penalty may not be imposed "unless on a presentment or indictment of a Grand Jury.") Nor had the Court itself, in the 181 years since the enactment of the Eighth Amendment, cast doubt on the constitutionality of the death penalty in a single decision.

Burger suggested that if state legislatures and the public wanted capital punishment, then they would have to make changes in the existing laws, providing "standards" for judges and juries to follow or by more narrowly defining crimes that deserve the punishment of death.

After Furman

State legislatures took the *Furman* minority's advice to heart, and over the next four years thirty-five states enacted new death penalty statutes, some making death mandatory, others trying to give juries and courts more specific guidelines for imposing death. The result: more than 460 new convicts moved into death row around the country.[10]

In 1976 the Court heard two more cases on the constitutionality of these new death penalty laws. The majority held in favor of two convicts who contended that North Carolina's and Louisiana's mandatory death penalties were inconsistent with *Furman*.[11] But, on the same day, the Court also concluded in three other cases that new death penalty laws in Georgia (which, after *Furman,* had revised its death penalty law), Texas, and Florida were *not* unconstitutional as such under the Eighth and Fourteenth Amendments as long as the statutes provided the defendant the chance to give the court information about himself, allow evidence of mitigating factors, point to guidelines for sentencing, and give a state appeals court the opportunity to review every death sentence.[12]

The majority opinion in the Georgia case (*Gregg* v. *Georgia*) stressed that both the framers of the Constitution and state legislators clearly saw a place for the death penalty. The Court felt that the Georgia legislature had worked hard to come up with guidelines to eliminate the capriciousness of the state's death penalty, proving that "it is possible to construct capital-sentencing systems capable of meeting *Furman*'s constitutional concerns."[13]

In the years since *Gregg,* the Supreme Court has reaffirmed its view that the death penalty is a disproportionate punishment for kidnapping and rape where the victim is not killed. The Court has also blocked attempts to keep executions mandatory when specific victims, such as a police officer, are involved.[14] Yet, no matter how hard state legislatures tried to come up with the kinds of "standards" that Chief Justice Burger had hoped for in his *Furman* dissent, the new laws were unable to satisfy a Court populated by so many justices who seemed personally and morally uncomfortable with the death penalty.

McCleskey[15]

In 1987 the Supreme Court reaffirmed, 5 to 4, in *McCleskey* v. *Kemp,* that the death penalty is constitutional despite statistical studies that killers of white people are much more likely to face execution than killers of blacks. Warren McCleskey, a black man, was one of four men involved in a 1978 robbery in which a white policeman was killed. Though McCleskey had admitted he was part of the robbery, he contended he did not pull the trigger. His lawyers argued that his capital sentence should be overturned because the race of his white victim played a major role in his sentencing.

The Court disagreed. In 1991, McCleskey's attorneys went to the

Supreme Court once again (*McCleskey* v. *Zant*), arguing this time that evidence had come to light that the police had used a jailhouse informer to obtain a confession from McCleskey, thus violating his constitutional right to counsel. Once again the majority of the Court was not impressed. In a 6 to 3 ruling, the justices pointed out that McCleskey should have introduced the evidence in an earlier appeal. The Court majority sternly noted that repeated petitions like McCleskey's "threatened to undermine the integrity of the habeas corpus process." The Supreme Court proceeded to set tough new standards that severely undercut a state prisoner's ability to get his claims that his constitutional rights have been violated before federal courts.

McCleskey died in Georgia's electric chair in September 1991— thirteen years after he was sentenced.[16] Opponents of capital punishment have pointed to his case as evidence of how arbitrary and therefore unjust capital punishment is in the United States. The McCleskey case, they have argued, proved that the death penalty was, as one law professor put it, echoing Justice Brennan's opinion in *Furman*, "like a lottery."[17]

It is a lottery that many sociologists and legal scholars believe that black Americans have too good a chance of winning.

Is the Death Penalty Racist?

The Supreme Court may not have accepted McCleskey's argument in 1987 that he was a victim of discrimination. The statistics, however, show that blacks who kill whites are much more likely to get the death penalty:

- Of the 253 executions since the death penalty was reinstated in 1976, only one white person has been executed for killing a black.
- Of the 16,000 executions in U.S. history, only 30 cases involved a white man sentenced for killing a black.[18]
- Though only 12.1 percent of Americans are black, according to the Justice Department's Bureau of Justice Statistics, 40 percent of those sitting anxiously on death rows are black.[19]
- In Columbus, Georgia, four white men in the district attorney's office have decided which cases should be prosecuted as capital crimes since 1973; 78 percent of their cases have involved white victims, though in 65 percent of the cases the murder victims were black.[20]

Proponents of the death penalty often concede that the criminal justice system has been known to be capricious, selective, even racist. But they argue that to prevent more crime guilty men should be punished.

Does It Deter?

Common sense and intuition would suggest that the prospect of being executed would deter criminals. Yet the empirical evidence that capital punishment deters murder is inconclusive. For years, abolitionists hammered away at the deterrence argument, showing that it had no basis in fact.

In 1975 the economist Isaac Ehrlich published a study, which actually began making the rounds in pro-death-penalty circles a couple of years before, that claimed to have found a correspondence between executions and deterrence.[21] The article caused a larger stir than the usual academic statistical analysis, and the fact that Solicitor General of the United States Robert Bork cited Ehrlich's report in a brief filed in amicus curiae in a death penalty case then before the Court as the support for what Bork called the "*a priori* logical belief" that the death penalty deters murderers.[22]

Citing the statistics from 1933 to 1967, Ehrlich concluded that the "tradeoff" from executing one murderer was seven saved lives. Activists eager to keep the death penalty (the "retentionists") were ecstatic. Almost immediately, counterarguments emerged, several taking Ehrlich to task sternly. Ehrlich published rebuttals, and his opponents batted them back in his face.[23] Some of his critics have offered statistical evidence that executions actually brutalize the public, an argument that is as old as Cesare Beccaria's contention that the death penalty is an example of "barbarity." One recent study of 692 executions and murders that took place in New York State between 1906 and 1963 concluded that each execution "adds roughly three more to the numbers of homicides in the next nine months. . . ."[24] Ehrlich's opponents countered that an execution adds three more deaths to the FBI crime statistics. And so it goes.

The Popular Appeal of Capital Punishment

For the ordinary American, particularly without training in statistics, the battle over deterrence in the scholarly journals and academic presses offers no help in resolving the dilemma: Does justice require that murderers be punished by death? Historically, academics have opposed the death penalty, and the public ignored their statistical arguments and presumed that most people are likely to be scared to do anything that would get them a seat in the electric chair.

This intuition, and that is all it is, even influences the views of Supreme Court justices. While the 7 to 2 majority in *Gregg* noted that the evidence for deterrence is "inconclusive," two sentences later Justice Stewart said that while death is not about to deter murderers who "act in passion," for others it "undoubtedly is a significant deterrent." In fact, capital punishment is still used so sparingly that it remains impossible to conclude that the promise of death actually deters. In 1990, the most recent year that has received complete statistical attention, states executed only 23 murderers— less than .001 percent of all those convicted of murder that year. The category of murderer comprised only .000004 percent of all violent criminals.[25]

Crime Increases, and So Do Executions

Executions have been up in recent years. Texas alone, the leader in executions, has executed an average of four convicts a year since 1982, when the state restored the death penalty. In 1994, 31 executions took place—257 since the Supreme Court held that the death penalty is constitutional in 1976. Every year in the United States, criminals murder 22,000 people. And every year 250 to 300 of them are sentenced to die. At the moment, 2,500 men and women are sitting on death row in the nation's prisons. Death row convicts in Texas, Florida, Louisiana, and Georgia are more likely to die.

Americans Believe in the Death Penalty

American public opinion has shifted in its enthusiasm for the death penalty. In 1953, 68 percent of the public was in favor of capital punishment; the number had fallen to 51 percent by 1960 and 42 percent in 1962.[26] A Gallup poll in 1994, however, indicates that support for the death penalty is back up to 50 percent.[27] Among the supporters are Presidents Ronald Reagan and George Bush. As governor of Arkansas,

Bill Clinton allowed the execution of a brain-damaged black man during the 1992 presidential campaign.

The Supreme Court, meantime, has turned more ambivalent. In 1994, Justice Harry Blackmun announced that he had finally decided that the Court's efforts to resolve capital punishment had been fruitless; he now regards capital punishment as unconstitutional.[28] That summer, in the case of a South Carolina man sentenced to death for the murder of an elderly woman, the Court ruled, 7 to 2, that if the state argued for the death sentence on the grounds that a convicted murderer was too dangerous to go free, it could not conceal from the jury the alternative sentence of life imprisonment without parole. Justice Antonin Scalia, in an angry dissent signed by Justice Clarence Thomas, wrote: "The heavily outnumbered opponents of capital punishment have successfully opened yet another front in their guerilla war to make this unquestionably constitutional sentence a practical impossibility."[29]

Yet only 13 percent of capital punishment advocates say they believe that the death penalty actually deters crime. Unlike most academic and legal supporters of the death penalty, the public is quite straightforward about why they support capital punishment: 69 percent say they prefer the death penalty for reasons of revenge or because it "keeps them from killing again."

In that poll there is an ironic echo of something the convicted murderer Richard Eugene Hickock, then on death row in the Kansas State Penitentiary for his and Perry Smith's savage shotgun murder of a family of four in 1959, said to Truman Capote in 1964: "Well, what's there to say about capital punishment? I'm not against it. Revenge is all it is, but what's wrong with revenge? It's very important. . . ."[30]

Is it? Is revenge a moral response to murder? And if revenge is a good reason for punishment, does it have to go so far as the ultimate in punishment—the death penalty? Such questions have been at the basis of the debate over capital punishment for the past 250 years. However, for anyone who believes in justice, the question remains: Does justice ever require the punishment of death?

IN FAVOR

"A Public Violation of Justice": Immanuel Kant[31]

The Penal Law is a Categorical Imperative; and woe to him who creeps through the serpent-windings of Utilitarianism to discover some advantage that may discharge him from the Justice of Punishment, or even from the due measure of it. . . . For if Justice and Righteousness perish, human life would no longer have any value in the world. . . . Whoever has committed murder must *die*. . . .

Even if a Civil Society resolved to dissolve itself with the consent of all its members—as might be supposed in the case of a people inhabiting an island resolving to separate and scatter themselves throughout the whole world—the last Murderer lying in the prison ought to be executed before the resolution was carried out. This ought to be done in order that everyone may realize the desert of his deeds, and that blood-guiltiness may not remain upon the people; for otherwise they might all be regarded as participators in the murder as a public violation of justice.

Useful and Just: Ernest van den Haag[32]

Capital punishment, like all other kinds of punishment, is selective and capricious. This is true—and unfortunate, but unavoidable.

Yet capriciousness is not a good enough reason to ban the death penalty. Industry, medicine, sports, and automobile traffic all cause the deaths of innocent bystanders. But we don't ban them. Why? Because they are all morally useful activities. "If the advantages sufficiently outweigh the disadvantages, human activities, including those of the penal system with all its punishments, are morally justified."

The debate over the death penalty is not about whether the courts are capricious or that juries may be racist. That is all a "sham." Abolitionists oppose capital punishment for the guilty, too. The real question is whether the death penalty is morally useful.

That the death penalty actually deters crime is controversial. Yet Ehrlich's work raises a *probability* that executions do deter, so prudence and morality command us to choose to trade the certain death of a convicted murderer against the survival of upwards of seven victims who are likely to be killed. "It seems immoral to let convicted murderers survive at the probable—or even merely possible—expense of the lives of innocent victims who might have been spared had the murderers been executed."

Our penal system rests on the proposition that more severe penalties deter the more severe crimes. This proposition is based on common sense: aware of danger, people are likely to avoid danger. If the more severe penalty deters severe crime, it follows that the most severe penalty—death—will have the greatest deterrent effect on the most severe crime—murder. "This may not stop an Eichmann after his first murder, but it will stop most people."

"WHO ACTUALLY BELIEVES THAT NO CRIMINAL DESERVES TO BE EXECUTED?"

Capital punishment abolitionists oppose the death penalty even for murderers guilty beyond a doubt. They would want us to believe that no human can be wicked enough to be deprived of life. "That takes egalitarianism too far." Stalin or Hitler deserves execution as his minimum punishment.

If life is sacred, then it must be protected, "by threatening with the loss of their own life those who violated what has been proclaimed as inviolable—the right of innocents to live." It cheapens human life to punish a murderer as you would a pickpocket—with prison. "Murder differs in quality from other crimes and deserves, therefore, a punishment that differs in quality from other punishments."[33]

Simply because "times have changed," and today we are less comfortable with corporal punishment, does not necessarily mean that corporal punishment is not right and useful. The kind of "retaliatory mutilation" that did not bother even such an enlightened eighteenth-century soul as Thomas Jefferson "would horrify us today. . . . Indeed we have become repelled altogether by any form of corporal punishment."[34]

But our contemporary reluctance for all punitive punishment, especially corporal punishment, may simply be an "emotional bias." We are more sensitive to cruelty than our ancestors. "Bodies have become private, intimate things, not to be invaded without consent for any public purpose."[35] Through the advances of modern medicine, we are less familiar with pain than our predecessors. And so we are more eager to rehabilitate our criminals than punish them; we would prefer to isolate them from the rest of us, take away their liberty, and if it is necessary to execute a particularly vicious criminal, we would prefer to do it as "humanely" as possible.

But just because some people do not think they are competent to decide matters of life and death does not mean death is not deserved. Those who reject capital punishment must prove that no crime deserves the ultimate penalty of death. "Never to execute a wrongdoer, regardless of how depraved his acts, is to proclaim that no act can be so irredeemably vicious as to deserve death—that no human being can be wicked enough to be deprived of life. Who actually believes that?"[36] Not to execute vicious murderers is a "failure of nerve." The courts must deal with life and death decisions "to do justice, to secure the lives of citizens and to vindicate the norms society holds inviolable."[37]

Righteous Anger: Walter Berns[38]

We want to execute the worst criminals for the same reason we want to execute Nazis like Adolf Eichmann who oversaw the murder of millions of Jews: "We want to punish them because we want to *pay them back.*"

And we want to pay them back because we are angry that they have broken laws that historically all reasonable men have agreed on, and we want to express that anger publicly. Utilitarians who argue that capital punishment is neither useful nor fair do not understand the connection between anger and justice. Anger is "a very human passion not only because only a human being can be angry, but also because anger acknowledges the humanity of its objects: it holds them accountable for what they do." By acknowledging that men are responsible for what they do, anger recognizes the dignity of human beings. "Anger is the passion that recognizes and cares about justice. Modern penology has not understood this connection."[39]

Penologists have ignored the role of anger in punishment because they have assumed that all anger is self-indulgent. Yet anger need not be so self-interested. It is anger that signals the existence of a community. Anger over robbery, rape, and murder proves that we care about someone other than ourselves.

"Can we imagine a people that does not hate murderers?" No one teaches us the "awesomeness" of the commandment "Thou shalt not kill" better than Shakespeare in *Macbeth*. The man who kills Macduff's wife and children must die. Who can deny this? Our "moral sense" says it must be so. The reason that Macbeth is such a good example is that as a ruler he is able to express his virtue—and his vice—fully and freely. He shows us the meaning and majesty of the moral law.

Criminal law must be more than a list of statutes enacted for utilitarian or self-interested reasons. Criminal law must have a special "dignity," it must be made "awful . . . inspiring. . . . It must remind us of the moral order by which alone we can live as *human beings,* and in America now that the Supreme Court has outlawed banishment, the only punishment that can do this is capital punishment."

Anger demands justice, and justice demands punishment. That is how a community works and protects itself.

AGAINST

"The sanctity of life" is a principle that plays a fundamental role in the Christian opposition to abortion and euthanasia. But many Americans who oppose abortion also favor the death penalty and justify the killing of innocent civilians during war. A growing group of American Christians, and some Jews, have argued eloquently that if life is indeed sacred, then it is sacred across the board—for convicted murderers, citizens of hostile governments, and cruel dictators no less than for innocent unborn. They have constructed a "seamless garment" in defense of the fundamental principle of the "sanctity of life," opposing poverty, war, and nuclear arms as well as abortion, and supporting women's rights as well as the rights of the unborn.[40] This same Christian view extends quite easily to opposing capital punishment:

Vengeance Is Not the Christian Thing: John Howard Yoder[41]

The Christian believes that life is sacred because "God made man in his own image" (Genesis 9:6). The very definition of "the sacred" is to belong to God, and, according to the Bible, life is not ours to take. Jesus' message in the New Testament is that "there is no moral difference between friend and enemy." Central to the Christian message is the obligation to love others as much as we love ourselves. Jesus demanded that the judges and executioners be sinless (John 8), and he himself traded places on the cross with the murderer Barabbas. According to Jesus, you hate the sin not the sinner: "Life is sacred because in the fallen world, Christ is our chance for repentance. To take a life is to deprive that person of a future and thereby of all possibility of being reconciled with God and humankind."[42]

Even the legendary vengeance of the Old Testament (blood for blood of Genesis 9:6 and "eye for eye, tooth for tooth . . ." of Exodus 21:24–25) can be seen more as a fact of primitive society which the progress of civilization and "God's grace" eventually limited. While in the world of the Old Testament the life of a murderer or enemy was far from sacred, "by Jesus' time most of these [retributive] penalties had evolved to the point that they could be absolved through payments of money."

In the Sermon on the Mount Jesus advised, "Do not take revenge" (Romans 12:19). Evil is supposed to be drowned with love. After Christ's own redemptive sacrifice of his life—perhaps the most famous example of capital punishment in history—"the cross has wiped away the moral and ceremonial basis for capital punishment." Capital punishment is mentioned explicitly only once in the New Testament—in John 8—where Jesus comes to the defense of a woman about to be stoned for adultery.[43] The implication here and in other references to divorce, war, and slavery in the New Testament is that "capital punishment is one of those infringements on the divine that will take place in society." Christianity demands a "new level of brotherhood" of humanity, and even though most people—and societies—may not be up to the Christian standard, it is still up to Christians to persuade them to change their ways.

The "forgiving ethics" of Christianity has its place in the civil order. Those Christians who have argued for the sacredness of human life cannot be silent on the issue of capital punishment.

The Prejudice Against Capital Punishment

Some find it absolutely impossible to justify the act of killing a human being under any circumstances. Such fundamentalist pacifists oppose war, of course, but they also find other kinds of killing such as euthanasia, terrorism, and abortion just as horrifying. They also oppose capital punishment absolutely. But most opponents of the death penalty are not absolute pacifists. They have no trouble going to war, for example, or even aborting a fetus. But they find in the kind of death involved in capital punishment unjustifiable cruelty.

The Supreme Court has had several opportunities to strike down the death penalty, now legal in thirty-nine states. But the Court majority has held that capital punishment is unconstitutional only when it is applied unfairly and capriciously and thus becomes "cruel and unusual punishment."

Two Supreme Court justices—William Brennan and the late Thurgood Marshall, the Court's first black member—have said that in their opinion the death penalty is unconstitutional. In 1994, before his retirement, Justice Harry Blackmun announced that he, too, had come to the conclusion that the death penalty is unconstitutional. Here are summaries of Brennan's and Marshall's arguments in *Furman* and *Gregg*:

"CRUEL AND UNUSUAL PUNISHMENT": JUSTICE WILLIAM BRENNAN[44]

We have little evidence of what the framers of the Constitution had in mind when they included the Eighth Amendment's provision against "cruel and unusual punishment." But for a constitutional provision to be "indefinite" and "vital" it should not be confined only to the evils of its time. Time works changes in society and the law. Four interrelated principles make a particular punishment "cruel and unusual":
   (1) "A punishment by its severity must not be degrading to human dignity"—torture, for example, the kind of punishment that the Eighth Amendment has always banned.
   (2) Any "obviously arbitrary" punishment such as a "reign of blind terror."
   (3) A punishment that is "totally rejected throughout society."
   (4) A severe punishment that is "patently unnecessary" and serves no purpose.
Since the adoption of the Bill of Rights the Supreme Court has judged only three specific punishments to be covered by the Eighth Amendment: twelve years in chains at hard and painful labor, expatriation, and imprisonment for narcotics addiction. Capital punishment today meets that test.

I. "Uniquely Degrading": Death is an unusually severe punishment, unique in its severity, finality, and enormity. Like expatriation, it destroys the individual's political existence and rights, but unlike expatriation it also destroys the individual himself. In prison, a convict retains his "right to have rights." The executed man loses this right. He also loses the right to be part of the human family. His punishment, unlike the prisoner's, is irrevocable. "Death is truly an awesome punishment. The calculated killing of a human being by the State involves, by its very nature, a denial of the executed person's humanity. . . . In comparison to all other punishments today, then, the deliberate extinguishment of human life by the State is uniquely degrading to human dignity."

II. *"A Lottery System"*: The evidence is "conclusive" that death today is an infrequent and thus extraordinary form of punishment, inflicted only in the "minute fraction" of the cases it is authorized for. (At the time of *Furman*, in many states death was the possible punishment for rape as well as murder.) "When the punishment of death is inflicted in a trivial number of cases in which it is legally available, the conclusion is virtually inescapable that it is being inflicted arbitrarily. Indeed, it smacks of little more than a lottery system."

III. *Out of Fashion:* The death penalty has been debated since the beginning of the nation. It has been a battle on "moral grounds"—the ancient belief in vengeance and retribution versus the eighteenth-century belief in the value of the common man and what motivates him. But the decline and rarity of the death sentence shows that "contemporary society views this punishment with substantial doubt." In fact, "the likelihood is great that the punishment is tolerated only because of its disuse."

IV. *Not a Deterrent:* Proponents of the argument that capital punishment deters murderers concede that deterrence works only when the punishment is "invariably and swiftly imposed." In the American system, the convicted murderer's death is no certainty but rather "remote and improbable," and thus no real deterrent. Nor does the death penalty seem to protect society by serving to show the community's outrage at the commission of such a hateful crime any more than imprisonment. In fact, rather than strengthen the community's moral code, the official, deliberate killing of humans is more likely to brutalize us. "That, after all, is why we no longer carry out public executions."

Nor is pure retribution (i.e., punishment regardless of its benefits to society) a sufficient reason for the death penalty. "The asserted public belief that murderers and rapists deserve to die is flatly inconsistent with the execution of a random few." The history of punishment in the United States shows that we do not want to kill murderers to get even with them, we want to execute them to *prevent* crime. There is no evidence that the death penalty prevents crime any more than the less severe punishment of prison.

"DENIAL OF HUMAN DIGNITY": THURGOOD MARSHALL[45]

Many Americans—and their state legislators—favor the death penalty for first-degree murder. This fact is important to the "moral acceptability" of the death penalty in this country. "But if the constitutionality of the death penalty turns, as I have urged, on the opinion of an *informed* citizenry, then even the enactment of new death statutes cannot be viewed as conclusive."

Public sentiment is not the final test of a law's constitutionality. Any punishment that is "excessive" is invalid under the provisions of the "cruel and unusual punishment" clause of the Eighth Amendment, regardless of public sentiment.

The Court has argued that two purposes make the death penalty "nonexcessive"—general deterrence and retribution. But the evidence that the death penalty deters is controversial. That the state satisfy man's inclination for vengeance in order to avoid such outlawed means as lynching and vigilante justice is a poor justification for the death penalty. "It simply defies belief to suggest that the death penalty is necessary to prevent the American people from taking the law into their own hands."

That the death penalty as an expression of "moral outrage" serves to reinforce the values of society is equally unconvincing. Any individual concerned about doing what society says is "right" is not about to fail to recognize that murder is "wrong" even if the penalty were life imprisonment rather than death. In fact, such arguments are not purely retributive but "essentially utilitarian": they present the death penalty as valuable because of its beneficial results. But society can gain those same results without the death penalty.

But let's take the purest retributive: "That the death penalty is appropriate, not because of its beneficial effect on society, but because the taking of the murderer's life is itself morally good." It is up to society to make that judgment. This is what is "fundamentally at odds with the Eighth Amendment," which demands that a punishment be more than merely acceptable to contemporary society. The Court has made it clear in the past that the death penalty must "[comport] with the basic concept of human dignity at the core of the Amendment. On this test, the taking of human life 'because the wrongdoer deserves it' surely must fail, for such a punishment has as its very basis the total denial of the wrongdoer's dignity and worth."

The death penalty promotes neither the goal of deterrence nor that of retribution, and is thus excessive.

The Injustice of Capital Punishment

Contemporary moral philosophers and philosophers of law have not taken kindly to the death penalty. In general, they worry about runaway utilitarianism that could justify any barbarity for "the good of the many." And even in the purest retributivist they detect a smidgin of utilitarianism, for when the retributivist is asked "Why punish?" he is inclined to answer, "To vindicate or reinforce society's moral principles." The Oxford philosopher H. L. A. Hart, perhaps the twentieth century's most influential commentator on the philosophy of law and theories of punishment, believes that the burden of proof is on the retentionist to prove that executing people is worth more than some other less "irrevocable" punishment.

"EVIL," ON THE FACE OF IT: H. L. A. HART[46]

In Great Britain and the United States, most of us share a "kind of qualified utilitarian" system of moral convictions which also extends to our attitudes toward punishment. Ordinary people believe that punishment benefits us all by protecting society. That is the justification for why we punish.

That does not mean, however, that society can resort to any punishment, even though the best protection for society might be the most barbarous one. It may be a fact that if all drivers who park illegally were tortured, the parking problem would be solved. Or it is easy to think of cases where it would be useful for the government to take an innocent man, fake his guilt, and execute him to warn others not to do something. But "clearly it is part of a *sane* utilitarianism that no punishment must cause more misery than the offense unchecked."[47]

Most people believe that punishment should be just, and that is why we tend to rule out penalties that we agree are barbarous or excessive. Punishing the innocent, no matter the social benefits, is also ruled out. "Indeed, so insistent is this demand that no system of rules which generally provided for the application of punishment to the innocent would normally be called a system of punishment."[48] And even those hard-liners who believe that a crime must be punished even if the punishment has no obvious effects (indeed, if the day after the punishment, society itself dissolves) because it reinforces the morality of the society are taking on a position that "trembles on the margin of a Utilitarian theory."[49]

Within these limits, this qualified utilitarian view seems to hold. As such it presents some serious problems for its advocates who believe that the death penalty is worth having in England and the United States, especially the United States. Three problems arise, in fact:

(1) Killing even a convicted murderer causes suffering, not only to him but to many others. This "*prima facie* evil" can be endured only if some good comes of it that could not be achieved by any other means.

(2) "The death penalty is irrevocable, and the risk of an innocent person being killed is never negligible."

(3) The death penalty is never administered certainly and quickly. In the United States especially, capital trials are interminable, and appeals can be drawn out for years. The costs are immense, not only to the public coffers, but also to the public's confidence in the judicial system. More worrisome, such long delays waiting to be executed constitute an unjust addition to the sentence of death.

The burden remains on those who insist on retaining the death penalty to prove that there is "positive evidence" that proves that the evil of the death penalty, a kind of premeditated murder in itself, is required because it serves some other valuable purpose that other punishments cannot.

Deterrence is often raised as the best proof, but according to studies in the United States and Great Britain, the evidence that the death penalty actually deters homicides remains inconclusive.[50]

"CAPRICE AND MISTAKE": CHARLES BLACK[51]

The issue of the death penalty in the United States stands on only one question: "Shall we kill those who are chosen to be killed by our legal system as it stands?"

The American criminal justice system is based on standards, but they are not clearly articulated. In practice, although one is presumed innocent until proved guilty, the prosecution is unlikely to go ahead with a case unless they think they can win it. Moreover, from the prosecutor's decision as to what crime to charge the defendant with or whether to offer him the opportunity to plead to a lesser crime (90 percent of cases are plea-bargained), to instructions to the jury that they may find the defendant guilty of a lesser offense than the death penalty, to the "insanity defense," which in every state is only vaguely defined, and to the governor's right to opt for clemency, virtually "full discretion" exists to select a defendant for the ultimate punishment of death, or excuse him.

Capital punishment is not a science. *Furman* wiped out one system; what arose in its place is still characterized by caprice and prejudice. Perhaps it might be otherwise if there existed a *perfect* system of criminal justice, pure of personal discretion, prejudice, luck, and circumstance, but such perfection is not to be. Perhaps it might be somewhat different if every state, at every stage, provided every capital defendant with the best counsel money can buy. But this, too, is unattainable. At this very moment death rows are filled with men who had awful legal representation from the start and are without the financial resources to hire lawyers to help them with their appeals.

No one wants to execute an innocent person. Few will not concede that in the past many innocent men have been executed. How does one make amends for such a horrendous mistake? And even if the state discovers that the police or prosecutor or jury has made an error, what good will it do for the man who has been executed? Yet the problem is not simply one of mistakes. ". . . the difficulty goes deeper. For our society is totally committed to executing, not all who have committed homicide, but only some, selected in accordance with certain procedures and certain criteria."[52]

The Death Penalty, Up Close and Personal[53]

Pure abolitionists can find their voice in George Orwell, author of the two twentieth-century classics *Animal Farm* and *1984*. In his famous essay "A Hanging," Orwell describes the day in Burma as a colonial policeman when he marched forty yards to the gallows behind a condemned man. Two things happened: Before the prisoner had gone ten yards, a dog bounded into the yard, barking and wagging, and then, before anyone could get in his way, ran up to the condemned man and tried to lick his face. "Everyone stood aghast," recalled Orwell. Two strong guards led the barefooted prisoner to the gallows. "And once, in spite of the men who gripped him by each shoulder, he stepped slightly aside to avoid a puddle on the path."

That moment changed Orwell's attitude toward capital punishment.

"THE UNSPEAKABLE WRONGNESS": GEORGE ORWELL[54]

> It is curious, but till that moment I had never realized what it means to destroy a healthy, conscious man. When I saw the prisoner step aside to avoid the puddle, I saw the mystery, the unspeakable wrongness, of cutting a life short when it is in full tide. This man was not dying, he was alive just as we were alive. All the organs of his body were working. . . . His eyes saw the yellow gravel and the grey walls, and his brain still remembered, foresaw, reasoned—reasoned even about puddles. He and we were a party of men walking together, seeing, hearing, feeling, understanding the same world; and in two minutes, with a sudden snap, one of us would be gone—one mind less, one world less. . . .

IN MY OPINION

> *The American public wants it. They're fed up with criminals getting away with "murder" and they want to see them pay.*
> —Pennsylvania Attorney General Ernest R. Preate

> *This is a democracy, you know. The people know what they are doing.*
> —Mississippi Assistant Attorney General Marvin White[55]

The latest poll shows that three out of four Americans favor the death penalty. Attorney General Preate is definitely right about the anger out there: most Americans have abandoned even lip service to the "deterrent effect" of the death penalty. Vengeance is what they are after. "They want to see them pay."

But do the people really know what they are doing? Should a society that believes it is the most free, open, and generous nation in the world execute even its most brutal and murderous convicts or put them away forever without parole? Perhaps more important: Should our leaders—clergy, politicians, judges, and lawyers—take their cue from public emotions, or should they initiate a national debate and try to shape the moral imaginations of the society? Finally, the issue of capital punishment comes down to one question: Can a society that presumes itself to be decent kill even its most vicious criminals?

Back to the Future

Morality, as most politicians and judges would quickly tell you, is not a popularity contest. After all, people used to want murderers tortured, dismembered, hanged, and then incinerated. Thousands died barbaric and agonizing deaths in France and England in the eighteenth century, where two hundred crimes, including robbery, arson, and counterfeiting, could get you the death penalty.

The modern liberal ideal—and the United States is considered its most brilliant result—was to create a future in which such cruelty is not institutionalized. The framers of the U.S. Constitution added the Eighth Amendment to outlaw cruelty.

They were in many ways far ahead of their time, but by not outlawing the death penalty (as the Quakers had done in the colonies of Pennsylvania and South Jersey), the great legal thinkers of the American Revolution only proved that they hadn't escaped the early eighteenth century.

But surely we, on the verge of the twenty-first, can. To argue for capital punishment because the founders did not argue against it more than two centuries ago seems not only absurd but to fly against the idea of America. Jefferson advised rewriting the Constitution every generation.

No nation with our kind and generous self-image can live with the death penalty, and if Americans do not yet understand that, it is the task of the nation's leaders to educate them. If several members of recent Supreme Courts have all been *personally* appalled by the death penalty, then it shouldn't take much to persuade millions of Americans why even some of the most conservative legal thinkers of our time find the death penalty unnecessary and barbaric.[56]

The polls show that Americans want vicious retribution for vicious criminals. The goal is to persuade our citizens that murdering murderers is beyond the kind of viciousness that we as a constitutional democracy want to sanction.

If the people no longer even want to pay lip service to the notion that the death penalty deters the most brutal murderers, if they want to punish for the sake of punishment, that is fine. States have the alternative of creating life sentences without the possibility of parole. But if the people want to punish someone for the sake of seeing him suffer—how often have we heard the murder victim's family scream, "I want to see him suffer!"?—if that is the goal, then it is not fine. It is torture.

The Barbarity of the Death Penalty

Proponents of capital punishment like Ernest van den Haag and Walter Berns, enemies of torture, suggest that anyone not willing to sanction the execution of a brutal murderer betrays a certain moral cowardice, "a failure of nerve," in van den Haag's phrase.

Yet why do men like Clinton Duffy, the longtime warden of San Quentin who oversaw many executions, become firm opponents of the death penalty? Why did the prison records officer at San Quentin say, "No matter how often I heard [the gallows trap snap open], it always shocked me out of my skin. Then in the dim light we would see the poor bastard plunge out of sight."[57] And why did George Orwell write in a letter about the hanging he saw, "There was no question that everyone concerned knew this to be dreadful, unnatural action. I believe it is always the same—the whole jail, warders and prisoners alike, is upset when there is an execution . . ."?[58]

Is this bad feeling at the scene of an execution the result of a general cowardice? Or is that nausea in the pit of everyone's stomach something quite different—civilization maybe?

Breaking Through the Metaphor

It is often and understandably difficult to throw off two thousand years of believing that the heinous crime deserves an equivalent punishment. Habits of belief, however, can be wrong. History is full of examples of beliefs strongly held for centuries that we now see as mistaken. All of us get trapped inside tight metaphors. The celebrated physicist Stephen Hawking has noted that physicists resisted the idea that the universe is expanding for two centuries: "This behavior of the universe could have been predicted from Newton's theory of gravity at any time in the nineteenth, the eighteenth, or even the late seventeenth centuries. Yet so strong was the belief in a static universe that it persisted into the twentieth century."[59] Einstein himself was so convinced that the universe had to be static that he modified his general theory of relativity in 1915 to allow for a static universe.

Metaphors are often so powerful that it usually takes a genius to destroy even the most moribund of them. That is how scientific and social revolutions are made. It was not long ago that U.S. law finally was changed to give black Americans equality with white Americans. Over the past twenty years we have slowly approached the view that women, too, are equal. These are huge social revolutions that seemed unthinkable a century ago.

Usually, such revolutions occur when people realize that the way they talk and think about the world is inadequate to the way things actually are or have recently been discovered to be. Someone comes up with a new way of describing what once seemed so obvious. Newton explained how the world works, Einstein pointed out that it is actually quite different. We could not imagine women in the boardroom or on the Supreme Court, until Betty Friedan exposed the "feminine mystique"; then we began to see how silly we had been. How many other things that seem so obvious and "true" about our lives will look ridiculous or barbaric or mad to our descendants—as barbaric as the once traditional punishments of disembowelment and breaking on the wheel? Or as barbaric as torture's traditional mate, the death penalty.

The death penalty, I believe, is trapped inside a discredited metaphor about justice, the ancient retributive notion of an "eye for an eye" and Rome's *lex talionis*—literally, the law of the same kind of punishment. Advocates of capital punishment do not suggest that rapists should be raped or wife beaters beaten. It would be too much like torture. Why do they have so much trouble seeing the death penalty in the same way?

Walter Berns's acceptance of the death penalty suggests that its proponents cannot yet break away from the metaphor of crime as the "big payback." Their view is that if the crime provokes the community's anger, which turns into hatred, the punishment should be as large, perhaps the maximum punishment—death. And while the death penalty camp concedes readily that punishment must be distinct from torture, a close reading of Berns's position (and similarly the utilitarian van den Haag's arguments) suggests that though they do not want to be in favor of torture, they really have a taste for a kind of macho cruelty.

"The Liturgy of Punishment"

Not caring that much about the debate over capital punishment and recognizing that among intellectuals (his people) support is rare, Berns reports that a moment came when he understood that the police and majority of Americans who favor the death penalty are right. He understood Nazi hunter Simon Wiesenthal's personal moral crusade "to bring the guilty ones to trial." Berns saw the connection between anger and punishment. "Anger is the passion that recognizes and cares about justice," he writes. We are angry when the Eichmanns are not brought to trial. And following Adam Smith, he notes that "we feel cheated" if a criminal should drop dead before he can be executed.

But do we? Berns mentions Jack Ruby's murder of JFK's alleged assassin, Lee Harvey Oswald. But did Ruby cheat us of the chance to punish Oswald? Berns does not say. But he does say that the Israelis would have felt cheated if Adolf Eichmann had been gunned down in Argentina instead of being hauled back to Israel to stand trial.[60] "Justice requires not only punishment," declares Berns, it requires the *forms of justice* [my italics]; "and the reason for this is that while the law might blame the crime by summarily punishing the criminal, it cannot praise the law-abiding without providing the solemnities of a trial." For it is the "majesty" of the law that will strengthen the habit of obeying the law among the people.

He is, I believe, half right here. The forms of justice are significant, and it was an important message that the Jewish state put a mass murderer of Jews on public trial. But why does this kind of ritual require an execution? Some might argue that the Israelis might have displayed a certain moral elegance by locking up Eichmann for life without parole, as a constant reminder of Jewish suffering. A display of justice is an essential part of the law and its power. But why must it be a bloody, torturous display?

And this brings us to what I think bothers Berns about giving up capital punishment: it deprives us of what Michel Foucault has called the "liturgy of punishment."[61] The true majesty of the law is the power that only his majesty the king once possessed: to call for another man's head. By admitting to this appeal of the rituals, the "solemnities" of punishment, Berns (unknowingly it appears) is throwing himself back into the Middle Ages when the atrocities of torture and execution were acceptable because they were part of the very kind of public ritual of punishment that Berns embraces.

As Foucault has shown in *Discipline and Punish,* the history of punishment has been progress from being "an art of unbearable sensations" to "an economy of suspended rights."[62] Once "paid back" by the most imaginative and horrible tortures and executions, convicts now simply lose man's most precious right—freedom. In the Middle Ages, the actual act of murder was often imitated at the execution. Men were actually brought to the scene of their crime to be put to death. The ritual was carefully planned: what the man wore, how he was conveyed to the scaffold, usually at a crossroads (all the better to confuse the condemned man's evil spirits), the reading of a decree, an opportunity for the condemned man to repent, the mutilation of the hands of murderers, disembowelment, drawing and quartering.

The public execution, as Foucault has pointed out in graphic detail, was as highly ritualized as the Catholic Mass. Indeed, medieval torture and executions had their theological dimension. The punishment of torture showed the condemned man—and his audience—what he could expect in hell. Foucault also points out that even as late as the eighteenth century, the public execution was as much a "political operation" as a legal one. The death penalty proved how much more powerful a king was than his subjects. The omnipotent monarch had the right—a *divine* right—to order a man's death. Jurists described public executions as "atrocities" without irony. That is what they were supposed to be—as horrible as the crime committed.

The achievement of the Enlightenment was to convince intelligent and powerful eighteenth-century men (men like the leaders of the American Revolution and the framers of the U.S. Constitution) that the atrocities of judicial torture and public executions were barbaric, shameful, immoral, and unnecessary. That kings could order torture and executions as a show of power was precisely the sort of thing to which the idea of America was opposed. In a constitutional democracy the people were to be sovereign, their rights would be sacred, and the unbridled power of leaders to punish might be judged, in the words of the Eighth Amendment to the U.S. Constitution, "cruel and unusual punishment."

That the framers did not explicitly cite the death penalty is only evidence that they were not as enlightened as they thought. After all, the founders believed all sorts of things that we find ludicrous (powdered wigs are attractive) and barbaric (slavery is morally justified). That a conservative jurist like Chief Justice Warren Burger would admit that if he were a legislator he would ban the death penalty indicates that if men as thoughtful as the original framers were to draft the Eighth Amendment today, they would ban the death penalty. (This is precisely why Jefferson believed that the Constitution ought to be revised every generation.)

The question that the rewriters of the Eighth Amendment would have to pose is plain enough. Walter Berns himself proposes it: "Does justice permit or even require the death penalty?"

The Limits of Moral Outrage

For Berns, "a moral community is not possible without anger and the moral indignation that accompanies it."[63] This kind of outrage is a sign that people care about the community. And when a murder occurs, it is this "natural moral sense" which infuriates us and makes us want revenge. Taking an unusual literary turn for a constitutional scholar, Berns points to Shakespeare's *Macbeth* as proof that "there is something in the souls of men—men then and now—that requires such crimes to be revenged [*sic*]." Berns eloquently (and rhetorically) adds: "Can we imagine a world that does not take its revenge on the man who kills Macduff's wife and children? (Can we imagine the play in which Macbeth does not die?)"

Berns deserves an answer. No, I cannot imagine the play in which Macbeth does not die. But I can easily imagine a world in which he is not executed. In Shakespeare's world—sixteenth-century Elizabethan England—criminals were tortured and hacked to death. In our world, that is not supposed to happen. As some might put it, "it is unimaginable." Imagining a world that does not take revenge on Macbeth is precisely what those who oppose the death penalty are asking Berns and all those other Americans who favor the death penalty to do—stretch their imagination.

That Berns cannot imagine such a world does not make the death penalty right or just. It simply suggests that Berns has a limited imagination—a limited *moral* imagination.[64] By talking of "our natural moral sense" and "something in the souls of men," Berns is begging the question. *His* natural moral sense might call for capital punishment. Orwell informs us that he—and every other policeman and colonial official on hand for that hanging in Burma—felt morally ill. In Berns's terms, something in Orwell's soul told him that execution was just plain wrong.

Berns has plunged into metaphysics here. He is assuming a "moral order" that he gives no evidence for; he does not tell us who set that moral order or where it came from. He is assuming that his "moral sense" (or even Shakespeare's) is shared by everyone. To be sure, we share many things. I, too, was outraged by the assassinations of the Kennedy brothers and Martin Luther King Jr. Nor am I tolerant of Nazi or Communist mass murderers.

Berns, however, does not seem to share Justice Marshall's sense of moral indignation over the statistical fact that a white man who has murdered a black man is not very likely to get the death penalty. But isn't the rage that blacks feel about the inequities of the death penalty just? One could take Berns's argument to places he would not want to go, for if what helps define a community is the moral outrage people feel when they are wronged, then surely this justifies insurrection and revolution. What are the riots in our ghettos if not mass displays of the moral outrage of the African-American community?

You do not even have to be "politically correct" to ask such questions. In moral argument, we must be careful about wearing blinders, about ignoring the facts. We must also be careful about limiting our moral imaginations. And we must also be careful about arguing for our opinions on the basis of mystical "moral codes" that work only for

Americans (and Shakespeareans), but might not fit the sense of justice of our enemies.

Is the moral code that guides Walter Berns really undermined by the fact that James Earl Ray and Sirhan Sirhan are imprisoned for life? (Let's not imagine the possibility that neither is solely responsible for his crime.) What would we Americans have gained if Texas had had the opportunity to send Lee Harvey Oswald to the electric chair?

Surely a Nazi Murderer Deserves to Be Executed?

I think Berns errs in building his case for capital punishment on the kind of moral outrage we feel over monumental acts of atrocity. Surely, it trivializes the monstrous crimes of a Hitler to compare them to those of an ordinary gunman or a husband who orders the murder of his wife or even a cold-blooded Mafia hitman. (It is not insignificant, I think, that Israel has banned capital punishment except for convicted Nazi murderers; the Israelis do not even execute terrorists.)

Did Rudolf Hess, who spent more than forty years in Spandau prison, suffer more than Eichmann? Was he punished more? Admittedly, the execution of Eichmann gave the Israelis (and the rest of us) more satisfaction. And that is the problem with vengeance: the more you prod and squeeze it, the more you strip off its layers, the more you describe it, the more it begins to look like pleasure.

"I want to see him suffer!" screams the family of the murder victim. But how much should one enjoy watching that murderer suffer? How much punishment is enough to satisfy Shakespearean vengeance? Okay, execute him. But should he, like Caryl Chessman, wait twelve years to die in the gas chamber? Or thirteen years like Warren Mc-Cleskey? Of course, the appeals stage prevents innocent men from being executed, but that an innocent man might be executed may be the best argument against capital punishment.

If the evidence that the death penalty deters murderers is inconclusive, to say the least, if the notion that executions somehow shore up some kind of ideal Platonic moral code requires a metaphysical commitment that is hard for many to buy, then why execute? Because we are angry and our anger is just, advises Berns. Perhaps. Who can deny there is a kind of justice in torturing a torturer? But even Berns will concede that such a punishment is repulsive and immoral. Torture is immoral because, as O'Brien, the professional torturer in Orwell's *1984,* says, "Torture is for the sake of torture." Since the tortured man, to end the pain, is likely to admit to anything, torture is a test of nothing but a man's capacity for pain. The goal of torture is suffering. Its side effects may be to humiliate the victim, to break him or her down into pieces he or she may never be able to put back together again.[65] What is that but psychic pain? Even worse, there is the double horror of knowing it is coming, and then it comes.

Unlike murder. And like execution. The horror of the Mob hitman is that he "executes" people. They see it coming. We are morally repelled by the Mafia murder (even of another Mafia member) but call the electric chair or the lethal injection "justice." Why? Because it is legal? Both seem equally cruel, and that is why capital punishment should be illegal.

The Wimp Factor

If the criminal must pay, as he must, why must he pay with his life with all the cruelty that execution calls upon us to condone, and with the awful (even if rare) possibility of the horrible mistake of executing an innocent person? Punishment may be valued for its own sake, as Berns argues, but why must it be corporal punishment?

At this point, the proponents of capital punishment begin to swagger and stick out their chins. Four-eyed academics they might be, but they are hard guys nonetheless. Resist capital punishment? "A failure of nerve," harrumphs Ernest van den Haag.[66]

Anyone who feels "queasy" about executing a criminal, no matter how depraved his acts, who believes that such a monster has a right to go on living "oppresses" van den Haag. He blames the eighteenth century, particularly those notorious sadomasochists de Sade and Rousseau (though van den Haag admits Rousseau was a "political thinker of the first rank"), who "sexualized" corporal punishment, and thus put it out of the reach of all good men.

Van den Haag is quick to admit that we are not up to such life and death decisions because "the irrevocability of a verdict of death is contrary to the modern spirit that likes to pretend that nothing is ever definitive, that everything is open-ended, that doubts must always be entertained and revisions made." Courts, however, do not have this luxury. Their business is to protect society, "to do justice," and "to vindicate the norms society holds inviolable."

At this point, van den Haag, a self-professed utilitarian, begins to sound like Walter Berns, who would not want to be called any such thing. But by claiming that his "pay-them-back" view of punishment will protect the moral code, Berns's position, too, "trembles on the margin of Utilitarian theory" (to borrow H. L. A. Hart's lovely phrase).[67] Both these proponents of the death penalty are convinced that it is the only way to keep our "moral code" from crumbling. Not only do abolitionists not have the guts to pull the switch, they are even nervous about letting the courts order an execution; they lack the "moral courage" to see that the deed is done.

In short, those who oppose the death penalty are wimps.

This wimp, however, is inclined to reach for his gas mask when he smells the kind of hot air that tries to attach me to the "modern spirit" or when he is asked to worry about the future of our "moral code." (In Chapter 6, "One Nation, Many Disagreements," I deal with the charge that those of us who are inclined to revise our "moral codes" do not tremble when we are attacked as "moral relativists.")

Is that the same wicked "modern spirit" that has wiped out disease, fostered universal education, and withstood the evils of fascism and totalitarianism? Is it the same moral code that, when I was in elementary school, would not allow black Americans to drink out of the same water fountain as whites, never mind enter the same voting booth? That treated sex as "dirty," that told my sister that a woman's place was in the home, that applauded Joe McCarthy?

Moral codes have a way of crumbling under the weight of their own absurdities. It is difficult to see how executing criminals will affect the future of such codes, whatever or wherever they are, for better or worse. For Berns, the "moral strength" required to favor the death penalty is the same sort of strong conviction that moved the Israelis to mount their brilliant commando attack against Arab terrorists at Entebbe. The same "moral courage" that the administrators at Cornell University in 1969, where Berns was on the faculty, did *not* have in the face of student demonstrators.[68]

What began as a thoughtful and fair discussion about the pros and cons of capital punishment culminates in a kind of intellectual mambo—the professor as macho man.

Let's forget that the Israelis, in spite of their strong convictions about not being pushed around by those they view as terrorists, only have the "moral courage" to execute convicted Nazis. And let's sidestep the presumption that the morally strong are by nature not supposed to have qualms about legal, premeditated torture. (According to doctors, the reason smoke comes out of the ears of the man in the electric chair is that his brain is literally being fried. That man struggling against his straps and turning blue in the gas chamber is suffocating before our very eyes. Is death by lethal injection really a "painless" alternative or only a chance to die like a dog? If that's what it takes to make one's moral courage weak-kneed, then call me a wimp.)

Murder deserves murder, according to van den Haag. "The worse the crime the higher the penalty deserved," he declares and then concedes in a footnote, "One may argue that some crimes deserve more than execution, and that on the above reasoning, torture may be justified."[69] I would like to hear van den Haag make the case for torture, but he steps around what even he admits is a logical implication of his own argument by noting that torture is no longer allowed "so the issue is academic."

But so is his discussion and mine. (Only in the Supreme Court, state legislatures, and governors' mansions is discussing the death penalty not academic.) But van den Haag has already whittled away at his own argument. He says: "Unlike the death penalty, torture has become repulsive to us."

But that's the point. *The death penalty has become repulsive to its opponents!*

We opponents of capital punishment have trouble distinguishing it from torture. We are also appalled that innocent people get executed. Any system of rules that allows innocent people to be punished, as H. L. A. Hart has noted, can hardly be called a system of punishment. A tragedy is what that is—a cruel tragedy.

Postscript: A headline in the *New York Times* in 1992 read: "2 CLEARED IN DEATH AFTER 17 YEARS IN PRISON." Both men had been convicted in 1974 of murdering a California highway policeman. Recent evidence that Los Angeles cops had coerced witnesses and manufactured the testimony of a prison informer to convict them was so strong that even the district attorney joined the defense lawyers in pressing the court to release the men. Both had been sentenced to life imprisonment—two years before California reinstated the death penalty.[70]

"Nothing can return to you the years irretrievably lost," the judge declared, informing the convicts, "you are free men."

A wonderful and terrifying moment, an impossible moment if those innocent men had been executed.

A related story the same day: James McCloskey, founder of Centurion Ministries, an organization whose goal is to help innocent men avoid life imprisonment or the death penalty, worked for years to free the two California men—the eleventh and twelfth men whose freedom he has helped win. In another case in 1987, McCloskey videotaped two witnesses who confessed that the police had coerced them into fingering a Louisiana man for murder. McCloskey showed the tapes to state authorities.

Two days later the man died in the electric chair, as scheduled.[71]

5. Racial Justice and Affirmative Action

THE ISSUE

In the 1960s, Presidents John F. Kennedy and Lyndon B. Johnson described racial discrimination in the United States as a "moral crisis" and "a crippling legacy of bigotry and injustice."[1] In response to initiatives from the White House, moral outrage against legalized racism in the South and de facto segregation in the North, and increasing social unrest among American blacks, Congress began enacting civil rights legislation to redress the balance. Today some argue that the United States has fulfilled its moral obligation to black Americans; even people opposed to racial discrimination have been concerned that further efforts to compensate African-Americans engender "reverse discrimination."

Do we still have a moral obligation to black Americans? If so, is it worth discriminating against some innocent white people to meet that moral obligation? Any answer to these questions requires a sense of the enormity of the injustices American blacks—American *citizens* after all—have suffered. It is easy to forget how bad things were, and for how long. Today race is viewed mainly as an economic or social problem, or a burden on the criminal justice system. But treating black people differently than white people is a *moral* problem—indeed, the greatest and most visible source of moral ugliness in a nation that too easily considers itself a "good society."

Racism

Racism was the invention of white men, morally upright *Christian* white men, eager to justify the institution of slavery. The effort to classify and deride one group of people as "inferior" to the rest of us by virtue of their skin color, shape of their head, or the size of their nose is a relatively new notion, invented in the late eighteenth century and polished to deadly perfection in the twentieth. (While state racism has been used to lethal effect against Jews and other minorities in this century, my focus in this chapter is on racism against African-Americans.)

In *Politics,* Aristotle declared that "some men are by nature free, and others slaves, and that for these latter, slavery is both expedient and right."[2] Greeks, of course, according to Aristotle, were by nature free men, and the first, in fact, as the historian M. I. Finley has pointed out, to create "an institutionalized system of large-scale employment of slave labor in both the countryside and the cities."[3] (The last "slave society" was in the American South.)[4]

Yet while the Greeks and Romans saw their slaves as property, they did not consider slaves as necessarily inferior. Greek and Roman slaves worked side by side with freemen. Slaves worked as doctors and policemen in antiquity, and the Romans had no problem putting slaves into top bureaucratic roles in the empire.[5] The Greeks derided the "barbarians"—non-Greeks (literally, those whose speech was an incomprehensible babble of "bah, bah, bah")—because they were *culturally,* and not biologically, different.[6]

The early Christians stressed the unity of humankind, that man was made in "God's image." Jesus advised men "to love your neighbor" and announced that he had not come to save only the Jews. "Go, therefore," said Christ, "and make disciples of all nations."[7] Christianity's greatest promoter, St. Paul, declared that God "hath made of one blood all nations in the earth to dwell."[8] For St. Augustine, born in North Africa and later a bishop there, every man is born a member of humankind, and "no matter what unusual appearance he presents in *color* [my italics], movement, sound . . . no Christian can doubt that he springs from that one protoplast."[9]

The first African slaves arrived in Europe in the fifteenth century, and the philosophers of slavery were not far behind with their intellectual and theological rationalizations for treating some men worse than animals. According to one writer in 1453, kidnapped Africans who had lived like beasts were "happy" to be spared damnation.[10] To the European eye, Africans were not only ugly, but their black skin became a metaphor for evil and corruption. Slaveholders pointed in error to the Book of Genesis 9, where Canaan, "the son of Ham," whose descendants populated Africa, was cursed (by Noah, actually, and not by God, as many claimed) to be "the lowest of slaves to his brothers"— his *white* brethren.

There were, however, dissenters to enslaving non-whites. Montaigne (1533–92) said of a Brazilian Indian: "There is nothing savage or barbarous about his nature save for the fact that each of us labels whatever is not among the customs of his own people as barbarism."[11] The Spanish Dominican and former conquistador Bartolomé de Las Casas (1474–1566) protested against enslaving American Indians, arguing that they were rational and perhaps even superior to the ancient Greeks and Romans. De Las Casas's tireless efforts on the Indians' behalf persuaded Pope Paul III to condemn the slave trade in 1537, declaring that Indians are "truly men" who should not be deprived of their freedom and property. Five years later the Spanish crown prohibited slavery by law.[12]

Spanish colonists, however, generally ignored the bans, and when Indian forced labor began literally to die out because of overwork and disease, the Spaniards began importing black Africans to the New World. By the end of the sixteenth century, Europe had developed an almost insatiable taste for sugar, and sugar profits soon justified the high cost of African slaves. The slave trade in Britain had the imprimatur of the Crown and the Church, creating some of England's greatest fortunes. By the middle of the eighteenth century, even David Hume, the great Scottish philosopher, could write without a moral twinge in his celebrated *Treatise of Human Nature*, "I am apt to suspect all negroes, and in general all other species of men . . . to be naturally inferior to the white. . . ."[13]

"Race"—a zoological term first used to classify different categories of men in 1749—is generally defined as a subcategory of a species which inherits certain physical characteristics that distinguish it from other categories of that same species. Thus, the Caucasian race is "different" from the Negro or Mongolian groups.[14] The claim that one race is superior, or inferior, to another is "racism." As a scientific theory, racism is intellectually absurd, as de Las Casas had argued as early as the fifteenth century and such great thinkers as Herder, Goethe, and Kant felt obliged to argue again at the end of the eighteenth century. Anthropologists who had actually gone out and lived with various "savages" in Africa, Melanesia, and the Antipodes concluded that in spite of cultural and physical differences, these "new" peoples were only different versions of us. Over the ages man's mobility and sexual urge had ensured hybridization of the species. Among man, there is only one race—the *human* race.[15]

"As American as Apple Pie"—and Racism

The first blacks in America preceded the *Mayflower* to the shores of the New World, arriving in Virginia in 1619. These twenty Africans were *not* technically slaves, but indentured servants. Other blacks soon followed, from England, Spain, Portugal, and the West Indies, worked out their periods of indenture, and began to accumulate property. Some of them even imported *white* indentured servants to work on their farms.[16] For the next forty years they lived among the settlers of Virginia—with the right to own property and to vote. (A few even held public office.)

In the North, the first blacks, also listed as "servants" and not slaves, arrived in New Amsterdam in 1626 and Massachusetts in 1638. Black and white servants worked together in the fields, intermarried, and were protected by the laws. While prejudice existed, racism did not. In the 1660s, Virginia and Maryland took the first step to assuring a surplus of black labor by passing laws forbidding intermarriage and making blacks slaves for life.[17]

Among early American religious leaders, there was hardly a discouraging word about slavery until the Revolution.[18] That blacks were slaves seemed to imply that they were fit to be nothing else.[19] In the South, where black slavery seemed crucial to the economy, the record of the Christian churches in opposing slavery was scandalous.[20]

All Men—Except Black Ones—Are Created Equal

The American Revolutionaries declared that "all men are created equal," though the author of those words, Thomas Jefferson, had a poor opinion of the black man's potential to be equal.[21] At the end of his life, however, Jefferson admitted that the issue of slavery filled him with terror, "like a firebell in the night."[22]

What was good for the slaveowner was good for the slave, and up to the Civil War wealthy slaveowners in the South resisted the moral arguments against slavery, parroting instead the words of such philoso-

phers of slavery as Thomas R. Dew, a professor of history, metaphysics, and law at William and Mary, and William Harper, who derided the view that all men are born free and equal. "Man is born to
subjection," declared Harper. "The law was created to keep certain
people in their place."[23] For scientific confirmation, the slaveholder
pointed to the work of Harvard's Louis Agassiz (1807–73), a Swiss-
born naturalist, and Josiah Nott (1804–73), a leading Alabama doctor
and "ethnologist" who wrote a much-quoted seven-hundred-page
tome asserting white superiority.[24]

Constitutional Racism in America

By the Civil War, the black population of the United States numbered
4 million.[25] Legal racism had become a "truth" crucial to an American
economy dependent on free labor. Even those Americans uncomfortable with slavery in the South had come to believe that a freed Negro
would not be fit for all the rights and privileges of even the dimmest
white citizen of the nation.

Among those well-intentioned doubters was the U.S. Supreme
Court. The landmark *Dred Scott* decision, written by Chief Justice
Roger Taney, is itself an analysis of the effects of American racism on
the law.[26] By the time of the Declaration of Independence and the Constitution, American Negroes, Taney reminds us, "had for more than a
century before been regarded as beings of an inferior order. . . . This
opinion was at that time fixed and universal in the civilized portion of
the white race. It was regarded as *an axiom in morals as well as politics,* which no one thought of disputing, or supposed to be open to dispute." [my emphasis]

So much for "traditional values." According to the pro-slavery
Taney, neither the Declaration of Independence nor the U.S. Constitution sought to alter that "axiom" of black inferiority. The Supreme
Court ruled, 7 to 2, among other things, that slaves were property protected by the Constitution.

Six years later, in the middle of the Civil War, President Abraham
Lincoln tried to sidestep the racism of the Constitution.

The Gettysburg Address: Lincoln Reinvents America

In his justly famous speech dedicating the Union cemetery at Gettysburg, Pennsylvania, in 1863, Lincoln—in 272 words—restated the proposition that "all men are created equal" and asserted that a reunified America would have a "new birth in freedom"—a freedom that emancipated slaves could share. The President, as Garry Wills has pointed out in *Lincoln at Gettysburg*, sought to "refound" America, to re-create the experiment in liberty, and to restate—and thus reinterpret—the values upon which the country was created. His critics knew and resented this.[27]

If *all* men are truly created equal, then those who by an accident of birth happened to have black skin could not be property, nor could they be derided as naturally inferior—as the Supreme Court and Southern ministers had concluded.

Legalized Racism: "Separate but Equal"

After the Civil War, Congress ratified the Thirteenth, Fourteenth, and Fifteenth Amendments to the U.S. Constitution, banning slavery, declaring all "persons born or naturalized in the United States" citizens with certain "privileges or immunities," including due process and the equal protection of the law, and assuring the right to vote regardless of "race, color, or previous condition of servitude." In 1875, Congress passed a "civil rights" act confirming that American blacks were citizens with rights that were guaranteed "equal protection" under the law.

At least they were in theory. In practice, however, the legislatures of the South worked hard and inventively *for the next half century to deprive black Americans of their rights*. More tragic still, the American legal system did not discourage such racism. In the landmark *Civil Rights Cases* decision of 1883 the Supreme Court gutted Congress's civil rights law by limiting "equal protection" to state action only.[28] In *Plessy* v. *Ferguson* (1896) the Supreme Court upheld Louisiana's right to require "equal but separate accommodations for the white and colored races" on railroad cars. According to the seven-man majority, the Constitution is not color-blind—and "Jim Crow" was born.[29] Racists took *Plessy* as a signal to solidify segregation not only in public transportation, but also in schools and public places.

The New Black Middle Class

At the turn of the century, the dominant African-American leader in the United States (indeed in white eyes, the *only* Negro leader) was Booker Taliaferro Washington, a former slave who had founded Tuskegee Institute, an industrial school for Negroes. Washington was soon opposed by a group of more militant black intellectuals including William E. B. Du Bois and Ida B. Tarbell. While Booker T. Washington counseled thrift, industrial training, and patience with Jim Crow for the black masses, Du Bois, a Harvard Ph.D. and a brilliant polemicist, proposed "the use of force of every sort: moral suasion, propaganda and where possible even physical resistance"[30] to achieve the rights promised to them by an amended Constitution. Murderous race riots in Atlanta and Springfield, Illinois, in 1906 and 1908 mobilized an even wider black leadership to form the National Association for the Advancement of Colored People (NAACP) in 1909.

By 1913, the nation's almost 10 million blacks had made some impressive gains: they owned hundreds of thousands of homes, farms, and businesses; more than 70 percent were literate and 1.7 million were in school. There were 35,000 black teachers, 17,495 black ministers, 3,553 black doctors, and 798 black lawyers and jurists.

Most whites were still unimpressed. In 1917, with four regiments of black men fighting in World War I, one of the bloodiest race riots in American history broke out in East St. Louis, Illinois, over the hiring of black workers. Encouraged to move to the "Promised Land" for jobs and genuine citizenship, blacks traveled the highways and railroads from the Mississippi Delta northwards to Chicago in growing numbers, 50,000 in the first eighteen months after World War I. The first wave of the "Great Migration" of blacks from the rural South to the factories of Chicago, a massive display of Negro freedom and industry, failed to impress most whites.[31] In the "Red Summer of 1919," twenty-six more race riots exploded around the country. The stock market crash of 1929 kicked the wind out of the Roaring Twenties. No group was harder hit than the blacks.[32]

Discovering Black Political Power

Black activists, however, continued to fight racism, boycotting and picketing businesses and public utilities, pressuring whites to hire blacks. In Harlem, Adam Clayton Powell Jr. led a four-year nonviolent campaign to force city businesses to employ more blacks. A. Philip Randolph organized the Brotherhood of Sleeping Car Porters, a black union. On the eve of another world war, Randolph threatened a March on Washington of 10,000 American Negroes unless blacks got their fair share of defense industry jobs and equality in the armed forces. Franklin D. Roosevelt resisted, but finally issued an executive order banning discrimination in defense industries in 1941—*the first such formal decree from the White House on race since Lincoln's Emancipation Proclamation.*

Once again blacks discovered that the only time they made a political, social, or legal advance was when they demonstrated, picketed, or threatened to take to the streets. Again, black soldiers fought bravely in a war against racism in Europe, and once again when black veterans returned home they were assaulted by racists in riots in Tennessee and Philadelphia. Congress continued to resist fair employment legislation. In 1947 the NAACP appealed formally to the new United Nations organization to pressure the United States on behalf of its persecuted minority. Randolph again threatened to lead a movement against the proposed peacetime draft, and President Harry Truman issued two more executive orders aimed at eliminating racial discrimination in federal employment and the armed services.[33]

In the Deep South, "separate but equal" still prevailed.

The Battle for School Desegregation

The first targets of the early civil rights activists were universities and professional schools that refused to admit the best and brightest black college graduates. In 1938 the Court had ruled that "equality" meant that black college graduates had a right to go to law school.[34] When Missouri and five Southern states tried to get around the law by creating separate law schools for blacks, the Court ruled them inadequate. And after the University of Oklahoma admitted a black law student and then proceeded to segregate him from white students through special seating arrangements in classes, the library, and the cafeteria, the Court concluded that this arrangement undercut the student's "ability . . . to learn his profession."[35] The year was 1950.

By midcentury the status of black America was grim and hopeless. But it took a Swedish sociologist named Gunnar Myrdal to point out that the situation of blacks was literally *un-American.* In his classic study of "the Negro problem," *The American Dilemma,* Myrdal

wrote: "From the point of view of the American Creed [i.e., the fundamental values of the Declaration of Independence and the Constitu-
tion] the status accorded the Negro in America represents nothing
more and nothing less than a century-long lag of public morals." For
Myrdal, "the American dilemma" was somehow to try to bring the nation's racial practices into line with its ideals. "The subordinate position of Negroes is perhaps the most glaring conflict in the American
conscience and the greatest unsolved task for American democracy,"
Myrdal wrote.[36] As long as the nation's blacks were oppressed, America's commitment to true "equality"—the most fundamental of its
principles—could only be seen as "lip service."[37]

In 1950, one in twenty black American *citizens* was registered to
vote. Most black American *citizens* could not work, live, eat, go to the
movies, or travel where they wanted to. Their elementary schools were
terrible; most blacks did not graduate from high school. Most black
American *citizens* were living in poverty, and whites seemed to be willing to do just about anything to keep their children from mixing with
black kids.[38]

The Battle for School Desegregation in the North and South

American blacks, led by the NAACP, kept suing—and winning. Finally, in 1954, the Supreme Court consolidated four suits against state
laws segregating elementary schools into *Brown* v. *Board of Education of Topeka, Kansas*. For a unanimous Court, Chief Justice Earl
Warren declared the separate but equal doctrine unconstitutional in
public education, concluding that segregation bred a sense of inferiority in black children and made it difficult for them to learn, thus
denying them the equal protection promised by the Fourteenth
Amendment to the Constitution. The Supreme Court's message to local school districts: Desegregate public schools "with all deliberate
speed."[39]

On March 11, 1956, ninety-six members of Congress from the South
issued a "Southern Manifesto" in which they condemned the *Brown*
decision as an "unwarranted exercise of power by the Court contrary
to the Constitution." They pointed out—with no apparent irony—that
Brown "had planted hatred and suspicion where there had been
heretofore friendship and understanding."[40]

With such thinly veiled racism and contempt for the Court at the
very top of the U.S. government, state legislators and officials, and lo-

cal school boards felt free to interpret "deliberate speed" as slow gear.[41] Some states simply used such "nonracial" measures as aptitude, grades, health, even "moral character" to control the number of blacks in schools. One school system closed down for five years until the Court declared the strategy discriminatory.[42] In the North, where legal segregation did not exist, civil rights activists charged the schools were segregated "in fact." The Court allowed districts to integrate grade by grade; thus some schools where de facto segregation thrived took twelve years to get blacks into the same classrooms with whites.

But, finally, history took a turn against the racists. In 1955, after Rosa Parks was arrested for refusing to yield her seat to a white on a bus in Montgomery, Alabama, a one-day protest grew into a year-long boycott of bus services led by a young black minister named Martin Luther King Jr. His strategy of "nonviolent" action spread to other cities in the South. In February 1960, four students from a black college sat down at a "white" lunch counter in Greensboro, North Carolina. Over the next year, 70,000 students staged "sit-ins" throughout the South; "freedom riders" traveled from city to city trying to integrate public places and register voters. Thousands were arrested.

There was no question in the 1960s that the standard of living of American blacks had risen: their schools were better, their job opportunities greater; they lived longer; fewer of their babies died at birth.[43] There were black letter carriers, black police officers, black army officers. Most blacks were attending high school. Black earning power had increased rapidly.[44]

But a hundred years after the Emancipation Proclamation, no step seemed to come without violence or the threat of it.

Taking to the Streets, Again

The most historic showdown between black and white America took place in 1963 in one of the South's most notorious centers of racism—Birmingham, Alabama. King and his people virtually scripted the battle, and city officials, especially the police commissioner Eugene "Bull" Connor, played their parts, sicking dogs on demonstrators, many of them children, and blasting them with high-pressure fire hoses. Arrested and denounced as an outside agitator by white Catholic, Protestant, and Jewish religious leaders, King responded with his brilliant "Letter from a Birmingham Jail" in which the thirty-five-year-old minister, citing St. Paul and Socrates, conceded that his

actions sought "to create a crisis"—that freedom "must be demanded by the oppressed."

In June, President Kennedy federalized the Alabama National Guard to escort two black students into the University of Alabama, despite the opposition of Governor George Wallace. That evening Kennedy went on television to declare that the nation faced a "moral crisis," that America could not say "that this is the land of the free, except for the Negroes . . . that we have no ghettos, no master race, except with respect to Negroes."[45] The President called for legislation and lawsuits to end segregation and protect the right of black Americans to vote.

Four hours later, as his family awaited his arrival to discuss the President's speech, Medgar Evers, a Mississippi NAACP official, was murdered in his front yard. On the day of Evers's burial, Kennedy sent his civil rights bill to Congress; it gave the attorney general the power to sue to force the nation to obey the Fourteenth and Fifteenth Amendments. The protests continued, culminating in the August March on Washington where Martin Luther King Jr., in front of the Lincoln Memorial, eloquently declared his "dream" of black equality in the United States where children would no longer be judged by the color of their skin, but by "the content of their character."

Civil rights activists turned up the pressure on Congress, and after John Kennedy was assassinated in November, his successor, Lyndon B. Johnson, pressed Congress to pass the Civil Rights Act of 1964, which banned discrimination in public places, the workplace, privately run establishments like lunch counters, and the voting booth.

Southern states sued and lost. In a series of cases, the Supreme Court declared discrimination unconstitutional in schools, hotels, motels, and other public accommodations, including eating establishments.[46] Over the next three years, the Johnson administration pressed Congress to act against discrimination in buying and renting houses and apartments.

"The Firebell in the Night"

While many well-intentioned Americans were patting themselves on the back for what they were doing for their black fellow citizens, it was all relative. And by the only comparison blacks had—namely, with whites—they fell hopelessly short. "The firebell in the night" that Jefferson had feared began to ring.

In the summer of 1964 racial anger exploded in Harlem, then Brooklyn, Philadelphia, Rochester, and Dixmoor, a suburb of Chicago. In December, Martin Luther King Jr. was awarded the Nobel Peace Prize. President Johnson pushed ahead with his plans for a War on Poverty.

Black activists were not about to let up, though. In the midst of a voter registration drive in Selma, Alabama, in 1965, Martin Luther King Jr. led a march from Selma to Montgomery to protest the killing of a civil rights worker in Marion. As King and six hundred marchers crossed the Pettus Bridge east of Selma—with television cameras looking on—two hundred state police and sheriff's deputies threw tear gas at them and then attacked the demonstrators with billy clubs and whips.

That same day millions of Americans, including President Johnson, watched the film of the attack on TV in horror. Before the month was out, Johnson went before Congress and in an emotional speech declared that Selma was a historical "turning point in man's unending search for freedom," like the Battles of Concord and Lexington and the South's surrender at Appomattox. The black struggle was every American's struggle because, said Johnson, "it's all of us who must overcome the crippling legacy of bigotry and injustice." Johnson urged that Congress assure blacks the right to vote. The result was the Voting Rights Act of 1965, which suspended the use of "literacy tests" and provided a federal mechanism for voter registration. At a speech at Howard University, President Johnson referred to the continuing poverty of most American blacks as "this American failure." He pointed out that "you do not take a person who, for years, has been hobbled by chains and liberate him, bring him up to the starting line of a race and then say, 'You are free to compete . . .' and still justly believe that you have been completely fair."[47]

In August 1965, in response to police brutality, a riot broke out in the Watts section of Los Angeles. The following summer, national guardsmen and police put down rebellions in Omaha, Chicago, Dayton, Cleveland, Brooklyn, Jacksonville, Philadelphia, Atlanta, and scores of smaller cities. In the "long, hot summer" of 1967, the rage accelerated in uprisings in the black communities of Newark (23 dead, 1,500 wounded) and Detroit (43 dead, 2,000 wounded), which lasted for a week. After examining the causes of the riots, a presidential commission concluded that the nation was "moving toward two societies, one black, one white—separate and unequal." The eleven-member commission concluded that the "explosive mixture" of poverty, dis-

crimination and resentment in the black community was the result of "white racism."[48]

On April 4, 1968, Martin Luther King Jr., thirty-nine, was assassinated in Memphis, Tennessee. More cities went up in flames.

The Fight for Equal Education Continues

In 1968, after fourteen years of concerted efforts on the part of the South to sidestep *Brown,* the Supreme Court declared that school districts were obliged to come up with realistic plans to create *not,* as Justice Brennan forcefully put it, "a 'white' school and a 'negro' school, but just schools."[49] In 1969 the Court overruled a lower court decision that allowed Mississippi to delay the integration of thirty-three school districts, declaring the *Brown* standard of "all deliberate speed" no longer "constitutionally permissible" and ordered desegregation "at once."

Busing would be necessary.[50] White families fled to the suburbs or enrolled their children in private schools.[51] Even supporters of integration began to wonder whether efforts to achieve educational equality for America's blacks had not gone too far—that is, to the point where the law had created "reverse discrimination" against *white* students.

The Battle over "Affirmative Action"

In 1978 the Supreme Court decided that a university may consider racial criteria as part of a competitive admissions process as long as "fixed quotas" were not used. Allan Bakke, an applicant to medical school at the University of California at Davis, charged that he had been rejected twice even though his qualifications were superior to those of most of the sixteen minority students—in violation of Title VII of the 1964 Civil Rights Act and the equal protection clause of the Fourteenth Amendment.[52]

The outcome confirmed that the Court itself was as severely divided about affirmative action as most Americans. Six of the nine justices filed separate opinions. Four decided that affirmative action programs violated neither the civil rights law nor the Fourteenth Amendment, and therefore Bakke should not be admitted to the medical school; four other justices said that the law permitted *no* racial discrimination, and that the school had rejected Bakke only because he was white. He should be admitted to the U.C. Davis Medical School. The ninth justice, casting the deciding vote, agreed that racial considerations were permissible, but that quotas were not.

Bakke went to medical school *and* affirmative action continued. The debate shifted to the workplace, where the Court seemed no less confused about how to proceed, ruling in 1979 that Title VII did not prevent race-conscious affirmative action plans.[53] In dissent, Justice William Rehnquist attacked his colleagues for interpreting that the words of Title VII—no racial discrimination—to mean exactly the opposite, that discrimination against whites, at least, was legal.

It was a conundrum that remained at the center of affirmative action cases throughout the 1980s. In one case the Court would tilt in favor of "reverse discrimination," arguing that evidence of "prior discrimination" was not necessary; then, in another case, it would tilt back, arguing that such evidence was necessary.[54] The Court decided that public funds for local and federal works projects could be set aside for black businesses. Yet the Court upheld seniority systems in the workplace when affirmative action plans threatened to promote black workers over whites with more experience. The Court seemed to oppose preferential hiring in some cases and support it in others where there was no evidence of prior discrimination.[55]

While the Court seemed flummoxed, the position of the Reagan administration was firm: affirmative action was, in the words of Attorney General Edwin Meese, "nothing short of a legal and constitutional tragedy."[56] But in 1987, in *Johnson* v. *Santa Clara County Transportation Agency,* the Court seemed to confirm its support of reverse discrimination by ruling, 6 to 3, that to remedy a statistical imbalance of women in its workforce, a public employer could set up an affirmative action plan without showing prior discrimination and still not violate Title VII of the Civil Rights Act.[57]

Opponents of the decision saw it as a clear example of "quotas"—that is, to mirror the racial and sexual composition of a community, employers would hire the same ratio of blacks and women, regardless of their ability. Public employers would have to widen their hiring, and for the first time the Court declared women, not just blacks, eligible for affirmative action. In its next two affirmative action cases, however, the Court soon took a swing *away,* deciding that evidence of "prior discrimination" was necessary.[58]

How to achieve color and gender blindness without discriminating against someone remained confounding. Nevertheless, thanks to affirmative action, the United States suddenly had a growing *black* middle class.[59]

The Increased Significance of Race

For most of American history, relations between black and white Americans have been based on race and racism. Racial oppression was deliberate, often institutional or legal, and impossible to deny. But, according to William Julius Wilson, the distinguished black sociologist at the University of Chicago, during the 1960s and 1970s the civil rights revolution waged in the courts and Congress helped create a growing black middle class. The "significance of race" declined; racial inequality became "class inequality."[60] New high-tech jobs in the cities required a highly educated workforce. Poor, badly educated urban blacks found themselves stuck in an "underclass," while well-educated middle-class blacks experienced unprecedented job opportunities. Affirmative action programs, Wilson pointed out, did not help the black underclass. It was the economy—and not racial discrimination—that came to play an increasingly dominant role in black-white relations.

Yet, as persuasive as Wilson's thesis seemed when it was published in 1978, racism would hardly appear so insignificant during the twelve years of Republican administrations beginning in 1980. Since Franklin Roosevelt's New Deal, the Democratic Party had created a political majority by funneling tax revenues to the poor, the working class, and the lower middle class. In the 1960s and 1970s, minorities—first blacks, then women, and later homosexuals and the disabled—fought for political recognition and found it in the Democratic Party.

Millions of Americans—generally *white* ethnic (and Catholic) Americans in the North and white lower-income Southerners—unable to live with this coalition, deserted the Democratic Party of Roosevelt, Kennedy, and Lyndon Johnson for the Republicans. What appealed to these "Reagan Democrats"—and turned them against Jimmy Carter, Walter Mondale, and Michael Dukakis—was the GOP cry of "no new taxes" and their all-out attack on the "tax and spend" policies of previous Democratic administrations which they thought favored black Americans at their expense. While President Johnson had eloquently stated that justice for black Americans was the responsibility of all

Americans, the Reagan Democrats believed that the nation had done enough for blacks; they particularly resented the "reverse discrimination" of federal affirmative action programs. Deftly exploiting this new wave of anti-black sentiment among traditional Democrats, the Republicans persuaded working-class Americans that solidarity was not with the black poor and working-classes, but with the well-to-do. Civil rights advocates saw the GOP's opposition to "busing," "quotas," "entitlements," "welfare queens," and "new taxes" and its support for "law and order" as code words for racism. Indeed, by dividing the nation on the basis of who supported more taxes and rights for minorities, GOP leaders gave racism a new legitimacy. The electorate bought it. For many, the Democrats became the party of the blacks; the Democrats seemed stymied, and the Republicans won the next three presidential elections. Reaganites bubbled over with talk of "trickle-down economics"—that as the rich got richer, their wealth would flow into the economy to help everyone. In fact, once the Congressional Budget Office tallied the effects of the "Greedy 1980s," it turned out that the top one percent of American families had pocketed 60 percent of the nation's economic gains. And while some Americans got richer than their wildest dreams, unemployment had skyrocketed, particularly among young black men.

In 1985, 31 percent of black families still lived below the federal poverty line. Only 11 percent of white families were stuck in poverty. The income of an American black in 1984 was only 57 percent of the nation's whites—the same relative position that blacks held in 1971.[61] Meantime, chances to escape poverty seemed to vanish. One crippling factor: in 1984, 75 percent of poor black children were living in a family headed by a woman. Just as typically, the black middle-class family featured two parents. Black college graduates did fine, while the earning power of their contemporaries with only a high school education fell between 1969 and 1984.

"Black conservatives" advised the poor not to depend on affirmative action. Black self-respect and salvation, the argument went, depended on black people helping themselves.

But is poverty the responsibility of *only* the poor? What is the community's responsibility? What do we owe the poor?

AGAINST

All Racial Preferences Are Evil: The Reagan Administration

You cannot wipe out injustice with another injustice. Affirmative action is reverse discrimination. Deciding anything on the basis of race risks taking us back to the days of "separate but equal," the very thing that the civil rights movement thankfully destroyed. The only criterion for selection should be "race neutral." Race consciousness will create "a racial spoils system in America," "stifle the creative spirit, and divide society rather than . . . bring blacks and whites together in racial harmony."[62]

Whenever we take race into account, we discriminate and "destroy the sense of self."[63] According to the U.S. Constitution, every citizen shall be entitled to equal protection of the law. "Equal means equal. Equal does not mean you have separate lists of blacks and whites for promotion, any more than you have separate accommodations for blacks and whites for eating."[64] Affirmative action policies are simply another form of racism. "There is no such thing as good racial discrimination." It is not all right to treat people of different races differently. "We had to construct tortuous rationalizations when we permitted blacks to be kept on the back of the bus—and the rationalizations to justify sending blacks to the head of the line have been just as tortuous"[65]—as many black intellectuals now realize.

"Equal Opportunity," Good; "Affirmative Action," Bad: Thomas Sowell

The "Civil Rights Vision" has been perverted, from "equal opportunity" to "affirmative action," from giving blacks an equal chance to getting an equal number of blacks—from reality to rhetoric. The historic 1954 Brown v. Board of Education Supreme Court decision that integrated American schools aimed to close the door on a morally ugly chapter of American history; instead it set off a revolution—a "Civil Rights Revolution"—that has gone in a direction that few predicted, the wrong direction.

The concept of "equal rights" is now applied not only to blacks but also to women, Asians, Hispanics, and American Indians. According to one estimate, *70 percent* of the population of the United States is entitled to preferential treatment under affirmative action policies. The civil rights vision is based on three major—and debatable—premises:

(1) Statistical disparities in incomes, occupations, education, etc. represent moral inequities, and are caused by "society."[66]

(2) Belief in innate inferiority explains why there are policies that treat blacks differently.

(3) Political activism is the key to improving the lives of the disadvantaged blacks.

However, large statistical disparities between groups exist *without* discrimination. Certain groups of Americans watch one television program rather than another, marry at a younger age than others, and hit more home runs in major league baseball games (blacks) than others (whites and Latinos). Discrimination has nothing to do with these results.

In the civil rights vision "the relationship between discrimination and economic, educational, and other disadvantages is taken as virtually axiomatic."[67] But throughout history ethnic groups with higher incomes and better education have been discriminated against (the Jews in Europe and America and the Chinese minority in Malaysia, Indonesia, Vietnam, Thailand, and the Philippines). Discrimination does not necessarily lead to poverty, and social and economic disadvantages do not imply discrimination.

Some differences are clearly due to cultural factors that can go back for centuries: traditionally, the Chinese have had a reputation as hard workers, Irish Americans have had a rate of alcoholism fifty times higher than that of Jews, and Germans have distinguished themselves in family farming and industrial technology. Group patterns are not necessarily stereotypes.

Nor is political activism the most effective route to economic equality. The Chinese in Southeast Asia rose from poverty, though they stayed away from politics; the same is true for Germans in Brazil, Australia, and the United States. "Jews were for centuries kept out of political rule in a number of countries, either by law, by custom, or by anti-semitic feelings in the elite or the populace."[68] South African Jews by and large opposed the racial policies of the Afrikaner government with little effect on their traditional economic prosperity. The Irish, however, were politically successful quite quickly in the United States, but their economic progress came later.

Virtually from the beginning of the civil rights revolution the goal of the Kennedy and Johnson administrations to wipe out racial discrimination by mandating "equal opportunity" *without* regard to race, sex, age, religion, etc. turned into selecting people precisely on such grounds. "Statistical parity" replaced a fair chance at getting a job. Equal opportunity requires that people be judged on the basis of their qualifications as individuals, regardless of race, sex, and such, whereas "affirmative action requires that they be judged *with regard* to such group membership, receiving preferential or compensatory treatment. . . ."[69]

In the debates preceding the passage of the Civil Rights Act of 1964, "Congress declared itself in favor of equal opportunity and opposed to affirmative action." Senator Hubert Humphrey, the legendary civil rights advocate, assured the Senate that the bill "does not require an employer to achieve any kind of racial balance in his work force by giving preferential treatment to any individual or group."[70] Congress was against "quotas," and so are the American people, including, according to some polls, most blacks and women.

Helping the shift from guarding rights to enforced quotas were LBJ's 1968 guidelines, which mentioned "representation" and "goals and timetable"—albeit for "prompt achievement of full and equal employment opportunity." But by 1970, new guidelines mentioned "results-oriented procedures." Before long the burden of proof was on the employer to show he was trying harder, and number totals of blacks or women were the easiest proof.[71]

But inequality is not necessarily the result of unequal opportunity. "Groups differ by large amounts demographically, culturally, and geographically—and all these differences have profound effects on incomes and occupations."[72] Asian-American students are more inclined to study mathematics, no matter their economic status, so it is hardly surprising that black, Mexican-American, and American Indian youngsters from families with incomes of $50,000 and up score lower than Asians from families whose incomes are just $6,000 and under.[73] "Cultural differences are real, and cannot be talked away by using pejorative terms such as 'stereotypes' or 'racism.' "[74]

Affirmative action cannot even be praised on the basis of its results, which have not been impressive. "The relative position of disadvantaged individuals within the groups singled out for preferential treatment has generally *declined* under affirmative action."[75] Of course, there are complex factors behind these numbers—the increase in fatherless families among the poor being the most significant—but the fact is that the results do not square with the civil rights vision. More significant is that life for the more advantaged got better and for the less advantaged worse. The incomes of two-parent black families rose faster in the 1970s than the incomes of white families. Well-educated and experienced black workers succeeded, while those without education sank.

Affirmative action did help blacks—those who needed the help the least. And the continued poverty and unemployment of poor blacks has very little to do with racism or discrimination.

Affirmative Action Hurts More Than Helps Blacks: Shelby Steele

"Affirmative action has shown itself to be more bad than good and that blacks . . . now stand to lose more from it than they gain."[76] The practice of giving blacks a more equal shot, after centuries of racism and discrimination, turned into a kind of "social engineering by means of quotas, goals, timetables, set-asides and other forms of preferential treatment."[77] What was a well-intentioned effort to do better soon began to distort our understanding of racial discrimination by giving preference based on color and not injury. The unfortunate result: the very thing we sought to wipe out—*discrimination* against blacks—has created a reverse discrimination—against whites.

An *equal* number of black employees does not mean that blacks are equal to whites on the job. We cannot expect an oppressed people to leap to the top in one try. They must first have the preparation that will allow them to achieve proportional representation on their own. Nor is "diversity"—the holy grail of the affirmative activists—the same thing as proportional representation. Too often the appearance of diversity masks disparity. Not enough of those black faces on campus are graduating. (Six years after admission, only about 26 percent of black students graduate from college.)[78]

Affirmative action implies inferiority, a lack of preparation that is due to a history of oppression and deprivation, to be sure, but still a kind of inferiority that feeds the self-doubt of blacks—and the racism of whites—in integrated job situations. The vicious circle is complete: whites are inclined to believe that blacks can never measure up, and the nagging suspicion among black workers that their white colleagues might be right is likely to impede the black worker's performance.

"Preferential treatment, no matter how it is justified in the light of day, subjects blacks to a midnight of self-doubt, and so often transforms their advantage into a revolving door."[79] Preference merely on the basis of color also creates the "illusion" that society owes you that job or place in the freshman class at Harvard. "Blacks cannot be repaid for the injustice done to the race, but we can be corrupted by society's guilty gestures of repayment."

Preferential treatment is bound to create a sense of *dependence* among blacks when what they really need is self-reliance. Affirmative action breeds two wrongs: allowing whites to feel superior and "stigmatizing the already stigmatized."[80] Talented black employees on their way to the top often run into the "glass ceiling"—reinforced by the suspicion of top management that black executives are not really up to the job.

The trouble with affirmative action is that "it tries to function like a social program." Devised to create "equal opportunity," it is now expected to establish racial parity—and a demand for black executives and students that far exceeds the qualifications of the pool. And while there might be social programs that can help young African-Americans to become better educated, increase their skills, and develop their motivation, affirmative action is not the ticket.

Equal opportunity ought to be the focus of government action, not "entitlement." To be skeptical about the benefits of affirmative action is not to approve of discrimination, an impulse that the American legal system has yet to wipe out. Discrimination is the evil. "Preferences only sidestep the evil and grant entitlement to its *presumed* victims."[81]

Forgetting the Real Victims of Racism: William Julius Wilson

The struggle of African-Americans is not, finally, about who goes to Harvard or Yale or who makes partner at a Wall Street law or investment banking firm. Well-educated middle-class blacks do not have any problem getting into the best colleges, corporations, or firms; in fact, they are likely to be the focus of bidding wars. The real problem with affirmative action is that it ignores the real victims of racism and discrimination—"the millions of struggling black Americans for whom affirmative action and entry into the professions are stunningly irrelevant"—the truly disadvantaged, the underclass.[82]

Fewer blacks are attending college and more are going to jail than a decade ago—despite affirmative action. Instead of trying to justify affirmative action to whites—and to ourselves—blacks should concentrate on the problems of people "outside the mainstream of the American occupational system."[83]

What is the alternative? It is "race-blind" policies to better the educational and economic development of the poor. On-the-job training is key. Blacks must also take responsibility for their own advancement.

"Affirmative Action Babies" in Dissent: Stephen Carter

The moment for affirmative action has passed. No matter how well intentioned preferential treatment is, it has become an embarrassment and insult to competent blacks, a potential confirmation of white racism, and, worse, a threat to black solidarity: the debate over the pros and cons of affirmative action in the black community serves only to divide the black middle class and intellectuals, diverting them from helping African-Americans progress in American society in the face of the inevitable obstacles of racism and discrimination.[84]

African-Americans who have benefited from policies of preferential treatment in education and employment—"the affirmative action babies"—would prefer a level playing field. Uncomfortable and exhausted by living with the resentment of fellow employees that they are not good enough or the self-doubt that maybe their colleagues are right, successful blacks would prefer to be judged *not* on the color of their skin but on their merits—according to the same standards used for everyone else. These standards should be explicit. And even if such standards are far from objective, sneak in cultural bias, or are racist, "we should aim to meet and beat them anyway."

"To rise to the pinnacle of professional success, a black person must function in an integrated world, but to do so is no more a betrayal of one's birthright than it is for white people to do the same thing."[85] The professional world is competitive. The market sets your worth. If you do the job, you'll succeed is the belief that all professionals, white and black, need to advance. As long as racial preferences exist, blacks will not know how competent or excellent they really are. Nor will the assurances of our white colleagues or bosses—"You're here on merit"—suffice. The current backlash among black professionals and the black middle class is a signal that preferential treatment, in its most extreme forms, has run its course. That is not to say that blacks do not want opportunities that they never had before or the preparation to compete; but what they want most is the ability to prove what they can do. African-Americans want to show that we can meet the standards of American life, the same standards that white people must meet.

For members of the black middle class, racism is receding.[86] *For members of the black middle class.* From the perspective of the "bottom of the well," that is not the case; for the poorest and most disadvantaged of blacks, racism is a fact of daily life, and a major, if not insurmountable, obstacle into the black middle class. Middle-class blacks and intellectuals have a right to dissent from the commitment of the traditional black leadership to affirmative action. Yes, we are beneficiaries of affirmative action; but preferential policies began as a *transitional* means to push black people up the ladder, to get them into positions of power. Now that we are there, now that we proved that blacks can compete, we would like to continue to test ourselves without any system of handicapping.

"Standards of excellence are a requisite of civilization." We were not defeated by slavery or Jim Crow, and the end of affirmative action will hardly be our end. Before affirmative action, blacks had proved they could be successful in virtually every field. We were going to college, we were making inroads in employment, we were creating a growing middle class. Ironically, with the law on our side, fewer blacks are graduating from college and the main growth in black economic life is in poverty. We could not do much worse without affirmative action, and we might just do better.

It is time for a new phase in the strategy of African-Americans to advance. We can either wait for white people to help us or help ourselves. And that includes the poorest among us. We successful members of the black middle class cannot turn away from the poorest members of our community. We cannot retreat into our individual success stories. If we want to prove that we have really made it on our own, we will also have to prove that we are leaders with some ideas—a vision—of the future of American society, black and white.

IN FAVOR

Preferential Treatment of Blacks Has a Historical Precedent[87]

Far from being against the principles of the Constitution, racial preference in the United States is as old as American efforts to recover from slavery. Less than a month after the U.S. Congress adopted the Fourteenth Amendment (and its famous "equal protection" clause) in 1866, Congress enacted eight laws granting preferences in land, education, banking, hospitals, and other areas to free slaves. "No comparable problems existed or were established for whites."[88] Opponents of the legislation, led by President Andrew Johnson, argued that such preference discriminated against whites.

Affirmative Action Is Just Compensation: Gertrude Ezorsky

"The paramount injustice against blacks"—enslavement—requires compensation. Blacks have a "moral claim" against society for past injury whose results are with us today.

> If the effects of that murderous institution had been dissipated over time, the claim to compensation now would certainly be weaker. From the post-Reconstruction period to the present, however, racist practices have continued to transmit and reinforce the consequences of slavery. Today blacks still predominate in those occupations that in a slave society would be reserved for slaves.[89]

For two thirds of the twentieth century, racism was virtually public policy. Government racism has encouraged racial discrimination at every level of society: in employment, schools, municipal services, in the courts, and among policemen who have treated black people brutally on the streets and under arrest. Residential segregation persists; even well-off blacks still find it difficult to get mortgages. Inner-city schools are a scandal and help ensure the vicious cycle of black poverty. Black workers, the "last hired," often only because of affirmative action guidelines, tend to be the first fired when the economy goes sour. As a result, even recent arrivals to the black middle class, without inherited nest eggs or an accumulation of assets, are "two paychecks away from poverty."

Is preferential treatment a just compensation? The U.S. and state governments have been giving veterans job preference for decades, long before federal affirmative action programs. In some states, where veteran preferences are widespread, nonveterans have little chance at the best positions.[90]

"Suffering can be endured and overcome, it cannot be repaid," argues Shelby Steele. Then withhold compensation from veterans and victims of industrial actions. What about Holocaust survivors? Since the 1950s cash compensation from Germany to Israel for survivors of Hitler's horrors—about $400 million a year—has helped keep the Jewish state solvent. No one suggested that payment would, as Steele has argued, "prolong the suffering."[91]

It is a curious argument against affirmative action that the people benefiting from the jobs will feel uncomfortable about getting preference or lose self-esteem. Blacks are refused jobs because they are too weak, but when they come back fighting, they are turned down because they are too strong. That is demeaning and enraging.[92]

Nor is it true that affluent blacks do not deserve preferential treatment.[93] Every black doctor, lawyer, and college professor can tell a story about being refused admittance to a posh store or steered off course by real estate agents or being hassled by the police or getting the runaround on a job.[94] While middle-class blacks may have suffered *less* discrimination than other blacks that does not mean they deserve no compensation. How many veterans pushed to the top of civil service lists served in noncombat roles? And unlike compensating veterans, giving blacks preference for past injustice "contributes to eradication of a future evil"—continued racism and racial discrimination, legacies of slavery.[95]

WHAT ABOUT THE EMPLOYER'S RIGHT TO HIRE WHOM HE WANTS?

"If the woman who later became my wife rejected another suitor . . ." for me, the Harvard philosopher Robert Nozick has argued, ". . . would the rejected less intelligent and less handsome suitor have a legitimate complaint about unfairness . . .? . . . (Against whom . . .? Against what?)"[96] When everyone has a right to things, one person's rights will clash with another's. Blacks have a right to more jobs; private entrepreneurs or corporations have the right to hire whom they think will do the best job. Whose right takes precedence? The American "libertarian" believes that we all have a right to go our own way without government interference.

But a person's right to share his or her life with someone else is a personal choice quite different from a corporation's practices. Companies are incorporated by a state—indeed, in the nation's infancy incorporation was a very selective process—and government has a right to make sure that companies are not abusing their employees or the law or public morality. Few Americans would concede that corporations have the right to pay their workers what they wish and work them as long as they would like. To the same extent, employers do not have the right to ignore qualified black candidates for jobs.[97]

The decent employer might be trusted not to exploit his employees and to fill jobs no matter the candidate's skin color, but what one of us has not met the businessman who, in order to maximize his profit, would try to keep his mother's paycheck as low as possible?

AS FOR THOSE WHITE "VICTIMS OF DISCRIMINATION" . . .

That generations of white Americans have benefited from institutional and overt racism (and sexism) in employment, housing, and education is undeniable. Yet, whites, too, have been hurt by racism. Corporate threats to find workers eager to work for lower pay have been a traditional negotiating ploy with dissatisfied workers. Over the past twenty years scores of businesses (and thousands of jobs) have moved to the South to take advantage of lower wages. The threat of hiring black workers has also, historically, been a successful ploy in keeping unions out of plants in the South.

Affirmative action is bound to hurt white workers, and some of them unfairly. They, too, should be compensated beyond unemployment insurance, as the courts have concluded in cases of civil service workers forced to forfeit their seniority because of affirmative action programs. Where should the money come from? One possibility would be "a federal progressive tax" that would distribute the cost of affirmative action throughout society equitably. Such tax money could also be used to pay for the transportation of workers from the inner city to the suburbs.

Whites who can prove that they have been passed over for a less qualified black candidate should also be compensated. How to determine the victims in such cases will be much more difficult than in cases of seniority. Companies often promote people who are not always the "best candidate"—that is, the best qualified in terms of skill or experience. Too many other factors enter into personnel decisions—personality, friendship, favoritism, luck, even nastiness (i.e., an executive recommends an enemy for a job in which he is sure to fail). Unless the qualifications for a particular job are clearly objective—an advanced degree, a special test, a blind review (orchestras now often audition musicians behind a curtain so that they will be judged only on their musical ability)—it will be difficult to prove who is the "best qualified." In certain jobs the candidate's personality could be more important than experience or education (e.g., public relations).

There is also the danger that overqualified whites might apply for jobs that they hope will be given to less (though perfectly) qualified blacks so that they can apply for compensation. A limit should be placed on the number of times an aggrieved white can receive this.

Ironically, affirmative action has often benefited whites just as much as blacks. In the famous *Weber* case, where a white worker sued because a position he wanted went to a less qualified black employee, it was revealed that the company had established a craft training program for whites (which they had been demanding for years) only after the company felt it had to institute an affirmative action program. The Bell Telephone Company instituted goals and timetables for women and blacks without any trouble. And race-conscious employment has worked in urban police and fire departments.[98]

Affirmative Action Is "Socially Useful": Ronald Dworkin[99]

"American society is over-all a racially conscious society." One effective way of canceling out the factor of race is to increase the presence of blacks in powerful professions such as medicine and the law. The most efficient way to achieve that desirable social goal is affirmative action admissions policies for professional schools.

Preferential treatment is justified not because it compensates blacks for past injuries or because they are entitled to special treatment, but simply because "helping them is now an effective way of attacking a national problem."[100]

The argument that preferential treatment violates the rights of white candidates is "a piece of intellectual confusion." In the past when blacks were excluded because of their race, it was because of sheer prejudice or racism. This is not true of the whites put at a disadvantage by affirmative action, which treats race as another criterion, not unlike the process by which a school selects someone who has particular test scores, lives in a certain part of the country, or is good at basketball. A person's race, of course, is not in his control, but neither is his intelligence or his natural athletic ability.

Nor does selecting a black candidate with lower test scores than those of some whites violate an applicant's right to be judged on merit. "Merit" is hardly an abstract concept that exists outside what a particular institution decides are the qualities that best serve its purposes. Intelligence is definitely a prime quality for doctors and lawyers, but it is by no means the only relevant criterion. "If quick hands count as 'merit' in the case of a prospective surgeon, this is because quick hands will enable him to serve the public better and for no other reason. If a black skin will, as a matter of regrettable fact, enable another doctor to do a different medical job better (e.g., minister to an urban ghetto population), then black skin ought to be taken as 'merit' as well."[101]

And while some may find it a dangerous precedent to count race as a form of merit, it is so "only because they confuse its conclusion—that black skin may be a socially useful trait in particular circumstances—with the very different and despicable idea that one race may be inherently more worthy than another." Whites will indeed be excluded for no other reason than they are white; nevertheless, this is permissible because it is not motivated by prejudice but by a "rational calculation about the socially most beneficial use of limited resources."[102]

Affirmative action serves the goal of society. And while no social goal, no matter how worthy, is justified if it violates another's rights, preferential policies do not do this. Race becomes one criterion among many, and "merit" depends on what an institution or society concludes is worthwhile.

Is America a Meritocracy or Not?

Not. Some critics of affirmative action have argued that true justice in the workplace is about hiring the most qualified people for a particular job. Intuitively, it does seem that the best people ought to get the best jobs—and not the "best blacks" or any black, regardless of how much discrimination black people might have suffered in the past. It also seems that if one is eager to be "race neutral," an "objective" standard for selection is required, and that "competence" is a natural candidate for such a standard. Some would even argue that "competence" is the most widely accepted criterion for hiring, and if a black worker is hired over a more competent white worker, it would be an act of reverse discrimination against the white, and thus an example of one injustice used to wipe out another.[103]

But the assumption that "competence" is a widespread standard does not square with the facts of business life. As anyone who has worked almost anyplace has noticed, it is not always the most qualified person who gets the job or the promotion. By and large, American employers still have the right to hire whomever they want, and "best qualified" is open to extraordinary qualification. One boss's idea of competence (ten years of experience) does not necessarily match another's (great golfer whom clients will love).

In many states, veterans get preference in civil service jobs, clearly beating out many better qualified nonveterans. Promotions, training, or layoffs based on seniority, by definition, ignore the concept of "merit." And universities and colleges have always accepted students who might be less academically qualified because of other desirable qualities (i.e., they can throw a football or play the violin, are an alumni son, have a famous or very rich father). "It's not what you know, it's who you know" may be a cliché about the frustrations (or joys) of job hunting, but it is a constant variable of employment decisions the world over.

Anyone who argues that "competence" ought to be the standard for employment will have to fight a battle not just against affirmative action but against preference for veterans, seniority rules, and hiring friends, relatives, and political supporters. "Merit" is a noble goal, but one that will be pursued in the face of some of the nation's most "traditional values."

In fact, one might argue that the way people are employed in this country is demonstrably unjust and that affirmative action is a reasonable way to give black people the kind of shot at success that whites have had since the first owner of a business put his idiot son in charge.

"JUSTICE AS FAIRNESS": JOHN RAWLS

Though many people think that the well-off among us deserve their wonderful lives, "this view is surely incorrect." No one *deserves* to be born rich any more than he *deserves* to be born smart. Nor does anyone *deserve* the "superior character" that enables him to work hard or succeed or get rich; nor does he *deserve* the riches he gains as a result of his character. "For his character depends in large part upon fortunate family and social circumstances for which he can claim no credit."[104]

No one can "deserve" anything because no one really possesses the assets that they claim to deserve: good looks, good birth, vast riches, great job. All are the result of things not in anyone's control. Institutions define a person's moral worth. Once a person accomplishes what an institution has encouraged, he is entitled to any honor the institution has established as a reward for that achievement. He does not deserve that reward, but rather has a "legitimate expectation" that he get it. He is *entitled* to it. Individuals have no "intrinsic worth" apart from what just institutions attribute to them. One's values and deepest convictions are also accidental features of life and not integral factors of his person. "That we have one conception of the good rather than another is not relevant from a moral standpoint," for even our conception of the good is set by the same kinds of accidents and luck that drop us into one gender or class rather than another.[105]

Justice is not getting what you deserve. "Justice is fairness." It rewards neither virtue nor natural talents. Nor is its goal to bestow only equal opportunity where natural talents or the accident of birth might give someone an unfair advantage. Justice is simply providing everyone with the basic conditions to realize his or her goals. The most talented must accept restrictions on how much they will benefit from their natural advantages in order to help the least advantaged.

The justice of social institutions is measured by their effort to balance out the natural inequalities due to birth, talent, and luck. All such advantages become "common assets" of the community in service of the common good—individual and political liberty, economic and social advantages, and self-respect. Justice depends on two principles: the greatest equal liberty and no inequality—except to distribute economic and social gain to everyone, in particular the least advantaged. (Liberty, however, is never to be sacrificed for economic or social advantages unless they are so scarce or unequal that it will be impossible to practice equal liberty until the economic situation is improved.)

So no white person *deserves* a job or a place in a university more than any black person. The reason for this is not, as religious people usually argue, because every person, no matter his or her race, is intrinsically worthy and deserving. No one deserves anything or is more worthy than anyone else because no one can be said to have anything that is not an accident of history or birth and the consequences thereof. What we are justified in expecting or are entitled to is only what just institutions establish.

A PRACTICAL SOLUTION IN AN UNJUST WORLD: THOMAS NAGEL

"The greatest injustice in this society . . . is neither racial nor sexual but intellectual."[106] No one *deserves* his or her high intelligence, so why should a person in any sense *deserve* the rewards that go with being really smart?

Conflicts of justice are bound to arise. In the case of affirmative action the conflict is between job and educational opportunities and economic and social rewards. Without a chance at higher education or better jobs, blacks are bound to suffer continued economic and social inequality. Something has to give.

We run into an immediate problem in a highly competitive and high-tech society like ours, where intelligence and the skills that accompany it are more likely to be rewarded. That is the way it works, according to the existing standards of supply and demand. While smart people may deserve "richer educational opportunity," they do not deserve to get rich. (The same goes for great athletes and beauties.) Of course, they do get rich, and we are unlikely to reform the current distribution of rewards, no matter how unjust they might be.

In fact, there might be no completely just solution available without "large alterations in the social system, the system of taxation, and the salary structure."[107] This may be the most just route, but it is not one that can be achieved by fixing hiring or admissions policies. In these areas, affirmative action efforts can be judged on the grounds of justice only if they compensate for specific disadvantages caused by injustice. Not only are such cases difficult to verify, but they also probably vary among individuals in the oppressed group. Moreover, it is not even obvious that where justification for preferential treatment exists, a pluralistic society is obligated to counteract such injustice by adopting discriminatory measures against another group.

If blacks have been discriminated against, is it unjust to discriminate against whites? No, at least not "seriously unjust"—that is, in the same way that making lots of money because you are really smart is unjust but not "seriously" so. Discriminating against whites is not unjust in the same way as discriminating against blacks. Racial (or sexual) discrimination "has no social advantages, and attaches a sense of reduced worth to a feature with which people are born."[108] The personal and social results are insidious: if it is socially disadvantageous to be black, then young blacks, who have no choice in the matter, begin to regard their blackness as an essential characteristic, and, worse, one that reduces their self-esteem. Others, too, will view them as unworthy (and themselves as better).

Reverse discrimination will not necessarily hurt the self-esteem or social esteem of white people and might even have social advantages: if the health needs of the black community could not be met without an increase in black doctors, then preferential policies in medical schools for blacks would be required—and qualified whites would lose out to black candidates. Such reverse discrimination might be unjust, but it would be *socially useful*. Nor is the injustice to whites as "strong" as that which blacks have suffered: the self-esteem of white society is not endangered, and while the interests of individuals are being sacrificed for a social goal, "it is the better placed who are being sacrificed and the worst placed who are being helped."[109] (It is an important feature of this "social utility" that the social position of the favored group is "exceptionally depressed with destructive consequences both for the self-esteem of members of the group and for the health and cohesion of society." Not every ethnic or religious group is in a position to benefit from preferential treatment, nor are all groups fair game for reverse discrimination. Native Americans are not likely to suffer reverse discrimination as easily as whites.)

Affirmative action in education and employment adopted to lessen a "grave social evil" and favor a group in a "particularly unfortunate social position" is probably not unjust. Such a policy of preference will, however, have its costs: resentment among the better qualified, lower self-esteem among blacks who feel that they did not deserve the job, plus self-doubt or lower self-esteem among those passed over for the job. These costs will be unavoidable but they can be tolerated "only so long as they are clearly contributing to the eradication of great social evils."[110]

AFFIRMATIVE ACTION IS NOT RACIST; BETTER STILL, IT WORKS: DWORKIN

American blacks have been the victims of racism; they know what discrimination looks like—and sixteen places in medical school out of a hundred in *Bakke* or 10 percent of federal work contracts in *Fullilove* does not look like discrimination to them. How do you compare such middle-class career setbacks to centuries of slavery, decades of "separate but equal," and current residential segregation and acts of discrimination in every area of society?

American blacks resent the comparison between racism and the "reverse discrimination" of affirmative action.

Justice has its costs—and one of them is that some white males may have to suffer. Why is it that citizens willing to suffer even death in a "just war" are unwilling to lose a few jobs to black people in a war against racism, discrimination, and poverty?

Few Americans complained when after World War II and Korea veterans went immediately to the top of civil service lists. After all, they deserved it; they were being paid back for their courage and service in the war. (It is important to recall that not all "veterans" saw combat, but all who served got job preference.) Preferential treatment for blacks is just recompensation for their long and vivid past of undeniable oppression and discrimination. Black Americans look around them and they do not see racial equality.

All an honest person has to do is ask: "What would things be like now *without* affirmative action?"

AFFIRMATIVE ACTION HELPS ALL BLACKS: EZORSKY

Affirmative action programs have helped blacks from every social level, as one look at the increased number of black faces on police forces, in fire departments, and in civil service jobs proves. The 1965 executive order banning discrimination by government contractors and Title VII of the Equal Employment Opportunity Act and its amendments have generated thousands of jobs for blacks, according to several studies in the 1970s.

The court-ordered decrees to check job discrimination have also generated new jobs for blacks.[111] Another look at the Bureau of Labor Statistics chart on "Occupation and Industry Employment for Black Men and Women, 1939–1984" shows huge increases in manufacturing jobs for blacks.[112] In the late 1960s preferential policies led women in the South to get off the farm and go into the textile mills, tripling their wages.[113] Studies also show that among the increased numbers of minority students in medical school are students from low-income families.

Affirmative action has boosted tens of thousands of young African-Americans into the black middle class who might otherwise be stuck in dead-end jobs or on unemployment lines.[114]

What about the "the underclass"? It depends whom Professor Wilson means by those "outside the mainstream of the American occupational system." The unemployable, the untrainable, will not qualify for Wilson's expanded economic development and "race-blind" educational and employment programs. But also languishing in the underclass are black workers who were laid off because they were the last hired or who had low-level or mechanical jobs that vanished because of technological or economic change (e.g., manufacturing jobs leaving the city). In 1984, 52 percent of unemployed blacks had been displaced from jobs. Frustrated and angry, too, are the young people and welfare mothers who have given up.

Can affirmative action bring these people into "the mainstream"? If affirmative action cannot qualify untrained industrial workers for the new high-tech jobs, will race-blind economic expansion prepare them better? Most of the 15 million net jobs created in the 1980s are routine "service" jobs: restaurant workers, bank, retail and supermarket clerks, computer assemblers, health-care personnel, fast-food employees. Former manufacturing employees as well as black teenagers could learn to do those jobs—if they knew they were available and had the "connections" to get their foot in the door. Young blacks in highly segregated inner-city areas, as Wilson has pointed out, tend to lack the "social networks" to put them in contention for available jobs.[115]

"Minority outreach" would create a pipeline to these jobs. And while corporations and businesses are unlikely to set up offices in the inner city, buses and other forms of transportation can ferry ghetto residents to jobs in the suburbs. More vigilance is necessary to catch employers inflating the educational requirements for certain jobs. Company on-the-job training programs can make up for lack of preparation, and special screening and testing programs could find out which candidates without college diplomas might have "college-level" abilities or work habits.

Without a doubt, increased education will make it easier for blacks to get better jobs. But if there are no jobs, or blacks do not know about them, then education is not enough. Nor is education always sufficient even when the jobs are there. In the past, the rates of unemployment have been higher among college-educated blacks than among white high school dropouts.[116]

This is precisely the sort of injustice that affirmative action was designed to wipe out. Wilson is incorrect when he suggests that there is an either/or choice at hand—affirmative action *or* race-blind programs for economic development and full employment. Increased economic opportunities for blacks *and* government policies to make sure they can take advantage of these new openings are both necessary.

"The record shows that without enforcement of AA training goals blacks are often excluded from such opportunities."[117] When employers resort to "race-neutral seniority" for training and promotion, the result is usually lily-white employees—precisely the reason the Supreme Court in *Weber* upheld the constitutionality of affirmative action programs requiring preferential seniority selection for training.

Precedent proves that when construction companies are not legally bound to offer apprenticeships to young blacks, white-dominated unions will continue to hand these well-paying entry-level jobs to their friends and relatives. (White opponents of affirmative action seem to forget the age-old "preferential" programs that have kept the union door open to sons and nephews since the beginning of the trade union movement; it is only natural, but, of course, unfair to blacks unable to get their foot through the door for a shot at a better job.)

Consider this analogy:

> Before bus desegregation, blacks could occupy only a relatively small number of seats in the back of the bus; hence they often had to stand. If there were more buses, blacks would have gained more seats, but Wilson certainly would not have advocated building more buses as a substitute for racial justice. Let us then not conceive of expansion in the number of jobs as a substitute for racial justice in the workplace.[118]

It is important to keep government pressure on employers.

"BEYOND AFFIRMATIVE ACTION": CORNEL WEST[119]

"Progressives should view affirmative action as neither a major solution to poverty nor a sufficient means to equality. We should see it as primarily playing a negative role—namely, to ensure that discriminatory practices against women and people of color are abated."[120] Without affirmative action, "it is a virtual certainty" that discrimination would return—"with a vengeance"—and black access to prosperity and good jobs would be even more difficult to obtain. This is based not on cynicism about white people, but on "America's historically weak will toward racial justice and substantive redistributive measures. An attack on affirmative action is an attack on redistributive efforts."

Ideally, a society eager to stamp out poverty would institute an *economic redistribution* program. "If there were social democratic redistributive measures that wiped out black poverty, and if racial and sexual discrimination could be abated through the good will and meritorious judgments of those in power, affirmative action would be unnecessary."[121] The American people and their representatives have resisted sharing the wealth with the "have-nots" and the "have-too-littles." Whenever "visionary progressives" push for ways to redistribute wealth in the United States—federal support to small farmers, federal housing loans to city dwellers, etc.—they are forced to compromise. Affirmative action was that kind of compromise. Without it, blacks would have to depend only on the "good will and fair judgment among the powerful."

Black economic progress also requires black self-respect. "The flagrant self-loathing among black middle-class professionals bears witness to this painful process." But progressives, too, must realize that transforming the attitudes of black people toward their black identity is as crucial as changing the economic system. Otherwise the black bourgeoisie will remain pre-occupied with the approval of white and black nationalists obsessed with white racism.

Affirmative action may be a compromise, but it is a necessary one. Without it, life for American blacks would be a whole lot worse.

IN MY OPINION

In a 1993 Supreme Court case involving changing legislative districts along racial lines, the majority decision expressed a sense of frustration and essentially asked the question, "Can't we get beyond race?"[122]

It seems a good question, a kind question. But, finally, it is not because it ignores too much of American history. In a strong sense, race and racism is a part of the nation. Black people have been part of the American experience since before the *Mayflower*. The "American dilemma" has nagged the nation from infancy. "Africanism," as Toni Morrison, the Nobel Prize–winning novelist, has pointed out, "provided the staging ground and arena for the elaboration of the quintessential American identity." Before the Civil War, to be American was, in one sense, *not* to be a black slave. To understand the notion of "freedom" requires the possibility of slavery.[123] "The Negro Problem," as the philosopher Cornel West has noted, will remain a chronic American condition as long as the nation continues to treat blacks as something less than "the fellow-Americans" they are.

We do not seem to be able to understand race. The one sure way to get beyond race may be to focus on poverty. If the United States can not be color-blind, perhaps we can at least focus on poverty. Half the black children in our nation are poor. This is more than a terrifying statistic; it is a moral failure.

Precisely what can be done about poverty (how the welfare system can be reformed, or what alternative strategies the government might take to help the poor) is beyond the scope of this book. What is central to this book's concerns, though, is the widespread view among Americans, including politicians, that government *ought not* to be in the business of helping the poor—that the poor ought to help themselves. This is definitely a moral issue, one riddled with confusion about poverty and race and the community's obligations. At the center of this confusion are some myths that have dominated the conventional wisdom.

Myth #1   After three decades of civil rights advances, white Americans owe nothing to black Americans. It is now time for black people to help themselves.

White People Still Owe Plenty

Black American history is a history of injustice and to suggest that enough has been done in the past thirty-five years to offset what has been done in the past 350 is absurd and morally suspect.

Black people have difficulty getting loans and mortgages. Residential segregation is a major contributor to street crime, violence, and wretched schools. Black men and women even in the most humdrum jobs cope with not so repressed racial hatred daily. For years at the Miller Brewing Company plant in Fulton, New York, over the paging system, a disembodied voice summoned "Harold . . . the ape." Harold Thomas, a production supervisor in the packaging department, is black, and the racial slurs began to bother him so much that a psychiatrist advised him to take a leave. When Thomas returned to his job in 1991, a voice announced over the paging system: "Welcome back, Harold, but you're still a nigger." According to a racial harassment suit against Miller, which was unable to catch Thomas's tormentor, such racial remarks over the pager to black male and female employees had been a common irritant for a decade. Moreover, such incidents are, according to a recent *New York Times* report, "remarkably common in the American workplace—and may even be on the rise."[124]

Historically, black Americans have done well—when the American economy has done well. Of course, even the blacks who were working never did as well as whites. In 1947 the median incomes of blacks were 51 percent of whites. By 1974, after years of economic expansion and the advances of the civil rights revolution, the income of black families stood at 62 percent of what white families were taking in. By 2000, if the trends of black and white income levels between 1974 and 1986 continue, the median income of black families would be 54 percent of white families—*the same as it was in 1960.*

Myth #2   Poor people get what they deserve—and they certainly do not deserve to get preferential treatment. A less qualified black person does not deserve to be promoted. Affirmative action is fighting injustice with injustice.

America, a Meritocracy—for the Lucky and Well Connected

Before I go any further, let me make a confession: I, too, was an "affirmative action baby." I am not black, nor was I born poor. I was a working-class kid of some intelligence who applied to college in the early 1960s when the nation's elite schools were looking for "diversity" and "geographical distribution." Luckily (and I don't see it as much more than that), I had a combination of traits that made me seem "different": I was the son of a letter carrier, the first on both sides of my family to go to college, and a Catholic.

I could also hit the curveball. While critics are now inclined to view college sports as a way to exploit black athletes, it is important to remember that during most of this century the "athletic scholarship" was the easiest way for a poor white boy (until "affirmative action" policies for women in the 1970s, only boys counted) to enter a prestige college or university and thus rise from the working class.

"The Meritocratic Ideal" that Stephen Carter and other members of the black bourgeoisie so revere does not exist, as John Rawls, Thomas Nagel, and Ronald Dworkin have eloquently pointed out. The fact is, hardly anyone in this world "makes it on his own merits."

Among affluent whites, the traditional route to success was the family business, the Ivy League, the "old boy network," and other lucky connections. Nor is "networking" limited to the Ivy League set. In the Massachusetts working-class white community I grew up in, the "good jobs" usually depended on "who you knew." If you had a relative in the local of the Bricklayers International, you had a shot at a good-paying job as a "brickie." Your uncle's a plumber or electrician or construction worker? No problem, you had an entree into those unions. Your brother-in-law on the city council or county commissioner's office could get you that job as a school janitor or on the county road crew or on the maintenance staff at the park.

In 1967 you could count the blacks at Amherst College, my alma mater, on one hand. (Two sets of hands would have covered the Catholics.) Ironically, two of those black students were from more distinguished backgrounds than most of the rest of us—their fathers were alumni of the college, one a federal judge, the other a university professor. I suspect that there were hundreds of blacks in America who *deserved* to be in that college more than I did: from better educated families, from better schools, and with better grades. Since the end of slavery, tens of thousands of brilliant, talented, or just competent blacks have not got their due. Most of them "deserved" better. Affirmative action was invented to alter this fact of American history.

Myth #3   Preferential treatment is detrimental to black progress and undermines black self-esteem.

The Black Middle-Class Hang-up

In *Reflections of an Affirmative Action Baby*,[125] Yale law professor Stephen Carter's second thoughts about affirmative action, he recounts a series of amazing, and humiliating, stories about the role color has played in his life: in spite of achieving the second highest score in the National Merit Scholarship qualifying test in his high school in the early 1970s, he was awarded the National Achievement Scholarship, an alternative for "outstanding Negro students"; accepted by the prestigious Yale Law School but rejected by Harvard, Carter was stunned when a Harvard representative called to apologize: "We assumed from your record that you were white."

Decades later, when most of us have put our SAT scores and graduate school triumphs behind us, Carter was still smarting at those slights. Yet, finally, it is not so easy to sympathize with Carter's plight: he grew up a "fac-brat" on the campus of Cornell University, where his father was a professor; he scored 800s on his college boards, went to Stanford and Yale Law School, and clerked for a Supreme Court justice.

These are the kinds of credentials that are likely to make any employer whistle in admiration. Carter is right to be annoyed that anyone might think he got where he is because of some government boost. But, as John Rawls and Thomas Nagel have argued, he is wrong to think he or anyone else deserves to be a Yale law professor. While some do make it to the top by virtue of their talent, as those who make the hiring decisions in the powerhouses of New York, Washington, and Los Angeles could tell you, planning to rise to the top on merit alone is likely to be the long way around. Like many other successful members of the black middle class, Carter has fallen victim to what W.E.B. Du Bois identified as "double consciousness"—looking at oneself through the eyes of white people, who are inclined to pity (or hate) blacks no matter what. Black conservatives would save themselves much frustration if they grabbed their opportunities and ran with them—just as the Irish, Italian, and Jewish beneficiaries of patronage (an earlier version of affirmative action) did before them, never worrying about whether they "deserved" to get a cushy job.

The envy or resentment that whites may feel when they see a black in a big job is their problem, not the black person's. Blacks have too many other better reasons to be angry.

Myth #4   Black violence, such as the 1992 Los Angeles riots, is unjustified and wrong.

Injustice Equals Rage

In the early 1980s, Charles N. Jamison Jr., the only black vice president at one of the top five ad agencies in the United States, was eager to invest in a condo. After a few minutes conversation on the phone with a top real estate agent, Jamison was asked, "Are you black?" When Jamison said he was, the agent, uncomfortably, informed him that the owner of the building did not want to sell to blacks, though she would be happy to talk about other properties. Jamison was enraged, "physically hot," he recalls. "No matter what I did, how far I climbed, how much money I made, the door was slamming in my face—again." He also confesses that, for a moment, he understood how someone as enraged as he could, in the words of a rap song, "just kill a man." According to Jamison, "every black male has felt the kind of rage that makes you want to put somebody's face through the wall." Mostly, however, black men, he says, keep such feelings to themselves.[126]

Black women, too, evidently feel the same rage. When Patricia Williams, a black law professor, pressed the door buzzer to enter a Manhattan clothing store, the young white employee refused to buzz her in. Like Jamison, Williams burned with humiliation and anger. "At that moment I literally wanted to break all the windows of the store and *take* lots of sweaters for my mother," she recalls in her book *The Alchemy of Race and Rights*.[127] Virtually every black person can tell a similar story. Rage and hatred toward whites seethe below the surface even in the most law-abiding blacks. For Martin Luther King Jr., it was when he was six and his best friend's father told his son, a white boy who had just entered Atlanta's segregated school system, that he could no longer play with King. "I was greatly shocked," King recalled, "and from that moment on I was determined to hate every white person."[128] He did not. For the Chicago bus driver Christopher Jones, the blind rage came when a white passenger spit on him. For Elsie Melvin, a registered nurse in Chicago, it was when white patients refused to let her touch them. "They don't care how sick they are," she said. "They'll say, 'I don't want any colored nurse working on me.' "[129]

For centuries, black people have swallowed this rage. And when at last, at some awful time, it finally bursts out, in, say, the kind of violence that occurred in Los Angeles in 1992, white America asks wonderingly why suddenly this rage.

We act according to and against certain principles; we act because we think we must. But often we do things because we are just plain angry. Philosophers, theologians, and lawyers so caught up in the argument and its logic too often ignore how much anger or resentment motivates people to do what they do, the good as well as the bad. And while the results of anger might be deplorable, as in Los Angeles in 1992, the anger itself can still be understandable—perhaps, we may imagine, justifiable.

Judith Shklar, a philosopher, argues that "injustice" itself is "the special kind of anger we feel when we are denied promised benefits and when we do not get what we believe is due."[130] "Mommy, I want to be white," said the daughter of a successful and powerful American journalist.[131] If the most advantaged of black kids feel this way, something is obviously wrong—and it is white America's moral obligation to fix it.

Myth #5   The government is too eager to tax hardworking people to spend their money on people not interested in working.

The Obligations of Community

A community, by definition, is a mutual protection society. Communities have a moral obligation to protect their weakest, poorest, and unluckiest members. The suggestion that there should be no public help for the disadvantaged is unacceptable. The difference between bad luck and injustice is that you can not do anything about the former, but the latter might actually be fixed. In a sense, as Michael Walzer has noted, "every political community is in principle a 'welfare state.' "[132]

The current American presumption that taxes are an evil (and not even a necessary one) is a perverse view of government. Taxing its citizens is how government pays for what individuals can not afford—defense, health care, support for the elderly, and government itself. In a democracy paying a fair share of income taxes is a citizen's moral obligation to the community, which includes its weakest and poorest members. Increasing taxes and programs for the poor may be politically stupid; it may even be political suicide, but it is the moral thing to do.

By definition, a community must treat its members better than non-members. The persistence of racism in the United States is proof of the failure of most Americans to accept blacks as members of their community, full citizens, part of that "us" that seems to exist only in the speeches of politicians.

Myth #6   The "free market" has its winners and losers; that's the way the world works. God—and the free market—helps those who help themselves.

"Socialism" for the Rich

The government intervenes constantly in our lives. And while American businesspeople and politicians sing the praises of "the free market," the market is never totally free. In fact, the market does not even satisfy the needs of the richest businesspeople or the most powerful politicians. The market will not educate their children, tend to their health, care for them in their old age, pay for their national defense, or keep their air free of pollution. The market does not care whom it rolls over, white or black, rich or poor.

Yet when the market does make mincemeat of the Chrysler Corporation or Boeing, or when rich Texans watch their oil prices plummet, the titans of industry who hate "socialism," fight the unions, scream bloody murder about taxes, and don't give a damn about the poor turn to Washington for a handout. The rich plunge in and help the rich, with the kind of loyalty and solidarity that would bring a tear to the eye of a good socialist.

Myth #7   Welfare causes "a culture of poverty."

A Brief History of Economics

Historically, grinding urban poverty—*Dickensian* poverty—arrived with capitalism's greatest triumph, the Industrial Revolution. When the capitalist economic system exploded in America's face with the stock market crash of 1929, President Franklin Roosevelt's New Deal came to its rescue, and the American "welfare state" was born. Social security, labor unions, the minimum wage, and unemployment insurance were all invented to *protect* us from the free market (and ensure that the workers' revolution that would follow the self-destruction of capitalism, as Marx also predicted, would not happen). For his social democratic policies, FDR was denounced as a "traitor to his class." Yet history shows that Roosevelt's policies have made the United States a more humane and just place (while preserving the market economy).

The progressive income tax encouraged the rich alumni of the Ivy League and its sister colleges to write checks to their alma mater rather than Uncle Sam, increasing scholarship money for working-class boys like me eager to be launched into the upper middle class. The postwar economic boom looked as if it would never end. President Johnson himself noted that the boom and bust days of the American economy were over. LBJ believed he could fight a war against poverty and North Vietnam, and afford them both. And then in the 1970s the economic growth that had bankrolled poverty programs vanished, and so did the poverty programs. By the 1980s, Americans had decided that they could no longer afford to support the poor. "Taxes" became a dirty word (almost as dirty as "government"), and an American president who had allegedly once supported FDR—and who was himself remarkably lucky—cut taxes and informed the poor and unlucky that they were on their own.

The only thing that seemed to grow in the economy was the deficit, and poverty.[133] The biggest victims were young people and children, *one fifth* of whom were numbered among America's poor. American conservatives claimed that the Republicans had created new jobs, but failed to note that most of them were service jobs, like flipping hamburgers, for the current minimum wage of $4.25 an hour or part-time employment. In 1989 more than 13 million full-time jobs—one in six jobs—paid less than it took to lift even a family of three out of poverty. These workers include carpenters, food processors, hospital workers, secretaries, and machine operators—in short, vital contributors to the "good life" in America. Such working poor add up, amazingly, to 60 million Americans—about *one person in every four.*[134]

Manufacturing jobs fled to the suburbs, increasing unemployment, injuring already wounded families, forcing women into the labor market, and hurting families even more. The new working class was mainly black and brown, its unluckiest members relegated to the much discussed, and dangerous, "underclass." Thirty-seven million Americans were without health insurance. Most workers were scattered throughout the cities of our nation, scratching together a living and, unlike the unionized workers of the past, not much interested in political action. Politicians ignored them, while the Reagan-Bush campaigns persuaded blue-collar workers that it was in their economic interest to align with the haves and not the poor (and black). "Taxes" became a code word for giveaways to the irresponsible and lazy, to "welfare queens" who had allegedly generated the filth, drugs, violence, and fecund teenagers plaguing American cities.

Myth #8　The solution to social chaos is to do away with welfare.

The Moral Obligation to Care for the Poor

Without welfare, no matter how flawed the current system, the social chaos of poverty would deepen.[135] The only thing standing between the poor and devastation (or worse, social unrest) is charity, private and public. A moral society—certainly one resting on traditional

Judeo-Christian values—must care for the poor. Two centuries ago Adam Smith argued in *The Wealth of Nations,* the bible of capitalism, that the moral justification of the free market was reciprocity. "It is but equity that they who feed, cloath [*sic*] and lodge the whole of the people, should have such a share of the produce of their own labour as to be themselves tolerably well fed, cloathed and lodged."[136] The current American economy ignores this moral principle. A capitalism concerned only with profits is a tyrant disguised as a banker.

Critics of welfare often argue as if government support of the poor was invented by Lyndon Johnson. But, as Michael Walzer has pointed out, fifth- and fourth-century B.C. Athens made provisions for the elderly, orphans, and war widows. Adding the compensation for missed work among artisans and farmers who had to serve in official positions in the Athenian democracy, the outlays could total *more than half* of the city's internal revenues. Among the Jewish community of medieval Cairo, there was one person on the dole for every four contributors to charity.[137]

The modern welfare system has to be reformed to avoid waste and corruption and to encourage people to get off the dole; but welfare must not be abandoned.

Myth #9   Surely, we need *less* welfare.

The Common Good

We need more government commitment to the poor, not less. Corporations, too, must recognize that dealing with poverty is in their long-term economic interest. It has become fashionable, particularly in politically conservative circles, to talk about the need for "community," "traditional values," and "the common good." Unfortunately, the boundaries of the conservative version of "community" stop short of the ghetto.

Confronting poverty in our nation is neither a liberal nor a conservative goal; it is for the common good. Is there an American CEO who would now dare argue—at least in public—that polluting the air and rivers is the cost of American affluence and mobility? It should become equally difficult to find corporate leaders who believe that decreasing poverty and its social effects is not in their economic interest. Liberals are right to expect the government to continue to help the poor. But the traditional liberal commitment to the kind of unbridled competition that built American capitalism will have to be at least restrained. Classic liberals will have to appeal to their better side, the part that values individual autonomy and treats people not as means but as ends in themselves.[138]

Conservatives are right to complain about the degradation of the American family and the old-fashioned values of hard work and good neighbors, but they also will have to concede the role corporations and the economy have played in that destruction. And those who contend that we all have to think less of ourselves and our own projects of self-creation and more about the community will have to admit that among that community there are bound to be poor and unlucky fellow citizens who need our help.[139]

This certainly does not mean simply throwing money at social problems or increasing the dole. What is required is an all-out moral commitment to simply *dealing* with poverty, treating it as a crisis, an emergency that must be remedied, a disease that must be wiped out, like fighting cancer or AIDS.

One remedy to help minorities get ahead has been affirmative action.

Myth #10   For the government to give inexperienced minority workers a boost over better-qualified white workers is racial discrimination in reverse. Affirmative action is fighting one injustice with another.

Affirmative Action: A Compromise Solution

Those who oppose affirmative action have to ask themselves if they could live with the moral ugliness that would have persisted without legal pressure on colleges, universities, professional schools, and employers to make places for blacks. Try to imagine what the United States would look like today without affirmative action.

By every measure—employment, income, education, health, and crime—a vast gap persists between American blacks and whites. It is safe to say that one hundred thirty years after the end of the Civil War, forty years after *Brown,* and thirty years after calls for "affirmative action" to push blacks into the American mainstream, most African-Americans are still treading water outside. Of course it is true that many black Americans are not trying hard enough to help themselves and their communities. But many others have had their ambitions crushed every step of the way. As all blacks know, and a surprising number of whites refuse to acknowledge, racism is still a prime obstacle to black success. And while it may be bad luck to be born in a ghetto, it is an act of injustice on the part of society to make no effort to wipe out ghettos. To expect blacks to start further back in the race than whites and still succeed is unjust. To force certain whites to stand aside while certain blacks are given a boost—so-called reverse discrimination—is also unjust.

Yet, as the philosophers Thomas Nagel and Cornel West have pointed out, reverse discrimination is in no way as unjust as the real thing. A more serious problem is that affirmative action was conceived as a beginning, a temporary measure that would eventually even the playing field. When? Apparently before now, as far as the opponents of affirmative action are concerned. But if they despise affirmative action, then they must provide an alternative, a better moral compromise.

I suggest an alternative—a war. Americans have always loved a good war.

One Nation . . .

When President Clinton in the summer of 1993 dumped Lani Guinier, his candidate to head the Civil Rights Division of the Justice Department, he said that her view of America was still one of "us versus them." Clinton's preferred vision was a nation of only "us." Who wouldn't prefer such a vision?

But, for the moment, it is only a rhetorical flourish of speeches by politicians—one that most blacks have lost patience with. While middle-class blacks seem as eager as whites to distance themselves from the ghetto, the bond between poor and wealthy blacks is their common experience of racism, discrimination, and humiliation. If rich blacks and poor blacks share the same anger toward white racism, we should at least be willing to concede there is a severe problem in need of attention.[140] Bill Cosby and Oprah Winfrey may be worth hundreds of millions, Michael Jordan can fly, Michael Jackson can moonwalk, Kathleen Battle sings like an angel, Maya Angelou writes sublime poems, and Toni Morrison writes great novels, but, as President Kennedy once pointed out, "who among us would be content to have the color of his skin changed?"[141] What white person has not driven through a black ghetto and thanked God he wasn't black? Racism is a subject about which we should listen more to black people.

"Solidarity," according to philosopher Richard Rorty, is an attempt to expand the number of people we identify as one of us, the people who are "we." It is easier to dig deep into your pocket to help your family, friends, and neighbors—"our kind." The challenge of race and poverty in America is to extend that community of "us" to the poor, black as well as white.

Nothing unites Americans faster than a national disaster.

Imagination of Disaster

The novelist Henry James once said that Americans lacked the "imagination of disaster." The twentieth century, however, seems to have expanded that side of the American imagination. The imagination of disaster may be the only thing capable of uniting a country that has become increasingly divided along racial, political, religious, and ideological lines.

Nothing brings America together faster than a *crisis*—the threat of war, or more likely, a flood, hurricane, or earthquake. Only in the face of disaster do Americans seem to grasp the notion of "community"— a mutual protection society. Disasters stimulate our moral imaginations: We can imagine ourselves escaping our flooded neighborhood in a boat, fighting a fire, crawling out of the rubble of an earthquake. We see on TV people like ourselves coping. We can imagine our own misery if one of our children were trapped in a well, our houses destroyed, our farms incinerated, our bridges down.

What Americans really lack is the imagination of being different, of being, for example, black and poor. Occasionally, a Martin Luther King Jr. or Cesar Chavez presses onto our imaginations a sense of what it might be like to be a grape picker or a black child who cannot go to school with white kids. The images of police dogs and fire hoses turned on innocent citizens in Birmingham seared the imaginations of millions sickened by what they saw on the television news. We also saw ourselves walking across the bridge outside Selma when the state troopers attacked. But when the crisis passed we forgot what it was like to be under attack simply for what we look like. Perhaps it is an impossible leap of imagination to conjure up being a black American. Yet it seems equally difficult for well-off American businesspeople or even for solid members of the middle class to picture themselves on an unemployment line or standing outside a soup kitchen.[142] But this lack of imagination, I think, can be remedied by a simple change of focus—from black poverty to poverty alone.

American crime, violence, guns, drugs, teenage pregnancy, fractured families, decaying cities, and welfare dependency have, to an exaggerated sense, been reduced to race, as if every one of those problems did not exist before the poverty of poor blacks dominated our idea of our cities (as if every one of those problems would not still exist if "the problem of race" were magically erased from the social agenda). Race has become the national scapegoat, the easiest explanation for all our social and economic problems.

Blackness, however, is hardly a necessary condition for being poor, for while *one half* of America's black children are poor, so are 40 percent of Hispanic children. *One out of five* American kids—20 percent—are poor. In fact, most poor people in our nation are *white*. Poverty exists in such relatively homogeneous societies as Great Britain and Germany (where the unemployment rate is even higher than in the United States).[143] In his recent analysis of race relations in the United States, the sociologist Andrew Hacker has pointed out that whites are catching up with blacks on almost every measure of poverty and dysfunction—unemployment, teen pregnancies, single-parent families.[144] Gang warfare has spread to the suburbs.

Blacks may only be the avant-garde of the poor. Our national preoccupation should not be race; it should be poverty. Most Americans support government aid for health care and the elderly. Who cannot imagine getting sick or old? If the politicians and communitarian critics of liberalism are sincere about wanting to turn the battle between "us" and "them" into a harmonious "we," they will have to expand their imaginations to include the poor in their vision of community. In fact, they have a moral obligation to do so. Communities are based on a social contract which is also a moral bond that ties the rich and the poor, the strong and the weak, and the lucky and the unlucky.[145]

The news that millions of Americans were starving to death would stun the nation. Of course, poverty has not reached that stage of disaster. But how much poverty is our nation willing to accept? I remember seeing a film of Robert Kennedy visiting an Appalachian family. As he arrived, Kennedy was your usual smiling politician. When he emerged from that Appalachian hovel followed by children with sad eyes, their bellies distended from hunger, he was one genuinely shaken rich white man. Clearly, Kennedy had seen a kind of poverty that he did not imagine existed in America. That visit to a poor family in Appalachia grabbed Kennedy's imagination. He did not think we should tolerate that kind of poverty.

We have to try to stretch our imagination of disaster beyond natural calamities to the grinding tragedy of poverty—unemployment, homelessness, family breakup, violent crime. For most of its victims, poverty is no less a tragic accident, or "act of God," than the latest flood in the Midwest or earthquake in California. Instead of looking at poor people and wondering why they cannot pull themselves out of their poverty, we have to look at them and imagine ourselves in their torn, or stolen, sneakers: what if you had been raised by a teenaged mother, what if you hadn't known your father, or if you did, he had lost the only job he ever had and didn't know how to go about finding another, what if you hadn't met that teacher, what if you hadn't been able to hit a curveball and get that scholarship?

It is hard to imagine such things because we get so rapt up in our own lives. Living well at the top of society often makes it easier to take a liberal view of things. A blue-collar worker who has scrambled his whole life to keep the bill collectors from his door is bound to resent an unemployed man living on welfare. The worker cannot imagine himself with his hand outstretched for a welfare check. Yet I suspect that the tens of thousands of once successful members of the middle class who have lost their jobs in recent years, who have benefited from unemployment insurance and even welfare, have had their imaginations of disaster expanded. The next step is to try to imagine what it is like to live hand to mouth, to be poor, even despised. Imagine your resentment, your anger, your sense of injustice.

To stand in that position is to see why justice requires that some of the nation's wealth must be redistributed. For most Americans this requires a brave leap of the imagination. But let our imaginations roam. Social security was once denounced as socialism or worse, and for good reason: it is tax money redistributed to the old. A few decades ago many Americans derided a national health-care plan as socialism or worse, and for good reason: it is also an example of redistributive wealth. But today most Americans agree that society has a moral obligation to care for the old and the sick. Yet many of them still resist the idea that they ought to pay higher taxes for social welfare programs. And while they would not suggest that the sick and the elderly are responsible for their condition, they still persist in their view that the poor are to blame.

But before we resist helping the poor, we should try to imagine the alternative, another kind of disaster that poverty can produce.

"The Fire Next Time"

After the Los Angeles riots in 1992, President Bush said, "I can hardly imagine . . . the fear and the anger people must feel to terrorize one another and burn each other's property."[146] But that's a failure of his imagination, not theirs. What really is hard to imagine is why blacks don't take to the streets more often. Black solidarity is based on the humiliation and rage African-Americans feel, middle class as well as poor. It is a rage justified by injustice. White leaders should ask—and fast—whether they want to bear the potential disastrous consequences of that rage or try to figure out how to allay it.

Black leaders might also consider how to turn that rage to their advantage. Reading various accounts of the civil rights battles of the 1960s as well as histories of the Kennedy and Johnson administrations, one is struck by the moral fervor and righteousness of the fight. Three decades later that moral intensity seems to have waned, even among the black leadership (indeed the black leadership itself seems to have disappeared). Yet the injustice of racism and discrimination is still with us.

The African-American leadership should take American history to heart and do the only thing that seems to force white Americans to recognize that African-Americans are part of the same country—namely, turn up the pressure.

Martin Luther King Jr. wrote in his "Letter from a Birmingham Jail": "Freedom must be demanded by the oppressed."[147]

It is time for another War on Poverty—without a doubt, a just war.[148]

6. One Nation, Many Disagreements

I never imagined there were so many screwed-up people.

An anti-abortion activist at a large pro-choice rally

Doubtless, the feeling was mutual. For that opponent of abortion, the fetus is an unborn child, a person, and why anyone would think killing a person is anything but murder mystifies him. His opponent, who approves of a woman's right to choose an abortion, cannot, of course, imagine why anyone would consider a month-old embryo a person with the same civil rights as you and I.

Both look across the barricades and see a criminal. I believe that any morality worth a damn must explain why we are so divided over so many issues and then bring us back together again, not in some perfect harmony (I believe that is impossible), but to the point where we would prefer to talk rather than fight. A theory of morality must explain why some people will fight for the lives of fetuses but be resigned to the fact that one half of the nation's black children live in poverty. Why do some people think it is wrong for a nation to ignore its poorest people, while others believe that the poor must take responsibility for their poverty? A theory of morality worth a damn must explain why some people look at a homeless person in the street with the feeling of shame and perhaps even an urge to help, while others avert their eyes or suggest to the poor wretch that he "get a job."

And above all, a theory of morality must tell us how we can shape a decent society from people who look across the moral barricades and see not a fellow American but a "screwed-up" person.

It might help to recognize that we do not always have to look so far to find someone to disagree with. Sometimes the clash of opposing views takes place in one's own mind, and the most "screwed-up" person we know turns out to be oneself. I, for instance, oppose killing innocent people—even in war. Regardless of the primary aims of war, the deaths of thousands of civilians—whether in Dresden, Hiroshima, Leningrad, or Baghdad—are the very definition of mass murder. I even recoil at the idea of B-52s bombing North Vietnamese or Iraqi soldiers into insanity. Yet I am no pacifist. Shooting the enemy may be necessary. Killing Nazis or cruel dictators can be a moral obligation.

And so may be killing an infant born without a brain or a terminally ill relative. Most of us are inclined to believe that we know right from wrong. But one "right" has a way of ending up conflicting with another. You argue that human life is sacred, but how can so many opponents of abortion be *for* the death penalty? Why isn't the life of a murderer sacred? If you cannot kill fetuses, why are you obligated to kill cruel dictators? And what about my terminally ill father? When he begs me to help him die can I turn him down and still call myself a "good son"? The sanctity of life versus filial obligation. Justice versus mercy. Justice as fairness versus justice as what one deserves. What is a good person to do?

This is the very definition of "moral dilemma"—two desirable goods that we cannot have at the same time. No matter how strong our principles or values, no matter how virtuous we think we are, moral dilemmas are more difficult to escape than the common cold. Which value is most valuable? Who is right? Where do we find the answers to such questions—in the Bible, in the life of Christ, in the works of Plato, Kant, Nietzsche, Marx, or more contemporary philosophers? Our moral standards are where? In the U.S. Constitution, in our own hearts, or in the stars?

Or are such questions as Who's right? and How do you know? even the right questions to ask? Can we create a decent society from so many people who disagree so violently with one another on such fundamental matters?

Americans are inclined to believe that if they discuss an issue long enough, they will come to a solution acceptable to everyone. But not all moral arguments are settleable, as I think I have shown. One man's "traditional values" (e.g., a woman's place is in the home) may be one

woman's idea of oppression. For the five nagging moral issues discussed in this book, I have shown, I believe, that *there are good arguments on all sides of these issues.* What is clear from these arguments is
that good people, smart people, even friends and spouses, can disagree
on major ethical issues confronting our society.

And this, I believe, is a good thing, for it is in disagreement, the
clash of values, that moral progress is made. And in America, I want to
argue, disagreement on moral matters is not only inevitable, it is what
the idea of America is about. No matter who we are or how establish-
mentarian we claim to be, we will always seem "screwed up" to someone.
In fact, the United States is, by definition, a nation of "screwed-up"
people. We are bound to disagree, not only fundamentally but especially fundamentally. I also want to argue that in a democratic society
more heterogeneous than the Greeks could have imagined, in our "one
nation under God" where the fastest growing religion is Islam, where
the white majority will soon be a minority, moral "knowledge"—the
idea that one individual's ethical standards provide the best way to
live, absolutely and indisputably—is the first step toward political oppression. No value in America is more "traditional" than freedom—
freedom to think, to speak, to choose, freedom to be "screwed up." It
is useful to keep in mind that "utopia" is Greek for "nowhere."[1]
"Common ground" may be a location no easier to find.

It is not surprising that on matters of life and death—like abortion,
suicide, euthanasia, the death penalty, even race—we are likely to get
excited. What is surprising is that we could be so arrogant to believe
that the world would be decent and peaceful if only others saw every
issue through our eyes.

In fact, we are more likely to create a decent society if, unable to
agree, we could at least see the issue through *their* eyes. "The task of
future philosophy is to clarify men's ideas as to the social and moral
strifes of their own day," said the American philosopher John Dewey.[2]
The route to such clarification requires tolerance—the glue that holds
a free society together. Thomas Jefferson, the philosopher of the idea
of America, once wrote, "it does me no injury for my neighbor to say
that there are twenty Gods, or no God."[3] But to understand why requires a great deal of imagination—what I want to call "moral imagination."

The Inevitable Clash of Values

If virtue is knowledge, as Socrates claimed, then we are bound to be wicked. The only constant in the history of knowledge is how little we seem to know (and how often we have been dead wrong).

If the great thinkers of history have not delivered on the ultimate answers to the problems that trouble us the most, why do we expect people of more modest intellectual talents (politicians or Supreme Court justices, for instance) to show us the way to The Truth? Religious people will argue that what is right is what God commands. What God's criteria are, of course, nobody knows. But some of us refuse to look to God for moral direction, either because we do not believe in God or have looked to God for direction and have been disappointed with the results. God is not always available when we need him most.

And while we would prefer to find one easy solution to our deepest moral dilemmas, many answers are available. The problem is, they are usually incompatible. This, however, is hardly a new problem, as the eminent historian of ideas and philosopher Isaiah Berlin has pointed out, often and eloquently:

> The history of moral, political, theological thought is a history of violent conflicts between rival claims of rival experts. Some men looked for the answer in the word of God as contained in his sacred books; others in revelation, or faith, or holy mysteries which we believe although we may not understand; still others in the pronouncements of the appointed interpreters of God—churches and priests—and if the churches did not always return the same answer, no one doubted that one or other of such answers must be true—if not the answer of this denomination, then of that one. Some found the answer in rational metaphysics, or in an infallible intuition of some other kind, such as the verdict of the individual conscience. Others again discovered it in empirical observation, in the scientific laboratory, in the application of mathematical methods to the data of experience. Wars of extermination were fought over rival claims to the true answers to these crucial questions. The price was, after all, the solution of the deepest and most important questions that any man could ask—about the true way of living; and for the sake of salvation men were ready to die . . . for to find the truth and live according to it was surely the ultimate goal of anyone capable of seeking it.[4]

According to Berlin, from the beginning of history, Platonists, Stoics, Christians, Muslims, deists, and atheistic humanists have all followed this "faith," and the results have been bloody. "Wars for principles and causes, both religious and secular, indeed human life itself," Berlin points out, "would have seemed meaningless without this deepest of all assumptions."[5] Yet Berlin argues that this "deepest of all assumptions"—that there is one true way of living—seems to be wrong. There is no one Truth, no one solution to life, no ideal state. As Berlin puts it, "In the house of human history, there are many mansions."[6]

The only certitude in Berlin's reading of history is that the values—"the goods"—some people cherish most are bound to collide with the principles other people value just as much.[7] "We can discuss each other's point of view, we can try to reach common ground, but in the end what you pursue may not be reconcilable with the ends to which I find that I have dedicated my life."[8] Sometimes the collision takes place closer to home—in our own minds: I oppose killing, but my father, dying of terminal cancer, asks me to help him die. I believe in justice and hate cold-blooded murderers, but I also believe in mercy and compassion and oppose all forms of torture (which the electric chair, gas chamber, and hangman's noose resemble too closely for my comfort). I am committed to the principles of liberty and equality. But how much liberty can I give to the titans of industry before they start exploiting their workers and trying to dominate me politically?

Still, we must choose. But how? On what grounds? What criteria do we use? If there is no one way of living, are all ways equally acceptable? The smart opponent of this pluralistic ideal is bound to point out that if no one's version of the truth is the final one, then there is no reason to fight for your beliefs, or a country, built on such a flimsy moral foundation.[9]

You are a "relativist."[10]

The Problem of Relativism

I like New York in June, how about you? I like a Gershwin tune, how about you?

Cole Porter

If you prefer Paris in June or rap music to a Gershwin tune, and cannot imagine why anyone would differ, you may begin to understand how often our prejudices pass for knowledge and why, since the time of

Protagoras, moral thinkers have argued that differences of opinion can be so fundamental even between people in the same society that "truth" or "knowledge" or "certainty" is simply impossible. It all depends on who you are, where you come from, what you believe, what you value as good. "Man is the measure of all things" (Protagoras). "The world has no meaning behind it but countless meanings" (Nietzsche).

The pure relativist argues that one man's view has no more status than another—that every belief is as good as every other. History and anthropology have taught us that all societies have their own standards, and what is good in one society may be different and even incompatible with what is good in another society, past or present. The virtues of a Homeric warrior were not the same as those of the best of men in Plato's ideal Republic. The fast-living Romans were puzzled by the sexual abstinence of the early Christians. Christians have preached a gospel of love thy neighbor and massacred the "infidel" Muslims, Jews, native Americans, not to mention fellow Christians who dared to question dogma. Similarly, abortion is murder, or self-defense. The fetus is a person, or a lump of cells. I have my opinion, you have yours. I like Paris in June. I'm okay; you're screwed up.

For this reason many people are inclined to throw up their hands in frustration in the face of moral controversy. As a journalist said to me when she heard the topic of this book, "It's not worth writing about these issues because people already have their minds made up." Yet people change their minds about the most fundamental issues of life all the time. Sometimes this change results from a scientific "revolution"—when a Galileo or Newton or Einstein proves to us that we ought to see the world in a radically different way. Sometimes the agent of change is a moral revolution, like civil rights, or a social revolution, like feminism. Sometimes we change because what was once only an abstract "social problem" becomes a personal issue: suddenly, our own daughter gets pregnant, our own mother is hooked up to a life-support machine, our wife attempts suicide, our son is slammed up against the wall by the cops, our own husband loses his job.

For most of us life is a series of changes—of place, employment, friendship, love, and belief. When I see my marriage in a new light, people call it "experience" or "growing up." But when my moral views mature from what my parents or church taught me to a more ironic view of the inevitable moral confusion of modernity, I am suddenly a big, bad "relativist." What does that really mean? Do I have any alternative? If not—if there are so many incompatible goods—does that mean that the notion of the "common good" is as out of date in our country as the powdered wig?

Who's Afraid of "Relativism"?

In one sense the pluralist cannot avoid being branded a relativist, but he does not care. As the philosopher Richard Rorty has pointed out, the charge is like calling someone who doesn't believe in God a "blasphemer."[11] But pure moral relativism implies that every view is equally right, and the pluralist does not make that claim. His view is much less positive: in a world of many truths, all of them might be *equally wrong*. But for a pluralist like Isaiah Berlin, at least one thing is for sure: "The notion of the perfect whole, the ultimate solution, in which all good things coexist, seems to me to be not merely unattainable—that is a truism—but *conceptually incoherent;* I do not know what is meant by a harmony of this kind. Some among the Great Goods cannot live together. That is a conceptual truth."[12]

It is also a truth experienced by anyone who has faced a major moral dilemma: the justice of the death penalty versus the mercy of a society that has put medieval torture behind it, the sanctity of life versus a doctor's compassion for a family whose baby has been born without a brain, discrimination against white workers to compensate for discrimination against black workers. Every day people make these kinds of moral choices. "We are doomed to choose," explains Berlin, "and every choice may entail an irreparable loss."[13]

But the question persists: How does one choose? The fundamentalist Christian can look to the Bible, the Marxist has his laws of history. To what criteria does the modern pluralist refer to make his choice? Berlin offers an answer that resonates for me:

> . . . the best that one can do is to try to promote some kind of equilibrium, necessarily unstable, between the different aspirations of different groups of human beings—at the very least to prevent them from attempting to exterminate each other, and, so far as possible, to prevent them from hurting each other—and to promote the maximum practicable degree of sympathy and understanding, never likely to be complete, between them.[14]

"Some kind of equilibrium," "necessarily unstable," "never likely to be complete," is, admittedly, a shaky foundation, but to expect something more solid is perhaps to expect too much.

I think the common distaste for relativism is due to the intuition that not every belief is as good as every other. In fact, the view that every belief is as good as every other is logically self-refuting, as many philosophers have pointed out: if every belief is as good as this one—relativism—then what's the worth of relativism (or any other belief)?

Another reason many are offended by relativism is that they presume there has to be at least one right view of things. But to claim that there are no indisputable moral truths is not to say that there is no right way of doing things. Is there anyone who is a pure relativist, who believes there is no such thing as right or wrong? That is not what is at issue. Certainty is the rub. You may be right, but don't ever bank on your "right way" being indisputably and absolutely right. You may also be wrong. To brand someone a "relativist" stands as a genuine criticism only if you can appeal to a standard that is not relative—some foundation or Archimedean point or ground zero from which you can judge all other views.

Truth is not something we *find* but simply the way a particular society—*our* society—describes how it justifies certain ways of doing things, how it determines what is right. Among philosophers, this is known as pragmatism, a way of looking at the world that is as American as this nation's greatest (and most American) philosophers, William James and John Dewey. In recent years pragmatism has had a philosophical revival thanks to the writings of Rorty, an articulate and prolific admirer of James and Dewey.[15] Traditionally, the pragmatist has been contrasted with the "realist," who argues that true beliefs are distinguished from false ones by grounding them in "reality"—an objective standard of the way things really are. Knowledge is different from opinion, true belief from false belief. To be truly rational is to progress through a series of justifications that lead to the truth, to a correspondence with reality, to the intrinsic nature of things, to the way things really are, to truth comparable to the truth of mathematics and physics. In moral matters, such justification must spring from "the nature of man."[16]

A Rorty pragmatist does not view "knowledge" as some kind of transcendental standard or Platonic form; Truth does not require the discovery of the "nature" or "essence" of man or his world. "For the pragmatist . . . 'knowledge' is, like 'truth,' simply a compliment paid to the beliefs which he thinks so well justified that, for the moment, further justification is not needed." For the Rorty pragmatist, knowledge is simply a "socio-historical account of how various people have tried to reach agreement on what to believe."[17] All you can do is justify your beliefs, given your customs, traditions, and values. And that's that. No further, or deeper, criteria are available. Or, to borrow from Ludwig Wittgenstein, one of this century's most influential thinkers: "I have reached bedrock, and my spade is turned."[18]

Thus, for Rorty, every theory "comes to be seen as one more vocabulary, one more description, one more way of speaking."[19] When values collide, Rorty's pragmatist recognizes that she is stuck inside the common language of her community, and suspects that the current vocabulary she is using may be inadequate and that she will have to come up with a new way of describing things.[20]

> If one grants these claims, there is no such thing as the "relativist predicament," just as for someone who thinks that there is no God there will be no such thing as blasphemy. For there is no higher standpoint to which we are responsible and against whose precepts we might offend. There will be no such activity as scrutinizing competing values in order to see which are morally privileged.[21]

In my terms, Rorty's pragmatist looks at her father lying in a hospital hooked up to a life-support system and says, "That is not my father, at least as I have known him all my life; that is not a living person, at least in the way that I have known living people; that man lying there, who is terminally ill, beyond care, being kept alive artificially, he is *formerly* my father, just in the way that the one-month-old embryo in my grandmother's womb seventy-three years ago was not my father, not even a person, but only potentially so."

Is that a relativist trick, some fancy philosophical sleight of hand? No, says Rorty; it's just the way language and culture work. It's also how scientific and moral progress take place. New metaphors cause changes in belief; metaphors make intellectual progress possible.[22] Language is all we have. The only way to rise above that language is not to appeal to some kind of "objective truth" but to come up with another word or phrase or "redescription" that breaks the logjam, that manages to explain things as no one has ever done before.

Einstein dreamed of riding a beam of light, and thus saw that time, space, and mass were not as "absolute" as Newton (and his successors) had thought. What is relativity theory itself but another metaphor? In Nietzsche's memorable phrase: "Truth is a mobile army of metaphors."[23]

In Rorty's terms, politics is about persuading people to adopt competing metaphors. In my terms, the work at hand is persuading people to drop the old metaphors—that the fetus is an "unborn child" or a "lump of cells," that the death penalty is appropriate "payment" for murder, that a patient living only by virtue of being hooked up to a life-support system is "living"—and come up with other ways of describing the situation that defuses the anger on both sides of the moral conflict. To repeat Dewey: "The task of future philosophy is to clarify men's ideas as to the social and moral strifes of their own day."[24]

There can be no clarity without talk and thought. Moral progress is the product of moral reflection.

The "Problem" with Democracy

To American conservatives, what I call "moral progress" is likely to look more like "moral chaos." For them, my cavalier attitude toward the truth—what they call "moral relativism"—is precisely what has wrecked our nation. They claim that the eagerness of "liberals," like Rorty or Berlin or John Rawls, to put the freedom of the individual before the demands of the community has created not just a "Me Generation" but a veritable "Culture of Narcissism." The kind of Rawlsian liberalism that establishes justice as the first virtue and rights as always trumping goods creates, according to two of liberalism's most sophisticated critics, Michael Sandel and Alasdair MacIntyre, a "collection of strangers" whose culture heroes are "the Rich Aesthete, the Manager, and the Therapist," who worship the individual conscience while ignoring shared traditions, values, beliefs, and the common good.[25] Separating the individual from the place where values and common goods are really shaped—the family, social organizations, the community—is to imagine a person, explains Sandel, "wholly without character, without moral depth." Such "self-interpreting beings" are bound to be so "thin" as to bear no resemblance to those of us trying to raise families, educate children, and keep our communities from turning into violent, drug-addicted armed camps.

These "communitarians" are equally appalled by the liberal political theorist's disregard for the central role that merit and reward have played in traditional societies. In the ideal liberal society where "justice is fairness," the powers that be are too likely to spread the wealth to people who have not proved they deserve it. Such "welfare state liberalism," the argument goes, may protect individuals, but it destroys a community's intuitive sense of justice—that each ought to get his due. Worse still, contends the sociologist Robert Bellah and his four coauthors of the best-selling analysis of the social effects of liberalism, *Habits of the Heart,* "this individualism may have grown cancerous, that it may be threatening the survival of freedom itself."[26]

The sacred book of this discontent with the liberalism that allegedly dominates American intellectual and political life is *Democracy in America,* the French Count Alexis de Tocqueville's brilliant reportage of his trip around the United States in 1831–32, only fifty-five years after the Declaration of Independence.[27] Tocqueville worried that American "individualism" (he was one of the first to use the word) might overtake the nation's commitment to other traditions—"habits of the heart" such as family life, religion, and participation in local politics—that had helped shape the American character. A great admirer of the infant democracy, the aristocrat Tocqueville warned that this dangerous tendency of Americans to pursue their own goals and personal projects—"enclosed in their hearts"—would isolate them from political activity, leaving government up to the "soft despotism" of professionals, thus endangering the very freedom that allowed their individualism to flourish.

Tocqueville's heirs among American philosophers and social critics have for years now been warning that Tocqueville's chickens have come home to roost. "We have committed," warns Bellah and his coauthors, "what to the republican founders of our nation was the cardinal sin: we have put our own good, as individuals, as groups, as a nation, ahead of the common good." Americans have followed their bliss and ignored the dream that has made such self-indulgence possible— "of living in a society that would really be worth living in."[28]

The communitarians protest too much. They have set up a straw liberal—a citizen too individual, too independent, too morally neutral, too cut off from his fellows to be believed, even by good liberals. They also point to the alternative of "community" and "common good" that is filled more with nostalgia than reality, and thus also too good to be believed, even by a candid communitarian. And while it is true that many of us can be selfish, self-absorbed, and unsympathetic to the goals of the society that protects us, neither liberalism nor individualism is wholly to blame. Often we are just running for cover from what some might call American business and politics as usual—from business leaders who care only about money and power, Wall Street littered with junk bonds, banks afraid to loan to small businesses or black people or women, lobbies who serve only their special interests, politicians with their hands in the pork barrel, and leaders who think that politics is only about politics.[29]

What sane citizen would not retreat into what Tocqueville called "the solitude of his own heart"?[30] But how do we form a community out of that? How in a society where everyone seems to disagree so fundamentally are we going to create any solidarity?

The first step, I think, is to recognize that we Americans are all democrats—*liberal* democrats, *communitarian* liberal democrats.

The "Liberal Communitarian"

No individual can be separated from the community where he lives and was educated, no matter how much the communitarian critics of liberalism try. Even Rawls's ideal legislator trying to reinvent a society with principles of justice that will help sort out the inevitable clash of values and ways of life is a member of a society with democratic political institutions like our own, as Rawls himself has pointed out since the publication of *A Theory of Justice:*

> . . . Since justice as fairness is intended as a political conception of justice *for a democratic society,* it tries to draw solely upon basic intuitive ideas that are embedded in the political institutions of a democratic society and the public traditions of their interpretation. Justice as fairness is a political conception in part because *it starts within a certain political tradition.* [my italics][31]

Rawls's original liberals, contrary to his critics, are hardly pure human essences, independent neutrals, standing outside history. They stand in a pluralistic democracy, like our own, and from these ordinary Americans who love freedom and hate oppression Rawls tries to create a principle of justice. Significantly, he feels no need to offer any philosophical or metaphysical justification for his attachment to American democracy.[32] (A moment's thought gives enough reason: to try to justify the advantages of democracy over a more authoritarian regime would be as silly as trying to explain why you are for freedom and against slavery.)

And so we are all "communitarians." Society is no mere collection of individuals, whether they are strangers or those bound by the ties of family, religion, and common goods. We adults enter the game who we are, and who we are has a lot to do with where we are from (and, I would add, whom and what we are running from). We make our debuts in society, humanized, *socialized*. But society, of course, requires more than people; *institutions* make a society as much as the people. Then again, institutions are not born; they are made—by people. Americans ought to understand this point more than any other people. Our institutions were created from the intellectual enthusiasms of an intelligent and idealistic—and exceedingly progressive—group of men. (Feminists would start an argument here, one that has merit, but that does not belong in this book.) Jefferson was passionate about "religious tolerance" because it had been in so little evidence in European history.

Individuals make society, and society makes its individuals. They are both products of the other's dreams, back and forth, forth and back. Society gives the world its meaning, creates full individuals who, in turn, dream up and create political constitutions that ground the society—until some revolutionary convinces them they have been doing it wrong. Americans founded the colonies, revolutionized that society with the Articles of Confederation in 1781, and six years later returned to the drawing board in Philadelphia, producing the Constitution of the United States, which remains the arbiter of "what's good" for America and a model for revolutionary democrats around the globe.

The Threat of Democracy

The future of communities, like people, depends on their instinct for survival. By nature communities are conservative, fearful of outsiders, hostile to rebels and dissenters. Democracy, however, is by nature revolutionary. "Conservative democracy" is, in fact (and in the long term), a contradiction in terms.

Democracy, as invented by the Greeks, is based on the freedom to question government. Discarding tyranny and keeping the gods in their place (on Mount Olympus and not at the head of the Assembly), the Athenian democrats turned power (*kratos*) over to the people (the *demos*) and the imaginative result was *demokratia*. Politics and creating a constitution (a *politeia*)—what citizens (*politai*) do—was about questioning the status quo: What is the best constitution? What is justice? What is good? were questions that Greek citizens were the first to ask. And thus the invention of democracy encouraged the birth of philosophy.[33] In fact, Athenian democracy's greatest thinkers and writers were its harshest critics. (Plato's *Republic* is, after all, an all-out attack on the "rule of the people"—that is, democracy; it was the Greek "sophists"—literally, "wise men" who made their living at teaching—who first raised the possibility of moral and epistemological relativism. ["Man is the measure of all things," wrote Protagoras.] And it was the anti-democrat Plato who argues that Truth is not man's to name, but an ideal that exists outside the world of appearances which a true lover of wisdom, a *philosophos,* might find.) Fifth-century Athens was the first "culture of complaint."[34]

It was Athens that invented the "individual"—and among its most grateful beneficiaries were the liberal arts graduates (typically the first of their family to attend a university) who met in Philadelphia in 1787 to put history's latest democratic constitution into writing. Like their models the Athenians, the men who dreamed up America knew that if God didn't rule man, then man himself would have to figure out the best way to do so. There were no sacred books in Athens, or in Philadelphia.

Like the Athenians, the men who invented America created democracy, freedom, and truth *as they saw it.* Democracy is a constant reconstitution of the political truth. For two thousand years a woman's place was in the home—and then, in 1993, the Pentagon announced that women will now be permitted to fly combat missions.

Communities resist revolutions and revolutionaries. In a strong sense, the individualist is a natural enemy of the established community. To question the standards of the community is to threaten its existence. To overthrow those standards is a revolution. Over the past century the rush of modernity has devastated communities, scattered families, and destroyed relationships no less than the American, French, and Russian Revolutions. The consequences of modernity, are that "all fixed, fast-frozen relations, with their train of ancient and venerable prejudices and opinions, are swept away, all new-formed ones become antiquated before they can ossify. All that is solid melts into air, all that is holy is profaned. . . ."

It is a feeling that many of us have felt as we survey the vanishing values and traditions of our childhoods—"*all that is solid melts into air.*" This striking attack on modernity is, of course, Karl Marx's famous description in *The Communist Manifesto* of the consequences of the bourgeoisie's transformation of production—and thus "all social relations." The success of capitalism produced more machines,

more products, more money—and more disaffection from the workers than the masters of industry could ever have imagined. "Everlasting uncertainty and agitation distinguish the bourgeois epoch from all
earlier ones," explains Marx, who believed that the social devastation
of bourgeois competition will force men to revolt against their capitalist masters.[35]

Ironically, this same "uncertainty and agitation" is what has driven
contemporary American conservatives and religious traditionalists
into a kind of reactionary political activism feeding more on nostalgia
than history. Memories of "the good old days" are usually false. Professor Sandel advises that we find our moral identity by reflecting on
"our moral experience" within our families, friendships, and other
communities in which we live. Yet too many of us look back on those
communities as prisons that tried to press every bit of our "experience," moral or otherwise, into their versions of the good. The age-old
response to the stifling life of a small community is to do what people
from every small town in America have done to save—or find—themselves: head for the big city, where "difference" more easily finds its
own community or creates a new one.

It is misleading at best and nostalgic claptrap at worst to claim that
American communities of the past were idylls of truth and harmony.
For every good neighbor, there was a drunk or wife beater or greedy
merchant or factory owner or corrupt politician stirring up or using
the community for his own ends.[36] Most American cities and towns
began or thrived with wanderers from other places, refugees from
other communities, immigrants from other lands, sometimes criminals, and often men and women who had run away from their families. Others were founded around a family factory or plant whose
owners lorded over the area like European nobility, the schools, the libraries, and other social entertainment the avocation or religious duty
of the presiding family. It has been the genius of America to take such
"communities of strangers" and turn them into Americans.

Typically, however, the only thing such people have in common is
their Americanness. They are inclined to differ on almost everything
else. The culture is presently experiencing the downside of its own pluralism: too many groups fighting for their own "rights" with little care
about the common good. Conservative commentators are quick to
point this out, and they are right to be dismayed by the intolerance of
the Left and the silliness of "political correctness." Yet this trend is not
individualism's fault or even liberalism's. The trouble is that everyone,
on all sides of every issue, Right and Left, conservative and liberal, re-

ligious and not so, thinks he or she is absolutely right. Nothing could be more destructive of the dream of a decent society than the illusion of omniscience. Moral progress requires disagreement.

The Oppression of Certainty

> For those who say I can't impose my morality on others, I say just watch me.
> Joseph Scheidler, executive director,
> Pro-Life Action League[37]

Such arrogance is all too common in what passes for moral debate in our nation these days, and not just on the issue of abortion. While Scheidler doubtless considers himself a "good American," what he really is is a good American fanatic. As John Stuart Mill noted in 1859, in his justly famous defense of freedom "On Liberty": "It is not difficult to show, by abundant instances, that to extend the bounds of what may be called moral police, until it encroaches on the most unquestionably legitimate liberty of the individual, is one of the most universal of all human propensities."[38]

The urge to interfere, to treat one's preferences and taste as the equivalent of a moral law, has achieved a kind of political, if not intellectual, sophistication in the United States of the late twentieth century. The "moral police" are impressively organized and influential. Patrick Buchanan, the former Nixon speechwriter, Reagan aide, presidential candidate, and self-professed "man of the Right," expressed his contempt in his recent autobiography for the question his enemies put to him: "Why are you always trying to impose your values on the rest of us?" Buchanan's typically antagonistic, and well-phrased, answer is:

> Among too many raised in the Judeo-Christian tradition, that taunt has engendered a moral disarmament and political paralysis. But . . . someone's values are going to prevail. Why not ours? Whose country is it, anyway? Whose moral code says we may interfere with a man's right to be a practicing bigot, but must respect and protect his right to be a practicing sodomite? Why should the moral code of modern secularism prevail? Simply because the militant homosexuals have come marching out of their closets is no reason for the saints to go marching in.[39]

In a televised speech during the 1992 Republican convention, Buchanan called on his supporters to wage a "cultural and religious war" against fellow Americans who believe that women have the right to choose abortion, that homosexuals do not necessarily choose to be so, that the lives of trees and rivers may be, in the end, as crucial to the future of humanity as the people polluting them. This is a war, he claimed, for the "soul of America." Buchanan called his Christian soldiers to arms (Buchanan's version of "Judeo-Christian values" rests heavily on the Christian side of the divide): "We must take back our cities, and take back our culture, and take back our country."

His culture!? *His* country!? "We are America," said Richard Bond, the Republican National Committee chairman, during the convention. "These other people [i.e., the supporters of the Democratic candidate Bill Clinton] are not America."[40] Jefferson and James Madison would have been dismayed to discover that America belongs to the 1992 version of the Republican Party. But, to be fair to the Buchananites, Jefferson and Madison would have been equally appalled by the inanities of "political correctness" on the leftward side of the American political spectrum. Ironically, the true believers on the American Right and Left share a taste for self-righteousness and intolerance. Their illusion of infallibility can be staggering.

One could envy Buchanan's and the PC gang's certainty that their values are right. But what if they are wrong? That those values might be the wrong ones, and that they might be forced on a minority (or a majority) was precisely what was bothering Madison when he argued for his version of the Constitution in The Federalist Papers. Indeed, someone's values will probably prevail, but preferably they will win out by debate and not by religious war. Apparently the Jesuit-educated Buchanan has forgotten St. Augustine's words: "No one ought to be constrained to believe." Surely he has forgotten that Martin Luther himself had quoted Augustine, not to mention John Locke's gloss on Augustine and Luther: "No man can be forced to be saved."[41]

Within a century Locke's view was embodied in the First Amendment to the Constitution's commitment to religious liberty: "Congress shall make no law respecting an establishment of religion, or prohibiting the free exercise thereof." Politics and religion are obliged to live free of each other. Generally, most Americans accept keeping the State out of the Church, but lately some have forgotten that it is a two-way street. Legally, my religious views are equal to Pat Buchanan's, even if we both think each other is nuts. In fact, in a democracy, the real nut is the person who presumes he and only he is right. This is the lesson of the tolerant man, the so-called liberal. (The word "liberal" has been so discredited, perhaps "tolerant man" should replace it.) As the philosopher Judith Shklar has expressed it, "Liberals have abandoned certainty and agreement as goals of a free people."[42] Once one side claims to have The Truth, the argument either must stop or turn into religious warfare.

Herein lies our salvation. The inventors of America were worldly men, more intellectually sophisticated than most of our own politicians. They were not only aware that freedom would breed conflicting values, incomprehension, incoherence, and hostility; they were expecting that such differences would secure the nation's future as a republican democracy, one that by its design would be a natural multiplicity of different and thus inevitably conflicting cultures.[43]

Free people can only hope for tolerance on all sides. As the Supreme Court Justice Oliver Wendell Holmes Jr. wrote in a dissenting opinion in 1929 (*U.S.* v. *Schwimmer*), there is no "principle of the Constitution more important than the principle of free thought—not free thought for those who agree with us but *freedom of thought for those we hate.*" [my italics][44]

This is the alternative to religious and civil war. In America, no moral identity is supposed to be dominant. Ideally, the liberal state (and America is history's ideal liberal state) is supposed to ignore the moral (and ideological) differences between Thomas Jefferson and Jefferson Davis, between George Washington and George Washington Carver, between Father Divine and Father Flanagan, between Arthur Miller and Arthur Godfrey.

To be sure, we are a "collection of strangers"—and it can be our glory rather than our downfall. Fundamental differences can divide a society, but they can also be the juice of democracy, what keeps the debate cooking, the political conflict inevitable, and change ever constant. For it is only in conflict that we might recognize the *legitimate* differences of others and thus open our own minds (and communities) to the possibility that we may be wrong and need to change.

What else is there for a free and decent society to do? Unlike the ayatollah, we have no sacred book to refer to. The first premise of a decent free society is tolerance. The first sparks of tolerance and decency, however, reside in the imagination—what I want to call the "moral imagination."

7. The Moral Imagination

Following a tour of the burned-out neighborhoods of South Central Los Angeles after the riots in the spring of 1992, President George Bush admitted, "I can hardly imagine—I try, but I can hardly imagine the fear and the anger that people must feel to terrorize one another and burn each other's property."[1] It is not surprising that a sixty-eight-year-old Connecticut-born son of a U.S. senator and an alumnus of Andover, Yale, the U.S. Congress, and the Central Intelligence Agency cannot put himself into the sneakers of a looter in South Central L.A. Yet any leader who claims, as ours so often do, to be committed to wiping out moral ugliness had better try, for while it might not be right to terrorize one another or burn one another's property, it is crucial—especially for presidents—to understand the urge.

I wondered if the President had read the op-ed essay in the *New York Times* the previous day in which the author noted, "White people sometimes think that if blacks could just act like whites, everything would be all right."[2] The author, of course, is black, which gives some authority to his comments about blacks. But what does he know about how whites think? Plenty, it turns out. His father, you see, is white. The author is also an eighth grader in a Chicago school. He is able to see the problem in a way that most of us cannot imagine. But that doesn't mean that, with the help of such reports from the much too distant world of black life, we cannot at least try to imagine the differences.

The facts are unavoidable: one in five American children lives in poverty, banks and other money lenders still discriminate against blacks applying for mortgages, white males are more likely to work at the best jobs for the highest salaries.[3] In 1989, President Bush vetoed a bill that over three years would have raised the minimum wage to $4.55 an hour. In 1991 that same president (who had once called for a "kinder and gentler nation") vetoed a civil rights act passed by Congress to set aside Supreme Court rulings that make it more difficult for women and minorities to win employment and discrimination suits.

Some things in any society are not worth "conserving." Surely, even conservatives do not oppose moral progress. I hear no one lamenting the passing of slavery, male suffrage, child labor, and indiscriminate pollution of the air and rivers. Yet these were all "values" that American society once lived with. It was the Civil War—not morality—that ended slavery. But today we recognize all of them as clear examples of moral ugliness and, in the case of slavery and child labor, cruelty. That we want to stamp out cruelty and the morally ugly is, I believe, a common trait of Americans, on the Right and the Left. Recognizing what is morally ugly is another matter. Our standards are typically different. Poverty may be an injustice for me and the breaks of the game for you. What does it take for people to recognize moral ugliness or cruelty?

God will not help us here; nor will some overarching sense of "community." Being a decent, compassionate, good person in a diverse community requires considerable imagination—"moral imagination."

We all have our ghettos to escape. It takes no less a leap of the imagination for a privileged white president to see his way into the ghetto than for a poor black to see his way out.

That our values are so different and incompatible is a fact of life in a pluralistic democracy, as I demonstrated in the previous chapter. But how such people who see the world in such different ways can live together peacefully in a society is one of philosophy's most vexing problems. I want to argue that the only peace available in American democracy is an unstable one. And to keep the peace, we must learn to live with our lack of moral knowledge and the inevitable clash of values around us. We must try to become the historians of our own society, the novelists of our own lives, the screenwriters of the suffering and humiliation on the streets, in hospitals, in abortion clinics, even on death row. We must try to feel the frustration and bitterness, the hatred and fear of the poor, the black, the female, the pregnant, the dying, and the condemned.

If that sounds too politically correct, let me add quickly that from the Left we must also try to feel the frustration and bitterness, the hatred and fear of hardworking, God-fearing, loyal, tax-paying Americans who, with good reason, question the crime, disorder, and social chaos in their midst. As I argued in the last chapter, neither liberals nor conservatives have a lock on The Truth. Liberals who press political correctness on their neighbors are no better than conservatives who want to impose their values on the rest of us. Both are strategies for religious and cultural warfare. Oppression is no less so when it comes from the Left.

Of course, there are those who do not want to listen, who have no interest in what the other side believes. They prefer shouting to civil conversation. But I am not talking about the extremists and fanatics. I am addressing the moral conversation that might take place between people with divergent attitudes who proudly call themselves liberal and conservative but also view themselves as people of good will who share at least the common goal of a decent society. To them, I suggest that the moral conversation is more likely to continue if we can imagine the world from the other side of the barricade. Standing among "the enemy" for a moment, we might be able to see similarities between them and us, not some common "human nature" or some ineffable "essence" shared by all men, but the fact that we are all bundles of opinions and beliefs, of theories and prejudices about how we and our world are or ought to be. To be able to make this imaginary leap is to have a well-developed moral imagination.

A few of us seem to be born with this kind of moral creativity—people with such natural compassion that they strike us as saintly (Mother Teresa comes to mind first, but pick your favorite "living saint"). But the rest of us can *become* more morally imaginative about what we might value and what others value. This should not be beyond our powers. Our moral adversaries are not ancient Greeks, medieval knights, warring Zulus, evil Russians, or any of the other people that historians and anthropologists claim to understand. These are our fellow Americans, indeed they are likely to be our neighbors, our relatives, even our very selves.

"Transcending Local Prejudices"

I hear the objections: If burning down another's place of business is wrong, what good does it do me to imagine the anger of a black looter? What's wrong is wrong. If I believe abortion is murder, then sympathizing with a murderer seems to be stretching it.

Yes, but what about the possibility that the L.A. arsonist might be justified in his anger (if not his actions)? What if abortion is not murder—and capital punishment is? To explore these possibilities, you have to understand more about the intellectual source of your moral conflict, listen a little harder to the other side of the story. By trying to understand a black person's rage, or why a husband feels morally obliged to kill his wife suffering from the pain of terminal cancer, you might see the possibility of sometimes being wrong. You don't have to change your mind about one issue or another. You don't have to believe that anything goes. (Who does?) But by developing your moral imagination, you will be less likely to burn your adversary at the stake for fear that no matter how strongly you feel that the death penalty is right, say, or that affirmative action is unjust, you may actually be wrong.

To create a decent society from millions of people who disagree with one another on matters of life and death requires getting comfortable with "screwed-up" people and their ideas. No one understood this better than the men who invented America. As Samuel Cooper, the influential Boston preacher, wrote in 1753: "Benevolence is the Cement and Support—of Families—of Churches—of States—of Kingdoms—and of the Great Community of Mankind. It is the single Principle that constitutes and preserves all the Peace and Harmony, all the Beauty and Advantage of Society."[4]

"Benevolence" (literally, "willing the good") was a virtue that dominated the imaginations of the colonial revolutionaries. The good will of Cooper and his fellow colonial intellectuals stretched beyond their communities to "mankind" at large; each wanted to be, in the words of George Washington, the most self-conscious Roman statesman among the revolutionary leaders, "a citizen of the great republic of humanity at large."[5] As the historian Gordon Wood reminds us, "the revolutionary generation was the most cosmopolitan of any in American history."[6] The men who made America wanted to be "citizens of the world"; they sought to transcend, in the words of Thomas Paine, "distinctions too limited for continental minds." According to Wood,

To be free of local prejudices and parochial ties defined a liberally educated gentleman. One's humanity was measured by one's ability to relate to strangers, *to enter into the hearts of even those who were different*. And Americans prided themselves on their hospitality and their treatment of strangers. Such cosmopolitanism was a consequence of civilization. [my italics][7]

Did this make the founders "relativists"? Here again the model was the Greeks, the first to recognize that different cultures, foreigners—the "barbarians" (i.e., the non-Greek speakers)—had their own rational way of living. (In the historical writings of Herodotus there is already the recognition of cultural pluralism.) The American revolutionaries may have rejected England's rule, but not European ideas. After all, they considered themselves men of the *European* Enlightenment.

Wood's description of the "cosmopolitanism" of the early American leaders—their ability to "enter into the hearts" of strangers—echoes Isaiah Berlin's account of the intellectual origins of "cultural pluralism" in the eighteenth century. According to Berlin, thinkers like Giambattista Vico in Italy and Johann Herder in Germany were the first to recognize that other cultures could be committed to different and incompatible values without being incomprehensible to one another. All it took was an "imaginative leap" into the cultural history of different national traditions, present and past. They knew they could learn from other traditions without committing themselves to any kind of moral relativism. Unlike the traditional relativist, they did not believe these different values were solely a matter of opinion or prejudice; such values could be justified, though only within the communities that cultivated them. Nor did they believe that outsiders were incapable of evaluating the forms of life in communities different from theirs. Vico, explains Berlin, believed that "what men have made others can understand" by "entering into" or "descending into" their minds. All it requires is "imaginative insight," what the Germans call *Verstehen,* a kind of personal understanding. Vico also called it *fantasia.* According to Berlin, *fantasia*

> is unlike the knowledge that Julius Caesar is dead, or that Rome was not built in a day, or that thirteen is a prime number, or that a week has seven days; nor yet is it like the knowledge of how to ride a bicycle or engage in statistical research or win a battle. It is more like knowing what it is to be poor, to belong to a nation, to be revolutionary, to be converted to a religion, to fall in love, to be seized by nameless terror, or to be delighted by a work of art.[8]

Without such "flights of the imagination," Berlin points out, historians would not be able to reconstruct, or evaluate, the past whose inhabitants saw the world so differently from us. Imagination is a "prerequisite for history," says Berlin. "Otherwise the past is dead."[9]

This same gift to penetrate the minds and beliefs of others is also what makes for a great novelist, the kind of writer who can help us understand the deepest thoughts, motives, and complexities of men and women. It is a prerequisite for art.[10]

Such "imaginative sympathy" is also, I believe, a prerequisite for democratic pluralists to meet Dewey's task of philosophy—"to clarify men's ideas as to the social and moral strifes of their own day." What I have in mind is the kind of imaginative leap it takes to understand what it is like to be poor, black, female, and pregnant without the option of abortion; it requires the kind of insight into the shame and defeat or numbing depression someone might feel when he decides he has no reason to continue living; it requires understanding what it is like to be terminally ill and kept alive by machines; it requires understanding what makes a person angry enough to burn down and loot his neighborhood in East Los Angeles. And it is also the same kind of imaginative leap required to understand why some Americans are appalled by feminists, abortion, euthanasia, and black people unable to find a job or so angry that they burn their neighbors' property.

Supreme Court Justice Thurgood Marshall once asked the deputy solicitor general arguing for the constitutionality of a regulation prohibiting people from sleeping in public parks whether *he* had ever been homeless. Marshall knew that sometimes even the imaginations of the most well-intentioned people, stunted by ignorance or inexperience, could use some prodding.

Moral Leadership

For centuries white Americans have found it difficult to understand the frustration, anger, indeed the hatred of some black Americans. Slavery, after all, once was legal in the United States and rationalized by the best political, philosophical, and religious minds of the day. Neither morality nor piety ended slavery; a murderous civil war did. And even after the Constitution was amended to grant black Americans their equal citizenship before the laws, state legislatures treated them as second-class citizens for the next century, until the civil rights battles of the 1960s helped expand our moral imaginations.

As I was writing this chapter, the newspapers reported the death of Thurgood Marshall, the first black Supreme Court justice who as the chief attorney of the NAACP had pursued the school discrimination cases that resulted in *Brown* v. *Board of Education,* the landmark reversal in 1954 of the "separate but equal" doctrine. The *New York Times* obituary quoted from a tribute to Marshall written by a former law clerk:

> He grew up in a ruthlessly discriminatory world—a world in which segregation of the races was pervasive and taken for granted, where lynching was common, where the black man's inherent inferiority was proclaimed widely and wantonly. Thurgood Marshall had the capacity to imagine a radically different world, the imaginative capacity to believe that such a world was possible, the strength to sustain that image in the mind's eye and the heart's longing, and the courage and ability to make that imagined world real.[11]

Apparently, Marshall's own imaginative powers were contagious. The obituary reminded me of another newspaper story about Marshall I had clipped months before: "LIBERAL GIANTS INSPIRE THREE CENTRIST JUSTICES" was the headline of a story about the personal reminiscences of Justices Anthony Kennedy, Sandra Day O'Connor, and David Souter—all Republican appointees to the Court and moderate conservatives—about their recently retired colleagues Justices Marshall and William Brennan.[12] O'Connor had written that she was surprised by the extent to which Marshall "would profoundly influence me" during the ten years they had served together on the Court. Discussing cases during conference, Marshall liked to tell personal stories that spoke to a particular issue before the Court. O'Connor recalled one example of racial prejudice and the miscarriage of justice in a death penalty case Marshall had handled as a trial lawyer. "His story made clear what legal briefs often obscure: the impact of legal rules on human lives," wrote Justice O'Connor, who described Marshall's stories as "a source of amazement and inspiration."

This is what makes great moral leaders: they amaze and inspire us and help us reimagine the world we think we know so well, until we realize that something is so wrong with it that we have to create a new world. This is what Justice Marshall did; it is also what Martin Luther King Jr. did, and it is what one of America's greatest leaders did.

Lincoln's Reinvention of "America"

The dogmas of the past are inadequate to the stormy present . . .

Abraham Lincoln[13]

At the end of 1862, in the midst of America's greatest catastrophe, the Civil War, Abraham Lincoln proposed legislation for the gradual emancipation and compensation of the slaves—the famous Emancipation Proclamation. More than 130 years later it is not easy to understand what an extraordinary proposal this was. Lincoln had ground his heel on the presiding metaphor of the times, which he himself had believed in—that black men and women were fit only to be the property of their white superiors.

"As our case is new, so we must think anew, and act anew," Lincoln declared. "We must disenthrall ourselves, and then save our country." To end the war, new ideas were necessary. A year later in his dedication of the Union cemetery at Gettysburg, Lincoln would simply take an old idea stated clearly in the Declaration of Independence—"all men are created equal"—and restate it so it seemed new. Lincoln declared that black Americans would have to be included in the class of "all men" for the country to live up to its commitment to freedom.

The nation, Lincoln announced, would have "a new birth in freedom." Lincoln would act as midwife. In his Gettysburg Address, Lincoln restated the values of the American experiment and reinterpreted them for his own age and the future.[14] While Jefferson himself might have owned slaves, and the Supreme Court had reaffirmed the constitutionality of slavery in the infamous *Dred Scott* decision, and the Constitution was at least ambiguous about the right of states to secede, Lincoln recognized that no nation could remain true to Jefferson's words without abolishing slavery—and along with it an American "truth" that had existed for two hundred years (i.e., that slavery was morally right).

It is Lincoln's version of America, his *reinvention*, as Garry Wills has pointed out in his analysis of the Gettysburg Address, that we cherish today.[15] In the face of political and editorial criticism, even hatred, Lincoln, I would suggest, stretched the *imagination* of America. What seemed radical and unconstitutional at the time—that slavery was morally wrong—is now a truth which everyone is so comfortable with that to state that slavery is wrong seems banal.

I want to argue that every moral decision we make involves some degree of imaginative effort on our part. It is our ability to imagine first the consequences of a certain act for ourselves that makes us rational beings. What makes us *moral* beings—and here is where moral leaders can help us—is being able to imagine the effects of our acts on others.

Creating a Moral Imagination

Why is it that certain acts—rape, child abuse, murdering innocent people, torturing even guilty people—seem wrong to all civilized people, no matter their religious beliefs, their national origin, their culture?

In a recent encyclical Pope John Paul II has rejected the notion that man freely creates his values.[16] For the Vatican (and, I hasten to add, for most philosophers since Plato), true values are inherent in God's ordered universe and only await discovery. Human morality ought to be directed by "natural law." The pope's encyclical is only the latest attack on the "moral relativism" of modernity. In the previous chapter I discussed the inadequacy of this charge. If I disagree with the pope that there is no evidence of any one Truth, then his calling me a "relativist" bears no sting (no more than if because I reject the infallibility of the pope, I will be insulted by the being called an "anti-papist." In my opinion, and with considerable historical evidence on my side, the pope may be well-meaning, but he is no more infallible than I on matters of morality. The Church has committed moral horrors throughout its two millennia, and a few popes have admitted as much).

But the pope is right to note that certain actions seem absolutely wrong to everyone. The reason, I think, such acts as rape or child abuse seem wrong to everybody is the universal discomfort with cruelty. Although throughout history, torture and cruelty have not always been so universally despised (to point to the Church's resort to torture during the Inquisition would be too easy), since the Enlightenment it has been a distinction of the "liberal" or "progressive" or "atheistic humanist" to oppose cruelty for any reason, even (or particularly) for dogmatic religious reasons. As Richard Rorty and Judith Shklar have pointed out, what the traditional liberal dislikes most is the idea of hurting other people, and not only physically. Rorty's good man "takes the morally relevant definition of a person, a moral subject, to be 'something that can be humiliated.' "[17]

Herein lies the "universal" immorality of certain acts—and here lies a connection between liberals and those who despise the label but consider themselves decent persons. Decent people recoil at rape or child abuse not because of some "natural law" written in the heavens but because they recognize such acts as cruel and humiliating. Some acts, like murder and rape, have seemed heinous to men from the beginning of civilization; others, like slavery and torture, took centuries before their cruelty was recognized. And while the founders may not have recognized that capital punishment was "cruel and unusual punishment," they did condemn torture. It is now time for Americans to expand their moral imaginations and understand that capital punishment is equally cruel and unusual.

It is this imagination of what it is like to be humiliated, oppressed, or treated cruelly that can provide the bridge between us and our moral enemies. While we know when we are being treated cruelly or have been humiliated, it is not always so easy to recognize our cruelty to others, nor how such cruelty has affected their lives. When President Bush saw what happened in Los Angeles in 1992, he could not imagine how people could burn one another's property; he could not look and understand their rage and hopelessness. When the novelist James Baldwin looked at his fellow blacks, he saw:

> the Negro's past of rope, fire, torture, castration, infanticide, rape; death and humiliation; fear by day and night, fear as deep as the marrow of the bone; doubt that he was worthy of life, since everyone around him denied it . . . rage, hatred, and murder, hatred for white men so deep that it often turned against him and his own, and made all love, all trust, all joy impossible. . . .[18]

It is all a matter of one's moral imagination. For Baldwin, the American Negro's violent past "contains, for all its horror, something very beautiful." Black Americans have survived, notes Baldwin in a startling image, "and produce children of kindergarten age who can walk through mobs to get to school." Martin Luther King Jr., too, knew from personal experience the rage and humiliation his fellow African-Americans felt. But he believed that we all needed to be redeemed—blacks from their rage, or their resignation, segregationists from their evil and irrational racism, and the rest of us from our moral and political complacency.

To understand the histories of ancient people, where the information is thin and the cultures so distant from our own, takes great imagination. Why should it be so hard to understand the histories of members of our own communities? The poor, the black, the accidentally pregnant, even the wickedly criminal do not have different kinds of emotions from the prosperous, the white, and the purely virtuous. How hard is it to understand the anger a black bus driver feels when white people snub him, or the humiliation of a black nurse when a white patient recoils to her touch? Why is an American president—and too many of the rest of us—unable to imagine the anger and frustration of black people, of all ages, in our cities? At first sight, to a member of the white middle class, the homeless black man seems so alien, so "screwed-up." But on closer look, the poor are like the rest of us, only less lucky. They have failed, they have been humiliated, they are threatening. We need not be sentimental about poverty or homelessness to recognize what we might share with the poor and the homeless. Many of us are just one bad break from misery. To get beyond the abstractions and the poverty statistics, we must become more like Graham Greene's whiskey priest in the great novel *The Power and the Glory* who remarked of his fellow prisoners: "When you visualized a man or woman carefully, you could always begin to feel pity—that was a quality God's image carried with it."[19]

Morality is a continuing *conversation* about how we can keep from stomping on one another's special projects of self-improvement. How will a good person know when she is hurting or humiliating her neighbors? Valuing freedom, tolerance, justice "requires me," says Rorty, "to become aware of all the various ways in which other human beings whom I might act upon can be humiliated."[20] It is not always easy, but tuning into the potential humiliation of others, including those on the other side of the moral barricades, ought to be easier than penetrating the customs of an aboriginal tribe or figuring out the daily lives of fifth-century Athenians. Figuring out what hurts or is likely to enrage another person may be the only way that people of good will who disagree fundamentally about basic values can avoid being hateful to one another. To achieve this, however, requires that we try to understand why they have the beliefs and values that they do.

Here, in the area of creating a moral imagination, I think Rorty and Berlin and the liberals who invented America converge. According to Rorty, his postmodern man of tolerance "needs as much *imaginative acquaintance* with alternative final vocabularies [Rorty-speak for systems of values that may be incompatible with yours], not just for her own edification, but in order to understand the actual and possible

humiliation of the people who use these final alternative vocabularies." [my italics][21]

In other words, we pro-choice advocates should not be too quick to
deride women who oppose abortion because they believe "the fetus is
a person" and "motherhood is a woman's highest calling." We may
disagree with such a "final vocabulary," but we have no right to humiliate or to be cruel to those who have adopted it. But to recognize that
deriding such values constitutes cruelty requires "an imaginative acquaintance" with another's system of values.[22]

What Vico called *fantasia,* what Berlin calls an "imaginative leap,"
what Rorty calls an "imaginative acquaintance" with another's value
system is what I want to call "moral imagination."[23]

I believe this idea of moral imagination is precisely the notion I
need to explain what I said at the outset any decent moral system must
explain: why the liberal winces at the sight of a homeless man lying on
the street, and the conservative tells him to get off his butt and get a
job. Since the worst thing that can happen to the traditional liberal is
to be oppressed or humiliated or treated cruelly, he certainly will not
want to hurt or humiliate anyone else. He hates cruelty and suffering
and never thinks, as others do, that suffering (or exploitation of workers or pollution of the environment) is a necessary condition or "the
downside" of the good life. In my terms, a woman wants to be able to
choose freely when to have a baby, she wants to be able to walk into an
abortion clinic without someone sticking a bottled embryo in her face;
similarly, the tolerant person will not rush into the cathedral and disrupt mass or blow up the offices of Operation Rescue. This kind of liberal avoids all dogmatism (including political correctness) and is
willing to hear the other side's case, as long as they will hear his, and
may the best group win in persuading the lawmakers to their point of
view. "Imagination," wrote Dewey, "is the chief instrument of the
good. . . ."[24]

But whose "good"? The question does not go away: What kind of
standards will guide our imaginations? We will have to choose, but
how? Without moral knowledge, from where do we draw our reasons
to choose, not to mention the strength to stick to our choices? The historian John P. Diggins, noting that Henry James once said that America lacks "the imagination of disaster," has suggested that a nation
which skipped feudalism and was born free ". . . may also lack the
imagination of oppression."[25] This gap in our national imagination
has, I think, fueled the nastiness of our politics and moral conflicts. Alleged conservatives want to impose their ideas on the rest of us. That's

one definition of "oppression." Some so-called liberals are equally eager to press their "politically correct" beliefs on schools and communities. That's another definition of oppression, and a call for humiliating people of opposing views.

Trying not to hurt or humiliate your opponents is what puts morality into us. It is what restrains us from doing whatever we damned well please. This is why my tolerant man cannot be charged with being a pure relativist who believes that anything goes, that nothing is wrong. In fact, this person, in spite of his skepticism about our ability to find The Truth, actually believes one thing to be certain: he knows that he does not want to be treated cruelly or to be humiliated. He has a definition of "bad" or "evil"—what hurts, oppresses, humiliates us. And thus he believes, strongly, that it is bad, wrong, evil to hurt and humiliate others.

That is a *common* moral standard, perhaps the only one. What is cruel or humiliating, of course, is typically a "relative" standard. But even that is not out of our reach—if we can manage to try to "enter into" the hearts and minds of our adversaries, understand their beliefs and opinions, their world-view, their "form of life," their "language games,"[26] and understand not necessarily that they are right, but that we might actually be wrong.

Populist Ethics: Taking Moral Thinking into Your Own Hands

The issues I have raised in this book were once the province of only a tiny fraction of the society—theologians, philosophers, doctors, constitutional scholars. And while intellectuals and the press mined one subject or another, most Americans had an opinion and went on with their lives. That is no longer true. Abortion, euthanasia, suicide, capital punishment, and race have raised fundamental questions about who we are as a people and where we are going. I think many people now realize this.

The fact that Americans have begun to debate these issues openly, and in some cases have taken their views to the streets, indicates a certain maturity in thought if not manners. It is as if the people, disappointed in the remedies of their politicians, educators, and religious leaders, have decided to take thinking into their own hands. (Evidence that they have taken the law into their own hands emerged in two jury trials in Los Angeles connected to the 1992 riots. After deliberating for days, two juries were equally lenient with three black men charged with beating a white truck driver and four white cops who beat up a black man. It seemed that in the absence of any political or moral leadership in Los Angeles, the juries decided to ignore their job of coming to a verdict according to the rule of law and instead tried to avoid causing a riot.)[27]

That tens of thousands of "ordinary Americans" have become passionate about issues that were once discussed seriously only in universities is in itself a blow to "traditional values." Doubtless, we were more innocent in the 1950s, but there is no going back. As Thomas Paine wrote in *The Rights of Man*, one of the founding documents of the American Revolution: "When once the veil begins to rend, it admits not of repair. Ignorance is of a peculiar nature: and once dispelled, it is impossible to reestablish it."[28]

Americans know much more today about moral issues, and, as Paine also noted, "though man may be kept ignorant, he cannot be *made* ignorant."[29] Among some Americans the desire to make people ignorant is strong. It is not only a losing battle, it is also a stupid one. For centuries, people believed that blacks are inferior to whites and women are inferior to men until moral thinking progressed to the stage where only extremists or moral morons would dare to say such a thing today.

Who is not for moral progress, for creating a more decent society? But moral reflection and its result, moral progress, is unlikely without the free exchange of ideas, indeed without moral disagreement. What is my standard for moral progress and the decent society? It is a simple one: an abiding hatred of moral ugliness.

Inspiring the Moral Imagination: The Force of Moral Ugliness

This brings me back again to the problem that I stated at the outset which challenges any theory of morality: Why is it that one American who thinks he is a good and virtuous man can step over a homeless man in the street and tell him to "get a job," while another American who has the same opinion of himself cringes at the defects of a society that allows its poor and unlucky to live in the streets?

For me, the real difference between these two Americans is their reactions to the morally ugly. The killer competitor believes that the morally ugly is an unfortunate, but *inevitable*, consequence of freedom and individualism, while the bleeding heart sees such social chaos and human devastation as an affront to freedom. One is willing to live with the morally ugly as a price of doing business; the other would like to figure out a better way of doing business.

What qualifies as the "morally ugly"? Turn to the morning paper; it's whatever tightens the lower half of your body. In this morning's *New York Times* I note a wire service dispatch buried on page 14, "1 in 4 Elderly Is Ill Fed, Poll Finds." A national survey to promote better nutrition by health-care providers not only found that one quarter of older Americans are malnourished, but also discovered that doctors and nurses estimated that *half of all hospital patients sixty-five and older and 40 percent of nursing home patients are malnourished.*[30] That's morally ugly. When Americans spend 14 percent of their GNP on a health-care system and still manage to leave 37 million people un-covered—that's morally ugly. So is American reluctance to raise taxes to provide for higher education for everyone qualified.

In June 1989, President Bush vetoed a bill that would have raised the minimum wage to $4.55 over three years; in October of that year he ve-toed a provision of a Medicaid bill that would have paid for abortions for victims of rape and incest; in 1992, Bush vetoed the family leave bill that would have entitled workers to time off, without pay, for family births or medical emergencies.[31] That's morally ugly. And so is the atti-tude of American business, that it can succeed well enough in the world market *without* training or educating ghetto youngsters. Moral ugliness is when a fifth of all the nation's children are poor, not to mention *half* of its black preschoolers.[32] When a mother and father both work and still cannot push their family income over the "poverty line"—and when that number might be as high as *one fourth of the nation*[33]—that's moral ugliness.

But not everyone, amazingly, sees it as such. If so, then it is a failure of moral imagination, an inability to see the humiliation in the other person's story. But when Americans get it, when moral ugliness stares us in the face and we blink, we usually try to do something about it. That is why videotape of starving children in Somalia and kids bleed-ing from shrapnel wounds in Bosnia enrage and sicken us, and inspire us to send money and food. For some reason the poverty, starvation, and increasingly violent deaths of young people in our own cities (where, unlike in Bosnia and Somalia, we might actually be able to do something about such violence and hunger) can no longer grab our imaginations. For some reason political leaders cannot envision a dif-ferent world, a world with at least less moral ugliness. Of course, it can

seem hopeless and intractable. Maybe it is. But it is our moral and social obligation to try to be as inventive as possible. As Lincoln said, "as
our case is new, so we must think anew and act anew."

The Not-So-Perfect-But-Decent Society

As I worked out my own response to each of the issues raised in this
book, I realized that "morality" was always only part of the answer.
Other factors interfere. No one really makes a moral decision by running it through his "moral system," like numbers through a computer
program. To any question of "How would you decide," the answer "It
depends . . ." is always a fair start. If the doctor emerges and says,
"The fetus or your wife?" I don't even have to think: my wife, of
course. Though I may be uncomfortable with 1.6 million abortions a
year, and think that is too much killing, whatever is being killed, a person, a lump of cells, or something (as I believe) in between, I know one
thing for sure: the relationship between my wife and me and the fetus
and me is different. I love my wife; I have only hope for the fetus. Similarly, if it is my teenaged daughter who is accidentally pregnant, I have
to think how that fetus threatens her future.

If my terminally ill father, in great pain, asks me to help him die, my
decision will not be based only on my views about assisted suicide.
Much more is involved: my love for my father, my responsibility to
him, fulfilling the only major request he has made of his son in his life.
I will also have to consider the consequences for me and my family
(i.e., if I am arrested and convicted of murder). That poor black man
on the street with no home, no prospects, what do I say to him? I'm
not quite sure, but it would probably begin with an acknowledgment
of how lucky I am not to be poor and, above all, not to be black.

So, unlike Pat Buchanan or Joseph Scheidler, the anti-abortion activist, so eager to force their values on me, I do not have clear answers
to any of my moral dilemmas. It is never as simple as that. I am prepared to be wrong, even laughably so. Like any traditional American
man of tolerance, I will think over my views, recommend them, but
never forget that what I see as the most important issue of the day in
another century (if not in another week) might turn out to be the
twentieth century's version of the theory that the Earth is flat.

The tolerant man (I suggest we substitute that description for the
now ridiculously—and unfairly—charged word that "liberal" has become) is not willing to believe that his age has finally created the intel-

lectual tools to find all the answers, to resolve all the problems. No matter how satisfied he is with his world (and at the end of the twentieth century democratic pluralism has the smile of a winner), he is still inclined to accept that liberalism is, as Mill put it, an "experiment in living." (Jefferson called America an "experiment," as did Dewey.)[34]

In this view of the not-so-perfect society much compromising and balancing is required. But, as you can see, not every claim deserves equal attention; not everyone is right. (I can reject the pleas of one homeless beggar because I know he is a lazy fraud, but show compassion to another who was laid off and took refuge in drugs. For me, daughters and wives generally take precedence over fetuses. Still, I can easily conceive of situations in which I would oppose abortion: my daughter decides to abort to hurt her boyfriend, or, worse, to take a cruise to the Caribbean. In between these two examples will be many more cases where I might oppose abortion.)

My general guidelines are few: I would rather not hurt someone else or humiliate him. I want to be right, not cruel. I may be wrong, but at least I try to be decent. And, yes, I have my "traditional values" to refer to, the form of life that we have adopted in modern America—the moral, social, and political priorities of pluralistic democratic society, a kind of democratic bottom line: We Americans love freedom and we hate oppression, and (a more recent moral advance for which not everyone has signed on) we hate discrimination against people on the grounds of religion, race, sex, and sexual identity. Our goal is a decent and caring society. Any move to stifle me and my beliefs cuts against that goal. And while I may have to concede to the majority position, I can continue to try to persuade others to come over to my side or reshape the debate.

I would also emphasize that my moral guidelines have a strong basis in Christian tradition. You do not have to be a devout Christian, for example, to cherish Christianity's commitment to the poor and the weak. When Christians rescued unwanted Roman babies exposed on hillsides, when they protested the brutal treatment of slaves and the cruelty of the Coliseum, the hard-hearted Romans were baffled. One might argue that the success of the Christian "revolution" could be explained by the universal appeal of decency to people who had learned only to expect cruelty and oppression and a lack of compassion from those in authority.

What I cannot accept from certain American conservatives and the most self-righteous of the Christian Right is their pretense of infallibility. Philosophers, theologians, historians, physicists, popes, and even

TV evangelists have not proved to be infallible. I cannot expect it from these American moralists. All I can hope for in the midst of a diverse, challenging society where values are colliding all around me is "promoting and preserving an uneasy equilibrium, which is constantly threatened and in constant need of repair," as Isaiah Berlin has said. As Berlin rightly points out, that effort to walk the line between the moral certitude of warring parties "is the precondition for decent societies and morally acceptable behavior."[35]

You may desire to commune with God, but man is what you are left with. He is mystery enough: difficult, unstable, in constant need of repair, though with an amazing capacity for decency in spite of all evidence that nice guys finish last.

If my view of how the good man copes with his fellows seems on the wimpy side, seems to lack *conviction,* I will concede that it definitely does not have the pugnacious passion of Buchanan's or Rush Limbaugh's vision of America. But even in my state of Berlinian "uneasy equilibrium" I do not think it would be hard to convince anyone of my commitment to freedom and tolerance and justice. I have no doubt I would fight very hard indeed against anyone who tried to mess with my freedom to live my life according to the values and traditions I choose. I could even entertain the prospect of being wrong about the value of freedom and justice and still fight like hell against anyone who tried to stifle or oppress me. Holding an infallible list of what is right and wrong or being told by some authority what one ought to do may be some people's version of happiness, but I would prefer the opportunity to think for myself.

The Benefits of "Incredulity"

Expanding our moral imaginations is bound to strip our debates of their moral arrogance. Moral conflict is a good thing; religious and moral *wars* are not, for there can be no moral progress without disagreements. Transforming society requires dissidents and revolutionaries.

We are inclined to see history as the progress of knowledge. In fact, history is the progress from one unknown to another—from flat earth to global, from ether to Einstein, from Europe to America, from communism to democracy. History has a way of taking each age's certainties and reducing them to absurdity. "Incredulity" is the sign of what the French philosopher Jean Lyotard calls our "postmodern condition." All around us absolute values clash. The traditionalist is thrown off balance—"all that's solid melts into air"—and he wants to return to "the good old days." The postmodern man knows that those days are gone forever, and good riddance. He knows that we must tolerate differences, values that will inevitably clash—such as my views of blacks and women and yours, our differences over abortion, my moral dilemma about helping my father to an easy death.[36]

Americans have once again discovered these "differences." The question is, can we learn to live with them? The route to moral progress, I have argued here, is moral reflection. Someday perhaps science will tell us more about how we make moral decisions. For now, however, in our ignorant, underdeveloped state of knowledge about moral matters, I am willing to concede that if there is Truth about anything it is so complicated and vast that we and the next few generations of thinkers will never pierce more than a small chunk of it.

Immoral men need not worry about moral dilemmas. Those of us who aspire to something better will have to make some hard choices. And that requires some serious thought, not to mention the willingness to give up some of the ideas we have cherished. I suspect that the best man is the one best able to expand his experiences of others; he is the man eager to continue the conversation of morality, not stifle it with dogmatism; he is the man who has developed a complicated moral sense, which, ironically, allows him to come to simple moral decisions. But such moral reflection and conversation are impossible without moral imagination.

Acknowledgments

A good book begins with a good idea, something that even the best writers can be short on. Fortunately, I have a smart wife, Marilyn Bethany, who is also a good writer and is never short on good ideas. This book is one of them.

On the way home from a dinner party where the guests had expressed strong opinions about abortion and capital punishment, Marilyn said, "No one knew what they were talking about." As usual, my wife was right. "Your next book should be about moral issues, dealing with the arguments on opposing sides," she advised. "Everyone needs that book." But did I need to write it? I had been out of the academic world for almost twenty years and considered the prospect of venturing my opinions on the biggest and most incendiary issues of the day with trepidation. Yet such a project would provide the opportunity to spend my days reading philosophy under the guise of work. I began a book proposal.

The result, for better or worse, is this book. "The just man pays his debts," says Plato's Socrates, and I would like to pay several off right here. Along with my wife, I'd like to thank my daughters Maisie and Nell for putting up with a father whose free time seemed to be spent mostly on "the book." In 1973, I went to my dissertation advisor at Princeton, Prof. Gregory Vlastos, the great Plato scholar who died not long ago pushing ninety, to inform him that I had decided not to take a job in philosophy but to head off instead into the hurlyburly of New York journalism. To my amazement, Gregory confessed that after

World War II he had almost done the same thing, and encouraged me to give it a shot. If there were such a thing as a Platonic Form of the just man, it would look a lot like Vlastos.

I first began thinking about several of the issues in this book while teaching a seminar in an introductory ethics course at Princeton in 1973 run by Thomas Nagel, an original thinker now at New York University who was a pioneer in applying philosophical argument to practical ethical issues. I summarize Nagel's arguments in support of affirmative action in chapter 5. Readers will also note my debt to Richard Rorty, another of my Princeton teachers, who is now at the University of Virginia and widely considered to be America's most eminent philosopher. His views on "solidarity," "truth," "irony," and "objectivity" (on the other side of the philosophical barricades from Nagel) resonated for this refugee from Philosophy (with a capital "p"). I would hope this book is an example of the kind of philosophy (with a small "p") for which Rorty is an eloquent advocate.

For helping me research chapter 5 on racial justice and pare down my section on euthanasia, I thank my old friend Andy Olstein, who was his usual thorough self. Jonathan Landreth also aided me in the labors of tightening the manuscript, and Jenner Bishop pitched in for some last minute research. I thank my copy editor, Charlotte Gross, for her careful reading of the manuscript, which saved me from many a howler.

Behind every successful book project is a good agent. Mine is Joy Harris, who understood my idea immediately, helped me shape the book proposal, sold the project, and then cheered me on during the research and writing. But my biggest debt is to my editor and friend Alice Mayhew, who quickly and enthusiastically saw a book in this idea. This is my second book for Alice, and I feel that I have achieved some success as a writer if only by having an editor as intelligent and skilled as Alice Mayhew willing to publish me.

The success of this book is due to all of the above; its failures are all mine.

NOTES

Introduction

1. Lionel Trilling, "Manners, Morals, and the Novel," *The Liberal Imagination* (New York: Charles Scribners, 1950), p. 222.

1. Abortion

1. See Laurence H. Tribe, "Two Centuries of Abortion in America," chap. 3 in *Abortion: The Clash of Absolutes* (New York: Norton, 1990), p. 32. The historical information in this chapter is from Tribe, from *Abortion: An Eternal Social and Moral Issue* (Wylie, Texas: Info Aids, 1988), and from Roger Rosenblatt, *Life Itself: Abortion in the American Mind* (New York: Random House, 1992), p. 49 ff, which was published after I had written my original drafts of this chapter and saved me from some mistakes. See also John Noonan, ed., *The Morality of Abortion: Legal and Historical Perspectives* (Cambridge, Mass.: Harvard University Press, 1970). When I began work on this book, I knew that Rosenblatt was finishing up his own long essay about abortion, and I was looking forward to including his argument for abortion in this chapter. But *Life Itself* turned out to be curiously thin on philosophical argument. In fact, Rosenblatt, always a fluent and insightful essayist, seems to view the controversy over abortion in America as a wholly sociological phenomenon. He seems to manage 189 pages on the subject of abortion without rehearsing one philosophical or constitutional argument for or against the subject. But he does correctly point to the ambivalence Americans have about abortion, not to mention their discomfort about fem-

inism and extramarital sex—two points I also make in my own argument, beginning on page 46. I also agree with Rosenblatt's opinion that "conflict of thought is thus not an accident of democracy but a necessary attribute" (Rosenblatt, p. 41). But while he attributes the American inclination to sidestep the traditional value of tolerance and impose one's values on everyone else to the nation's tradition of individualism (p. 109), I attribute it to an epistemological mistake. I explore the good—and bad—consequences of this inevitable collision of values in the final two chapters of this book. As a historical primer on abortion and for insight into the religious and psychological obstacles Americans have to agreeing to disagree about abortion, *Life Itself* is useful, but anyone looking for philosophical and constitutional arguments will be disappointed.

2. It was not until 1869 that Pope Pius IX proclaimed that those responsible for abortion were automatically excommunicated—a punishment that remains the official position of the Catholic Church. Until then Catholics adhered to St. Thomas Aquinas's view that the fetus was not "ensouled" until it took human shape, about forty days into the pregnancy for males, eighty days for females. For more on Aquinas and the changes in Catholic doctrine, see "A Liberal Catholic's View," pages 34–36. It is likely that the recent scientific discovery of fertilization influenced the Church's position that the soul enters the body at conception. The Church's new doctrine of the Immaculate Conception—that Jesus' Mother, Mary, was also conceived without sin—fits right in with science's view of conception as well. See Tribe, p. 31. Also Noonan and the *New Catholic Encyclopedia* (Washington, D.C.: The Catholic University, 1967), pp. 27–31.

3. The woman was Sherri Finkbine. After her abortion Swedish doctors informed her that the fetus was indeed deformed.

4. Tribe, p. 39.

5. Ibid., p. 38. See also Rosalind P. Petchesky, *Abortion and Woman's Choice: The State, Sexuality, and Reproductive Freedom* (New York: Longman, 1984), p. 79.

6. Alaska, Hawaii, New York, and Washington went so far as to legalize all abortions done by a doctor for any reason within a certain cut-off point between twenty and twenty-six weeks into the pregnancy.

7. *Bellotti* v. *Baird*, 443 U.S. 662 (1979).

8. One anti-abortion group, Operation Rescue, was convicted of trespass, criminal conspiracy, and disorderly conduct. A federal

court of appeals found that the abortion protestors' behavior amounted to extortion under a federal law devised to prosecute racketeers. According to the National Abortion Federation Public Action program, between 1977 and 1987 there were thirty-two bombings and thirty-eight cases of arson against abortion clinics.

9. In a separate opinion, O'Connor wrote that she was willing to uphold any regulation on constitutional abortions as long as it was not an "undue burden" on the woman's abortion decision.

10. Linda Greenhouse, "5 Justices Uphold U.S. Rule Curbing Abortion Advice," *New York Times,* May 24, 1991, p. A1.

11. John P. MacKenzie, "What the Doctor Ordered," *New York Times,* June 4, 1991.

12. By the summer of 1991, abortion advocates were challenging laws against abortion in Louisiana, Pennsylvania, Utah, and Guam, and warning that the reconstituted Reagan-Bush Supreme Court was ready to overturn *Roe.* In August a federal judge in New Orleans struck down Louisiana's strict new anti-abortion law, contending that it was unconstitutional under the terms of *Roe* v. *Wade.* The Louisiana law banned all abortions except to save the life of the mother and in pregnancies resulting from rape and incest; physicians convicted of breaking the law would have been liable for a maximum prison sentence of ten years and fines up to $100,000. See "U.S. Judge Strikes Down Louisiana Abortion Law," *New York Times,* August 8, 1991, p. A15.

In October 1991 a federal court of appeals in Pennsylvania upheld the state's hard-nosed abortion law requiring that women under eighteen have parental consent and that women had to give "informed consent" to an abortion by getting pre-abortion counseling from a doctor and then waiting twenty-four hours before the abortion is performed. (The appellate court agreed with the lower court that the provision in the Pennsylvania law that required women to notify their husbands before an abortion was unconstitutional.) See Michael deCourcy Hinds, "Appeals Court Upholds Limits for Abortions," *New York Times,* October 22, 1991, p. A1.

13. Poll after poll shows widespread support for legal abortion, even among Catholics who personally oppose it. For a summary of the survey results since *Roe,* see Rosenblatt, pp. 183–89.

14. Alan Guttmacher Institute.

15. John J. Powell, S.J., *Abortion: The Silent Holocaust* (Texas: Argus Communications, 1981), passim. This is the hard-line version of

the Catholic pro-life view that attacks supporters of abortion for pushing a "new ethics" that values the "quality of life" over life itself.

16. Most of these arguments can be found in the Vatican's "Declaration on Procured Abortion" (AAS 66 [1974]: 738), prepared by the Sacred Congregation for the Doctrine of the Faith, the Vatican's official mouthpiece on matters of faith and morals, in 1974 and ratified by Pope Paul VI. I have used the Vatican translation published in the United States by the Daughters of St. Paul, Boston. The current pope, John Paul II, has confirmed the Church's position that abortion is murder. See the Vatican's *Charter of the Rights of the Family*, *L'Osservatore Romano*, November 25, 1983.

17. Cited in "Declaration on Procured Abortion." Original source: Epistle to Diogentus, ed. Funk, *Patres Apostolici* I, 399: S.C. 33.

18. Ibid., Didache Apostolorum, ed. Funk, *Patres Apostolici*, V.2. The Epistle of Barnabas, IX, 5 uses the same expressions.

19. Ibid., Athenagoras, *A Plea on Behalf of Christians*, 35; Tertullian: "To prevent birth is anticipated murder; it makes little difference whether one destroys a life already born or does away with it in its nascence stage. The one who will be a man is already one." Tertullian, Apologeticum (IX, 8PL I, 371–72: *Corpus Christi*, I, p. 103, 1, 31–36).

20. Pope Paul VI, *Gaudium et Spes*, 51 (AAS 58 [1966]: 1072). The 1983 *Charter of the Rights of the Family* confirmed that "human life must be absolutely respected and protected from the moment of Conception" when, as the science of genetics has discovered, the ovum is fertilized, and a new human being comes to life. See *Charter of the Rights of the Family*, 4. See also the *Declaration of Procured Abortion*, 12–13. Here the Vatican, not always a friend of science, accepts the view of some geneticists that at conception what we will become genetically is already present.

21. Gabrielle Glaser, "John Paul Angrily Scolds the Poles over Abortion," *New York Times*, June 4, 1991, p. A13.

22. Sripati Chandrasekhar, *Abortion in a Crowded World* (Seattle: University of Washington Press, 1974), p. 110. Information also cited by Tribe in chap. 4. New York *Village Voice* columnist Nat Hentoff, a classic political liberal and outspoken defender of civil liberties, has attacked abortion often in his columns; Christopher Hitchens, a columnist for *The Nation* and a well-known

left-wing critic of U.S. domestic and foreign policy, is also publicly opposed to abortion.

23. From congressional testimony in April 1981. See Powell, p. 68 ff.
24. Facts cited by Dr. A. W. Liley and quoted in John Lippis, "The Challenge to Be 'Pro-Life,' " National Right to Life Committee Educational Trust Fund's main pamphlet (1982), p. 3. Liley is described as a "world-renowned research professor of Fetal Physiology at the National Women's Hospital in Auckland, New Zealand, and known as the 'Father of Fetology.' "
25. *Life*, April 30, 1965. The picture was of an eighteen-week-old fetus. The National Right to Life Committee features several such photographs in its educational literature. See ibid.
26. Paul Ramsey, "The Morality of Abortion," in Robert M. Baird and Stuart E. Rosenbaum, eds., *The Ethics of Abortion* (Buffalo: Prometheus, 1989), p. 62. Originally appeared in Daniel Laddy, ed., *Life or Death—Ethics and Options* (Seattle: University of Washington Press, 1971). Collected elsewhere, too.
27. *Scott v. Sandford*, 19 How., 60 U.S. 393 (1857).
28. This is the summary of the argument in "History Repeats Itself" featured in "The Challenge to Be 'Pro-Life,' " p. 7.
29. The following descriptions are paraphrased from ibid., pp. 7–8.
30. To avoid being sued for "wrongful death," doctors used to smother the live fetuses with the placenta or drown them in a bucket of water. But in 1979 the Supreme Court ruled that a woman's constitutional right to an abortion prevented the state from preserving the rights of babies who survived abortion. See *Colautti v. Franklin*, 439 U.S. 379 (1979).
31. The institutional center of the pro-choice movement is the National Abortion Rights Action League. What follows tries to summarize the choice position, using NARAL's literature and guidelines as a kind of outline of the points that ought to be covered, particularly NARAL's 1983 pamphlet "Legal Abortion: Arguments Pro and Con." This document lists fifty-four arguments against abortion with the pro-choice movement's counterarguments right next to them.
32. Charles A. Gardner, "Is an Embryo a Person?" *The Nation*, November 13, 1989.
33. Tribe, pp. 125—28.
34. "Mother Cleared of Giving Cocaine to Child at Birth," *USA Today*, May 3, 1991. The article claims that about fifty similar cases have been brought in twenty states. Only one woman, Jen-

nifer Johnson of Sanford, Florida, has been convicted of delivering drugs through the umbilical cord. She has appealed her fourteen-year probation. A Michigan court of appeals overturned a lower court decision to prosecute a Muskegon woman for delivering drugs to her son; she had smoked crack hours before his birth.

35. The feminist literature on abortion is vast. The modern philosophical source is Simone de Beauvoir's classic *The Second Sex* (New York: Knopf, 1953). De Beauvoir argues that the "freedom from reproductive slavery" is the sine qua non of women's liberation. *Ms.* magazine has run literally hundreds of articles about abortion since its founding in 1972.

36. See Kathleen McDonnell, *Not an Easy Choice* (Boston: South End, 1984). She provides a thoughtful feminist's reconsideration of the abortion issue in face of some tough arguments from the other side.

37. See Carol Gilligan, *In a Different Voice* (Cambridge, Mass.: Harvard University Press, 1982). She argues that for centuries women's lives have been "anchored in passivity" (p. 68). According to her, birth control and abortion have given women a choice—or at least "the dilemma of choice"—about how to lead their lives.

38. Katha Pollitt, "When Is a Mother Not a Mother?" *The Nation,* January 31, 1991. She raises these points in a well-argued piece on surrogate motherhood.

39. Lindsay van Gelder, "Cracking the Women's Movement Protection Game," *Ms.,* December 1978. For a list of the not so prudent things feminists have said in the ideological heat of battle about the status of the fetus, see Jason DeParle, "Beyond the Legal Right," *Washington Monthly* (April 1989), pp. 28–44.

40. Kathleen McDonnell's book is essentially a mea culpa for feminist excesses in an effort to regain some of the moral high ground from the right-to-life camp.

41. Gilligan, p. 21.

42. Ibid., p. 103.

43. Ibid., p. 71 ff.

44. Tribe, p. 135; originally from Drew Jubera, "Kate's Choice," *Atlanta Constitution,* October 4, 1988, p. 1D. Michelman has told her dramatic story often in recent years, and I have seen her quoted in other newspaper and magazine accounts of the abortion battle. See also DeParle, p. 37.

45. To gain that control Kate Michelman committed herself to the

fight for legalized abortion and is now the executive director of the National Abortion Rights Action League, the main Washington lobby for abortion rights.

46. Philip J. Hilts, "Birth Control Safer Than Unprotected Sex," *New York Times,* April 23, 1991. It summarizes the findings of a 129-page report from the Alan Guttmacher Institute, 111 Fifth Avenue, New York, NY 10003—the first major statistical picture of contraception in the United States.

47. See "Abortion in the United States: A Statistical Study," chap. 4 in Abortion: An Eternal Social and Moral Issue.

48. Judith Jarvis Thompson, "In Defense of Abortion," *Philosophy & Public Affairs,* Fall 1971, pp. 47–66. Also collected in Baird and Rosenbaum, pp. 29–44. The following page references are to the *Philosophy & Public Affairs* version.

49. Thompson, p. 52.

50. Feminists for Life of America publishes a quarterly newsletter called "Sisterlife." The group has also published the book *Prolife Feminism: Different Voices.* The group is headquartered at 811 East 47th Street, Kansas City, MO 64110. JustLife's address is 713 Monroe Street, NE, Washington, DC 20017.

51. One of the most articulate, and persistent, proponents of the Catholic feminist position on abortion is Sidney Callahan. See her "Abortion and the Sexual Agenda," *Commonweal,* April 25, 1986, pp. 232–38. Also collected in Baird and Rosenbaum, pp. 131–42; and Patricia Beattie Jung and Thomas A. Shannon, eds., *Abortion, Catholicism: The American Debate* (New York: Crossroad, 1988). See also Kay Castonguay, "Pro-Life Feminism," *Political Woman* (Summer 1986), pp. 11–15. Castonguay is president of Feminists for Life of Minnesota.

52. See Castonguay and the literature and brochures of Feminists for Life, which feature anti-abortion remarks from such members of the feminists' hall of fame as Susan B. Anthony; Elizabeth Cady Stanton; Mattie Brinkerhoff; Victoria Woodhull; Emma Goldman; even Margaret Sanger, the founder of what is now Planned Parenthood; and Simone de Beauvoir, the philosopher queen of feminism. See also Mary Seger, "Abortion and the Culture: Toward a Feminist Perspective," in Sidney and Daniel Callahan, eds., *Understanding Differences* (New York: Plenum, 1984), pp. 229–52.

53. S. Callahan, "Abortion and the Sexual Agenda," in Baird and Rosenbaum, p. 136.

54. Ibid., p. 140.

55. See Castonguay, p. 13.

56. Joseph F. Donceel, S.J., "A Liberal Catholic's View," in Joel Feinberg, ed., *The Problem of Abortion* (Belmont, Calif.: Wadsworth, 1984), pp. 15–20.

57. See Aquinas's *Summa Contra Gentiles* II, 88–89; *De Potentia* Q. 3, Art. 9–12; *Summa Theologica* I, Q. 118, Art. 1–3.

58. Donceel, p. 16.

59. Ronald Dworkin, *Life's Dominion: An Argument About Abortion, Euthanasia, and Individual Freedom* (New York: Knopf, 1993).

60. Ibid., p. 10.

61. According to a Wirthlin poll commissioned by the United States Catholic Conference in 1990, a total of 33 percent of those surveyed found the statement "All human life, including that of the unborn, should be protected" not very convincing or not convincing at all. (Thirty-one percent found the statement extremely convincing, while 29 percent found it very convincing.) Those polled were similarly divided over the statement "Every unborn child has a basic right to life." See Rosenblatt, pp. 188–89.

62. Dworkin, pp. 34–35.

63. Ibid., p. 13.

64. Ibid., p. 74–75.

65. Ibid., p. 78.

66. Ibid., p. 89.

67. Ibid., p. 91.

68. Ibid., p. 99.

69. Though Dworkin doesn't mention it here, I assume he believes that those teenagers deserve education and other kinds of help to prevent them from finding themselves in another situation where abortion is required.

70. Dworkin, p. 99.

71. Ibid., p. 101.

72. Cardinal Joseph Bernardin, "The Consistent Ethic: What Sort of Framework?" *Abortion & Catholicism: The American Debate* (New York: Crossroad, 1988), pp. 260–67.

73. Bernardin notes that U.S. bishops have argued for such a "consistent ethic" since they began their Respect for Life Program in 1972, inviting Catholics to focus on "the sanctity of human life and the many threats to human life in the modern world, including war, violence, hunger and poverty." (See National Conference of Catholic Bishops' resolution, April 13, 1972.) This view

was further elaborated in the 1986 "Respect for Life" brochure and the bishops' pastoral letter "The Challenge of Peace: God's Promise and Our Response," in which they link abortion and the threat of nuclear war to the "many faces" of violence: oppression of the poor, deprivation of basic human rights, economic exploitation, sexual exploitation, neglect or abuse of the aged and the helpless.

74. Ibid., p. 262.

75. Ibid., pp. 263–64.

76. Here Bernardin leans heavily on the extensive writings of the Jesuit historian John Courtney Murray on the role of the Catholic Church, by nature an ancient, dogmatic, undemocratic institution, in the religious and intellectual pluralism of American democracy.

77. Bernardin, p. 265.

78. Tribe, especially chap. 5, "Finding Abortion Rights in the Constitution." See also Dworkin, chaps. 4–6.

79. Tribe, p. 81.

80. Ibid., p. 83.

81. These citations are from two landmark privacy cases: *Meyer* v. *Nebraska* 262 U.S. 402 (1923) and *Pierce* v. *Society of Sisters* 268 U.S. 535 (1925). In *Meyer* the Court struck down a law that during World War I prohibited Nebraska's German minority from teaching their children German; *Pierce* invalidated a law that would have closed parochial and secular private schools as alternatives to Oregon's public school system. The law was aimed primarily at Catholic schools.

82. *Griswold* v. *Connecticut* 381 U.S. 479 (1965); *Eisenstadt* v. *Baird*, 405 U.S. 438, 453 (1972). Dworkin argues that *Griswold*, widely accepted by Americans, is evidence that the Court has interpreted the Constitution to protect an individual's privacy. See p. 106 ff.

83. See Dworkin, p. 113 ff.

84. Tribe, p. 105.

85. See Catharine A. MacKinnon, *Toward a Feminist Theory of the State* (Cambridge, Mass.: Harvard University Press, 1989). The following summarizes MacKinnon's argument in chap. 10, "Abortion: On Public and Private," pp. 184–94.

86. Ibid., p. 191.

87. Ibid., p. 194. The similarities here in the argument between the radical feminist MacKinnon, who supports abortion, and the Catholic feminist Sidney Callahan, who opposes it.

88. Ibid., pp. 185–86.

89. Catholics, to their credit (logically if not compassionately), stick to their guns: abortion is always murder, no matter the cause of pregnancy.

90. This point is central to Dworkin's argument, as I have shown. It also plays a central role in my own argument, though in a slightly different way.

91. Recently, feminists have latched onto this point. For example, see Mary Gordon, "A Moral Choice," *The Atlantic,* April 1980; reprinted as "Abortion: How Do We Really Choose?" in Gordon's collection *Good Boys and Dead Girls: and Other Essays* (New York: Viking, 1991).

92. Robert M. Veatch, *A Theory of Medical Ethics* (New York: Basic Books, 1981), p. 246. Although I take a less absolutist view of prohibiting killing than Veatch, I share his belief that the early fetus has no moral standing under the "no killing" rule. That moral standing requires as its minimum "consciousness" is also a view held by Jonathan Glover, *Causing Deaths and Saving Lives* (London: Penguin, 1977), p. 46 ff. Glover says he finds it "natural to regard life as being of value only as a necessary condition of consciousness." Without it, he notes, "life" would be very much like death.

93. Thompson, p. 52.

94. Roger Rosenblatt's *Life Itself* is a notable exception. See p. 121 ff.

95. See Kristin Luker, *Abortion and the Politics of Motherhood* (Berkeley: University of California Press, 1984). Luker, who studied pro-life and pro-choice activists for five years, argues that both sides come from "different parts of the social world," and bring with them different "visions" of the world and their role in it. A concise summary of her work appears in "Abortion and the Meaning of Life," in *Abortion: Understanding Differences.*

96. A pro-life activist in Luker's study, cited in *Abortion: Understanding Differences,* p. 33.

97. S. Callahan, "Value Choices in Abortion," in ibid., p. 288.

98. See Robin Lane Fox, "Living like Angels," chap. 7 in *Pagans and Christians* (New York: Knopf, 1986). Many highborn, and highminded, Romans embraced Christianity because of its horror of infanticide, mainly in the form of exposing unwanted children. See also Elaine Pagels, *Adam, Eve, and the Serpent* (New York: Random House, 1988), chaps. 1–4 on early Christian attitudes toward sexuality and virginity.

99. See Pagels, chap. 5, "The Politics of Paradise," in which she gives

a careful reading of St. Augustine's attitude toward sexual matters, which, she argues, was far from being in line with the conventional wisdom of most Christians of his era.

100. In "Paradise," according to Augustine, women are free of the pain of childbirth and can enjoy marriage without oppression and coercion. God had punished Eve. "I will greatly multiply your pains in childbearing . . . yet your desire shall be for your husband, and he shall rule over you" (Genesis 3:16). This is the Christian justification for oppressing women. Instead of being seen as man's helper or his equal with the same kind of rational soul, woman became a temptress. See Pagels, p. 113 ff.

101. See Pagels, chap. 6, "The Nature of Nature," in which she points out that at the time of Augustine the "orthodox" view of sexuality was that of the Catholic ascetic from Britain Pelagius—namely, that God, being just, would not punish the whole human race for Adam's sin. Nor was women's pain and suffering due to the Fall.

102. *Abortion: Understanding Differences,* p. 295.

103. Ibid.

104. Ibid., p. 291.

105. Ibid., pp. 300–301.

106. See Luker, passim.

107. *New York Times*/CBS Poll, *New York Times,* August 3, 1989, p. A18; and September 29, 1989, p. A13.

2. Suicide

1. Albert Camus, *The Myth of Sisyphus and Other Essays,* trans. J. O'Brien (New York: Vintage, 1953), p. 3.

2. *Odyssey,* Book II, 271 ff. Virgil's *Aeneid,* Books I and IV. Thucydides, *The Peloponnesian War,* trans. John H. Finley Jr., III, 13:49, p. 235.

3. Plato, *Laws,* 873d. Some have argued that because Socrates had a chance to escape Athens, by staying he in effect committed suicide. This seems churlish. While Socrates, a man who had devoted his life to the discussion of virtue and knowledge, could have left town or even chosen to worship the state's gods or given up teaching altogether (and "corrupting the youth"), he decided to take a more heroic tack and force the leaders of Athens into the hateful position of executing him. Moreover, Plato, a lifelong opponent of suicide, certainly did not believe his mentor Socrates to be a suicide.

4. Robin Lane Fox, *Pagans and Christians* (New York: Knopf, 1986), p. 435. Original source: Tertullian, *De Anima*, 55:4–5.
5. Ibid., p. 440.
6. Ibid., p. 437.
7. See "Persecution and Martyrdom," chap. 9 in ibid., pp. 419–91.
8. Edward Gibbon, *The Decline and Fall of the Roman Empire,* vol. 1 (New York: Modern Library, 1932), pp. 721–22. For details on Augustine's battles with the Donatists, see Peter Brown, *Augustine of Hippo: A Biography* (Berkeley and Los Angeles: University of California Press, 1966), p. 218 ff.
9. See A. Alvarez, *The Savage God* (New York: Random House, 1970); and George Howe Colt, *The Enigma of Suicide* (New York: Summit, 1991), whose references to the Donatists suggest the group was a minor sect of, as Alvarez calls them, "lunatics."
10. John Donne, *Biathanatos,* in *The Complete Poetry and Selected Prose of John Donne* (New York: Modern Library, 1952).
11. For a lengthy examination of Donne's views on suicide, see A. Alvarez's own study of suicide, *The Savage God,* pp. 149–69.
12. It was the French philosopher Montaigne (1533–92) who offered the first explicit counterarguments to the Church's opposition to suicide. Written in 1608, Donne's *Biathanatos* (the subtitle is *A Declaration of that Paradoxe, or thesis, that Self-homicide is not so Naturally Sinne, that it may never be otherwise, Wherein the Nature, and the extent of all those Lawes, which seeme to be violated by this act, are diligently surveyed)* was not published until after 1646, fifteen years after Donne's death.
13. Donald Ramsay Roberts, "The Death Wish of John Donne," *Publications of the Modern Language Society of America,* vol. 62 (1947), pp. 958–76. Cited by both Alvarez and Colt.
14. Alvarez, p. 149.
15. Colt, p. 168.
16. Even many who believed suicide to be wrong, however, found the legal punishments of suicides and their families barbaric and unjust. In 1770, Geneva abolished the practice of mutilating the corpses of suicides, and France did the same. Twenty years later the French National Assembly, under the influence of Montesquieu, Diderot, and Voltaire, repealed all laws against suicide.
17. See Colt, p. 179. His source is R. Bartel, "Suicide in 18th Century England: The Myth of a Reputation" (*Huntington Library Quarterly,* February 1960), pp. 145–58.

18. Colt cites an array of "scientific" theories for suicide and possible cures, pp. 183–86.

19. Sigmund Freud, *Mourning and Melancholia* (1917), vol. 14 of *The Standard Edition of the Complete Psychological Works,* ed. James Strachey (London: Hogarth, 1953–65).

20. Freud, *The Ego and the Id* (1920), vol. 19 of *The Complete Works.*

21. "Declaration on Euthanasia," prepared by the Vatican's Sacred Congregation for the Doctrine of the Faith, originally published in the Vatican official newspaper *L'Osservatore Romano* (English edition), May 5, 1980. The National Conference of U.S. Bishops distributes the English-language version in the form of a pamphlet published by the Daughters of St. Paul in Boston.

22. Ibid.

23. Daniel Goleman, "Missing in Talk of Right to Die: Depression's Grip on a Patient," *New York Times,* December 4, 1991.

24. Ibid.

25. *Phaedo,* 61E–62C. The translation is my own, from the Oxford Classical Text.

26. Plato, *Laws,* 873c–d. The translation is my own.

27. Aristotle's *Nicomachean Ethics,* III.6 1115a 24–35. Also my own translation.

28. Aristotle, *Nicomachean Ethics,* V.11 1138a4–a14.

29. Augustine, *City of God,* Book I, 17–27. The text I have used is the abridged version of the translation by Gerald G. Walsh, S.J., et al. (New York: Doubleday Image Book, 1958), p. 53 ff.

30. Ibid., p. 58.

31. Thomas Aquinas, "Whether It Is Lawful to Kill Oneself," in *Summa Theologica* (New York: Benziger; London: Burns & Oakes, 1925), Part 2, Question 64, A5.

32. Kant addresses the issue of suicide in his "Lectures in Ethics," trans. Louis Infield (New York: Harper & Row, 1963), pp. 147–57. Also collected in John Donnelly, ed., *Suicide: Right or Wrong?,* Contemporary Issues in Philosophy (Buffalo: Prometheus, 1990), pp. 47–55.

33. Ray Monk, *Ludwig Wittgenstein: The Duty of Genius* (New York: Free Press, 1990), p. 188. See also Rush Rhees, *Recollections of Wittgenstein* (Oxford: Oxford University Press, 1964), Wittgenstein to Russell, July 7, 1920. A year or so before, after World War I, during which Wittgenstein, who fought on the German side, had been a prisoner of war, he also talked of suicide. See Monk, pp. 171–72.

34. Monk, p. 579.

35. Ludwig Wittgenstein, *Notebooks* (1914–1916), trans. E. Anscombe.

36. Monk, p. 187. Wittgenstein to his friend Paul Englemann. See also Rhees, June 21, 1920.

37. Terence M. O'Keefe, "Suicide and Self-Starvation," *Philosophy* 56 (1981): 349–63; also collected in Donnelly, pp. 117–34. The page references here are to the Donnelly collection.

38. O'Keefe, p. 124.

39. Ibid., p. 131.

40. Philip E. Devine, *The Ethics of Homicide* (Ithaca, N.Y.: Cornell University Press, 1978), pp. 138–43. Also collected in Donnelly, pp. 201–205.

41. Ibid.

42. Joyce Carol Oates, "The Art of Suicide," in *The Reevaluation of Existing Values and the Search for Absolute Values. The Proceedings of the Seventh International Conference on the Unity of the Sciences* (New York: International Cultural Foundation Press, 1978), pp. 183–90. Also collected in Donnelly, pp. 207–12. Like Devine, Oates raises questions about the rationality of suicide: "But can one freely choose a condition, a state of being, that has never been experienced except in the imagination and, even there, *only in metaphor?*" See Donnelly, p. 212.

43. Donnelly, p. 208.

44. Seneca, "On the Proper Time to Slip the Cable," *Epistulae Morales,* vol. 2, Loeb Classical Library (Cambridge, Mass.: Harvard University Press, 1920), Epistle 70, pp. 56–72.

45. David Hume, "Of Suicide," in *Essays Moral, Political and Literary* (Oxford: Oxford Univeristy Press, 1973), pp. 585–96; also collected as "Reason and Superstition," in Donnelly, pp. 37–45.

46. Joseph Fletcher, "In Defense of Suicide," in Albin Eser, ed., *Suizid und Euthanasie* (Stuttgart: Enke, 1976), pp. 233–44. Also collected in Donnelly, pp. 61–73.

47. Ibid., p. 63.

48. Ibid.

49. Ibid., p. 71.

50. Ibid., p. 73.

51. Jonathan Glover, *Causing Deaths and Saving Lives: The Moral Problems of Abortion, Infanticide, Suicide, Euthanasia, Capital Punishment, War, and Other Life-or-Death Choices* (London: Penguin, 1990), p. 175. The following is a summary of chap. 13, "Suicide and Gambling with Life."

52. Colt, p. 202.
53. William Styron, *Darkness Visible: A Memoir of Madness* (New York: Random House, 1990), p. 38.
54. Alvarez, p. 249.
55. Cited by Michael Mandelbaum, "Coup de Grace: The End of the Soviet Union," *Foreign Affairs*, vol. 71, 1 (1992).
56. *Phaedo*, 62b.
57. "Declaration on Euthanasia."
58. "Of Suicide."
59. Oates, in Donnelly, p. 212.
60. It is curious that Joyce Carol Oates, holder of the most fertile and prolific imagination in contemporary American literature (and whose teenaged heroine in *You Must Remember This*, a beautiful novel, carefully plans her own suicide, makes the attempt, but is saved), cannot conceive of an adult so miserable, so burdened by life, that even "brute, inarticulate Deadness" is preferable to life.
61. See "Declaration on Euthanasia," Part III, "The Meaning of Suffering for Christians and the Use of Painkillers."
62. See Judith Shklar, *Ordinary Vices* (Cambridge Mass.: Belknap Press of Harvard University Press, 1984). She argues that the measure of the good "liberal" in a world without moral certainties is her opposition to cruelty in all its forms. In the final chapter of this book, I discuss the notion that cruelty is the one standard for morality that both conservatives and liberals can agree upon. It is also the key to a decent, modern democracy.
63. Gerald Dworkin, "Paternalism," in Richard Wasserstrom, ed., *Morality and the Law* (Belmont, Calif.: Wadsworth, 1971).
64. See John Stuart Mill's famous essay "On Liberty," collected in innumerable editions. For a useful collection of essays on the "enforcement of morals" and "paternalism" that includes "On Liberty," see Wasserstrom.
65. Brown, p. 221. The original source is Augustine's *Nine Sermons of the Psalms*, 95, 11.
66. See the summary of Augustine's argument, pp. 74–75; also *City of God*, Book I, 27.

3. Euthanasia

1. By 1976, 70 percent of Americans died in hospitals (see John C. Fletcher, "Ethics and the Cost of Dying," in Aubrey Milunsky and George J. Annas, eds., *Genetics and the Law II* [New York

and London: Plenum, 1980], p. 192). By 1980, according to the President's Commission for the Study of Ethical Problems in Medicine and Biomedical and Behavioral Research, "perhaps 80 percent of all deaths in the United States now occur in hospitals and long-term care institutions, such as nursing homes" (see *Deciding to Forgo Life-Sustaining Treatment: A Report on the Ethical, Medical and Legal Issues in Treatment Decisions* [Washington, D.C.: U.S. Government Printing Office, 1983], pp. 17–18). See also the Supreme Court's decision in *Cruzan v. Missouri*, where three of the dissenting justices cite that 80 percent die in hospitals. That 70 percent of the estimated 6,000 deaths that occur in the United States daily involve an agreement to withhold life-sustaining treatment was reported by Andrew Malcolm in "Right-to-Die Case Nearing a Finale," *New York Times*, December 7, 1990, p. A24. For a longer discussion of the changing trends in how and where people die, see Robert W. Weir, *Abating Treatment with Critically Ill Patients* (Oxford: Oxford University Press, 1989), chap. 1. See also Robert W. Wennberg, *Terminal Choices: Euthanasia, Suicide, and the Right to Die* (Grand Rapids, Mich.: Eerdmans, 1989); and Robert M. Veatch, *Death, Dying and the Biological Revolution*, rev. ed. (New Haven: Yale University Press, 1989). For a less pedantic, more thoughtful and readable look at the moral issues surrounding euthanasia, see Daniel Callahan, *The Troubled Dream of Life: In Search of a Peaceful Death* (New York: Simon & Schuster, 1993).

2. The National Opinion Research Center asked the question, "When a person has a disease that cannot be cured, do you think doctors should be allowed by law to end the patient's life by some means if the patient and his family request it?" Fifty-nine percent of the respondents said yes; 36 percent said no. (Note: "Cannot be cured" does not necessarily mean "terminally ill," though most surveyed probably did not perceive the difference.)

3. Edward Tivnan, "Family Value Survey," *Family Circle* (March 10, 1992).

4. See Danielle Gourevitch, "Suicide Among the Sick in Classical Antiquity," *Bulletin of the History of Medicine* 43 (1969): 501–18.

5. Plato, *The Republic*, 295 and 297.

6. See section on "Suicide" for Plato's exceptions to his ban on suicide in the *Laws*, 873 c–d.

7. Aristotle's *Nichomachean Ethics,* Book III, vii: 130; Book V, xi: 200–201. Both Plato and Aristotle, like most Greeks, approved of infanticide.

8. Fred Rosner, "The Jewish Attitude Toward Euthanasia," in Fred Rosner and J. David Bleich, eds., *Jewish Bioethics* (New York: Sanhedrin, 1979), pp. 253–65. See also Basil F. Herring, *Jewish Ethics and Halakhah for Our Time* (New York: KTAV, 1984), pp. 67–90; and Weir, footnote 40.

9. The primary and secondary literature on the history of euthanasia is vast. For a recent book-length summary of the history of views about "mercy killing" and the political and legal responses, see Derek Humphry and Ann Wickett, *The Right to Die: Understanding Euthanasia* (New York: Harper & Row, 1986). The Hemlock Society, now based in Eugene, Oregon, reissued the book in 1990. A pro-euthanasia organization, the Hemlock Society has a definite axe to grind, but the book is well researched, and the footnotes will direct anyone interested in exploring related topics to the appropriate primary and academic sources.

10. See "Fortune Survey: Mercy Killings," *Fortune* XVI (July 1937): 106; "The Quarters Polls," in Mildred Strunk, ed., *The Public Opinion Quarterly* XI (Fall 1947): 77. The British Institute of Public Opinion's survey results were reported in the *New York Times,* April 23, 1939. A brief summary of these surveys may be found in Humphry and Wickett, pp. 18–19.

11. Joseph Fletcher, *Morals and Medicine* (Princeton, N.J.: Princeton University Press, 1954), pp. 172–210. See also Fletcher, "The Patient's Right to Die," in A. B. Downing, ed., *Euthanasia and the Right to Death* (Los Angeles: Nash, 1969), pp. 61–70; Fletcher, "Ethics and Euthanasia," in Robert H. Williams, ed., *To Live and to Die* (New York: Springer, 1974), pp. 113–22; Fletcher, "The 'Right' to Live and the 'Right' to Die," in Marvin Kohl, ed., *Beneficent Euthanasia* (Buffalo: Prometheus, 1975), pp. 44–53; Fletcher, "Euthanasia," in *Humanhood: Essays in Biomedical Ethics* (Buffalo: Prometheus, 1979), pp. 149–58 (also published as "The Courts and Euthanasia," in Robert M. Baird and Stuart E. Rosenbaum, eds., *Law, Medicine, and Health Care* 15 (Winter 1987–88): 223–30.

12. Pope Pius XII, "The Prolongation of Life," in Stanley Reiser, Arthur Dyck, and William Curran, eds., *Ethics in Medicine* (Cambridge, Mass.: MIT Press, 1977), pp. 502–503.

13. James F. Gustafson, "Mongolism, Parental Desires and the Right

to Life," *Perspectives in Biology and Medicine* XVI (1973): 529–59. Cited in Richard A. McCormick, "To Save or Let Die," in Thomas Shannon, ed., *Bioethics,* (New York: Paulist Press, 1976), pp. 123–33.

14. Raymond S. Duff and A.G.M. Campbell, "Moral and Ethical Dilemmas in the Special Care Nursery," *New England Journal of Medicine* 289 (October 25, 1973): 890–94.

15. The AMA House of Delegates endorsed the statement on December 4, 1973. See the complete text in the *Journal of the American Medical Association* 227 (1974): 728.

16. *Time,* October 27, November 3, November 24, 1975. For detailed discussions of the Quinlan case in the context of the euthanasia debate, see C. Everett Koop, "The Case of Karen Ann Quinlan," *The Right to Live; The Right to Die* (Wheaton, Ill.: Tyndale, 1976), pp. 102–11. Also collected in Baird and Rosenbaum. See also Paul Ramsey, "In the Matter of Quinlan," *Ethics at the Edges of Life* (New Haven: Yale University Press, 1978), pp. 268–99.

17. See Ramsey, p. 272, who quotes from the court decision (137 N.J. Superior Court 227, November 10, 1975).

18. Ibid., p. 294 ff. Ramsey also cites legal critics of the Quinlan decision.

19. *Deciding to Forgo Life-Sustaining Treatment,* p. 3.

20. Choice in Dying, a right-to-die organization based in New York City.

21. See *Cruzan* v. *Missouri,* 110 S.Ct. 2841 (1990). Chief Justice Rehnquist states this explicitly in his opinion for the five-judge majority.

22. The details of the case's history in the Missouri courts are taken from the U.S. Supreme Court decision *Cruzan* v. *Missouri.*

23. "Man Cleared of Murder in Aiding Wife's Suicide," *New York Times,* May 11, 1991, p. A9.

24. Peter Steinfels, "At Crossroads, U.S. Ponders Ethics of Helping Others Die," *New York Times,* October 28, 1991.

25. Pieter Admiraal, "Justifiable Active Euthanasia in the Netherlands," *Free Inquiry* 9, no. 1 (Winter 1988–89), reprinted in Baird and Rosenbaum, pp. 125–28. See also Callahan, pp. 112–16 and Marlise Simons, "Dutch Survey Casts New Light on Patients Who Choose to Die," *New York Times,* September 11, 1991, p. C12. For a book-length critique of the Dutch situation, see Carlos F. Gomez, M.D., *Regulating Death: Euthanasia and the Case of the Netherlands* (New York: Free Press, 1993).

26. *New York Times,* September 11, 1991.

27. Man is made "in the image of God" (Genesis 9: 5–6), and life is God's gift to man, and thus God's responsibility (Matthew 6:25–34, Jeremiah 1:4–5, Psalms 139:13–16, Ephesians 1:4–5). See "The Religious Argument" against abortion, p. 20.

28. See Immanuel Jakobovits, *Jewish Medical Ethics* (New York: Bloch, 1975); Fred Rosner, *Modern Medicine and Jewish Law* (New York: Yeshiva University Press, 1972); Seymour Siegel, "History of Medical Ethics," in Warren Reich, *Encyclopedia of Bioethics* 4 (New York: Free Press, 1978): 895–97; Rosner and Bleich. See the summary of some of these views in Weir, p. 221 ff.

29. The Central Conference of American Rabbis in New York, a Reform rabbinical group, periodically publishes "Responsa" (or answers) to major moral issues to aid members in advising their congregations. The group has published documents on euthanasia since 1950.

30. See "Introduction" to the "Declaration on Euthanasia," prepared by the Vatican's Sacred Congregation for the Doctrine of the Faith, originally published in the Vatican official newspaper *L'Osservatore Romano* (English edition), May 5, 1980, Part II, "Euthanasia"; also in *Official Catholic Teachings: Update,* 1980, p. 180. The National Conference of U.S. Bishops distributes the English-language version in the form of a pamphlet published by the Daughters of St. Paul in Boston.

31. W. Abbott, *The Documents of Vatican II* (Piscataway, N.J.: New Century Publications, 1966), p. 226.

32. Romans 14:8; cf. Philippians 1:20.

33. "Declaration on Euthanasia," Part II, "Euthanasia."

34. See "Declaration," Part III: "The Meaning of Suffering for Christians and the Use of Painkillers."

35. The report is available on request from the National Conference of Catholic Bishops, Committee for Pro-Life Activities, 1312 Massachusetts Avenue NW, Washington, DC 20005.

36. See *Active Euthanasia, Religion, and the Public Debate,* a report from Chicago's Park Ridge Center for the Study of Faith, Health, and Ethics, p. 53 ff. See also the Southern Baptist Convention's Christian Life Commission Board, *Policy and Procedures Manual of Christian Life Commission of the Southern Baptist Church* (1987); also "Christian Life Commission Staff Guidelines for the Publishing of Materials on Abortion and Euthanasia," revised version (September 1988), no. 4.

37. None of the other large Baptist denominations—the National

Baptist Convention U.S.A., the National Primitive Baptist Convention, or the Baptist Bible Fellowship—has an official position on euthanasia. The General Association of Regular Baptist Churches, a smaller group, however, opposes "mercy killing," declaring that "life and death belong in the hands of God." But the group does allow that every person has the right to die with dignity and opposes prolonging terminal illnesses unnecessarily. See Park Ridge Center report, p. 53 ff.

38. Leon R. Kass, M.D., "Why Doctors Must Not Kill," in *Euthanasia: Washington State Initiative 119* (A Special Supplement to *Commonweal*) August 9, 1991, pp. 472–76; see also in the same issue Albert R. Jonsen, "Initiative 119: What Is at Stake." Both authors are ethicists specializing in biomedical issues and have written and spoken about the dangers of legalized "aid-in-dying." See also Kass et al., "Doctors Must Not Kill," *Journal of the American Medical Association* 9, no. 14 (April 8, 1988): 2139–40. Also collected in Baird and Rosenbaum. See Jonsen's letter to the Washington State Medical Association in response to Initiative 119, reprinted in *Active Euthanasia, Religion and the Public Debate* (Chicago: Park Ridge Center for the Study of Faith, Health and Ethics, 1991), pp. 100–105. Like Daniel Callahan, Jonsen argues against reintroducing "private killing," and like Kass questions the role of doctors in killing, suggesting more aggressive research into pain-killing research and care for the dying.

39. See Kass, p. 473.

40. Ibid, p. 474.

41. Ibid, p. 478.

42. See Jonsen.

43. See Kass, p. 476.

44. See Daniel Callahan, *What Kind of Life: The Limits of Medical Progress* (New York: Simon & Schuster, 1990), chap. 8, pp. 221–49. He refines and elaborates his view on the social risks of private killing. Also Callahan, "Aid-in-Dying: The Social Dimension," in *Euthanasia: Washington State Initiative 119*.

45. See "Aid-in-Dying," p. 477.

46. See Robert Barry, O.P., "The Ethics of Providing Life-Sustaining Nutrition and Fluids to Incompetent Patients," *The Journal of Family and Culture* 1 (Summer 1985): 31. Barry, a Catholic medical ethicist, is the main and most prolific opponent of withdrawing food and fluids. See also Barry, "Facing Hard Cases: The Ethics of Assisted Feeding," *Issues in Law and Medicine* 2 (1986). Barry, "Closing the Circle: *Humanae Vitae* and Feeding

the Comatose," *Homiletic and Pastoral Review* (July 1986). Barry, "Pulling the Tube: Mercy or Manslaughter," *Medical Ethics for the Physician* 1 (August 1986). Barry, "Euthanasia: The Domino Falls," *National Catholic Reporter,* February 1, 1987. See also Joseph Piccione, *Last Rights: Treatment and Care Issues in Medical Ethics* (Washington, D.C.: Free Congress Research and Education Foundation, 1984).

47. "Closing the Circle," p. 56.

48. See Daniel Callahan, *Setting Limits* (New York: Simon & Schuster, 1987), pp. 187–93.

49. Daniel Callahan, "On Feeding the Dying," *Hastings Center Report* 13 (October 1983), p. 22. See also *Setting Limits,* pp. 187–93.

50. See footnote 1 in *Cruzan v. Missouri* where the Court cites the Missouri Supreme Court's description of Cruzan's condition. See also *Cruzan v. Harmon* (Mo. 1989).

51. Justice Brennan's dissent in *Cruzan v. Missouri.* He was joined by Justice Marshall and Justice Blackmun. Justice Stevens delivered a separate dissent.

52. See Justice Stevens's dissent in *Cruzan v. Missouri.*

53. The argument is the Oxford philosopher Jonathan Glover's. See *Causing Death and Saving Lives* (London: Penguin, 1990), pp. 39–59.

54. Ibid., p. 46.

55. Ibid., p. 52.

56. Here I am following the mainstream pro-euthanasia argument. See Fletcher, *Humanhood: Essays in Biomedical Ethics,* pp. 149–58. Also collected as "Sanctity of Life versus Quality of Life," in Robert M. Baird and Stuart E. Rosenbaum, eds., *Euthanasia: The Moral Issues* (Buffalo: Prometheus, 1989), pp. 85–95.

57. Joseph Fletcher poses this question in Baird and Rosenbaum, *Euthanasia,* p. 91.

58. Fletcher stresses that the psychological qualms common to decisions on euthanasia are unrelated to its ethics.

59. Glover, p. 200.

60. The moral distinction between active and passive euthanasia was first argued by Joseph Fletcher more than three decades ago. "A decision *not* to keep a patient alive is as morally deliberate as a decision to *end* a life." See Fletcher, "The Patient's Right to Die," *Harper's* 221 (October 1960): 140. Fletcher, *Moral Responsibility: Situation Ethics at Work* (Philadelphia: Westminster, 1967), p. 51. Here Fletcher argues that withholding treatment and directly inducing death are morally the same. Recent commenta-

tors, however, tend to refer to James Rachels's more recent re-statement of the argument. See Rachels, "Active and Passive Euthanasia," *The New England Journal of Medicine* 292, no. 2 (January 9, 1975): 78–80. Also collected in Baird and Rosenbaum, *Euthanasia,* pp. 45–51. See also Rachels, "More Impertinent Distinctions," in Baird and Rosenbaum, *Euthanasia,* pp. 61–68; also Rachels, *The End of Life: Euthanasia and Morality* (Oxford: Oxford University Press, 1986).

61. See Rachels, "More Impertinent Distinctions," pp. 62–64.

62. Marvin Kohl, *The Morality of Killing* (Atlantic Highlands, N.J.: Humanities Press, 1974).

63. Rachels, *End of Life,* p. 187.

64. See Derek Humphry, *Let Me Die Before I Wake* (Los Angeles: Hemlock Society, 1982), "The Hemlock Manifesto," Appendix C, p. 99.

65. Based on a detailed study of the positions of mainstream religions reported in Part 4 of *Active Euthanasia, Religion and the Public Debate.* Available from the Park Ridge Center, 676 N. St. Clair, Suite 450, Chicago, IL 60611.

66. General Assembly of the Unitarian Universalists, *1988 Proceedings,* 74; also cited in Park Ridge Center report on euthanasia.

67. See Park Ridge Center report.

68. The argument that follows is mainly a summary of one presented by Richard A. McCormick in an often cited article, "To Save or Let Die," originally published in the Jesuit magazine *America,* July 4, 1974. The article is also collected in Shannon, *Bioethics,* pp. 123–33. McCormick is clearly influenced by Ramsey.

69. Statement by Pope Pius XII to physicians on November 24, 1957; cited by McCormick, in Shannon, p. 128.

70. McCormick's interpretation of Pius XII's remarks have been challenged by fellow Catholics, along with the Protestant ethicist Paul Ramsey. (See Ramsey, " 'Euthanasia' and Dying Well Enough," chap. 4 in *Ethics at the Edges of Life,* p. 171 ff. Also in note 33 Ramsey refers to several articles by McCormick's Catholic critics.) Essentially, they charge that McCormick is taking the pope's appeal to the traditional ordinary/extraordinary distinction and turning it into a precursor of the "quality of life" argument made by contemporary advocates of active euthanasia. "The spiritual ends" to which the pope refers mean "eternal life." His point is that if a patient's health prevents him from the pursuit of eternal life, it is time to die.

I have focused on McCormick's argument because he is an example of a major Catholic ethicist who has moved away from traditional Catholic discomfort with active euthanasia toward the views of some of the more controversial euthanasia advocates like Joseph Fletcher, who uses "quality of life" as the prime criterion for choosing to live or die.

71. The following is from Daniel Maguire, "The Freedom to Die," *Commonweal,* August 11, 1972. Also collected in Shannon, pp. 171–80.

72. See Maguire, in Shannon, p. 174.

73. Ibid., p. 175. I quote his exact words here as an example of how an otherwise measured, academic theologian can rise to a passionate defense of a kind of euthanasia that the majority of the Supreme Court could not muster in *Cruzan.* Significantly, according to Maguire, the dissenters in the case take this position apparently without realizing that they are backed by Pius XII and a long tradition of Catholic ethicists.

74. "The wall of their own solitude" is Paul Ramsey's evocative phrase.

75. The prominent Catholic theologian Charles Curran has made this point in *Politics, Medicine, and Christian Ethics,* pp. 161–62.

76. These are the views of Arthur J. Dyck, applauded by the well-known late Protestant ethicist Paul Ramsey in *Ethics at the Edges of Life,* pp. 147–48. See also Arthur J. Dyck, "An Alternative to the Ethics of Euthanasia," in Robert H. Williams, ed., *To Live and to Die* (New York: Springer, 1973), pp. 98–112.

77. See Ramsey, p. 148.

78. See Arthur J. Dyck, "Conflicting Views of Beneficence in the Euthanasia Debate," chap. 4 in *On Human Care: An Introduction to Ethics* (Nashville: Abingdon, 1977), pp. 72–90. Here Dyck explains how he differs from Kohl's version of "beneficent euthanasia" where we have a prima facie obligation "to act kindly" toward the terminally ill, and sometimes that can mean helping them die painlessly and more quickly. Dyck applauds Kohl's ethic of kindness, but he opposes inducing death, preferring simply to care for the dying.

79. See Ramsey, p. 153 ff. He argues against these distinctions eloquently and in great detail.

80. Ibid., p. 155.

81. Ibid., p. 201.

82. Ibid., p. 153 ff. Ramsey's commitment to the standard of what is "medically indicated" pervades his writings on euthanasia. See also the index.

83. Ibid., p. 206.

84. Ibid., p. 207.

85. Paris, a Jesuit priest and professor of medical ethics, is the main opponent of the view that withdrawing food and essential fluids from patients is tantamount to involuntary euthanasia. A consultant to the President's Commission for the Study of Ethical Problems in Medicine and Biomedical and Behavioral Research and an expert witness in three major court cases on this issue, Paris has also written widely on the subject. Often attacked by extreme right-to-life advocates, he still views his position as a "consensus view" in line with Catholic moral theological teachings developed since the sixteenth century, not to mention the medical profession and the President's Commission. See Paris, "The Withdrawal of Intravenous Feeding: Murder or Acceptable Medical Practice?" in Patricia H. Werhane et al., eds., *Philosophical Issues in Human Rights* (New York: Random House, 1986). Also Paris, "When Burdens of Feeding Outweigh Benefits," *Hastings Center Report 16* (February 1986); Paris and Richard A. McCormick, "The Catholic Tradition on the Use of Nutrition and Fluids," *America* 156 (May 2, 1987): 358.

86. Paris, "When Burdens of Feeding Outweigh Benefits," p. 31.

87. Paris, in Werhane, p. 94.

88. Paris and McCormick, p. 358.

89. The following argument has been made often and elaborately by Paul Ramsey in *The Patient as a Person* (New Haven: Yale University Press, 1970), pp. 161–64, and *Ethics at the Edges of Life,* pp. 187–227.

90. *Ethics at the Edges of Life,* p. 218.

91. Ibid., p. 212 ff.

92. Ibid., p. 214.

93. "On Dying Well: An Anglican Contribution to the Debate on Euthanasia" (London: Church Information Office, 1975), p. 2. (Church House, Dean's Yard, SW1P 3NZ, London, England.) Ramsey quotes this in *Ethics at the Edges of Life,* p. 218.

94. *Ethics at the Edges of Life,* p. 219.

95. See Robert M. Veatch, "Prolonging Living and Prolonging Dying: A Distinction That Is Not Decisive," in Milunsky and Annas, pp. 184–85. See also Veatch.

96. James Childress, *Who Should Decide?* (New York: Oxford University Press, 1982), p. 164. He has written extensively on this issue. For details on his views about the traditional distinctions of ordinary/extraordinary means, letting die/killing, and the

ethics of stopping artificial feeding and hydration, see *Priorities in Biomedical Ethics* (Philadelphia: Westminster, 1981), p. 45; Joanne Lynn and James Childress, "Must Patients Always Be Given Food and Water?" *Hastings Center Report 16* (February 1986), pp. 17–21; Childress and Steven L. Dalle Mura, "Caring for Patients and Caring for Symbols: Reflections on Artificial Nutrition and Hydration," *BioLaw 1* (August 1986), sec. 4.

97. Childress, "Love and Justice in Christian Biomedical Ethics," in Earl Shelp, ed., *Theology and Bioethics* (Dordrecht, the Netherlands, and Boston: D. Reidel, 1985), p. 227.

98. Childress, "Civil Disobedience, Conscientious Objection, and Evasive Noncompliance: A Framework for the Analysis and Assessment of Illegal Actions in Health Care," *Journal of Medicine and Philosophy* 10 (1985), passim.

99. The following outline in great detail the aims and achievements of the hospice movement: Samuel Stoddard, *The Hospice Movement* (New York: Random House, 1978). Cicely M. Saunders, ed., *The Management of Terminal Disease* (London: Edward Arnold, 1978). Saunders, Dorothy H. Summers, and Neville Teller, eds., *Hospice: The Living Idea* (London: Edward Arnold, 1981). Saunders, "Hospices," in A. S. Duncan, G. R. Dunstan, and R. B. Welbourn, eds., *The Dictionary of Medical Ethics,* 2d ed. (New York: Crossroad, 1981), p. 219. Jack M. Zimmerman, M.D., *Hospice: Complete Care for the Terminally Ill* (Baltimore and Munich: Urban & Schwarzberg, 1986).

100. Cicely Saunders, M.D., "The Moment of Truth: Care of the Dying Person," in Francis G. Scott and Ruth M. Brewer, eds., *Confrontations of Death: A Book of Readings and a Suggested Method of Instruction* (Corvallis, Oreg.: Oregon Center for Gerontology, 1971), pp. 118–19.

101. Ronald Dworkin, *Life's Dominion: An Argument About Abortion, Euthanasia, and Individual Freedom* (New York: Knopf, 1993), p. 217.

102. Ibid., p. 179.

103. Ibid., p. 192 ff.

104. Ibid., p. 195.

105. Ibid., p. 196.

106. Ibid., p. 207.

107. Ibid., p. 213.

108. Ibid., p. 216. Similarly, aborting a fetus might show more respect for the life of a woman, for her investment in her own life, than

bearing that child. See my summary of Dworkin's argument for abortion, pp. 35–39.

109. Ibid., p. 216.

110. Ibid., p. 217.

111. The success of modern medicine has persuaded us that we somehow can cure death, which, of course, is absurd. For a sensitive and measured effort to reconcile modern medical advances with the notion of what he calls a "peaceful death," see Daniel Callahan, *The Troubled Dream: In Search of a Peaceful Death* (New York: Simon & Schuster, 1993).

112. See "The Religious Argument for Passive Euthanasia," pp. 120–121.

113. Thomas D. Sullivan, "Active and Passive Euthanasia: An Impertinent Distinction?" in Baird and Rosenbaum, *Euthanasia,* p. 57. Originally appeared in *Human Life Review,* 1977.

114. Marvin Kohl has called this "beneficent euthanasia"—helping someone die out of kindness. See Marvin Kohl, ed., *Beneficent Euthanasia* (Buffalo: Prometheus, 1975). The Harvard Divinity School philosopher Arthur Dyck has invented the word "benemortasia" (from the Latin for "good" and "death") for his notion of "caring" for the dying person. "Benemortasia seeks to reduce pain and suffering as much as possible but not to the point of directly inducing death." See Dyck, *On Human Care,* p. 86.

115. Glover, p. 189.

116. "Last Rights," *Newsweek,* August 26, 1991, p. 40.

117. See "Dr. Death," *Time,* March 31, 1993.

118. I came across Dyck's view of "only caring" after writing a couple drafts of this section. While I think I am more sympathetic to those who want to assist people in dying, in rare cases I think that Dyck's idea of helping people face death—a position of "caring only"—is a compassionate alternative for those psychologically or morally incapable of taking an active part in hastening another's death.

119. Callahan, "The First Illusion: Mastering Our Medical Choices," chap. 1 in *The Troubled Dream of Life,* pp. 23–56.

4. Capital Punishment

1. Jan Gorecki, *Capital Punishment: Criminal Law and Social Evolution* (New York: Columbia University Press, 1983).

2. Leon Radinowicz, *A History of English Criminal Law and Its Administration from 1750,* vol. 1 (London: Stevens, 1948).

3. Ibid., p. 24.

4. Michel Foucault, *Discipline and Punish* (New York: Pantheon, 1977), pp. 3–5.

5. Voltaire published a commentary on Beccaria's book.

6. See William J. Bowers, Glenn L. Pierce, and John F. McDevitt, *Legal Homicide: Death as Punishment in America 1864–1982* (Boston: Northeastern University Press, 1984). Their section "Deterrence of Brutalization: What Is the Effect of Execution?" echoes Beccaria and Rush.

7. Hugo Adam Bedau, ed., *The Death Penalty in America,* 3d ed. (New York: Oxford University Press, 1982), p. 8.

8. *Ralph* v. *Warden,* 438 F. 2d 786 (C.C.A. 4th Cir., 1970).

9. *Furman* v. *Georgia,* 408 U.S. 238 (1972).

10. J. R. Browning, "The New Death Penalty Statutes: Perpetuating a Costly Myth," *Gonzaga Law Review* 9 (1974): 651–705. The same figures are cited by the Supreme Court in *Gregg* v. *Georgia,* 428 U.S. 153 (1976).

11. *Woodson et al.* v. *North Carolina* 428 U.S. 280 (1986); and *Harry Roberts* v. *Louisiana* 431 U.S. 633 (1977).

12. *Gregg* v. *Georgia; Jurek* v. *Texas,* 428 U.S. 262 (1976); and *Proffitt* v. *Florida,* 428 U.S. 242 (1976).

13. *Gregg* v. *Georgia.*

14. See *Coker* v. *Georgia,* 433 U.S. 485 (1977) in which the Supreme Court held, 7 to 2, that a mandatory death sentence for rape when the victim is not killed is unconstitutional. In *Harry Roberts* v. *Louisiana,* the Court ruled, 5 to 4, against the mandatory death penalty in specific cases, this one the murder of a police officer.

15. *McCleskey* v. *Kemp* 481 U.S. 279 (1987); *McCleskey* v. *Zant* 111 S. Ct. 1454 (1991).

16. In retirement, Justice Lewis Powell said in an interview that the decision he regretted most was voting for McCleskey's execution.

17. Jill Smolowe, "Race and the Death Penalty," *Time,* April 29, 1991, p. 68.

18. Ibid.

19. "40% on Death Row Are Black, New Figures Show," Associated Press dispatch in *New York Times,* September 30, 1991, p. A15.

20. David Margolick, "In Land of the Death Penalty, Accusations of Racial Bias," *New York Times,* July 10, 1991, p. A1. The statistics

in this Georgia county were compiled by the Death Penalty Information Center in Washington, D.C.

21. Isaac Ehrlich, "The Deterrent Effect of Capital Punishment: A Question of Life and Death," *American Economic Review* 65 (1975): 397–417.

22. The case was *Fowler* v. *North Carolina* 428 U.S. 904 (1976).

23. Bedau includes two of the most prominent attacks on Ehrlich on p. 116 ff. The original references: Hans Zeisel, "The Deterrent Effects of the Death Penalty: Facts v. Faith," in Philip B. Kurland, ed., *The Supreme Court Review* (Chicago: University of Chicago Press, 1977), pp. 317–42; Lawrence R. Klein, Brian Forst, and Victor Filatov, "The Deterrent Effect of Capital Punishment: An Assessment of the Estimates," in Alfred Blumstein, Jacqueline Cohen, and Daniel Nagins, eds., *Deterrence and Incapacitation: Estimating the Effects of Criminal Sanctions and Crime Rates* (Washington, D.C.: National Academy of Sciences, 1978), pp. 336–60. The classic statistical argument *against* deterrence, and the focus of the attacks on Ehrlich, is Thorsten Sellin's work revised and updated in *The Penalty of Death* (Beverly Hills, Calif.: Sage, 1980). Sellin argues that the evidence shows no advantage in deterrence of the death penalty over life imprisonment. See also William J. Bowers with Glenn L. Pierce and John F. McDermott, *Legal Homicide: Death as Punishment in America, 1864–1982* (Boston: Northeastern University Press, 1984), a careful and extensive analysis of Ehrlich's data which also goes so far as to suggest that the statistical evidence shows that far from deterring crime, the death penalty probably has a brutalizing effect on the populace, an argument as old as Cesare Beccaria.

24. See Bowers, Pierce, and McDermott.

25. "Death, Life and the Presidency," *New York Times,* January 25, 1992, p. A22.

26. Criminal Justice Statistics 1974, 1975. See also Gorecki, tables 2–109, p. 223.

27. Gallup Organization, Princeton, N.J.

28. Linda Greenhouse, "Death Penalty Is Renounced by Blackmun," *New York Times,* February 23, 1994, p. A1.

29. Linda Greenhouse, "High Court Overturns a Death Sentence, Signaling a Turn Away from the Conservatives," *New York Times,* June 18, 1994, p. A13. The case is *Simmons* v. *South Carolina,* 92 U.S. 9509 (1994).

30. Truman Capote, *In Cold Blood: A True Account of a Multiple*

Murder and Its Consequences (New York: Random House, 1965), p. 335.

31. Immanuel Kant, *Metaphysical Elements of Justice* (1787), trans. Ladd (1965), p. 102.

32. Ernest van den Haag, *Punishing Criminals: Concerning a Very Old and Painful Question* (New York: Basic Books, 1975), pp. 323–33. Also van den Haag, "In Defense of the Death Penalty: A Practical and Moral Analysis," in Bedau. This is an excerpt of "In Defense of the Death Penalty: A Legal—Practical—Moral Analysis," *Criminal Law Bulletin,* 14, no. 1 (January–February 1978): 51–68. The references here are to Bedau, which is more easily available.

33. Bedau, p. 331.

34. *Punishing Criminals,* p. 199.

35. Ibid., p. 201.

36. Ibid., p. 332.

37. Bedau, p. 333.

38. Walter Berns, *For Capital Punishment: Crime and the Morality of the Death Penalty* (New York: Basic Books, 1979). An excerpt of Berns's book has been published as "The Morality of Anger," in Bedau, pp. 333–41. Also collected in Robert M. Baird and Stuart Rosenbaum, eds., *Philosophy of Punishment* (Buffalo: Prometheus, 1988), pp. 85–93.

39. *For Capital Punishment,* p. 152.

40. It is a Quaker view of the world. Among this group are the Christian feminists who oppose abortion on the grounds that society is morally obligated to protect the "weak and the powerless," and who is weaker or more powerless than the unborn child? See the "feminist pro-life" view in chapter 1, "Abortion," pp. 30–33, as well as Cardinal Bernardin's "seamless garment" argument there, pp. 39–41.

41. John Howard Yoder, "A Christian Perspective," in Bedau, pp. 370–75.

42. Ibid., p. 371. All the following quotes are from this article.

43. Romans 13 addresses the principle that Christians should submit to established civil authorities.

44. See Justice Brennan's separate decision in *Furman* v. *Georgia,* 408 U.S. 239 (1972).

45. See Justice Marshall's dissent in *Gregg* v. *Georgia.*

46. H. L. A. Hart, "Murder and the Principles of Punishment: England and the United States," chap. 3 in *Punishment and Responsibility: Essays in the Philosophy of Law* (Oxford: Oxford

University Press, 1968), pp. 54–89. (This section was originally written in 1957, but Hart has updated certain facts and points out in a footnote that "the comparisons of murder and its treatment in the United States still hold good." This is still true twenty-seven years after the publication of Hart's book.) Few contemporary discussions of punishment and the death penalty do not mention Hart's contribution.

47. Ibid., p. 76.
48. Ibid., p. 80.
49. Ibid., p. 235. Hart makes this useful point in a postscript.
50. Hart, p. 65 ff. He is arguing from evidence that predates Ehrlich's studies by almost twenty years. Nevertheless, his point remains well taken. "We must remember how blunt are our sociological tools for assessing the quantity of crime of any type, and in particular the crime of homicide," says Hart. Our tools have not become any sharper, and the statistical case for deterrence awaits its Einstein.
51. Charles Black, *Capital Punishment: The Inevitability of Caprice and Mistake* (New York: Norton, 1981); see also Bedau, "Death Sentences and Our Criminal Justice System," pp. 359–64, an excerpted version of "Reflections on Opposing the Penalty of Death," *St. Mary's Law Journal* 10 (1978): 1–12.
52. Black, in Bedau, p. 363.
53. See Ernest van den Haag and John P. Conrad, *The Death Penalty: A Debate* (New York: Plenum, 1983). Van den Haag is pro capital punishment, Conrad is con. A sociologist and criminologist, Conrad dates his opposition to the death penalty to his work as a young psychiatric social worker at San Quentin prison. His most memorable task: interviewing inmates on death row to prepare their "psychiatric social histories." Conrad also witnessed an execution and had the opportunity to talk to many at San Quentin whose job it had been, like Orwell, to participate in executions. See his introduction "Before the Killing Stopped," pp. 1–12.

For a governor's own reservations about sending men to their deaths, see Edmund "Pat" Brown with Dick Adler, *Public Justice, Private Mercy: A Governor's Education on Death Row* (New York: Weidenfeld & Nicolson, 1988). Brown, who defeated Richard Nixon for the governorship of California in 1962 and himself lost to Ronald Reagan in 1966—when there were sixty-four condemned men on death row in San Quentin, the state record—looks back on his decision to commute the sentences of some men and send others to the gas chamber. Before leaving office, abolitionists put pressure on Brown to commute the death sentences of those men. Brown, the father of Edmund "Jerry" Brown Jr., Ronald Reagan's successor as California governor and erstwhile presidential candidate, examined the merits of each case and decided that five ought to escape death. "The longer I live," wrote Brown at eighty-three," the larger loom those fifty-nine decisions about justice and mercy that I had to make as a governor . . . I realize that each decision took something out of me that nothing—not family or work or hope for the future—has ever been able to replace." (p. 163)

54. "A Hanging," in vol. 1 of *The Collected Essays, Journalism, and Letters of George Orwell*, ed. Sonia Orwell and Ian Angus (New York: Harcourt Brace Jovanovich, 1968), pp. 44–48.

55. "Execution Pace Climbs as Appeals Run Course," Associated Press dispatch in *New York Times*, March 27, 1992, p. B16.

56. As pointed out earlier, Justices Marshall, Brennan, and, more recently, Blackmun are on record that they believe capital punishment is unconstitutional. At the time of *Furman* in 1972, Chief Justice Burger said that though he believes execution to be constitutional, he himself is personally opposed to it. On the current Court, only Justices Scalia and Thomas seem to support the death penalty without reservation.

57. Van den Haag and Conrad, p. 8.

58. Orwell and Angus, vol. 3, p. 267.

59. Stephen Hawking, *A Brief History of Time* (New York: Bantam, 1988), p. 40.

60. *For Capital Punishment*, p. 147.

61. See Foucault, chap. 2, pp. 32–69.

62. Ibid., p. 11.

63. *For Capital Punishment*, p. 156.

64. I expand upon this idea and its role in creating a moral theory for a pluralistic democracy like ours in chapter 7.

65. For a fascinating study on the psychology and metaphysics of torture, see Judith Scarry, *The Body in Pain* (New York: Oxford University Press, 1985).

66. See van den Haag, in Bedau, p. 332.

67. Hart, p. 234.

68. *For Capital Punishment*, pp. 6–7.

69. Ibid.

70. See also "2 Inmates Wrongly Convicted Go Free," *New York Times*, March 27, 1992, p. A14.

71. Iver Peterson, "Freeing Innocent Is Centurions' Mission," *New York Times,* April 1, 1992, p. B6.

5. Racial Justice and Affirmative Action

1. John F. Kennedy, Presidential Papers, June 11, 1993; Richard Reeves, *President Kennedy: Profile of Power* (New York: Simon & Schuster, 1993), p. 522. LBJ speech cited in Lerone Bennett, *Before The Mayflower: A History of Black America* (New York: Penguin, 1988), p. 416; *New York Times,* March 16, 1965, p. 30.
2. Aristotle, *Politics,* Book I, 1255a 1–3.
3. M. I. Finley, *Ancient Slavery and Modern Ideology* (New York: Viking, 1980), p. 67. Finley is a renowned expert on ancient economics and slavery.
4. "Slave societies" are a relative rarity in history, with only the Caribbean, Brazil, and the American South following the ancient Greeks and Romans in their economic dependence on chattel slavery.
5. A freed Roman slave automatically became a Roman citizen. In Greece, manumitted slaves remained political aliens. The children of ex-slaves were known to climb to the top of Roman society without any obstacles other than social sneers. We know of at least one Roman senator whose father was an ex-slave, and the poet Horace was also the son of a freedman. See Finley, p. 93 ff.
6. The Greeks were more inclined to base their prejudices on environmental, cultural, and even climatic differences rather than color. These and the following remarks about the history of "racism" are from "The Origin of the Concept of Race," chap. 1 in Ashley Montagu's landmark study *Man's Most Dangerous Myth: The Fallacy of Race,* 5th ed. (New York: Oxford University Press, 1974), and Thomas Gossett's *Race: The History of an Idea in America* (Dallas: Southern Methodist University Press, 1963). Montagu's book was first published in 1942 and has been updated.
7. Matthew 28:18–20.
8. Acts of the Apostles 17:26.
9. St. Augustine, *The City of God,* trans. Marcus Dods (New York: Modern Library, 1950), pp. 530–31.
10. Gomes Eannes de Azurara, *Chronicle of the Discovery and Conquest of Guinea 1453,* vol. 1 (London: Hakluyt Society, 1896), pp. 84–85. Cited by Montagu, p. 19.

11. Louis Ruchames, *Racial Thought in America* (Amherst: University of Massachusetts Press, 1969), p. 5.

12. Gossett, p. 15. For a recent article on efforts to have de Las Casas declared a saint, see Tom Bates, "Sainted Obsession," *Los Angeles Times Magazine,* October 11, 1992.

13. David Hume, *A Treatise of Human Nature*, ed. L. A. Selby-Bigge and P. H. Nidditch (Oxford: Oxford University Press, 1981).

14. The French naturalist Georges Buffon, by all accounts, was the first to introduce the term "race" to the field of natural history. No "racist," he recognized that all human beings belong to the same species. See his *Histoire naturelle, générale et particulière* (Paris, 1749–1804); trans. William Smellie (London, 1812); see also Montagu, chaps. 1 and 2.

15. Montagu, p. 19 ff. Johann Friedrich Blumenbach's *On the Natural Variety of Mankind,* published in 1776, noted the apparent differences between various peoples and concluded that such differences were only that—apparent and skin-deep. Blumenbach's pupil Alexander Humboldt confirmed the relative mental and physical equality of all men, and Ralph Waldo Emerson said much the same in *English Traits,* published in 1856.

16. Bennett, *Before the Mayflower,* p. 35 ff.

17. Ibid., p. 45. See also Gossett, chap. 2, "England's American Colonies and Race Theories." For an even more scholarly study of American attitudes toward Negroes and the evolution of slavery in Virginia, see Oscar Handlin, *Race and Nationality in American Life* (Boston: Little Brown, 1957).

18. In 1706 the legendary Puritan Divine Cotton Mather wrote that slaves who became Christians did not deserve to be free because Christianity allowed slavery. Cotton Mather, "The Negro Christianized," in Ruchames, p. 67.

19. Ruchames, p. 14.

20. Not even John Wesley's personal opposition to slavery persuaded the American branch of Methodism to oppose it. Similarly, Baptists, also strong in the South, moved quickly from theological opposition to slavery to acceptance. Southern Presbyterians believed that slavery would eventually be abolished, but the church did not pursue that goal with any passion. See H. Shelton Smith, *In His Image but . . . , Racism in Southern Religion, 1780–1910* (Durham, N.C.: Duke University Press, 1972), p. 36 ff.

21. As much as he tried to give the Negro's potential for genius the benefit of the doubt, Jefferson suspected that men, like plants and animals, could be graded, and black Africans were "inferior

to whites in body and mind . . . a powerful obstacle to the emancipation of these people." Jefferson, "On Negro Ability," in *Notes on the State of Virginia,* in *The Writings of Thomas Jefferson,* ed. H. A. Washington (Washington, D.C., 1854); collected in Ruchames, pp. 162–69. Among Jefferson's fellow founders were friends of the black man, most notably John Jay, a committed abolitionist who was known to buy slaves simply to free them and who as governor of New York signed into law the abolition of slavery in his state. The Quaker Benjamin Rush, a signer of the Declaration of Independence and the most brilliant doctor of his time, founded the Pennsylvania Society for the Abolition of Slavery in 1774 and thirty years later helped persuade Congress to outlaw slavery above the Mason-Dixon line.

22. Cited in Bennett, p. 141.
23. Christian apologists for slavery, with a straight face, argued that slavery was a God-given way to improve the Negro race. Thomas Dew went so far as to argue that slavery actually helped elevate women from beasts of burden to the "animating center of the family." See Smith, pp. 146–47.
24. Josiah Nott, et al., *Types of Mankind: or, Ethnological Researches, Based upon the Ancient Monuments, Paintings, Sculptures, and Crania of Races, and upon Their Natural, Geographical, Philological, and Biblical History* (Philadelphia, 1854). This is from a selection in Ruchames, p. 467.

   The most influential European proponent of racial differences was a professional French diplomat, Count Joseph Arthur de Gobineau, an unabashed opponent of democracy. In 1856 a proslavery propagandist from Alabama published his translation of the first two volumes of Gobineau's four-volume *Essay on the Inequality of the Human Races* in Philadelphia under the less incendiary title *The Moral and Intellectual Diversity of Races.* Josiah Nott contributed an appendix. Gobineau quickly became the intellectual source of several generations of racists, the most famous among them the great German composer and anti-Semite Richard Wagner and his son-in-law Houston Stewart Chamberlain, author of *The Foundations of the Nineteenth Century* (1899). Gobineau's and Chamberlain's views quickly found their disciples in the United States. Adolf Hitler seized upon Chamberlain's view that certain races were destined to a certain end, and, for Hitler, German destiny was universal domination.

25. Bennett, p. 46.

26. *Scott* v. *Sandford,* 19 How., 60 U.S. 393 (1857), p. 407. The text of the decision is also found in Ruchames, p. 397 ff.

27. Garry Wills, *Lincoln at Gettysburg: The Words That Remade America* (New York: Simon & Schuster, 1992).

28. *Civil Rights Cases,* 109 U.S. 3 (1883).

29. *Plessy* v *Ferguson,* 163 U.S. 537 (1896). The vote was 7 to 1, with the ninth justice not participating. "Jim Crow" comes from a refrain in a popular plantation song, ". . . jump Jim Crow."

30. Bennett, pp. 332–33. See also *The Autobiography of W.E.B. Du Bois* (New York: International Publishers, 1968).

31. For a fascinating book-length treatment of the "Great Migration," see Nicholas Lemann, *The Promised Land: The Great Black Migration and How It Changed America* (New York: Vintage, 1991), p. 16. By the middle of World War II, another 5.5 million Southern blacks had moved North, to Chicago, Detroit, Gary, Pittsburgh, Philadelphia, and New York.

32. During the Depression 65 percent of Atlanta's blacks were on welfare. In Norfolk, Virgina, 81 percent. See Bennett, p. 359.

33. Melvin Urofsky, *A Conflict of Rights: The Supreme Court and Affirmative Action* (New York: Scribners, 1991), p. 16.

34. In *Missouri ex rel. Gaines* v. *Canada,* 305 U.S. 337 (1938). The Court reaffirmed *Gaines* in *Sipuel* v. *Board of Regents of the University of Oklahoma,* 332 U.S. 631 (1948).

35. The Court ruled, in *Sweatt* v. *Painter,* 339 U.S. 629 (1950), that the law school Texas established for blacks was not comparable to the University of Texas School of Law. *McLaurin* v. *Oklahoma State Regents,* 339 U.S. 637 (1950), signaled that "separate but equal" was on its last legs.

36. Gunnar Myrdal, *The American Dilemma: The Negro Problem and Modern Democracy* (New York: Harper Brothers, 1944). This quotation is from the 1962 edition, p. 21.

37. Myrdal's commentary on the incendiary state of race relations in the United States was only a gloss (albeit a thousand-page one) on Jefferson's worry that racial injustice would be the nation's "firebell in the night," and Alexis de Tocqueville's conclusion after his own visit to the United States in 1831–32 that "the danger of a conflict between the white and black inhabitants perpetually haunts the imagination of the Americans, like a painful dream." Alexis de Tocqueville, *Democracy in America,* trans. Henry Reeve and ed. Philips Bradley (New York: Vintage, 1956).

38. See *A Common Destiny: Blacks and American Society* (Washington, D.C.: National Academy Press, 1989).

39. *Brown* v. *Board of Education,* 347 U.S. 483 (1954).
40. 102 *Congressional Record* 4255, 4515, 4516 (1956).
41. In *Cooper* v. *Allen,* 358 U.S. 1 (1958), the Court made it clear that it would not tolerate postponement of court orders even in the face of violence, no matter how "ingenious" the efforts were to continue to discriminate against black schoolchildren.
42. Prince Edward County in Virginia (one of the school districts in *Brown*), rather than desegregate, closed its public schools in 1959—for the next five years! While this move was fought in the courts, white schoolchildren attended private segregated schools largely bankrolled by the state. The black community rejected a similar program—namely, the segregation that the Supreme Court had declared unconstitutional in *Brown*—and thus their children had no formal schools until the Supreme Court declared the Prince Edward County strategy discriminatory. See *Griffin* v. *School Board of Prince Edward County,* 377 U.S. 218 (1964).
43. In 1940, out of 1,000 black births, almost 73 children died; in 1960 only 43.9 babies died—the same number of white babies that had died in 1940. Andrew Hacker, *Two Nations: Black and White, Separate, Hostile, Unequal* (New York: Scribners, 1992), p. 231.
44. See *A Common Destiny,* pp. 335 and 336 for statistics on black education levels. For comparative earnings, see pp. 299 and 300.
45. John F. Kennedy, Presidential Papers, June 11, 1993; cited in Reeves, p. 522.
46. See *U.S.* v. *Jefferson County Board of Education,* 372 F. 2d 836 (1966). For the Fifth Circuit Court of Appeals, Judge John Minor Wisdom declared that the Civil Rights Act "imposes an absolute duty to integrate" public schools. *Heart of Atlanta Motel, Inc.* v. *United States,* 379 U.S. 241 (1964), and *Katzenbach* v. *McClung,* 379 U.S. 294 (1964).
47. Cited in Bennett, p. 417.
48. See Bennett, p. 421 ff.
49. *Green* v. *County School Board of New Kent County, Virginia,* 391 U.S. 430 (1968).
50. *Swann* v. *Charlottte-Mecklenburg Board of Education,* 402 U.S. 1 (1971); see also *North Carolina State Board of Education* v. *Swann,* 402 U.S. 43 (1971), where the Court unanimously struck down a North Carolina law forbidding the "involuntary bussing of students." In at least two other cases, the Court made it clear that it would not stand for Southern school districts trying to

reestablish separate white schools. In *Keyes* v. *Denver School District No. 1,* 413 U.S. 189 (1973), the Burger Court put *Northern* school systems, many as segregated as those in the South before *Brown,* on notice.

51. The Court did not seem as eager to bus children outside the city limits. Justice Thurgood Marshall, who had been chief counsel for the NAACP in the *Brown* case, was outraged; for him, public education was a state function that school districts were created only to administer. Their lines were hardly sacrosanct in the face of the state's duty "to achieve the greatest possible degree of desegregation." See *Milliken* v. *Bradley,* 408 U.S. 717 (1974).

52. *Regents of the University of California* v. *Bakke,* 438 U.S. 265 (1978). See also McGeorge Bundy, "The Issue Before the Court: Who Gets Ahead in America?" *The Atlantic,* November 1977, p. 41, cited in Urofsky, p. 45. The Supreme Court was to have heard a similar case four years earlier, but the University of Washington Law School decided to admit a white student before the case got to the High Court.

53. *United Steelworkers of America* v. *Weber,* 443 U.S. 193 (1979). For a discussion of this and subsequent affirmative action cases related to employment, see Urofsky, p. 46 ff.

54. See *Johnson* v. *Santa Clara County Transportation Agency,* 480 U.S. 616 (1987).

55. *Fullilove* v. *Klutznick,* 448 U.S. 448 (1980). In 1977, Congress recognized the evidence of large-scale discrimination in the construction industry and passed a law requiring that 10 percent of public funds for local public works projects be spent with black-controlled businesses. The Court majority, led by Chief Justice Burger, held that Congress had the right, in the proper circumstances, to establish set-aside programs. In 1984 the Court voted, 6 to 3, in *Firefighters Local Union No. 1784* v. *Stotts,* 467 U.S. 561, to uphold seniority systems *against* affirmative action plans, as Title VII itself provided. Soon, however, the Court proved it remained just as divided as it was in *Bakke* by apparently opposing preferential hiring (*Wygant* v. *Jackson Board of Education,* 478 U.S. 1014 [1986]) and then confirming that such remedial plans that benefited people who were not the actual victims of discrimination were constitutional (*Firefighters* v. *Cleveland,* 478 U.S. 501 [1986] and *Local 28 Sheet Metal Workers* v. *EEOC,* 478 U.S. 421 [1986]). The sheet metal workers union not only discriminated but refused repeated federal orders to stop discriminating.

56. Cited by Urofsky, p. 109. "High Court's Five-Way Verdict," *U.S. News & World Report,* June 2, 1986.

57. *Johnson* v. *Santa Clara County Transportation Agency.* For a book-length discussion of this particular case and its role in the judicial history of affirmative action, see Urofsky.

58. *Martin* v. *Wilks,* 490 U.S. 755 (1989); *Richmond, Va.* v. *J. A. Croson Co.* 488 U.S. 469 (1989).

59. For a general discussion of the scholarly data, see *A Common Destiny,* p. 315 ff.

60. See William Julius Wilson, *The Declining Significance of Race* (Chicago: University of Chicago Press, 1978).

61. *A Common Destiny,* p. 274.

62. William Bradford Reynolds, assistant attorney general in the Reagan administration in charge of the Civil Rights Division of the Justice Department. Cited by Herman Schwartz, in "Affirmative Action," in Leslie W. Dunbar, ed., *Minority Report: What Happened to Blacks, Hispanics, American Indians, and Other Minorities in the Eighties* (New York: Pantheon, 1984), p. 63.

63. Linda Chavez, the executive director of the Reagan administration's Civil Rights Commission. Cited by Schwartz, p. 63.

64. *New York Times,* January 18, 1984.

65. Charles Murray, "Affirmative Racism," *The New Republic,* December 31, 1984. Reprinted in Bruno Leone, ed., *Racism: Opposing Viewpoints* (San Diego: Greenhaven, 1986), p. 159. The references here are to the Leone text, available in most libraries.

66. Thomas Sowell, *Civil Rights: Rhetoric or Reality* (New York: William Morrow, 1984), p. 15.

67. Ibid., p. 19.

68. Ibid., p. 31.

69. Ibid., p. 38.

70. Ibid., p. 39.

71. In *Weber* the Supreme Court rejected "a literal interpretation" of the 1964 act, and instead saw its "primary concern" as the economic problems of blacks. The majority ruled that "temporary, voluntary, affirmative action measures" to eliminate racial imbalances were not barred by the 1964 act.

72. Sowell, p. 42.

73. Asians as a group also score higher than white students on their SAT math tests.

74. Sowell, pp. 44–45.

75. Ibid., p. 51.

76. Shelby Steele, *The Content of Our Character* (New York: St. Martin's, 1990), p. 113.
77. Ibid., p. 114.
78. Ibid., p. 116.
79. Ibid., p. 118.
80. Ibid.
81. Ibid., p. 124.
82. The black sociologist and analyst of the "truly disadvantaged" William Julius Wilson is the most eminent proponent of this view. See his book *The Truly Disadvantaged: The Inner City, the Underclass, and Public Policy* (Chicago: University of Chicago Press, 1987). See also his *The Declining Significance of Race.* Other black intellectuals have climbed on his bandwagon. See Carter, p. 7. and Steele.
83. *The Truly Disadvantaged,* p. 8.
84. See especially Carter, chap. 10, "Special but Equal," pp. 213–35.
85. Ibid., p. 229.
86. As Shelby Steele has argued.
87. Schwartz, pp. 65–66.
88. Ibid., p. 66.
89. Gertrude Ezorsky, *Racism and Justice: The Case for Affirmative Action* (Ithaca, N.Y.: Cornell University Press, 1991), p. 74.
90. Ibid., p. 76, and Robert Fullinwinder, "The Equal Opportunity Myth," *Report from the Center for Philosophy and Public Policy* (College Park: University of Maryland, Fall 1981).
91. Shelby Steele, "A Negative Vote on Affirmative Action," *New York Times Magazine,* May 13, 1990.
92. Patricia J. Williams, *The Alchemy of Race and Rights* (Cambridge, Mass.: Harvard University Press, 1991), pp. 48–49.
93. Bernard R. Boxill, *Blacks and Social Justice* (Totowa, N.J.: Rowman and Allanheld, 1984), chap. 7.
94. Ezorsky cites the experiences of Laurence Thomas, a black university professor of philosophy, p. 78. See Thomas, *New York Times,* op-ed, August 13, 1990. Patricia Williams, a black law professor, has described her own rage at being refused entry into a New York boutique (p. 45).
95. Ezorsky, p. 80.
96. Robert Nozick, *Anarchy, State, and Utopia* (New York: Basic Books, 1974), p. 237.
97. Ezorsky, p. 80. Here I have added to Ezorsky's criticism of Nozick's libertarian defense of employers a couple of other counterarguments: the common intuition that left to their own devices

the greediest of employers would exploit workers to their heart's content. This is why unions and minimum wages were invented. (Of course, some libertarians oppose them, too.)

98. Cited by Schwartz, pp. 68–71.

99. Ronald Dworkin, "Why Bakke Has No Case," *New York Review of Books,* November 10, 1977, pp. 11–15.

100. Ibid., p. 12.

101. Ibid.

102. Ibid.

103. For a discussion of the rights of the most "competent," see Alan Goldman, "Limits to the Justification of Reverse Discrimination," *Social Theory and Practice* 3 (1975). He argues that when affirmative action violates "some *presently accepted rule for hiring,*" it will be an example of reverse discrimination and thus unjust. "The most competent candidate" is an accepted rule of selection, according to him.

104. John Rawls, *A Theory of Justice* (Cambridge, Mass.: Belknap Press of Harvard University Press, 1971), p. 104.

105. John Rawls, "Fairness to Goodness," *Philosophical Review* 84 (1975), p. 537.

106. Thomas Nagel, "Equal Treatment and Compensatory Discrimination," in Marshall Cohen, Thomas Nagel, and Thomas Scanlon, eds., *Equality and Preferential Treatment* (Princeton, N.J.: Princeton University Press, 1977), p. 12. What follows is a summary of Nagel's well-known defense of preferential treatment in this article.

107. Ibid., p. 13.

108. Ibid., p. 15.

109. Ibid., p. 16.

110. Ibid., p. 17.

111. See *A Common Destiny,* p. 315 ff.

112. Ibid., "Blacks in the Economy," p. 273.

113. See Ezorsky, p. 65; see also Richard L. Rowan, "The Negro in the Textile Industry," in Herbert R. Northrup et al., *Negro Employment in Southern Industry: A Study of Racial Policies in Five Industries,* Studies of Negro Employment 4 (Philadelphia: University of Pennsylvania Press, 1970).

114. Ezorsky cites as support for this William A. Taylor, "*Brown,* Equal Protection, and the Isolation of the Poor," *Yale Law Journal* 95 (1986):1713–14.

115. See *A Common Destiny,* p. 321. Ezorsky refers to this, but misses the irony of her own reference: the authors of *A Common Des-*

tiny cite Wilson's *The Truly Disadvantaged* as a source for their point that young ghetto blacks do not have the "social networks" to find out about new jobs. Wilson is also one of the panel members who helped compile *A Common Destiny*, a useful "report card" on the status of black America.

116. Ezorsky cites 1980 as an example, referring to "I Feel So Helpless," *Time*, June 16, 1980, p. 21.

117. Ezorsky, p. 70.

118. Ibid., p. 71.

119. West, formerly a professor of religion and head of Afro-American Studies at Princeton and now at Harvard, is one of the brightest young intellectuals in the black community. What follows summarizes his argument in "Beyond Affirmative Action: Equality and Identity," in *Race Matters* (Boston: Beacon, 1993), pp. 63–67.

120. Ibid., p. 64.

121. Ibid., p. 65.

122. Neil A. Lewis, "Unresolved on Race," *New York Times*, June 6, 1993. The case in question was *Shaw* v. *Reno* (1993).

123. Toni Morrison, *Playing in the Dark: Whiteness and the Literary Imagination* (Cambridge, Mass.: Harvard University Press, 1992). A collection of the three William E. Massey Sr. Lectures given at Harvard University. See also Orlando Patterson, *Freedom* (New York: Basic Books, 1991).

124. One hastens to add that for American blacks racial harassment is hardly "remarkable"; more than 6,000 complaints of racial harassment were filed with the Equal Employment Opportunity Commission in 1992. See Michael Janofsky, "Race and the American Workplace," *New York Times*, June 20, 1993, sec. 3, p. 1, for an account of the Miller suit.

125. Stephen Carter uses the phrase "Meritocratic Ideal" throughout his book *Reflections of an Affirmative Action Baby* (New York: Basic Books, 1991).

126. Charles N. Jamison Jr., "Racism: The Hurt That Men Won't Name," *Essence*, November 1992.

127. Williams, p. 45.

128. Clayburn Carson Sr., ed. *The Papers of Martin Luther King, Jr.*, vol. 1 (Berkeley: University of California Press, 1992), pp. 32–33.

129. Isabel Wilkerson, "Black Neighborhood Faces White World with Bitterness" (second of two articles "2 Neighborhoods, 2 Worlds"), *New York Times*, June 22, 1992, p. A1.

130. See Judith N. Shklar, *The Faces of Injustice* (New Haven: Yale University Press, 1990), p. 83.

131. Jack E. White, "Growing Up in Black and White," *Time*, May 17, 1993, pp. 48–49.

132. Michael Walzer, *Spheres of Justice: A Defense of Pluralism and Equality* (New York: Basic Books, 1983), p. 68.

133. David Stockman, Reagan's own budget director, has attacked the fiscal process he helped put into motion as "decadent" and called Capitol Hill's claims to want to cut spending a sham. Reagan's tax cuts were a disaster, according to Stockman, and the Democrats' concessions "a tremendous mistake, dramatically reducing the revenue base of the United States government, preventing the funding of programs they already had, not to mention any unfinished agenda. . . . They were like an army in the heat of combat disarming itself. Why did they do it? It's unfathomable." See Sidney Blumenthal, "Sorcerer's Apprentices," *The New Yorker*, July 19, 1993, p. 29.

134. See John E. Schwarz and Thomas J. Volgy, "Above the Poverty Line—but Poor," *The Nation*, February 15, 1993, pp. 191–92.

135. Welfare and other "entitlement" programs are the favorite whipping boys of conservatives, black as well as white. Cf. Charles Murray's *Losing Ground: American Social Policy, 1950–1980* (New York: Basic Books, 1984).

136. Cited in Schwarz and Volgy.

137. Walzer cites M. I. Finley, *The Ancient Economy* (Berkeley: University of California Press, 1973), p. 173. Walzer also discusses the commitment to the poor among medieval Jewish communities. "You must help the poor in proportion to their needs," according to one citation from the Jewish community of old Cairo. See Walzer, p. 73.

138. Here, of course, I am referring to Immanuel Kant's view that morality requires that we cannot treat people as mere objects or tools of our desires. Historically, capitalism has traded on the traditional "liberal" views of John Locke and Thomas Hobbes that the individual is free to go his own way and pursue his own interests, and that private property is sacred. But Kant showed us liberal individualism's softer, more human, more, if you will, "communitarian" side. It is a part of their vision that liberal democrats ought to cultivate more.

139. This is the view of a contemporary attack on traditional liberalism called communitarianism. The line was drawn in the sand by Robert Bellah et al., *Habits of the Heart: Individualism and Commitment in American Life* (Berkeley: University of California Press, 1985). For a recent popular manifesto of the communi-

tarian ideal, see Amitai Etzioni, *The Spirit of Community: Rights, Responsibilities, and the Communitarian Agenda* (New York: Crown, 1993). For a deeper, though more academic, discussion of the view that American political action has focused on individual rights to the detriment of a "community responsibility," see Harvard law professor Mary Ann Glendon, *Rights Talk: The Impoverishment of Political Discourse* (New York: Free Press, 1991). Popular conservative columnists like George Will and John Leo side with the communitarians. (I will discuss the liberal-communitarian clash in more detail in the final chapters of this book.)

140. See Ellis Close, *The Rage of the Privileged Class* (New York: HarperCollins, 1993), which is an anecdotal account of the anger and humiliation successful African-Americans have experienced playing the game by all the rules.

141. John F. Kennedy, Presidential Papers, June 11, 1963; cited in Reeves, p. 522. Andrew Hacker also makes a similar point in *Two Nations*, noting that for most white Americans there is no advantage to being black. See p. 31 ff.

142. Walzer makes a similar point in his explanation of why societies are more comfortable providing health care and programs for the elderly. "Disease is a general threat," he writes, "old age, a general prospect. Not so unemployment and poverty, which probably lie beyond the ken of many well-to-do people. The poor can always be isolated, locked into ghettos, blamed and punished for their own misfortune" (*Spheres of Justice*, p. 80). I address this failure of what I call "moral imagination" at much greater length in the final chapter of this book.

143. According to the *New York Times*, July 26, 1993, unemployment had risen in the United States to 7 percent of the workforce. In Germany, the unemployment rate was 8.2 percent; in Britain, 10.4 percent; and in Canada, 11.3 percent.

144. Hacker, chaps. 5, 6, and 7. Also, "The Myths of Racial Division," *The New Republic*, March 23, 1992, pp. 21–25.

145. Walzer, p. 82.

146. "Excerpts from Speech by Bush in Los Angeles," *New York Times*, May 9, 1992.

147. Martin Luther King Jr., "Letter from a Birmingham Jail," in *What Country Have I?*, ed. Herbert J. Strong (New York: St. Martin's Press, 1970), pp. 119–31.

148. President Lyndon Johnson was right to choose the metaphor for war in his own fight against poverty. See LBJ's comparison of the

fight for civil rights to the Revolutionary and Civil wars, p. 190. Simply because the Johnson administration did not end poverty does not mean the war was neither necessary nor just.

6. One Nation, Many Disagreements

1. "Utopia" is from the Greek *ou topos*, "not a place."
2. Richard Rorty cites this remark from Dewey in *Contingency, Irony, and Solidarity* (Cambridge: Cambridge University Press, 1989), p. 58. The source: John Dewey, *Reconstruction in Philosophy* (Boston: Beacon, 1948), p. 26. Rorty is the contemporary philosopher who has done most to revive Dewey's ideas. I knew Rorty when I was a graduate student in philosophy at Princeton in 1969–73, before he became the force for good or bad, depending on your opinion of the state of contemporary American philosophy. In the twenty years since, Rorty has been prolific. I have read his work carefully and Rorty's ideas resonate for me strongly, and they loom large in the following.
3. Thomas Jefferson, *Notes on the State of Virginia,* Query XVII, in *The Writings of Thomas Jefferson,* ed. A. A. Lipscomb and A. E. Bergh (Washington, D.C., 1905), 2:217. This section owes much to the writings on the ideals of liberal democracy in Isaiah Berlin, *The Crooked Timber of Humanity,* ed. Henry Hardy (New York: Knopf, 1991), p. 65 ff; John Rawls, *A Theory of Justice* (Cambridge, Mass.: Belknap Press of Harvard University Press, 1971); and the writings of Richard Rorty on the role of liberalism and philosophy in politics, especially Rorty's essay "The Priority of Democracy to Philosophy," in *Objectivity, Relativism, and Truth: Philosophical Papers,* vol. 1 (Cambridge: Cambridge University Press, 1991), pp. 175–96. In this article Rorty cites Jefferson's remarks about "gods" and proceeds to defend the Rawlsian notion of "justice as fairness" in a society like our own where there is a plurality of conflicting, indeed incompatible, goods. For these three authors, a "perfect society" is an incoherent notion. The world is comprised of a variety of different cultures and incompatible ways of life. Each of us, too, has ideals that are incompatible, and we live in societies where our own beliefs clash with the beliefs of others. For these writers, the true liberal is the man who can live among these different or incompatible beliefs, valuing, above all, freedom and tolerance.

4. Berlin, "European Unity and Its Vicissitudes," *The Crooked Timber of Humanity,* pp. 182–83. See also a speech Berlin gave, collected in the same volume as "The Pursuit of the Ideal." His passionate commitment to liberal pluralism runs throughout most of his writings, particularly those on Machiavelli and the eighteenth-century thinkers Johann Herder and Giambattista Vico. See the other essays in *The Crooked Timber,* particularly "The Decline of Utopian Ideas in the West" and "Giambattista Vico and Cultural History." See also Berlin's essays on Machiavelli and Vico in the earlier collection of his work edited by Henry Hardy: *Against the Current: Essays in the History of Ideas* (New York: Knopf, 1980).

5. Ibid.

6. According to Berlin, Machiavelli was the first to argue in the sixteenth century for at least two mansions of incompatible values—pagan and Christian: a ruthless prince, as even a Christian would have to concede, was no match for a Christian one. Two centuries later Johann Herder, a German, and Giambattista Vico, an Italian, made their cases for "cultural pluralism"—namely, that the traditions of cultures and communities within certain cultures were bound to collide.

7. The inevitable collision of ideas is a refrain in virtually everything Isaiah Berlin has written. Chronologically, the first place one runs across Berlin's argument against "the ultimate solution" is in the justly famous inaugural address he gave upon assuming the Chichele Chair of Social and Political Theory at Oxford in 1958 and published that year by the Clarendon Press as "Two Concepts of Freedom." The essay was first collected in Berlin, *Four Essays on Liberty* (Oxford: Oxford University Press, 1969), pp. 118–72. I still have my own paperback copy which I bought in Oxford that year when the essay was assigned as part of my reading in a philosophy course.

    Berlin repeats the same ideas in almost all the essays collected in *Against the Current: Essays in the History of Ideas* (New York: Viking, 1979) and his most recent collection, *The Crooked Timber of Humanity.*

8. "The Pursuit of the Ideal," p. 12.

9. As the reader might suspect, critics have made this argument, though their main target has been not Berlin but John Rawls, author of the most discussed book on political philosophy over the past twenty years, which also happens to be a deep and complex defense of liberalism, *A Theory of Justice.* See Michael Sandel,

ed., *Liberalism and Its Critics* (New York: New York University Press, 1984), p. 8. Sandel also attacks Rawls in *Liberalism and the Limits of Justice* (Cambridge: Cambridge University Press, 1982). Rorty counterattacks in "The Contingency of the Community," in *Contingency, Irony, and Solidarity*, pp. 44–69. He also defends Rawls against the communitarian attack in "The Priority of Democracy to Philosophy," in *Objectivity, Relativism, and Truth*, pp. 175–96.

10. "Relativism" has become almost as much a dirty word in American moral debate, at least at the popular level, as "liberalism." The most recent attack on so-called relativist views of morality and cultural values (disguised as tolerance, the author argues) was Allan Bloom's surprise best-selling critique of college education in America, *The Closing of the American Mind* (New York: Simon & Schuster, 1987). I will not argue specifically against Bloom, but my defense of my version of "tolerance" against even more popular American conservatives as Pat Buchanan and George Will, I think, will stand up to Bloom's fulminations. I think it is safe to place Bloom on the opposite side of the political spectrum from Berlin. (In terms of learning and the power of their minds, I hasten to add, there is no contest.)

11. I have borrowed this from Richard Rorty, whose influence I acknowledge later.

12. "The Pursuit of the Ideal," p. 13.

13. Ibid.

14. "The Decline of Utopian Ideas in the West," p. 47.

15. Rorty's bibliography is extensive; his main writings on how his pragmatism fits into his view of morality and politics have been recently collected: *Contingency, Irony, and Solidarity; Objectivity, Relativism, and Truth*; and *Essays on Heidegger and Others: Philosophical Papers*, vol. II (Cambridge: Cambridge University Press, 1991). Rorty's most systematic statement of his view of pragmatism can be found in *Philosophy and the Mirror of Nature* (Princeton, N.J.: Princeton University Press, 1979) and *The Consequences of Pragmatism* (Minneapolis: University of Minnesota Press, 1982). References to specific articles about Rorty's political and ethical views will appear in the notes.

16. Rorty, *Objectivity, Relativism, and Truth*, "Solidarity or Objectivity," p. 24. The dispute between realists (also called representationalists) and pragmatists (also called ethnocentrists and anti-representationalists) remains a major battle (some would argue *the* major battle) in contemporary philosophy. Most of Rorty's

work in the past twenty years has been aimed at ridding professional philosophy of this representational urge, trying to prove
that such a "mirror" image of truth and knowledge has been
fruitless and is thus undesirable. He has his critics and opponents, needless to say. See Thomas Nagel, *The View from
Nowhere* (New York: Oxford University Press, 1986). Nagel
charges that Rorty's pragmatism asks too little of philosophy; he
believes that "trying to climb outside of our minds" is "philo-
sophically fundamental" (p. 9). See also Bernard Williams,
Ethics and the Limits of Philosophy (Cambridge, Mass.: Harvard University Press, 1985). My own sympathy with the Rorty
point of view is obvious, but it is impossible here to rehearse a
philosophical dispute that seems to have split professional philosophy right down the middle (with very smart men and women
on both sides).

17. Ibid.
18. Ludwig Wittgenstein, *Philosophical Investigations*, trans.
G.E.M. Anscombe (New York: Macmillan, 1953), No. 217. The
"spade turned" is a much discussed remark in Wittgenstein. I am
hardly offering an exegesis of Wittgenstein here; the comment
simply seems to fit.
19. Rorty, "The Contingency of Community," p. 57.
20. See Rorty, "Private Irony and Liberal Hope," in *Contingency,
Irony, and Solidarity.*
21. See *Contingency, Irony, and Solidarity*, p. 50.
22. Here Rorty is following Donald Davidson's views on truth. See
Davidson, *Inquiries into Truth and Interpretation* (Oxford: Oxford University Press, 1984), p. 185. Also Davidson in "A Coher-
ence Theory of Truth and Knowledge," in Alan Malachowski,
ed., *Reading Rorty* (Oxford: Blackwell, 1990), pp. 120–37. For
Rorty's views on Davidson, see "Pragmatism, Davidson and
Truth," in *Objectivity, Relativism, and Truth*, pp. 126–50. For
more on metaphor and scientific progress, see Rorty's discussion of
Davidson's and Mary Hesse's views in "Unfamiliar Noises: Hesse
and Davidson on Metaphor," in the same volume, pp. 162–72.
23. This is a famous line from Nietzsche (and a favorite of Rorty's).
Nietzsche saw truth as "a mobile army of metaphors,
metonyms, and anthropomorphisms—in short, a sum of human
relations, which have been enhanced, transposed, and embell-
ished poetically and rhetorically and which after long use seem
firm, canonical, and obligatory to a people." Friedrich Nietzsche, "On Truth and Lie in an Extra-Moral Sense," *Viking*

Portable Nietzsche, Walter Kaufmann, ed. and trans. (New York: Viking, 1954), pp. 46–47.

24. Rorty cites this Dewey remark in *Contingency, Irony, and Solidarity,* p. 58. The source: John Dewey, *Reconstruction in Philosophy,* p. 26.

25. The main target of the intellectual hostility to liberalism is embodied in John Rawls's *Theory of Justice.* See my brief summary of Rawls's argument that "justice is fairness," pp. 207–209. Michael Sandel's *Liberalism and the Limits of Justice* (New York: Cambridge University Press, 1982) is an articulate and sophisticated attack on Rawls. See also Alasdair MacIntyre, *After Virtue* (South Bend, Ind.: University of Notre Dame Press, 1981), pp. 232–33. According to MacIntyre, "Modern society is often, at least in surface appearance, a collection of strangers, each pursuing his or her own interests with minimal constraints." MacIntyre, a major figure in Anglo-American philosophy who would prefer an Aristotelian state to a liberal one, derides the liberal heroes as aesthete, manager, and therapist.

26. Robert N. Bellah et al., *Habits of the Heart* (New York: Harper & Row, 1985), p. vii.

27. Alexis de Tocqueville, *Democracy in America,* trans. George Lawrence, ed. J. P. Mayer (New York: Doubleday Anchor Books, 1969).

28. Bellah et al., p. 285.

29. My reading of Tocqueville indicates that it is not "individualism" per se that forces Americans into the "solitude of their hearts," but *democracy.* The aristocrat Tocqueville was concerned that the competitive individualistic businessman of nineteenth-century America would not give a damn for his fellow citizens and workers (unlike the European aristocrat who could at least feel a moral and Christian obligation to the workers and peasants on his estates). It was this same greedy, selfish spirit that offended the aging Thomas Jefferson and his fellow founders, who saw their ideal democratic republic descending into a nation of greedy entrepreneurs. One might argue that from the start in America the values of "community" were not much valued. See Henry Steele Commager's *Commager on Tocqueville* (Columbia, Mo.: University of Missouri Press, 1993).

30. Tocqueville, p. 508.

31. John Rawls, "Justice as Fairness: Political not Metaphysical," *Philosophy and Public Affairs* 14 (1985): 225–26.

32. Rorty was among the first to point to the historicist, nonuniversalist communitarian side of Rawls. See Rorty, "The Priority of Democracy to Philosophy." Rawls explicitly wants to stay away from questions about "the essential nature or identity of persons." The Archimedean point for his imaginary designers of the just society is a democracy that assures its citizens freedom.

33. For a fascinating account of the "invention" of Greek democracy and philosophy, see Cornelius Castoriadis, "The Greek Polis and the Invention of Democracy," in David Ames Curtis, ed., *Philosophy, Politics, Autonomy* (Oxford and New York: Oxford University Press, 1991), pp. 81–123. I stumbled across Castoriadis, a French thinker unknown to me, in my general reading for this book. His ideas about political institutions as "social-historical imaginary institutions" square with my own intuitions about the revolutionary role of the "moral imagination" in a pluralistic democracy. See *The Imaginary Institution of Society* (Cambridge, Mass.: MIT Press, 1987), a rich, complex examination of how men "create" history, and history—and its societies—create men, which begins with a detailed criticism of Marx.

34. For a recent brief and entertaining introduction to the thought of classical Athens, see Bernard Knox, *The Oldest Dead White European Males and Other Reflections on the Classics* (New York: Norton, 1993). "Culture of complaint" is an allusion to the art and social critic Robert Hughes's lectures on the name-calling in contemporary culture machines, published as *The Culture of Complaint* (New York: Oxford University Press, 1993).

35. *The Communist Manifesto*, in *The Marx-Engels Reader*, 2d ed. (New York: Norton, 1978), pp. 475–76. The translation here has been slightly altered by Marshall Berman in *All That Solid Melts into Air: The Experience of Modernity* (New York: Penguin, 1988), p. 21.

36. Anyone needed to be cured of nostalgia for the good old days in the heartland should take a look at Michael Lesy, *Wisconsin Death Trip* (New York: Pantheon, 1973), a collection of photographs and newspaper stories from a small town in Wisconsin. The news of the day seemed to be a startling series of stories of infant mortality, mad women, drunks, and suicides.

37. Planned Parenthood Federation of America mailings in 1992.

38. John Stuart Mill, "On Liberty" (New York: Penguin, 1982), p. 152.

39. Patrick J. Buchanan, *Right from the Beginning* (Boston: Little, Brown, 1988), p. 342.

40. Cited by Norman Mailer in "By Heaven Inspired," a personal report on the Republican convention published in *The New Republic,* October 12, 1992, pp. 26–27.
41. Martin Luther, *Secular Authority,* in *Martin Luther: Selections from His Writings,* ed. John Dillenberger (Garden City, N.Y.: Doubleday, 1961), p. 283; John Locke, *A Letter Concerning Toleration,* introduction, Patrick Romanell (Indianapolis, 1950). See a discussion of this in Michael Walzer, *Spheres of Justice: A Defense of Pluralism and Equality* (New York: Basic Books, 1983), chap. 10.
42. See Judith Shklar's discussion of liberal democracy in *Ordinary Vices* (Cambridge: Harvard University Press, 1984), pp. 247–49.
43. Ibid., p. 247.
44. *U.S.* v. *Schwimmer* 279 U.S. 644 (1929).

7. The Moral Imagination

1. "Excerpts from Speech by Bush in Los Angeles," *New York Times,* May 9, 1992.
2. Jason C. Deuchler, "Race, Hate and My New Bike," *New York Times,* May 6, 1992, p. A29.
3. See Andrew Hacker, *Two Nations: Black and White, Separate, Hostile, Unequal* (New York: Scribners, 1992), passim.
4. Cited in Gordon S. Wood, *The Radicalism of the American Revolution* (New York: Vintage, 1993), p. 220.
5. Ibid., p. 221.
6. Ibid., p. 222.
7. Ibid.
8. Isaiah Berlin, "Giambattista Vico and Cultural History," *The Crooked Timber of Humanity,* ed. Henry Hardy (New York: Knopf, 1991), p. 62.
9. Ibid., p. 64.
10. As the literary critic Lionel Trilling pointed out in *The Liberal Imagination.* For Trilling, because the novel alerted people to the varieties and contradictions of human experience, it was an important agent of the moral imagination. See my Introduction, p. 9.
11. Linda Greenhouse, "Thurgood Marshall, Civil Rights Hero and Former Justice, Dies," *New York Times,* January 25, 1993, p. B8.
12. Linda Greenhouse, "Liberal Giants Inspire Three Centrist Justices," *New York Times,* October 25, 1992, p. A1.

13. From Lincoln's Annual Message to Congress on December 1, 1862, in which he presented the Emancipation Proclamation. See *Lincoln: Selected Speeches and Writings* (New York: First Vintage Books/Library of America Edition, 1992), p. 364.

14. *Lincoln: Selected Speeches and Writings*, p. 405. See Garry Wills, *Lincoln at Gettysburg: The Words That Remade America* (New York: Simon & Schuster, 1992), chap. 4, pp. 121–47.

15. Wills, chap. 4, pp. 121–47.

16. See Peter Steinfels's "Beliefs" column in the *New York Times*, October 6, 1993, p. A9. Also his follow-up, "Papal Encyclical Says Church Must Enforce Basic Morality," *New York Times*, October 16, 1993, p. 11. In the encyclical *"Veritatis Splendor"* ("The Splendor of the Truth") the pope argues for a "basic morality" that transcends all eras and all cultures—a logical impossibility in the minds of modern philosophers like Isaiah Berlin and Richard Rorty. According to Steinfels, the pope "rejects the idea that human freedom and human reason create values on their own, or impose them on nature, rather than discover the values that are inherent in the order of the universe God has created." This is the view that has dominated the Church and most of philosophy since Plato—and is precisely the view that American pragmatism and post-Nietzschean philosophy was invented to demolish.

17. Richard Rorty, *Contingency, Irony, and Solidarity* (Cambridge: Cambridge University Press, 1989), p. 91.

18. James Baldwin, *The Fire Next Time* (New York: Vintage, 1992), p. 98. (Originally published by the Dial Press, 1963.)

19. Graham Greene, *The Power and the Glory* (New York: Penguin, 1991), p. 131. The novel was originally published in Great Britain in 1940.

20. Rorty, p. 92.

21. Ibid.

22. This looks like Rorty's version of Viconian *fantasia*. Rorty seems to confirm this when he later writes, "For the liberal ironist, skill at *imaginative identification* does the work which the liberal metaphysician would like to have done by a specifically moral motivation—rationality, the love of God, the love of truth" [my italics]. Ibid., p. 93.

23. Neither Rorty nor Berlin uses "moral imagination" in the way I am suggesting. I have detected one appearance of the phrase in one of Berlin's essays on the logical incoherence of expecting that there is some kind of ideal solution to every moral and polit-

ical problem; "some values cannot but clash." Berlin notes that the Marxist attempt to create a community based on the same values, no clashes allowed, deprives us of other not so trivial values: "In a society in which the same goals are universally accepted, problems can be only of means, all soluble by technological methods. That is a society in which the inner life of man, the *moral* and spiritual and aesthetic *imagination*, no longer speaks at all. Is it for this that men and women should be destroyed or societies enslaved?" [my italics]. See Berlin, "The Pursuit of the Ideal," in *The Crooked Timber of Humanity*, p. 15. But his explanation of Viconian *fantasia* as, by analogy, being able to understand what it is to be poor or to fall in love squares with my use of "moral imagination."

24. I had missed this quotation from Dewey cited by Rorty in my first few readings of *Contingency, Solidarity, and Irony*, p. 69. The rest of the quotation reads: ". . . art is more moral than moralities. For the latter either are, or tend to become, consecrations of the status quo . . . the moral prophets of humanity have always been poets even though they spoke in free verse or by parable." John Dewey, *Art as Experience* (New York: Capricorn, 1958), p. 348.

25. John P. Diggins, "Theory and the American Founding," in Leslie Berkowitz, Denis Donahue, and Louis Menand, eds., *America in Theory* (Oxford: Oxford University Press, 1988), p. 22.

26. "Form of life" and "language games," two phrases favored by the great twentieth-century philosopher Ludwig Wittgenstein that have become part of the modern philosophical language, refer to how the limits of the languages we speak and think, the concepts of our own communities, define our beliefs and "knowledge."

27. See Susan Estrich, "The Sympathy Defense," *New York Times*, October 24, 1993, p. E15; also Jim Newton, "L.A. Trials Show 'Blind Justice' Is Hard to Achieve," *Los Angeles Times*, October 24, 1993, p. A1. Of course, the cases I am referring to here are the infamous—and much televised—attacks on Rodney King and Reginald Denny.

28. Thomas Paine, *The Rights of Man*, Part I (London: Dent, Everyman Library, 1958), p. 104.

29. Ibid.

30. *New York Times*, April 26, 1993, p. A14.

31. E. L. Doctorow, "The Character of Presidents," *The Nation*, November 9, 1992, p. 535.

32. Peter Steinfels, "Seen, Heard, Even Worried About," *New York Times,* December 27, 1992, sec. 4, p. 1.

33. A family of four with a household income below $13,920 was counted as poor in 1991, though independent researchers have argued that the minimum a family needs to purchase the bare necessities is more like $21,600. Using the $21,600 figure, the number of American poor increases from 14 percent of the nation to more like one in four. See John E. Schwarz and Thomas J. Volgy, "Above the Poverty Line—but Poor," *The Nation,* February 15, 1993, p. 191.

34. See Rorty, "The Priority of Democracy to Philosophy," in *Objectivity, Relativism, and Truth: Philosophical Papers,* vol. 1 (Cambridge: Cambridge University Press, 1991), p. 183; also Henry Steele Commager's *Commager on Tocqueville* (Columbia, Mo.: University of Missouri Press, 1993), p. 47, where he also cites Jefferson's description of the "American experiment."

35. "The Pursuit of the Ideal," p. 19.

36. Jean Lyotard, *The Postmodern Condition: A Report on Knowledge,* Geoff Bennington and Brian Massumi, trans. (Minneapolis: University of Minnesota Press, 1984), *passim.*

Index